PIGSKIN PULPIT

A Social History of Texas High School Football Coaches

Ty Cashion

Foreword by O. A. "Bum" Phillips

Texas State Historical Association

Austin

For my father

Copyright 1998 Texas State Historical Association
All rights reserved. Printed in the United States of America
First published in paperback, 2006
ISBN 978-0-87611-221-2

The Library of Congress has cataloged the hardcover editon as follows:

Cashion, Ty, 1956–
  Pigskin pulpit: a social history of Texas high school football coaches / by Ty Cashion.

  p.   cm.
  Includes bibliographical references (p.   ) and index.
  ISBN 0–87611–168–1 (alk. paper)
  1. Football—Coaching—Texas—History. 2. Football coaches—Texas—History. 3. School sports—Coaching—Texas—History. 4. Football—Social aspects—Texas—History. I. Title.

  GV956.6C38 1998   98–20976
  796.332'62'09764—dc21   CIP

5 4 3   06   07   08   09   10

Published by the Texas State Historical Association in cooperation with the Center for Studies in Texas History at the University of Texas at Austin.

Book design by Holly Zumwalt Taylor. Dustjacket design by David Timmons.

∞The paper used in this book meets the minimum requirements of the American National Standard for Permanence of Paper for Printed Library Materials, z39.48—1984.

Frontispiece: Masonic Home, 1953. Jim Bowlin, left, Coach Jack Whitley, Joe Lloyd, Max Blankenship. Whitley played for the Mighty Mites in the 1930s and returned to the school, an institution for orphans and needy dependents of Masons, as a coach. *Photograph courtesy Jack Whitley.*

Table of Contents

Part IV: An Era of Change and Crisis: The 1960s and Beyond

Preface

During the eight years since the Texas State Historical Association published *Pigskin Pulpit*, a disheartening number of the voices that contributed to this work have fallen silent. Although I professed an appreciation for the urgency of this project at its inception, it never occurred to me that posterity would arrive so quickly. Even as this edition goes to press, my own father joins them. With his passing and that of each old-time coach, it becomes more difficult to understand, much less appreciate, the collective ways and values they imparted to young men in an earlier era. Generally, Texas high school football coaches of that bygone time enjoyed wide admiration, and the great majority even felt beloved by players who experienced some kind of life-affirming lesson from their association with the game and these men who built a social institution around it.

Some of the lessons I describe in these pages, however, suggest that longing for the past might be more appropriate than trying to recreate it. After all, not many coaches today would think of lighting oil on the surface of a pool and working it into a swimming lesson. Then again, it would be safe to venture that not many coaches today have found themselves bobbing up and down on a fiery ocean after having a ship blown out from under them. The emotional baggage of economic depression, racism, and even some of the benighted manifestations of that old-time religion are better left behind us as well.

Yet, every Texas high school football coach today inherited his profession from men whose society possessed an intimate familiarity with the conditions and circumstances of survival, deprivation, prejudice, and ignorance. If we are to understand the past in the context of those who lived it, then it is important to know something of their wider experience, and their motives and inspirations. It is just as important to gain an appreciation for the fact that society placed its trust in football coaches. No one, apparently, even questioned the judgment of the man who sent that child for a swim beneath burning oil simply to impart a lesson he felt was important. Evidently it took. The boy grew up to be a coach himself, John Reddell, whom I hope you will come to admire as much as I did. He shared with me his human weaknesses as readily as the memories that brought him lasting satisfaction. And now he, too, exists only in memory.

I am grateful to see *Pigskin Pulpit* appear in paperback for the opportunity it gives me to reach a wider audience. Receiving feedback from
readers who had some personal connection with football coaches,
whether as admirers or critics, strengthens my conviction that what is
written here represents a faithful interpretation—biased perhaps, but not
nearly so tendentious as the ill-conceived works produced by conflict
theorists in the field of sports sociology. Even though *Pigskin Pulpit* represents an analytical social history, I have nevertheless tried to make it
the old coaches' story by giving them a voice that will endure, as far as
good judgment and accuracy allows, in the way they wanted it told.

One concern I earlier expressed, regarding the immediate need for further research on related issues, has since been addressed, but only in part.
Walter Day, who coached at the segregated I. M. Terrell High School in
Fort Worth, compiled records of the African American experience for a
two-volume work that augments the archival holdings of the Prairie View
Interscholastic League at Prairie View A&M University. There is a fasci-
nating story there awaiting someone with the skill and enthusiasm to tell
it. My friend and colleague, Jorge Iber, chair of the department of history
at Texas Tech University, became interested in the career of Coach E. C.
Lerma, who was among the first Tejanos in the state to coach high school
football. Iber is close to completing this important biography. Others
have produced less scholarly books on the lives of coaches as well as volumes that have illuminated some aspects of the game during its formative
years. Surely there is much work left to be done, and the day when we are
no longer able to consult those with memories of the experience will
arrive too soon.

Ty Cashion
2006

Foreword

By O. A. "Bum" Phillips

There is something about high school football in Texas that captures the essence of what the sport is all about. It's about pride; it's about boys playing for the love of the game; it's about entire communities coming together for a common cause. In the college and professional ranks you lose some of that. There's just nothing like the pure essence of high school football.

And there's something about high school coaches in Texas, too. I've seen football from the bottom to the top, and I say that Texas high school coaches overall are the best set of coaches anywhere at any level. They're better trained, they're better disciplined, they've got a better work ethic, and they're closer to each other than any group of coaches anywhere. And I've been around enough to know. I'm as proud to have been a high school coach in Texas as I am to have gone on to the NFL.

It was at the high school level—at Nederland, Port Neches, Jacksonville, and Amarillo—where I learned how to be a professional coach. In high school you learn to take the material you've got and build a system that fits your boys. In professional football, the coaches who are not successful are the ones who try to make their players fit their system. In high school, perhaps we'd have a good passer one year, so that year we'd have a good passing attack. Say the passer graduates, and the next year we wouldn't have a single guy who could throw the ball ten yards end-over-end, so obviously we'd have to develop a good running game and a strong defense or we didn't win. You had to work with what you had on hand. That's what I learned in high school, and that's what I did in college and professional football. I was never lulled into thinking our system was going to win for us. We felt like the players were going to do that. We'd ask them to do the kinds of things that they did well, not necessarily those that we wanted.

When I got to the college and professional level, I didn't really change anything. At the bottom line, I still tried to get every young man to do better than he thought he was capable of doing. To do that, you've got to understand him and truly know him, or you can't get him to perform at a notch higher than he thinks he can. And he has to have a reason for wanting to do it. If that reason is that he's got good friends on the team, then it's because you, as a coach, developed that close relationship with the players, and the players with each other. Everybody plays with pride, but they also play to not let their buddies down. Those were all lessons I learned at the high school level.

Like any coach—at every level—people expected me to win. In its own way, the pressure was no less at Nederland High School, where I started out, than it was at New Orleans, where I finished up my NFL career. Yet only in the high school ranks did I truly feel pressure from the community to juggle the demands of winning with the equal responsibility of keeping sight of the kids who played the game. From high school to the pros, the men I have known and admired have balanced those demands. But it's the high school coach who is in the toughest spot, and I don't think most people stop to think about it. He's got to win, but he also has to keep the kid number one. It's a tricky job and one that most coaches do very well.

I guess that's why it bothers me to know that so many critics today are attacking football—coaches included—as representing something that's bad and destructive. Until I read *Pigskin Pulpit,* I didn't realize the extent of what some people have been saying. A goodly number fancy themselves experts, and what they seem to be saying is that we, as coaches, have set our sights on winning at the expense of the players and everything else. As one who has worked with young men all my adult life, I can tell you that such condemnation could not be farther from the truth. The vast majority of coaches I have known are good men, and they have taught good values. Of course, any coach will tell you this, so that's why it's important to have a book like *Pigskin Pulpit,* by a guy who wears a square hat and a tassel, to say some of these same things.

Pigskin Pulpit has given us old coaches the opportunity to talk about our careers and what it was like to coach high school football in another era. Only a coach's son could have written a book like this. On the one hand the author, Ty Cashion, grew up with football, and he got to see a side of it that few people see. On the other hand, he is enough of an outsider to look objectively at the game and the profession. Whether he set out to do it or not, Cashion has defended the coaching profession, and he's done it without sounding defensive. He has also conceded that there is a downside, but he's put it into perspective, and in proportion, to what it really is. The book does not hide from the truth or make excuses, but it does explain why coaches are the way they are.

As for this old coach, I don't know what would have become of me had it not been for football. And I think that's true for most of the Texas high school coaches that I knew growing up in the profession. Most of us were farm boys or had rural roots, and we loved to play football. It changed our lives, and it opened doors that we never would have walked through otherwise. A lot of us didn't have anybody in our families who had even graduated from high school. *Pigskin Pulpit* is

O. A. "Bum" Phillips. *Photograph courtesy Bum Phillips.*

right on the mark when it tells how most of us would not have even realized we were capable of going to college if it weren't for football. Football gave every one of us a chance to earn a college degree, and I can safely say that nobody knows the value of an education more than some of these old Texas high school coaches.

I enjoyed reading about all the guys I used to coach with. We coached at a great time, and we shared a closeness that was truly special. Most of the guys you coached against were the same ones that you had played in high school or college, or at least you had seen them play or read and heard about them. Some of the best memories I have of high school football are the bull sessions we'd hold in those hotel rooms during coaching school. We'd pack in as many guys as could fit into the room and talk football until the sun came up. It was fun, and that's good, because football is a game, and it's supposed to be fun. But there were a lot of hard times, too, and I think *Pigskin Pulpit* has covered the water-front. I think that any football fan will enjoy reading this book. And, I hope that any young coach or any young man wanting to get into the profession will read it to know where he came from, to gain a sense of tradition, and to be aware that he has a responsibility to keep the "good game" good.

Introduction

igh school football in Texas emerged during the twentieth century as one of the state's identifying institutions, a pastime shaped in the image of its coaches. Yet coaches themselves, alternately revered and vilified, always have been members of a closed society, its ranks encompassing men who remain enigmas. We think of coaches in caricatures, but we do not really know them in their complexities.

Pigskin Pulpit opens the profession to historical scrutiny by weaving together the voices of a representative sample into a narrative that discusses their lives and careers. While this work does not dodge the tough questions critics of the game have posed, it is largely the coaches' own story, often in their own words, describing the way they fit into this once sacrosanct institution. The interviews concentrate on an extended generation that entered the profession around the time of World War II through the 1950s, although I interviewed a handful who started even earlier. All of them shared the experience of coaching at a time when their methods went unchallenged, their players did not question them, and parents supported them almost unconditionally. Most of their careers extended into the 1960s, and many into the decades that followed. The ones who experienced the social upheaval of those years found that their rigid code was no longer uniformly accepted by an urban, pluralistic culture that was less consistent in its own ways and less confident of its own values.

Collectively, the old-time coaches interviewed for this work provide a character study of a unique breed of men whose deeply planted values were nurtured in the common experiences of traditional Texas culture, economic depression, and times of war. Part I, an overview, allows the coaches to express their beliefs, philosophies, and intentions as well as to reflect on their methods and the lessons they imparted to their players. This section also surveys the portrayals and perceptions of Texas high school coaches in popular culture and scholarly works. Part II traces the development of high school football in the state alongside the coaches' lives and experiences, thus explaining how this schoolboy avocation wove itself so tightly into the fabric of Texas culture. It also examines these coaches' backgrounds and the resulting influence of those experiences on the profession's lockstep code. In Part III the coaches discuss the game at its peak, an era that began with victory in World War II and ended

1

sometime during the late 1960s. Three successive chapters concentrate on the game, the coaches' careers, and their families. Concluding the book, Part IV reflects on the social changes that have affected the nature, and diluted the importance, of Texas high school football. It also gives the coaches a final word in addressing a number of issues—among them education, corporal punishment, brutality, and competition—over which critics have lately condemned the coaching profession and the game of football itself.

The coaches interviewed here cross many boundaries, both figuratively and literally, within the state and in some cases outside of it. Their voices include those of Anglos, African Americans, and Hispanics. Geographically, they blanket the state. These old coaches began their careers in junior and senior high schools at places as diverse as Bowlegs, Oklahoma, and Houston, Texas, and some of them hung up their whistles only after reaching the college and professional ranks. Among these coaches were men who amassed prolific won-loss records as well as others who lamented having most often lost on the scoreboard, but professed security in having won some larger victories by guiding young men through their formative years.

Texas high school coaches in their heyday wielded an influence on society out of proportion to their numbers. Their successes at times united citizens hard pressed by economic calamities and war, while their failures too often erupted into quarrels that tore towns apart. In many cases the harvest that coaches reaped from the football field even determined the self-perception of entire communities as well as how outsiders viewed those places. If you had walked into any office building in Texas as late as the mid-1960s, moreover, you probably would have found that the man in charge was a Texan who had played high school football. Chances are, too, that his experience had been a good one for him, one that he felt reinforced his values.

Walk into an office today, and chances are that even if a man is in charge, he might not be a Texan. Even if he is, he might not have played football. And even if he had played, so many other experiences would have shaped his youth that the sport, and its coaches, might have influenced him only negligibly.

This supposition implies no value judgment. It does, however, underscore the bygone importance of high school football in Texas, and, as a consequence, the men who coached the game. Decreasing numbers of leaders in today's society have backgrounds in athletics. And as more women deservingly take positions of leadership in corporate and public life, football's influence will wane even further. As long as the game exists, however, coaches will continue to imprint upon their players the traditional values of hard work, sacrifice, physical courage, and teamwork—values they learned from their own mentors. *Pigskin Pulpit* explores this continuity of values and the concessions to new mores that coaches have had to make in a changing society.

All coaches, of course, do not subscribe to the values of their fraternal society, and others have at times betrayed those ways. Year in and year out newspapers and television broadcasts trumpet some coach's objectionable behavior or censure a coach for refusing to suspend a player for committing some sort of disgraceful offense.

In contrast to this boorish, win-at-any-cost image, however, are many more examples of coaches as protectors of traditional values. For example, Southlake Carroll's Bob Ledbetter, amid howls of protests from angry parents, suspended twenty-two players from his 1994 play-off-bound team for merely attending a party where alcohol was served. And just down the road, in 1996, Arlington's Bill Keith assured himself a dismal season by dismissing several players from his squad after they confessed to more serious after-game revelry. Former players of these coaches would have expected no less of them. Ledbetter commented: "Sometimes you just have to get the message across to your kids that there are a different set of rules they have to live by." Keith felt the same way and expressed that he was the product of his mentors, John Reddell and Bill Carter— old-time coaches I interviewed, coaches whose ways and values *Pigskin Pulpit* makes familiar.

In both cases Ledbetter and Keith prompted a spontaneous chorus of public support from their colleagues. Commerce's Steve Lineweaver, a former assistant of Ledbetter's, added: "There are so many times stuff like that happens, and the newspapers don't pick it up. Coach Ledbetter had done the same thing in 1992. And a few years before that, he had to kick four boys off the team for a drug violation—now, three of these were two-way starters—and that was the only years I was there that we didn't make the play-offs." A litany of such commending statements as Lineweaver's demonstrates the commonly-held belief among coaches that football still teaches the timeless lessons of character, but coaches no longer feel secure that they retain the faith and confidence of society.

However superficial, any behavior that reinforces the negative stereotype of coaches continues to draw the attention of indignant critics who denounce football as an archaic endeavor, one whose negative lessons of violence, unfair competition, and inflated self-importance outweigh any positive message that the sport may impart to its participants. In the vast majority of cases, however, coaches' rough exteriors belie men who are doing a good job, even if their methods do not evoke images of Mr. Chips.

Take Roger Benefield, for example. Walk into Grapevine High School on any particular day, and you might find a boy dangling over a garbage can in the hallways, clutched firmly by the ankles in Benefield's grasp. The coach's unspoken message is clear: "Keep it up, son, and this is where you will end up." The casual observer might see only a six-foot-three, three-hundred-pound bully. Students, however, see Benefield as a caring teacher with a sense of humor, who is quick with words of encouragement as well as with admonitions—and even some good-natured physical intimidation when the need arises. His athletes see him as a dedicated coach to whom they can turn for advice and assurance. His fellow teachers at this upscale suburban school regard Benefield as a supremely capable peer whom they recently feted with the school's "Teacher of the Year" award. Only Benefield's associates on the coaching staff know that he gives so much of himself to his students while teaching drivers' education and taking other odd jobs in the summer so that his wife can remain at home with their severely disabled son. And it is at home, not on the field, that the demands on him are greatest.

Roger Benefield recently turned forty years old. Yet in the classroom and on the field he behaves like a man truly cut from an older piece of cloth. What has made him such a good coach and teacher is the instinct to "read" kids. He knows which ones need a kind word and which ones need a firm push. By the way, a few of his fellow teachers, in mock angst, have walked down the hall to complain to government teacher Mike Sneed—who is also Grapevine's head football coach—that their students have deliberately provoked Benefield "'to do them,' so they can brag about being trashed by 'Big Daddy Fat Cat.'"

Benefield's ways and actions are reminiscent of many old-time coaches. In the 1940s, it was Perry Fite of Crozier Tech who could not seem to get one of his "jug-butted tackles moving." So he walked over to the edge of the practice field and broke a dead limb off an oak tree, which he then proceeded to break into smaller pieces across the backside of his laggard lineman, who "all of a sudden" bowled over the player on the other side of the line. Such ritualistic expressions of manly overkill come most often from loving hands, and players take them for what they are worth. And again, good coaches know when, and on whom, those kinds of messages work.

Regardless of what the old-time coaches say about themselves, their ways, and their game, football's critics will no doubt remain skeptical of the profession and the sport. *Pigskin Pulpit* does not ignore the darker manifestations that arise from the game, or even from the most earnest actions and philosophies of coaches. Yet neither does it dwell on the profession's black marks. Most of the old coaches agree that sometimes they erred, and that there existed as many "bad apples" in their profession as in any field. Joe Washington, of Port Arthur, attempting to reconcile the bad with the good, stated: "Anything that's different in a negative way will stand out. The good things are often overlooked because they are expected." He conceded that football, by its very nature, is detrimental in some ways. "But know this," Washington declared, "football has done good to the point that it has overpowered the bad things that have happened."

Texas high school football coaches long have contended with a formidably negative stereotype, one reinforced by literature and film. Coaches invest long and intense hours preparing for the forty-eight minutes on Friday night in which most parents and spectators experience their closest, but nevertheless impersonal, contact with them. The coaches' often frenzied behavior on the sidelines, as well as their "Pollyanna meets General

Patton" interviews prior to big games, certainly have inspired all manner of impressions. When fictionalized, coaches are routinely constructed on such superficial observations, and the force of these repeated portrayals has established a casual acceptance of that stereotype.

Scholarship, moreover, has hardened the negative image. When the first of the old-time coaches interviewed for this study began retiring in the 1950s, the field of sports sociology did not even exist. Only during the next decade did that discipline emerge. It gained momentum during the 1970s and today has blossomed into a prolific field of study. Within sports sociology a vocal and influential group of scholars consistently has concluded that involvement in athletics has contributed nothing to building character. Scholars also contend that studies affirming the positive lessons of athletics, and those of football in particular, are either flawed methodologically or draw from small samples.

Historians who trespass into the field of sociology stand accused of producing unsystematic narratives that fail to place their work into a theoretical context. I am a historian, and to the extent that *Pigskin Pulpit* crosses academic disciplines, this work is guilty as charged. And, while the text may often appear anecdotal, the examples nevertheless draw from an irresistibly strong and overwhelmingly consistent pattern.

I established my dialogue with the old coaches by sending them a questionnaire that covered the many themes and issues I wanted to explore, but also gave them the freedom to introduce other topics. The text that emerged from countless hours of taped interviews with more than eighty coaches, as well as follow-up calls, periodic correspondence, and casual conversations, represents the first scholarly treatment of Texas high school coaches as a social group. And, because several of them have died since I began the interviews in 1993, *Pigskin Pulpit* might well be the final word based on such personal reflections.

Regarding documentation, I did not clutter the text with endnotes on the sources created from interviews and personal correspondence. The text normally attributes comments to the appropriate interviews—all but seven conducted by me. The exceptions were conducted by Texas Tech's Southwest Collection during the 1970s. While striving to quote the old coaches precisely, I have on occasion taken the liberty of changing words for the sake of clarity or of conveying the intended meaning. In cases where coaches spoke in confidence, I have respected their wishes. At times I have relied on the work of sportswriters and scholars, whose words added resonance or counterpoints to the interviews. In every such case I have cited these written works.

In many places *Pigskin Pulpit* treads across some ground that has not previously been explored. In other places only scanty secondary sources exist. Constructing a balanced narrative, of course, dictated a broad sweep. Informed readers will no doubt note many issues that sorely merit further research and illumination. The African American experience embodied in the Prairie View Interscholastic League, for example, begs a book-length work. Similarly, because male gender studies lag far behind those in the field of women's history, different aspects of the coaches' lives raise many questions that need to be addressed. Even the origins of football remain hazy in many respects and provide a rich field for popular study. Where room exists for more depth, I hope that historians and sociologists will seize the opportunities for further inquiry.

Regarding a less ponderous matter, my professors as a rule always taught me to identify someone the first time I mention his or her name. I apologize for occasionally forsaking their instructions. The fact that in every such case the unidentified men are coaches presents only part of the problem. The word "nomadic" often arises when discussing members of the profession, and this quality also made geographic identifications of my subjects difficult. Take Frank Pulattie, for example. Throw a dart at a map of Texas and you will likely hit a spot only an inch or so from some place where he coached. And if one gets away from you and hits Sacramento, California, well, he coached there, too. The appendix, however, includes all the coaches I discuss as well as their dates of birth, the years spanning their careers, and all the schools where they worked.

Again, the story that unfolds in *Pigskin Pulpit* represents the coaches' collective memory. Over a period of four years, I conducted almost two hundred hours of interviews with coaches and received numerous letters relating their coaching experiences. Oral history, however, is an inexact science. I have diligently attempted to verify facts where sources allowed, yet the eyes of astute observers will no doubt catch occasional mistakes in the coaches' recollections of names, dates, places, and other matters. For these errors I take full responsibility. And while the coaches did a faithful job of recreating their impressions of life as they remembered it, the task of remaining true to life was more difficult. Retrospection certainly colored the coaches' recollections and sometimes allowed their psyches to winnow out life's pains and to magnify the good times.

Bum Phillips, for example, told how legendary Alabama coach Bear Bryant once skewered him by good-naturedly stretching the truth. Phillips had served on Bryant's staff at Texas A&M, but decided to take the head coaching job at Jacksonville High School in East Texas rather than follow his mentor to Alabama. The two nevertheless stayed in touch, and in one of their occasional phone visits Bryant greeted his former protégé by asking, "What are you doing good, Bun?"—for some reason "Bear always called me Bun," Phillips remarked. "Man-to-man football" was the reply. Bryant, a firm believer in zone coverage, nevertheless became intrigued by Phillips's defensive innovations, and after an hour or so on the phone, he insisted on flying Phillips out to talk to his staff.

The next spring the two met at a clinic in Washington state. At the crowded airport terminal Phillips spotted his mentor waving him over. "We were both pretty tall and could see each other's eyes over the tops of other people's heads," he remembered. "So there he is hollering over a bunch of coaches standing around, listening, and he says—'Bun!

Whenever you tell me something, tell me the whole damn thing!'"
Phillips called back: "What are you talking about coach?" To which
Bryant growled: "You and your man-to-man defense. Didn't you see the
Orange Bowl with that receiver running right down the middle of the
field for a touchdown?" Somewhat sheepishly, Phillips set himself up as
the butt for the punch line that he knew was coming: "Yes, sir, I did."
"Well," Bryant finished, "who's supposed to cover him?' Of course,
everybody gave me the horse laugh," Phillips recounted.

"The next morning at breakfast, we're sitting there at the counter, and
I asked him, 'What [defensive] coverage were y'all in?'—there's a jillion
man-to-man coverages. And Bear said, 'Hell, Bun, we weren't in man-to-
man, we were in a three-deep zone and busted it!'" When Phillips
protested, his old mentor just smiled. "Well, hell, Bun, it just made a better story!" I suspect that a few of those "better stories" found their way
into the text. Nevertheless, even the occasional exaggeration conveys
underlying truths.

Judging the old coaches' product compared to what society is turning
out today, it stands to reason that they had to have been doing something
right. Nevertheless, most of them admitted that some of their boot-camp-
tough methods, if practiced today, would be appropriately condemned as
barbaric. Most all of the old coaches insisted that as the times dictated
change, they, too, changed, even if somewhat grudgingly. To judge what
they did in an earlier era outside of the context of those times, however, is
unfair. I hope that after relating these men's backgrounds, the times in
which they coached, and their code of beliefs, *Pigskin Pulpit* will at least
put a human face on these men, even if the more critical readers are
thankful that their day has passed.

What some of the old-time coaches were doing, or about to do, when I
called on them provides a final indication of their interests and character.
Most of them remain active. Golf, predictably, seemed to be a favorite
pastime, since it allowed them a chance to socialize with old allies and
rivals alike. For example, when I told sportswriter Bill McMurray that I
had interviewed his friend Bob Barfield, he stated that he had recently
admonished the coach to get his old nemesis Darrell Tully "away from
that domino table." Barfield did, and the three of them met at the golf
course and played a round.

When I called on retired Wichita Falls coach Bill Carter, he was resting
from a workout. He is a national pentathlon champion for his 70-to-74-
year-old age group. After interviewing another former West Texas coach,
Gene Mayfield, I called back to ask him a few more questions, and his
wife told me: "He can't come to the phone right now, he's out riding his
bicycle." When I reminded her that a biting blue norther was at that very
moment hurtling through their Panhandle town of Levelland, she just
laughed. "He won't let anything stop him from getting his exercise in."

Donald Jay, a former executive director of the Texas High School
Coaches Association, took a break from working on the Special Olympics

to visit with me. I learned in the course of our conversation that at other times he conducts Bible studies at the THSCA office. Several others remain active in the Fellowship of Christian Athletes. And Jap Jones, in addition to sitting on the boards of three organizations and putting together a basketball tournament that generates scholarship money for underprivileged youth, was busy chronicling the records of the Prairie View Interscholastic League. Still others, such as James Brewer, Joe Bob Tyler, and Quin Eudy, were volunteering their services part time to help young coaches establish their programs.

When I first called Clarence McMichael, he had just returned from Gary, Indiana, where he had been visiting former player Buford Waterhouse, now an athletic director. McMichael remarked that "I had a hard time with him when he played for me. He could have gone either way. But he went on to Drake and became a success." Emory Bellard's trip still lay ahead when we visited. The week following our interview he flew to Washington, D.C., where he stayed with Buddy Lewis, a former player he had coached at Ingleside. "He had quit, and two days later he came back and said he'd made a mistake," Bellard commented. "Of course, I let him back on the team. . . . Later he became an aide to President Reagan."

As a coach's son who grew up in a locker room, I am admittedly humbled by the experience of having become acquainted with these men, many whose names I recall from my youth. Each interview comprised a brief biography of the coaches, and in no case did anyone question my motives or intentions. Many of the old coaches knew my father, and even more of them knew my namesake, Ty Bain. With no guarantees about what the eventual product would say, they were exceedingly forthcoming and simply let me know that they would do anything to help me.

Among the men I interviewed was Brooks Conover, born in 1907. A trip that our Kilgore Bulldogs made to Cleburne, where we played Conover's Yellowjackets, provided my first memory of football. It was 1958, and I was not quite three years old. Through the mists of time I cannot recall what our own stadium looked like, but I distinctly remember being overawed by the home-side bleachers' stone exterior and fence surrounding the Cleburne field. I also remember my mother carrying me high into the top rows of the stadium just prior to the game, and being terrified of falling through the cracks in the rickety stands covered by that impressive facade. I told Conover that somewhere in there I saw an analogy.

In conceiving this project, I never intended to produce anything akin to a football coaches' apologia. My initial goal—and one that I feel has been achieved—was to produce a social history that would examine the men whose rites and doctrines largely shaped my own outlooks and values along with those of several generations of Texas schoolboys. More often than I care to remember, my upbringing was more "push" than "pull," and this work has indeed provided a catharsis of sorts. At the same time, I discovered during the course of my research that a consistently positive pattern emerged in the old coaches' interviews. Critics of football might feel that I have not gone far enough in examining particular coaches or episodes that embody the profession's worst characters and characteristics. Yet I ardently believe that, figuratively, I have climbed high enough in the stands to see that such examples are exceptions and do not represent the traditional values that Texas high school coaches in general espouse. Going into this study, I was apprehensive about what I was going to learn, wondering if perhaps the game's critics were right. Yet, to complete the analogy, it was not long before I realized that, despite an occasional rickety bleacher slat, the old coaches' rigid facades are held in place by solid undergirding.

This book could not have been produced without the advice, support, and encouragement of many colleagues, friends, and "football people." Of course, I owe each of the coaches interviewed a tremendous debt of gratitude for lending their voices to this oral history project. Eddie Joseph, now retired, of the Texas High School Coaches Association supported the endeavor from its inception and worked to open many doors. Bailey Marshall, former coach and retired director of the University Interscholastic League, also gave me his blessing. In addition, several coaches gave advice well beyond their interviews: Jap Jones, Hoot Smith, Darrell Tully, Joe Bob Tyler, and my own father, Bob Cashion, in particular. Many others proofread all or portions of the manuscript and contributed illustrations.

As a coach's son, I began accumulating contextual knowledge about this subject since before I can remember. Along the way, several coaches influenced me tremendously—Hugh Hamm, father of my lifelong friends Buddy and Kirk; Maurice Cook; Prince Scott; and Ty Bain, whose name I carry proudly. Remembering others who coached with my father, or who coached me once I began playing, brings back many warm memories.

Several sportswriters and others close to the game are due acknowledgment for helping me craft this work. Among the former journalists are Fred Cervelli, Ted Battles, Blackie Sherrod, Bill McMurray, and George Breazelle. Others include Vernon Ritchie, Perry Goolsby, Hunter Kirkpatrick, Max Goldsmith, Steve McCarty, James Allen, Gary Gaines, Randy Mayes, John Wilkins, David Murrah, Charley McCleary, John Miller Morris, J. O. Fudge, David Boyd, Billy Fowler, Darrell Garrison, Joseph Hedrick, Jerald McCanlies, John Myers, Raymond L. Patrick, Janice Perez, Dan Pulattie, T. A. Thornburg, Nancy Walker, Doris Walters, and John Wills.

I am especially indebted to the Texas State Historical Association, not only for its enthusiastic support, but also for the enduring relationships that continue to grow out of what became a common endeavor. Ron Tyler and George Ward, as TSHA director and publications director, respectively, nurtured this project in ways that I have come to realize far exceeded the attention authors normally receive in this industry. J. C. Martin and Kent Calder have ably succeeded them, and they continue to make me feel that I am part of their team. The book's designer, Holly Taylor, who also edited the original work and helped assure that *Pigskin Pulpit* would enjoy a second life in paperback form, has earned my undying gratitude as well. Moreover, her sharp eye for inconsistencies and grammatical miscues saved me many an embarrassing moment. My warmest regards also extend to the dependable and ever-cheerful Sandra Gilstrap, the association's secretary. Finally, David Timmons, who designed the dustjacket, deserves praise for helping the TSHA develop a reputation for producing eye-pleasing volumes.

Finally, I acknowledge the loving support of my wife, Peggy, and son, Sam, whose ceaseless inspiration kept me on track as well as my "football family"—my parents Bob and Jo and sister Michelle.

Part I

Overview

Chapter 1

The Coaches and the Game

Buzz Allert, coaching at Houston's Northbrook High School in the 1970s, had a big tackle on the team, "just an average player . . . the kind of player that you had to push real hard, both on the field and in class." The boy seemed to resent Allert's insistence that he perform to his potential, "which was fine with me, because I was really doing what was best for him." Some games the boy started, other contests found him standing on the sidelines. "I didn't particularly think that the kid cared much for me," Allert recalled, "but there's a big difference between being liked and respected." The young man never won any honors, but he lettered two years and later graduated from Houston's police academy.

While on patrol late one cold and wet Christmas Eve, the young officer received a call that a convenience store was being robbed. Arriving just in time to catch sight of the fleeing suspects, he chased them out of Houston and onto a narrow farm-to-market road. Meanwhile, the misting rain had turned to freezing drizzle. At a sharp curve the squad car hit a patch of ice and careened down the bar ditch, spinned and rolled through fence and field, and finally settled wheels up, well out of sight from the road. "So he's laying there with both his legs broken . . . and he's partially in and out of the car," Allert continued. Shaking uncontrollably with fear, and exposed to the harsh weather, "he just says, 'Well, I'm going to die.'" Then, "all of a sudden, something came to him that 'If I don't get out of here, and it gets out that I lay here and let myself die without trying, then I know one guy that's really going to be teed off at me!'" Summoning all his strength and will, the officer crawled to the road where passersby rescued him.

That "guy," of course, was Coach Allert. "That's the way the story came back to me," he said. "I would never have thought that I would have any influence on that youngster. You just never know . . .," his voice trailed. "I want my players to like me, but the ultimate is that I want them to respect me. . . . You want to do what's right for that player."

A Microcosm Of Life

To a generation of Texas high school football coaches who grew up and reached maturity in times of depression and war, the things that were "right"

Leon Vinyard. *Photograph courtesy Texas*   Ed Logan, Haltom High School, 1961.
High School Coaches Association, Austin.   *Photograph courtesy Ed Logan.*

revolved around the values of *self-reliance, sacrifice, discipline, accountability,*
and *survival*—in a word that coaches so often used, manliness, in its most
positive sense. The coaches whose careers began around the time of World
War II and continued through the tumultuous social changes in the decades
that followed possessed a conviction that football imparted the qualities that
would turn fuzzy-chinned boys into stalwart young men.

At the heart of their philosophies lay a firm belief that the game presented to their players the same obstacles that would confront them "later
on," as many put it. Longtime Mesquite coach Charles Qualls asserted:
"For almost all kids who play, high school ball is their last athletic experience, so teach them something about life while they're here." Hawkins's
Robert Lowrance taught *self-reliance*: "Success comes through hard work,
whether it's football or life. Nobody ever gives you anything—you have
to earn what you get." Taskmaster Leon Vinyard of Terrell stated:
"Football has a great deal of bearing on staying hitched to the wagon—
you know, not quitting when things get tough."

Former Birdville coach and administrator Ed Logan said that through
football "young men learn they can do something if they want to badly
enough." Eddie Joseph, executive director of the Texas High School
Coaches Association, added that football, "to the players, too, was more
than a game; it had to be, otherwise the *sacrifices* would not be worth it. . . .
If football were only fun and games, you wouldn't spend the money, time,
and effort to do it." Panhandle's Stocky Lamberson remarked: "I teach history in the morning. In history you try to show how our forefathers reacted
under pressure. In athletics you can experience it for yourself. The most sat-
isfying moment is seeing a young person achieve something he didn't think
he could. He had a doubt in his mind, and all along the way you tried to
convince him he could do it."[1]

At the core of those beliefs lay a conviction that *discipline* and a sense of *accountability* were the keystones of character—and that it was football's job to teach those lessons. Chatter Allen, whose career began at La Grange in 1932, asserted: "Most kids do crave discipline and in later years brag about how tough the coach was on them, the number of times they got their 'butt busted,' and the number of laps they had to run." Ray Overton could identify with Allen. After thirty-five years at Paint Creek, Haskell, and Abilene Cooper, he landed at Irving MacArthur in 1982. Toward the middle of the season he had to counsel two players who had been fighting. When he learned they had also been drunk, he called a team meeting. Concluding his stern lecture, Overton told them: "If you were drinking at that party, show up at the track in the morning." Thirty-two of them reported, and he ran them for six weeks—even into the play-offs. "I didn't lose one kid out of that bunch," he stated. Bill Shipman, more father figure than drill sergeant, nevertheless believed that "the tougher coaches are usually the most caring." Shipman applied to football the lessons he learned in the army. "Kids want to prove themselves by accomplishing difficult things," he said; "you've got to let a kid measure up."

Ex-Marine Ray Akins, who fought at Okinawa, believed that football could reinforce a sense of *survival,* the most basic of human instincts. "In the war I saw a lot of boys give up who could have kept going," he said. "I wonder if their mamas could have seen them at that time, ten thousand miles away, if they hadn't wanted them to play football."[2] And even though survival in the post-World War II era of prosperity lost some of its relevance, the lessons of football could still come in handy, as Allert's player-turned-policeman illustrated. Eddie Joseph, moreover, related that during the Vietnam War he occasionally received letters from former players who told him how football helped them cope with combat. One wrote: "All around me I see people who have surrendered, but I can't, because you never let me quit."

Similar backgrounds and experiences through the childhood years and adolescence largely fashioned the morally certain values and self-perceptions that most Texas high school football coaches embraced. While broad social groups normally represent many walks of life, the vast majority of these men—whether white, black, or brown—hailed from humble, and in many cases outright destitute, environments. Typically they possessed a rural southernness that included strong fundamentalist religious roots. They also shared a sense of athleticism and became accustomed to the military regimen that characterized their youth. Even the exceptions could point to some hardscrabble mentor who breathed into them the ways and outlooks of a life honed and hardened by privation. Certainly, their own formative development marked the old coaches' character as adults. And, once in the profession, they sought to imprint upon their players the mores derived from their common social, religious, and economic backgrounds.

The coaches also believed that an even older heritage stamped a uniquely Texan brand on their institution. As the twenty-first century

dawns, it is difficult to appreciate that most of these men's fathers were
born in the nineteenth century. That legacy, many old coaches said, is
more important in Texas than in some other places. Darrell Tully, who
played or coached in almost every part of the state, declared that "here, a
pioneer way of life extended well into the twentieth century in ways of life
and attitudes." Bum Phillips agreed. "Both of my grandfathers went up
the Chisholm Trail," he related, and when he was a boy they relived those
days with him. Bill Shipman added that "Texas itself is historically somewhat rowdy and virile, and also extremely competitive." And with the dis-
covery of oil, freewheeling confidence and a roughneck disposition reinforced those hardy pioneer traditions and imposed their ways upon the
game. "Wherever there seemed to be a good oil producer," said Wichita
Falls's Joe Golding, "you'd find a good football team." The confluence of
folkways and attitudes as well as a lingering frontier identity compelled
Texans to project onto the football field all the exaggerations that they
had come to believe about themselves.

In general, athletics also provided old-time coaches the upward mobility
necessary to escape the vestiges of the rural, nineteenth-century environment
that had trapped their undereducated and underemployed parents. Before
Congress passed the G.I. Bill during World War II, athletics provided one of
the few paths to college for young men of modest means. And even then, in
a rigid, class-conscious society, most had not realized that they were college
material. Football, to young men for whom even a high school diploma was
outside their family's experience, opened the door to a new life, the likes of
which they had never conceived.

No wonder that by the time football became their livelihood, coaches
viewed the game as analogous to life itself. Port Arthur's Joe Washington
insisted that "there is no difference between athletics and life. The same
desires, motivations, disappointments, and successes are the same—they
carry over." "It is manly to withstand the problems of football," said John
Reddell, who used athletics as a ticket out of Oklahoma's Dust Bowl. "It
introduces success, failure, excitement, work ethic, and respect for group."
Almost all of the old-time Texas coaches possessed a firm belief that the
game presented their players a microcosm of life's future obstacles.

Coaches in Literature and Film

The coaches' point of reference, of course, harkened back to an earlier
era, a time before the social changes of the 1960s magnified the country's
moral diversity and left Americans a more sophisticated people. The world
view the coaches embraced was shaped before the time when Texans, like
other Americans, began to question their institutions. Football was one of
the first to fall under the microscope. Critics of the game have gone so far
as to contend that football imparts none of the values that the old coaches
supported. They assert that football's spartan attitudes promote brutality
and unhealthy competition and lead young men to have an overinflated

sense of their own importance. They have painted coaches as abusive troglodytes who used up their players in the pursuit of winning, no matter what the costs.

Writers, especially, in literature and in screenplays have created a shallow and distorted perception of Texas high school football coaches, whether unintentionally or by design. Most have written from observation rather than experience, and they invest no sympathy in the men whom they portray. As bit players in larger stories, coaches often appear as nothing more than cliché-barking caricatures.

Larry McMurtry's Herman Popper in *The Last Picture Show*, on the other hand, left a dark and lasting impression of a pitiful man—an ineffectual coach, an incompetent civics teacher, and a cuckolded husband. Although Hollywood abbreviated the coach's role, the novel on which the movie was based further portrayed Popper as a latent homosexual, who compensated for his perceived flaw by affecting abusive mannerisms and methods. The fictional Thalia (Anarene in the screenplay) and its coach provided vehicles for McMurtry to lampoon the institutions and values of Archer City, where he grew up during the 1950s.[3]

Toby Wood, who coached at Archer City the year that *The Last Picture Show* appeared in print (1966), found McMurtry's fictional coach disgusting. "He was fat and lazy," Wood hissed. "I can't imagine a coach acting like that. . . . He didn't impress me as being a Neanderthal, he was just a slob."

Eddie Morris coached with Wood at Archer City and succeeded him. He even outfitted "Anarene" for the movie, released in 1971. At first "it was all just a Hollywood thing to me," but "over the years, I became very defensive about coaches because they were stereotyped . . . I never worked with coaches of the stereotype. Certainly not at Archer City. . . . We cared about our kids, and we took care of them. We didn't mistreat them. We never cussed a kid, and we tried to set a good example for them."

It was McMurtry, admittedly, who had grown jaded. Quite simply, his fictional coach provided a convenient lightning rod to suffer some of the manifestations of social decay that the author identified with post-frontier West Texas. Morris remarked that McMurtry indeed "mixed and matched" his experiences. "When Larry was in school, there was a player that had an affair with one of the administrator's wives; so, it really wasn't the coach, he just transferred it to him."

On the other hand, McMurtry imparted to rancher and pool hall owner Sam the Lion the positive qualities of character that many football players have routinely found in their coaches, qualities that McMurtry could not have learned on the football field in Archer City because he did not play the game. "In high school I did a number of things mediocrely," the author stated modestly, but football was not among them.[4] If the actual theater at Archer City went belly-up, perhaps it was because townspeople were buying their popcorn down at the stadium. At the same time that McMurtry was conceiving the decadent little village portrayed in *The Last*

Picture Show, Archer City was busy celebrating the Wildcats' 1964 Class 1-A state championship.

In the movie *Dazed and Confused* (1993), set in the drug-influenced 1970s, one of the themes revolved around a moral dilemma facing "next year's" quarterback. He had to decide whether to pay lip service to the demands of his coach, a man who raged in and out of scenes, berating the would-be star for falling in with "a bunch of losers." He continually renewed his ultimatum that the player sign a pledge refraining from alcohol and drugs or "doing anything to hurt the team."

This Texas-based coming-of-age film burlesqued the coach as the embodiment of everything "uncool," a grown man immersed in a boys' game, out of touch with a distracted and self-absorbed youth who had more important things to do. The movie ended with the quarterback deciding to remain loyal to his friends and honest to himself. After impudently telling the coach what he could do with his pledge, the triumphant teens headed out to buy tickets to that evening's Aerosmith concert.

Most recently, Hollywood's back lots produced a vision of contemporary Texas football in the National Broadcasting Company's short-lived series *Against the Grain* (1993) that occasionally took a sideswipe at old coaches. The weekly drama revolved around the trials of Ed Clemons of fictional Sumpter, Texas, the former quarterback and hero of some ancient championship season. When their team lost its coach, fellow citizens prevailed upon Clemons to answer the higher calling by taking up clipboard and whistle and turning his insurance agency over to his wife. Every episode had the reluctant coach facing some crisis that forced him to cut "against the grain" of a football culture that expected him to put the game above grades, the students' welfare, and everything else.

One of the first things "Coach" Clemons did, however, was to install his sophomore son, Joe Willie, into the quarterback slot, placing the team's star in a less glamorous position in the backfield. In another episode, when the former quarterback—now a star running back—was suspended, the coach begged a rules committee to overlook the violation because its members did not understand the extenuating circumstances. Clemons was routinely portrayed as a noble individual because he was not really a coach, but a high-principled businessman bucking an abusive system. Implicating everybody from coaches and players in general to fans and school board members specifically, he proclaimed to the rules committee: "We created this system and our fathers before us." After convincing the tribunal that he had his priorities straight, Clemons won the appeal.

The episode as well as the series itself reflects the way most people probably perceive Texas high school football as an institution. In real life, coaches have not survived attacks by the kinds of angry parents and boosters portrayed in the series. And if Ed Clemons were a real-life coach, he would not have been lecturing some nebulous committee assembled at the Sumpter high school gymnasium when his star player broke the rules;

rather, he would have found himself facing the University Interscholastic League in Austin. Any coach that has appeared on the carpet would tell NBC that the UIL holds to some hard-and-fast rules that seldom accommodate extenuating circumstances. In the end, the fictitious coach survived the old-fashioned way—by coming out on top on the scoreboard. Ironically, the series aired on Friday nights, when Texans who enjoy football were watching their own local dramas unfold.[5]

Portrayals of Texas high school coaches in sports histories and non-fiction works present a mixed bag of images. Histories before the present generation concentrated on the game itself and its heroes. Coaches played prominent roles in their teams' successes, but the stories seldom looked beyond the playing fields. Recently, authors have expressed little concern over the numbers on the scoreboard. They have begun producing more penetrating accounts about football and its effects on players and even entire communities. Writers have recognized that in many cases coaches wield absolute control over their programs, and, as a consequence, they can profoundly manipulate the fragile psyches of their young players.

Sportswriter Harold Ratliff covered Texas athletics for almost half a century and produced several books. He began his career as sports editor for the Cleburne *Times-Review* in 1929, and ended it in 1968 as an Associated Press correspondent. While he covered Southwest Conference football games as well as basketball and track, it was his attraction to community gridirons around the state that earned him the title "Mr. High School Football." In *Autumn's Mightiest Legions* (1963) and *Texas Schoolboy Football* (1972), he traced the development of the high school game by extolling the great players and mythologizing the big games. The coaches in his narratives earned recognition by producing the kinds of teams and individuals that made Texans, as he declared, "the greatest football race in the world."[6]

Bill McMurray of the Houston *Chronicle* deservingly inherited Ratliff's title. His *Texas High School Football* (1985) remains the game's authoritative reference work. Like Ratliff, McMurray was determined to record and preserve the sport's high-water marks. He not only renovated the older work, but also produced a more substantive account, much wider in scope and more inclusive in detail. In addition to compiling records and discussing the game's uniquely Texan aspects, he summarized the careers and accomplishments of fourteen of the state's most successful coaches.

Texas's favorite pastime compelled both Ratliff and McMurray to regale their readers with riveting vignettes of greatness on the high school gridiron. And while both were eminently capable, it was not their purpose to probe behind the scenes and examine the nature of the game or the methods of its field marshals. Nevertheless, at times they acknowledged the human qualities in coaches, whose shepherding of their charges contributed noticeably to their success.

Contemporary with McMurray's encyclopedic work were some mono-graphs that placed particular Texas high school coaches under the micro-scope. R. E. Blount and Carlton Stowers illustrated the extremes. Blount, who enjoyed huge success as a University of Texas player during the late 1940s, recalled a bitter high school experience in *Mamas, Don't Let Your Babies Grow Up To Play Football* (1985). He painted a deplorable picture of "Ole Sarge," a man whom his West Texas community held in higher esteem than "the mayor, the sheriff, the chief of police, the pastor of the First Baptist Church, [and] the presidents of both banks."[7]

"I feared him," Blount reflected, because "he constantly dwelt on my inadequacies and failings—imagined and otherwise." Among the personal humiliations that the author described were instances of "Ole Sarge" chal-lenging players to fight him, of threatening to leave one behind during a road game, of ordering a player to sit with the band, and of ridiculing his charges just when they thought they had finally done something worthy of his praise. "You keep telling a sixteen-year-old he's sadly and pitifully lack-ing and a no-good turd, and it's not difficult to ultimately convince him that his sum total equals a piece of shit," the author concluded.[8]

"Ole Sarge," evidently, was a chip off the old block. As an assistant coach he had apprenticed under Dewey Mayhew, whose Abilene Eagles annually contended for state titles during the 1930s. After painting Mayhew with the same brush as his understudy, Blount proffered: "I would conservatively estimate that one-fourth to one-third [of high school coaches] were not fit to oversee a prison chain gang."[9]

Blount later admitted that his condemnation of the profession was overzealous. "I did not mean to just throw all coaches into one barrel. Goodnight, no!" The author conceded that he had based his judgment on observing mannerisms in coaches that reminded him of "Ole Sarge." Some of the coaches he respected most, "men that I absolutely loved . . . never gave you a pat on the back." The difference, he sur-mised, was that he could sense underneath those granite exteriors that the good ones truly cared for their players. "Ole Sarge," quite simply, let him down. Blount expressed both surprise and approbation upon learning that among almost two hundred names in the Texas High School Coaches' Hall of Honor, those of Dewey Mayhew and "Ole Sarge" do not appear.[10]

A quite different high school experience inspired Carlton Stowers to write *Friday Night Heroes*. While most of his idols ran up and down the playing field, a few of them jumped up and down on the sidelines. Among them was Stowers' own coach, Abilene's Chuck Moser. During the 1950s, Moser had taken over the very program that Dewey Mayhew had long since departed. And, like Mayhew, Moser once again brought the Eagles to prominence, winning three Class 4-A state championships in a row.[11] Comparing the accounts of Stowers and Blount, any similari-ties between the two men ended there. Where Mayhew's abuse and bro-ken promises inspired his players to open revolt, Moser "made everyone

Chuck Moser cuts a cake with his Abilene staff after winning the district title in 1954. A state championship would follow that season, and again in 1955 and 1956. *Photograph courtesy Texas Sports Hall of Fame, Waco.*

aware . . . starter or sub alike . . . that we had a contribution to make to the team." The day after Moser's bid for a fourth straight state championship fell short in a 1957 semifinal match with Highland Park, he was at church delivering a lesson to his junior high girls Sunday School class "about how everything happens for the best."[12]

Somewhere between the portrayals by Blount and Stowers lies Jan Reid's *Vain Glory* (1986). In three parts—dealing separately with the high school, college, and professional ranks—he alternately satirized and praised the eccentricities of Texans and their relationship with football. The author's admittedly cynical "character studies, impressions of football people, obscure and famous," reflected his middle-aged disillusionment. "The social trappings that we hang on a weekend diversion arouse the spoilsport in me," he remarked in his preface. This rambling narrative seemed to ask: "What's all the fuss about?" If the book's title failed to express fully that message, then his opening epigraph made it imminently clear. He quoted Don Quixote: "Do you not hear the neighing of the steeds, the braying of the trumpets, the roll of the drums?" To which Sancho Panza replied: "I hear nothing but the bleating of ewes and sheep." Like the two Spaniards, Reid implied, some Texans see giants, others only windmills.[13]

Coaches, as a rule that Reid acknowledged, see giants. Those he introduced in this alternately condemning, praiseworthy, and indifferent account were neither saints nor villains, except for Bum Phillips. Reid's "blue-collar folk hero" seemed to be the only man at any level who kept the game in perspective. He was also the only coach whose background Reid thoroughly investigated.[14]

In a later interview, Phillips himself insisted that he drew his values from an environment typified by the men whose ranks propelled him out of obscurity as Elbert Pickell's assistant coach at Nederland High School to head-coaching fame in the National Football League.[15] Reid did not invest that same understanding in his own high school coach, Joe Golding. A self-professed "scrub" on Wichita Falls' B-team as a junior in 1960, the author never gained access to the Coyotes' mentor. In fact, Reid's career ended prematurely when an assistant coach, worried that he might get hurt, suggested that he stick with baseball.[16]

From arm's length, Reid gently mocked Golding for manifesting the stereotypical traits of his profession. At the beginning of every season, he wrote, the old coach would tell the booster club: "Football is a man's game, and there is nothing which makes men out of boys as quickly as does football." He would finish his speech by relating the ultimate lesson that the game imparted: "Football players are not quitters, on the field or later in life." At other times Reid was not as kind. "It was kind of chicken-shit the way old Joe did it. All those kids starting out at the junior highs and coming up through the system, and then he only played the best fifteen."[17]

The author constructed his sketch through the troubled player-coach relationship between Golding and the Lavender brothers, Jay and Keith. Neither of them ever weighed much more than 150 pounds in high school, but even the biggest, meanest kids in town would give them a wide berth. Streetwise kids from the wrong part of town, they gained reputations for picking fights just for the fun of it. For some reason the elder Lavender, Jay, learned to keep his mean streak on the football field. That virtue escaped his younger brother Keith, who showed the same promise, but could not avoid trouble. One night, after he whipped a serviceman from nearby Sheppard Air Force Base, the police were dispatched to the brothers' home. And after provoking both of them into a brawl on the Lavenders' front lawn—which left one officer with a broken jaw and another fumbling for his gun—the police "retired to their squad cars and radioed downtown for instructions."[18]

Where critics have lately taken coaches to task for not holding their players accountable, Reid condemned Golding for booting Keith Lavender from the team. The Coyotes' linebacker coach, Joe Bob Tyler, let the Lavenders know that the staff was "not running a halfway house for outlaw football players," wrote Reid. "As a social institution," Tyler estimated, "football has to reflect accepted values in the community." Golding evidently agreed and cashiered the younger Lavender brother for violating those standards.[19]

Reid's portrayal of Golding fell short. As an outsider to varsity football, he never understood the kinds of relationships high school football coaches form with their players. However close to the principals in his character sketches, the author slipped discursively from one topic to the next, as if the answer lay somewhere between the lines. He could never quite fathom why Jay Lavender strove so hard to please Golding when the coach seemed to treat him so shabbily. "I was never on Golding's top shelf," the diminutive former linebacker admitted to Reid. "He knew I ran with the wrong crowd . . . but he liked me because he knew . . . I would go put the bonnet on somebody." Reid acknowledged that some larger, unspoken bond nevertheless tied the two. Lavender, he noted, eventually started a construction business, the JaBeau Corporation—named after the way Golding affectionately pronounced "Jay Boy."[20]

The same fascination with football that inspired Jan Reid to write *Vain Glory* compelled H. G. Bissinger "to discover the essence of high school football. . . . A variety of names came up, but all roads led to West Texas, to a town called Odessa," he declared. So, in 1988, he arranged to take a year's hiatus from his editor's post at the Philadelphia *Inquirer* to satisfy that obsession. Two years later he published *Friday Night Lights*.[21]

Most Texans themselves have long regarded Odessa's Permian High School as having built the best program in a football-rich state. And although the Permian Panthers suffer occasional down cycles, it at least seems as if they are always contending for gridiron championships. Yet the Panthers are actually perennial underdogs. They never send as many kids to the college ranks as the one-season wonders they face in the play-offs. Rather, they win consistently with precision-tooled but outmanned players, exhorted to victory by a band, cheerleaders, and a community following that would make many colleges envious. "Mojo"—an incantation of Permian High spirit whose origins no one quite seems to know—became the manifestation of the Panthers' mystique. The tingling chant arising from the throats of ten thousand or more black-and-white-clad fans has induced perhaps scores of aspiring dynasties to append such twists as Cujo, RoHo, and Pojo onto their mascots in hopes that the same Panther magic will rub off on them.

Friday Night Lights, however, cast a pall over Odessa's "east side" and the object of its pride. For four months the author lived among their team and its coaches—he ate with them, he prayed with them, he celebrated with them, he commiserated with them, but ultimately, in their view, he betrayed them. Odessans, believing that Bissinger was going to write a Texas version of *Hoosiers*, instead found themselves the objects of ridicule and condemnation. Certainly there exists a continuity between the game as it grew out of an earlier era and the distorted vision that Bissinger conceived. And no doubt his own values and expectations clashed with a people and an institution that he viewed as radically out of step with the times.

As for Odessa itself, the author painted a derisive picture of a semi-rural backwash with its priorities woefully out of balance—"an armpit" of a place, a description that "was actually a few rungs up from its usual anatomical comparison with a rectum." Within its city limits lived a society scarred by many cancers: racism—"There were some whites in town who found the use of the word nigger offensive, but they were so far removed from the mainstream that no one took them very seriously"; a rigid, unforgiving ideological and fundamental right-wing conservatism— "It sometime seemed surprising that Lanita Akins . . . an active Democrat, a Unitarian, an ex-hippie, and a Dukakis supporter . . . wasn't forced to walk around town with a shaved head and wearing a pair of striped pajamas like the French collaborators of World War II"; religious hypocrisy—its 109 Protestant churches provided "an excuse for people to come together and be made comfortable with their own social beliefs in racial and gender bigotry"; derelict educators—"It was not uncommon for teachers at Permian to teach for only a quarter or a third of the period and then basically let students do whatever they wanted as long as they did it quietly"; and the crass materialism of suddenly prosperous oil field trash who "wear gaudy jewelry and belt buckles big enough to eat their lunch off of . . . There were stories of them marching into Gibson's . . . and plunking down $2,000 or $3,000 to redecorate their mobile homes from head to toe."[22]

Odessans complained that any hostile and biased observer with a keen eye and a sharp pen could have singled out the poor and working class citizens of any southern-cum-western town and said the same thing that Bissinger wrote about them. Many old-time Texas high school coaches hailed from such origins and places, and their values no doubt reflect those of their communities. And while far from perfect, both the towns and their inhabitants certainly possess a catalog of virtues to match their vices.

Whether the author told the truth as he saw it, only he could say. Yet, in painting his impression, Bissinger seemed to use only the Permian black and white. His characters seemed to be either victims or predators; his situations seemed always to contrast the laudable and condemnable. The gray on his palette, from which most of life is truly painted, remained untouched. Any place Bissinger might have seen gray, complained townspeople, he painted it black every time.

The only thing he needed to make his dark portrait complete was an "Ole Sarge," but he did not find one in Odessa. Gleaning the lines of *Friday Night Lights* actually yields a quite positive portrayal of Permian's coaches, their approach to the game, and their relationships with the players. The entire coaching staff continually made sure that the kids kept their experience in perspective. They praised but they did not coddle; they criticized but they did not condemn; they prodded but they did not push. Yet rather than praise Permian's staff, the author drew a caustic comparison between the coaches and Jaime Escalante, the inner-city Los Angeles teacher Hollywood portrayed in the movie *Stand and Deliver*. Bissinger concluded that in Odessa such methods were wasted on the football field rather than invested in the classroom.[23]

The author's criticisms of Odessa's football-mad culture, however, could not hide that fact that its program rested on the shoulders of a man who embodied the picture of personal dignity, professional dedication, and paternal concern. Bissinger described head coach Gary Gaines as "methodical and meticulous about everything, the kind of coach, the kind of man, who prepared for every possible situation through tireless work." Not once did any rabid "Kill! Kill! Kill!" creep into his motivational messages. In fact, Gaines sounded eerily like the fictitious Ed Clemons. Before the first big game in *Against the Grain*, Clemons had said: "This is what it's all about fellas. . . . Have fun out there." In that same situation Bissinger noted that Gaines's last words of advice were "short and sincere: 'Nobody rest a play, men. Don't coast on any play. You're on that field, you give it everything you got.'" And right before turning them loose, "with a little smile still on his lips," Gaines said: "Let's have a great one."[24]

And, that evening, a great one they had. But the rest of the way was not always smooth for the Panthers. Even though they fought their way to the semifinals before being eliminated by the eventual state champions, they lost two other games. The first was a non-district contest that showcased Permian and East Texas powerhouse Marshall. Gaines's bunch, Bissinger estimated, should have been up by twenty-one points at halftime, instead of three. Yet in the dressing room Gaines remained calm. "Our own mistakes are the reason we're behind now. . . . We just need to bow up." He and the other coaches then grabbed some chalk and began diagraming adjustments on the blackboards—no chairs thrown through windows, no belittled players, no Gipperisms. At halftime in another game, Gaines confronted a running back who had just fumbled away two scoring opportunities. Taking him into "the little coaches' room," the author wrote, Gaines "threw him a football. 'Hold on to it,' he said." An assistant coach later took the boy aside and told him: "Just put that behind you. If you worry about it, it's gonna screw you up. It's history."[25]

Many other bright linings appeared on the edges of Bissinger's 364-page critique, but perhaps nothing shone more than Gaines's reaction to Permian's three losses. At the first setback the coach took all the blame upon himself. "I'll do a better job next week," he told his players. And when arch-rival Midland Lee beat them, he took in stride seven "For Sale" signs he found in his yard. Only when he learned that a disgruntled fan had punched a sign into a player's lawn did he become visibly upset: "That's sick to me . . . I just can't understand it." Finally Dallas Carter beat the Panthers in the semifinals. "It seemed corny" earlier in the season, the author remarked of Gaines's talk about the team building family-like bonds, "but it didn't now. They were together, white and black and Hispanic, rich and poor, and they would stay that way for as long as they were a team." Yet, by then it was all over. There was nothing for Gaines to do but lead a final benediction imparting a message of pride, character, and overcoming setbacks.[26]

Ways and Outlooks

Bissinger occasionally mentioned an assistant coach, Randy Mayes, who spent countless hours going over film, and at halftimes would fill up entire chalkboards diagraming plays. The description no doubt inspired images of a much older, mature man. Yet Mayes was only thirty-two years old at the time. His own high school coach at Lewisville, Bill Shipman, recalled him as the "5' 7", 150-pound captain of my 1972 team." He also recalled Eddie Mullins, who was six inches taller and fifty pounds heavier. "Eddie was a tremendous blocker, the only one who went both ways. These two stayed after workouts and battered each other regularly to get extra practice." Once Shipman asked Mayes, "Do you ever block Eddie?" To which his pint-sized captain answered nonchalantly, "Sure, coach; about half the time." Shipman expressed amazement: "That's better than just about anybody that's played against him." Unimpressed, Mayes continued: "Yeah, coach, the other half of the time we trade off, and he blocks me."

At thirty-nine, Mayes inherited Permian's program after a brief tenure as head coach at Ennis. Despite remarkably youthful looks, if he has retained any of the naiveté that Shipman fondly recalled, it remains hidden behind an aura of intensity. Mayes has already experienced many of the same ups and downs that marked his old mentor's career. As head coaches both of them have gone all the way to the state finals only to fall short. In 1995, Permian went to the wire in a heartbreaker against San Antonio's Converse Judson. In 1972, Shipman's Lewisville Farmers lost to Uvalde "by two feet." The old coach remembered that after the game both sides were so exhausted "they just didn't have much emotion left." At breakfast the next day Shipman and the Uvalde coach "agreed that it was a shame either team had to lose." That afternoon the Farmers returned home and everybody got off the bus. When they were all gone, Shipman said, "I sat down in the equipment room and cried for a long, long time, . . . and I'm sure a lot of other coaches have done the same thing in the privacy of their own place." Randy Mayes could commiserate with him. Of the Judson game, he said: "That was the worst I've taken a loss since 1972." And, he admitted, just as Shipman did: "I had a good cry when I got by myself."

Randy Mayes, like Gary Gaines, has adapted the ways of an older generation of coaches to modern times. And even though their kids know the meaning of physical sacrifice, gone are the boot camp ways of these coaches' mentors. Nevertheless, they still try to impart those same fundamental life lessons. Modern coaches, however, must convey football's instruction to a generation less receptive to the values of self-reliance, discipline, and accountability. Privation and survival remain largely outside of their players' conceptual frameworks.

John Reddell, who coached from one end of the Red River to the other, commented that even into the 1970s "most of the fathers worried about their sons being manly. They wanted them to be tough and learn how to handle adversity and 'get back up' if something bad happened to them. And they depended a great deal upon football to do that." What has changed, he insisted, is that parents, "instead of depending upon someone else to make the kid 'do this and that,' . . . began making excuses for them. They came to distrust the coaches as well as the teachers as well as the policemen as well as any type of authority. As a result, they pretty well took away the opportunity to give those kids something to build on."

Almost every old-time coach felt that kids today have been raised to "ask why." Jewell Wallace asserted that "questioning authority is not so bad. They have a right to know." Not many kids today, moreover, buy into the simple contrivances that coaches once regularly used. As Ed Logan put it: "These players know that that boy on the other side of the line doesn't even know his momma—so, how is he going to know she's a whore? You have to reach them in different ways."

Bissinger related that twice, before the two most emotionally charged games of the season, Gary Gaines did it by drawing parallels instead of feeding off base emotions. Before playing crosstown rival Odessa, he told the boys an instructional story about two opposing Civil War scouts. The second time, before facing white-collar Midland Lee, he related an inspiring object lesson, rather than indulging his mostly blue-collar players. He told them about Olympic swimmer Steve Genter, who "split his stitches" competing at Munich with a collapsed lung. His players, like Genter, "had come too far to let it all go."[27]

Old coaches long have used such confidence builders. Bill Shipman, in fact, relied on them. At the helm of the Lewisville Farmers, he created "Big John," patterned after Pecos Bill. "The first time I used him, we were playing Boswell, so it was a showdown with 'Bully Boswell,' Bully 'called him out' and they fought, and when they fell down it measured 7.0 on the Richter scale," he laughed. "Every Thursday after practice, I'd tell them another Big John story, and each week it was against the opposing team's mascot."

The ruse failed, however, when he later tried the same thing at Abilene in 1975. Shipman had concocted the legend of an Indian spirit he called "Aquilla." The week before his Eagles played crosstown rival Cooper, he got the idea of enlisting the Indian mascot at McMurry University to bring the character to life. "This was only about a three-week-old tradition," an apologetic Shipman intoned. "McMurry was having their homecoming, and they had this guy with a full headdress and an Indian pony. I explained the situation, and said, 'How about you coming over on Thursday at three o'clock? You get on your pony and ride through the practice field and throw your spear through the goal post. Then disappear just like you were a spirit—don't let the kids see the horse trailer or anything.' So I waited and waited. No Indian. We stayed out there covering punts so long that the kids were beginning to wonder what was going on, so I finally told them to go to the house." That night Shipman sat brooding in front of the television. When the sports came on, a reporter interviewed Ray Overton, head coach at Abilene Cooper. "When they asked him 'How's it going, coach?' he said, 'You'll never believe what happened today. . . .'"

With the "big game" looming ahead, old-time coaches pitched to their players' emotions in any number of ways. Day-to-day, however, they motivated more by stick than by carrot. Shipman remarked that "most of the time I coached, parents didn't question the fact that their kids worked hard and followed rules, and the kids didn't question, and a lot of times they would work out on their own." Bill Hartley of Columbus added: "Practices in the beginning lasted as long as you wanted it. There was no such thing as an hour-and-a-half of practice. If you got out there at 3:30, you could stay out there 'till 6:30. Everybody accepted that."

Bill Carter, a Joe Golding assistant in the 1950s, remembered that once, "after two hours into a bad workout one day, Golding stopped practice and told them to circle up; they were going to start practice over—and his practices usually lasted four hours." Bill Bookout, who coached at Hurst Bell and Trinity, played on that same Wichita Falls practice field during his high school days. "We called it the 'Hell Hole.' It was down in the river bottoms. Breezes seldom reached it, and it was rough land—a lot of river, but not much water." Of his coach, and the way he worked his players, Bookout remarked: "Joe Golding was tough, but it didn't seem that way because we were used to it."

"Football is a spartan-type game, and it's meant to be played by spartan-type people," declared Eddie Joseph. Nevertheless, he conceded, "I look back at some of the things we did, and I think about when I was in high school myself, and it's a wonder we didn't kill children. It was tougher than it had to be—to the point that it was stupid. . . . You were soft, and you were a sissy if you had to drink water in 110-degree weather. They used to think that drinking water would make you sick. Now we know that if you don't drink water, the consequences could be much worse than just getting sick. . . . Some of the silliest, stupidest things that we thought you had to do to become tough—it's a wonder that we had anybody survive!"

Yet even before Joseph retired in 1981, both the old coaches and their progeny had largely adapted to new conditions. "Nowadays you don't have to practice being miserable," Joseph commented. "Even in football you have to change with the times. Some fundamental things never change; it's still a game of blocking and tackling. But you don't have to treat a kid poorly for him to be a good football player. . . . A long time ago we started telling them that if you fly like an eagle on Friday nights, we won't treat you like a turkey during the week."

A consensus of old coaches believed that those today who continue to rely on the practices of twenty and more years ago are out of step with the times. New conditions require new methods. "You cannot intimidate and badger someone into being tough and playing," exclaimed John Reddell; "you can, however, develop enough pride in them that they'll fight to the death." Reddell commented that the "stuff of survival," its values, and its ways have become the province of men who have no business coaching. Still, images of Bear Bryant and Vince Lombardi die hard, and a popular perception lingers that "winning at all costs" dictates methods that border on abuse.

Criticism directed at today's worst coaches underscores that image. The worst peewee coaches are so terrible because they mimic some misshapen ideal; the worst professional coaches consider football a business that employs "players." Blurring the line between the game and business occurs somewhere at the college level and can certainly be found at many high schools. And since the "business" of football is winning, and because coaches earn their livelihoods by working toward that goal, the public mind has conjured up some vague idea of coaches as abusive drillmasters.

During the 1981 football season, ABC Entertainment demonstrated just how well ingrained those perceptions are. When its morning news program planned to run a segment on violence in sports, the network invited Brownwood's Gordon Wood, then the country's winningest coach, to represent the counter viewpoint. While the American Broadcasting Company insisted that "it has never been the policy of *Good Morning America* to 'ambush' guests," it nevertheless admitted "in this case, that policy was violated." Staff members, no doubt thinking this particular cause was a good one, did not invite Gordon Wood to enlighten them, but rather to have him for breakfast.

When the old country coach from West Texas took his seat, he found himself extending a hearty handshake to Harvard Law School professor Arthur Miller and a tentative howdy to two other guests, both victims of paralyzing football injuries. When the producers rolled a thirty-second clip of an abusive Florida high school coach slapping his players and railing at them, host David Hartman reeled. Unprepared for the day's segment, he assumed that it was Wood whom he was watching in action. Hartman indignantly began censuring the old coach, finally demanding that he explain. Rather curtly Wood responded to the effect of: "Well, that's not me, and if that were a coach of mine, I'd fire him."

A thoroughly perplexed and embarrassed Hartman finally allowed Wood to respond without browbeating him. And before the old coach was finished, the other members of the panel actually found more room for agreeing with him than disagreeing. They seemed to commiserate with Wood when he reflected: "I have been fortunate in my career that no serious injuries have occurred on my teams." And when he claimed that "a youngster has a better chance of getting hurt in an auto coming home from school than on the field," the others offered only tentative rebuttals.[28]

Gordon Wood came out all right. He, like any other coach, has lived on the griddle, and nothing turns up the heat like pressure to win. Winning provides communities a yardstick by which to measure their coach's success; it also determines whether towns fire a coach or lose one to a school that pays more money and has better facilities. Those who

Gordon Wood, Brownwood High. *Photograph courtesy Texas Sports Hall of Fame, Waco.*

know coaches only casually generally assume that since their job is to win, they will do anything to achieve that objective. Actually, they are right. Where folks miss the mark, however, is the way they interpret "anything."

Sports analyst Beano Cook, recently explaining why the Southeastern Conference was under a cloud of NCAA sanctions, laid blame on the demands of winning. "There's more pressure to win in SEC football than there is in any league in any sports. Except maybe high school football in Texas."[29] If the timeworn dictum of "winning at all costs" is true, then one might expect that those coaches who have won the most games have left the largest number of human casualties strewn in their wake.

If you search the top of the list, however, men like nine-time state champion Gordon Wood and Chuck Moser, who won championships at Abilene High School in 1954, 1955, and 1956, found that winning flows naturally as a product of achieving more important and long-lasting objectives. Moser stated: "I'm proud of the things we accomplished. But not as proud as I am of what so many of those kids have grown up to be. They're good, solid citizens. Something rubbed off back there, and that fact gives me a warm feeling." Said Gordon Wood: "Over there at Stamford, if I could take a team picture [from 1956] and show you, it's absolutely unbelievable the achievements that those kids have made— [U.S. Congressman] Charles Stenholm, he was an all-state end for me. I must have had twenty doctors and lawyers out there. In that little ol' country town, I think there's thirty-three kids in that picture, and I believe about twenty-eight of them graduated from college."

Mesquite's Charles Qualls said: "You've got to put the kids first—you teach values, responsibility, and discipline—and winning will take care of itself." Texas coaching legend Tugboat Jones, who produced winners at virtually every level, added that "I always put the kids first. . . . To get the best out of a kid, he's got to feel that he's loved." Jones regularly told his assistant coaches not to let their players go home upset, "you pat him on the back and tell him he'll have a better day tomorrow."

Texas High School Coaches' Hall of Honor member Buzz Allert, who both won and lost his share of games in Southeast Texas, mentored many young men into the profession. "I'd always tell my coaches, whatever you do, don't reflect on whether you win or lose. Don't ever cheat your players. Always work them in the right way. Always discipline them properly." Allert insisted: "Winning the game is secondary with me; it always has been. Winning the kid is first—getting a commitment, a good attitude, and a one-hundred-percent effort. . . . You always coach for the double win," he stressed. "Sure, you want to win that game; you're going to do everything humanly possible as a staff to have your kids prepared to win the football game—that's your first win. Your second win is that you coach for that kid to be a winner. I've walked off many a football field when that scoreboard didn't read in my favor, but I've loaded more winners on my bus than the other team did, by their character, by their effort, by their attitude, by their commitment, by their work habits. And all these things are things they're going to carry with them the rest of their lives."

Allert's expressions represented a common theme among the old coaches. At Riesel during the early 1900s, Frank Pulattie's Indians were hosting "a very salty team that was a twenty-point favorite." He remarked that when he went to his opponents' dressing room right before the kick-off to see if there was anything they needed, "I heard the boys cussing and being crude right in front of their coach." Pulattie went back to his dressing room and told his players: "'Men, we can beat this bunch. They've got no character.' And we did, too, 30–23."

Gordon Wood's formula for winning was simple. "You have to be real fair with [players], and you try to instill self-confidence in them, and you have to increase their team spirit. Every kid is really a better athlete than he thinks he is, so you try to get them to believe in their own ability and what they're capable of doing. As far as the values that you try to teach them, you try to improve their self-image, which is so vital to any success they might have as an athlete or as a person. And, you want to make sure they're as good a student as possible and as good a person as possible."

Very early in his career, Wood said, "a little ol' deal that I got into over some kids' grades changed my attitude, because I suddenly realized that we're supposed to be doing some things for kids besides just coaching football." It was at the Northwest Texas town of Rule in 1940 that he learned of three "regulars" who were facing academic suspension. "So I went to the superintendent and told him, 'I've worked like a dog to build up a program, and now I've got one, and if these three kids fail, I'm going to resign.'" After telling Wood he'd see what he could do, the administrator reported the next day that he had "worked it out with the teachers and they were going to pass." As one of the players waited on the news, Wood heard him repine: "If they're not interested enough in me and my football to let me pass, then they don't care much about it." At that, Wood said, "I turned around and went back in there and told the superintendent that now, if any one of them does pass, then I'm going to resign.

"And that is the last time in my lifetime that I ever tried to influence a teacher in helping a kid over grades." In fact, when the state began tightening its academic standards just before Wood retired, a band director complained "he'd lost so many that he couldn't have his spring band concert." Wood lost only one, for he long had subjected his players, "from the seventh grade on up," to weekly grade checks. The forms not only asked teachers if the boys were failing, but if so, "is it because he's not trying, or because he's misbehaving in class?" Wood added: "If they were misbehaving, then we'd bust their tail with a board. I'm not saying that's right or wrong, all I'm saying is that it's effective. It worked."

Morris Southall, who coached beside Wood for many seasons, told how he and his wife toured all over the Southwest with the Brownwood high school choir. One of the stops was at San Angelo, where the coach "was not having much luck with his program." Evidently, many of the faces in the choir looked familiar to the San Angelo coach, and "right in the middle of that thing, he stopped it and told the audience, 'I want you to see how many of these kids are football players.' There were twelve of them, and five were all-staters in 1965."

Reflecting on a very different image than that projected by Wood and Southall, another longtime West Texas coach, Moon Mullins, stated: "It burns deeply to be blasted by all the misperceptions." In the old days "the coach was cornerstone of the community along with the preacher and the mayor. He had access to the kids and guided their lives. In return, coaches got their respect and were even beloved. And the parents trusted you with teaching moral lessons."

Coaches were given a free hand to instruct their players, and they reached them in any number of ways. Ed Logan asserted that the coach had "more direct control over kids than any other teacher, and even clergymen. Parents would come and tell him about their kids' problems and get him to help." Herb Allen said: "When I was in college, my own coach told me that you have to treat them fair, but you can't treat them all the same. You've got to scream at some, slap some, pat some, and console some. This is the hardest part of coaching. All kids are different, and you've got to know which buttons to push."

Garland's Homer Johnson related that after thirty years, a former all-state tackle came back to visit him. "He said: 'Coach, I always thought you liked me, but at halftime you'd shake me until I was just about ready to hit you, and then you'd turn me loose and walk over to Bobby Norvell and hug his neck.'" Johnson responded: "Your daddy thought you were the greatest thing that ever walked, and all he ever did was brag on you. If I wanted to get anything out of you, I'd have to get your attention. Bobby Norvell's daddy didn't even know he existed, and if you said anything crossways to him, he wouldn't hit a lick. But if you bragged on him, or hugged his neck, he'd run through the wall for you."

Bill Shipman said: "At one school, I coached a boy with a great deal of ability, but he was 'fluffing it off.' I pushed him, I talked with him, I stuck notes in his pocket, I wrote to him, I praised him, I criticized him, and he became first team all-state and eventually a coach. At another school, I had a super specimen at fullback who could have made all the difference. I pushed, and I pushed, until I pushed him off the team. The same tactics will not work with every young man."

Teenagers could be sensitive, and sometimes their coaches pushed buttons unknowingly. At Anson, for example, Moon Mullins had a boy on the team who was so big—almost three hundred pounds—that no uniform would fit him. "I ended up having to go over to Abilene Christian to get him some pants, and this meant a lot to him." Yet during practice one day, when the boy hurt his shoulder, "I kidded him that his problem was that he was so fat." The next day "we were both at church, and I put my arm around him and gave him some encouraging words." Only years later, when they happened to run into each other, did Mullins learn that the kid had "swelled up and wanted to quit—and would have except for what I had told him at church."

Joe Bob Tyler found that occasionally he had to push that button very firmly. As the B-team coach on Joe Golding's staff, he learned that he was about to inherit from one of the junior highs "an ornery kid who had earned a bad reputation." The first day of practice, "I pulled him out of the group and berated him. I was surprised to see how little he was, but he was the team leader. I told him that if he ever got out of line, I was going to throw him bodily over the fence, and then jump over it and kick his butt all the way home. And you know, he never did a thing to disappoint me from that time on—on the field, or even off the field for that matter."

When that player, Jay Lavender, moved up to Golding's team, his mentor came along as the team's new varsity linebacker coach. "I was right there with him," Tyler remarked, "and I'm telling you he was a hitter and a fighter all the way, and he'd always knock that running back on his tail and then pick him up. He even won a sportsmanship trophy one year." And when Lavender graduated from college, he joined Tyler's staff. Perhaps the old coach's version of their relationship provided the missing element that author Jan Reid seemed to have searched for in vain. From that very first day of practice, the volatile linebacker had always been on Tyler's "top shelf." Lavender himself told Reid: "People don't seem to understand the positive effect that coaches can have on these kiddoes." Reflecting on old high school friends, he remarked: "Half of 'em hoodlums and criminals to this day. . . . I hate to think where I might have ended up if it hadn't been for guys like Joe Golding and Joe Bob Tyler."[30]

Scholars' Views and Coaches' Philosophies

There was a time when imparting life's lesson seemed natural to the old coaches. These men, who had grown up with nothing, taught their players to be resilient; these men, who had been fed old-time religion, encouraged their players to act on their emotions; these men, most of them veterans, many of whom had killed other human beings in combat, treated their players like soldiers; and they felt that passing on those lessons was in the best interest of the kids. Yet critics of football coaches see the players' sacrifices as abuse and the coaches' mannerisms as cartoonish and barbaric.

Eddie Morris, who split his career between Archer City and Gainesville, stated: "I really felt that any kid that didn't play football was cheating himself out of something that was very valuable. There were lessons to be learned in football that you can't learn anywhere else." "Functionalists" in the field of sports sociology would largely agree; they believe that sports fills the needs of athletes and society for the same reasons that coaches so often cite.

On the other hand, another, more vocal, group of sociologists—"conflict theorists"—have drawn some consistent and disturbing conclusions that seem to mock the fundamental beliefs of coaches such as Eddie Morris. The entire field of sports sociology has emerged since the late 1960s, with its existence turning on examining the role and influence of sports on society. In *Lessons of the Locker Room* (1994), anthropologist Andrew Miracle and physical education professor Roger Rees surveyed the most current research through the lenses of "conflict theory" and concluded: "We find little empirical evidence that sport builds character or has any positive influence on youth." Through the work of sports sociologists, the authors critiqued what they called a "sports myth"—that "one becomes number one . . . through hard work, dedication, following orders, and sacrificing self for the good of the team."[31]

The sweeping report card that *Lessons of the Locker Room* issued to high school athletics posted abysmally failing grades. Scholars, the authors contended, steadfastly denied that high school athletics served its purpose, that is, "that it pays off in terms of character development, educational aspiration, educational attainment, and occupational advancement." A catalog of those conclusions included: "Being an athlete . . . does not make poor students good students or good students even better"; "Every success story could be balanced by one of failure"; "Athletes tended to be less sportsmanlike than non-athletes." Positive "character changes" such as "self-esteem or valuing academic achievement . . . may be offset by increases in antisocial tendencies such as an increase in aggression or a decrease in self-control"; "There is nothing in the high school sport experience per se that prepares [the athlete] for the world of work"; "Athletics can teach independence or dependence or nothing at all." Sports sociologists also have implied that athletic directors and coaches are paying lip service to character building, while their programs actually concentrate on "winning at all costs." Again, at the bottom line, wrote Miracle and Rees: "The consensus . . . is that there is no evidence to support the claim that sport builds character in high school."[32]

The authors also stated that their "examination of the beliefs that commonly surround the question of sport in American schools [is] based on the best available data." A review of the scholarly works they cite, however, reveals that sports sociology is a nascent field of study that has largely examined a post–1960s culture. And, like examining the relationship between Christians and the Christian experience without putting the preacher into the equation, this field has similarly portrayed athletes and the athletic experience without listening to the voices of coaches. In 1988, bibliographer Paul Redekop annotated the sports sociology works represented in eighty-two scholarly journals. In compiling his section, "Sport and Culture," not one title surveyed coaches and their values. Andrew Miracle himself illustrated how far removed he was from the source by once asking: "Why is it that this term for an occupation ['coach'] is so often used as a title of respect?" He did not consider that society conferred that form of address upon these men in a much earlier age, at a time when his "sports myth" might have possessed more substance than it does today.[33]

The disparity between the assessments of sociologists and the old-time Texas coaches underscores some fundamental questions that historians have raised about their professional cousins in the social sciences. Historians complain that sociologists in general construct their arguments in a vacuum and often fail to incorporate primary or archival sources. And, by shoehorning their data into models and theorems, they distort historical reality. The disciplinary canons of sociology, moreover, have all but ignored social change over time. Today's high school athletes certainly bear the crosses of a society that has lost accountability, possesses disrespect for authority, and rests on shaky moral pillars. Such was not the case in an earlier age, say the old coaches. Reality no doubt lies somewhere between the two camps. Nevertheless, if what old-time Texas coaches have said embodies any truths, and if sports sociology possesses any validity, then perhaps the two voices together provide a measurement of how far our society has deteriorated.[34]

Confronted with that dual image, Fort Worth's James Brewer insisted that "coaches are generally good people and have the kids' interests at heart. They are also generally optimists and project their values onto the kids. If the average person understood the coach, they would just back off and let him do his job."

A boy that Brewer coached at North Side High School later became a Church of Christ minister in Friendswood, between Houston and

Bill Ellington, 1957. *Photograph courtesy*   Eddie Joseph. *Photograph courtesy Texas*
Homer Johnson.   *High School Coaches Association, Austin.*

Galveston. The coach keeps a framed sermon on his wall that the minister wrote about him. In biblical terms, it told of a relentless man who heaped upon his players all the trials of Job. "Give your heart to momma," he greeted his new players annually, "because your body is mine for the next three years!" In the end, the boy who had come to Brewer realized that the old coach was sending him away a man. The minister concluded his sermon by saying that he truly believed "the Good Lord put Brewer on this earth to coach."

"Since the time that I first put on a football suit, to the time I quit coaching," reflected Bill Hartley of Columbus, "there was a certain trait of character that was supposed to go with that football suit that was preached by the old coaches. I tried to instill that same philosophy in these boys. Through this game of football, we are going to make good citizens—or better citizens—and we stressed this point. We looked after these boys not just at school, and not just on the football field, but where they were at night, what they were doing. If we caught them out of line, we were on top of it the next day. I think that gave me more worry . . . I worried more about their attitude than whether we were going to win a ball game or not. And I don't know how many times I've had them come back to me and say how much they appreciated that."

In 1991 Hartley was master of ceremonies at Columbus's homecoming. "People of all time came; we had a big parade and all that," he said. "Then, I looked up and one old player jumped off a float and three or four others saw me and ran over and hugged me and shook my hand. That meant a lot to me; they really didn't say anything to me, but what they did said they still had some respect for me."

Morris Southall. *Photograph courtesy Texas High School Coaches Association, Austin.*

Bill Patrick. *Photograph courtesy Raymond Patrick.*

Ask any old coach: "What was your philosophy about football?" Almost to the man, they will rattle off words they have lived by, ranging from clichés to original thoughts—and they will do it without hesitation, without so much as an "uh . . . " or a "hhmmnnn . . . ." Most of their credos related to the boys they have coached. Jewell Wallace: "Try to make them become better citizens and live a life that means something to them. Honesty and a hard work ethic." John Reddell: "My philosophy centered around thinking well of everyone, and it borrowed from Bud Wilkinson— 'You don't have to be tough, mean, or ugly, just have pride in what you do.'" Bill Patrick: "Find something to believe in and stick with it." Homer Johnson: "Every kid needed to be involved in something, whether it was football, the band, drill team, or something—find something to be a part of." E. C. Lerma: "Good conduct, good living!" Eddie Joseph: "You treat every single kid like they're your own." Joe Hedrick: "Coaching was getting kids to do what they didn't want to, to achieve what they wanted." Morris Southall: "Values are very important—honesty, hard work, ethics, be on time, follow rules, and contribute." Allen Boren: "If it's right, do it; if it's wrong, don't do it. Kids can tell the difference because they have a conscience." Emory Bellard: "The key is to create a situation where the kid wants to do what you want him to do. You've got to be able to play with confidence. Confidence is a 'result,' not something that precedes the other." Bill Ellington: "Teach without injuries and keep it simple."

What football players learned depended upon what they were receptive to, what they needed, or what they expected to get out of football. Eddie Joseph, commenting on making men out of boys, said: "I've seen it a thousand times; you know it's happening, but I don't think there's any thunderbolt out of the sky." And chances are, it will happen off the field as readily as on it. A big part of a coach's job, Joseph stressed, is counseling. "I've had so many of them come up and say: 'Coach, I don't think I want to play football anymore.' If a kid did not truly want to play and there was a reason, then fine, he shouldn't play. But most of them are mixed up, and they don't know exactly what they want to do, and they can't talk to anyone at home, and he has no one else to go to. And you sit and counsel with them, and you find out they didn't really want to quit, they just wanted someone to talk to. I've had them come back in twenty years and say: 'Coach, you probably don't remember, because it wasn't a traumatic thing in your life, but I remember going in your office and telling you I didn't want to play anymore.' They would say something like: 'That was a turning point in my life, because I was just about ready to give up on everything; I was about ready to crater, and I remember you telling me that the first time you quit something, every time after that, it becomes a little bit easier.'

"I don't care who you are, you're going to have adversity come," Joseph continued. "Football, more than anything else, teaches you never to quit." Herb Allen declared: "All athletics is life played in the form of a game. You get knocked down, you have to get up. If you get knocked down seven times, you have to be prepared to get up eight times."

Perhaps no team, Joseph said, embodied that belief any more than the state's most consistent loser, Houston's Jefferson Davis, who "lost eighty straight ball games." After a late October victory by a single point in 1993, however, they were "one-and-eight and happy. . . . Of course, they poured the ice bucket on the coach, and those kids were just absolutely exuberant. Those kids thought some way, somehow, that they were going to win, and they did. What I'm saying, is that when you're 0-and-80, it's hard to stay 'up,' it's hard to even be in the contest. I really believe they were just as happy and got just as much out of that win as a lot of people do winning state championships."

Many coaches echoed Joseph, insisting that losing strengthened character, as long as it did not become a habit. Gordon Brown, who produced a state champion at Katy, stated: "My biggest regret is that worthy coaching friends in some cases were not appreciated for their abilities simply because the scoreboard was the final evaluation." Ray Overton, who enjoyed many ups and downs, said: "You're not going to win every battle, but you're going to win the wars. You don't have to walk off the field the winner, but even when you lose you can walk off a winner."

Joe Bob Tyler declared: "If our purpose in life is not to leave whatever we've found a little bit better for our having passed that way, then there's not much purpose for our lives. Football just happens to be the vehicle that I chose." And even though Tyler won many more games than he lost, he cannot point to a display case full of district championship trophies to reflect his successes both on and off the field. "When you don't set the woods on fire winning, you're kind of obscure in this business.

Which is fine with me," Tyler remarked.[35] "I feel good about myself because I was honest. Regardless of the mistakes that I've made—and I've made a lot of them—I was at least honest in all of them."

This concern for players did not mean that the old coaches coddled them. Far from it. "If you can get over the mental part, the physical part is easy," remarked Joe Bob Tyler. A nightmarish experience as a World War II prisoner of war made him an authority on that subject, as did working under Joe Golding at Wichita Falls. "If we worked them unreasonably hard," Golding said, "it was our effort and our philosophy that this is what was required in order to have your youngsters physically conditioned for the rigors of combat and football."

Those rigors, recounted Bill Shipman, consisted of such exercises as "the 'Meat Grinder,' 'Edge of the Earth,' and 'Top Guns'—fearsome names for hard contact drills," he laughed. Yet "most coaches had enough judgment not to overuse drills that invited injury and discouragement," Shipman said. Charles Qualls conceded that football "is a game of hitting, and it is a tough sport," but he also insisted that "you could still make that part of it fun, too." His "Hamburger Drill," for example, pitted two blockers and two tacklers nose-to-nose in down stances, with a ball carrier standing up behind one pair, and a linebacker behind the other. "We'd stick them between some dummies and give them three chances to score in five yards, and everybody rotated." This activity gave linemen a chance to carry the ball and running backs an opportunity to see what it was like in the trenches. "The kids loved it; it was like a mini-game, and it was fun to watch."

Both Shipman and former Dallas Woodrow Wilson coach Cotton Miles noted that sometimes, however, the line between good judgment and bad wore thin. Shipman, who saw many coaches come and go, stated: "You can't always tell how they'll work out. . . . Many years ago I had hired a young man to coach at the junior high level. Outward indications were that he would be a successful coach. The season had just begun when he decided to identify all those he considered non-hitters by painting a yellow stripe down the backs of their practice jerseys. He did not finish the season, and not by his own choice." Miles, on the other hand, used the same idea, but as a reward. "We'd give red shirts to the hitters," he said. "Others would want to be identified the same way, and they would strive to do so."

Jewell Wallace, who coached San Angelo to a state title in 1943 and San Antonio Jefferson in 1949, stated: "The bad ones didn't last long. The kids and parents wouldn't stand for it." Eddie Joseph, on the other hand, countered: "It would be naive to say they were all good men. They weren't. A lot of them had the morals of an alley cat and didn't last, but some did and were even successful."

Charles Qualls told of a colleague who enjoyed "great success, but he had no business coaching. He was a great motivator, but his ethics and personal life were bad." The man would never stay at one school very

long, and he built a winner at every place he ever landed. But "he left the
program in shambles because he took from the communities."

After taking a hiatus to sell sporting goods, this coach returned to the
game but kept his new avocation as a sideline. "Right before we played
him," Qualls said, "he tried to sell me some equipment. I asked him how
he did it, and he said he'd get someone to watch his class so he could go
on the road. . . . The last place he coached someone told me: 'The reputation of the profession has gone down a hundred percent.'"

When coaches go too far, the state's enforcement arm, the University
Interscholastic League, often steps in. Former director Bailey Marshall
insisted that "most rules are written for the five percent. The UIL hates to
have to enforce the rules when it ruins teams but they still have to hold
the line." The rules, he insisted, "protect the schools, kids, and the sport.
Actually, the UIL takes pressure off coaches by setting standards."

Marshall's main concern centered on "moral illiterates," whose loose
ethics inevitably filter down to their players. "If you're a dirty coach,
you've taught kids to lie and cheat," declared Ed Logan. For example:
"Teams that worked out during the off-season were cheating. Everybody
in town knew it, but nobody talked. If you do things like this, you've
destroyed the purpose of what you're trying to teach your kids."

Buzz Allert asserted that the "black eyes to the profession today are the
ones who say: 'If he can move the chains, then he can play for me.'" After
Allert retired from the game, a young backfield coach came to him for
advice about his star fullback, who was cutting classes and missing practice. "He says: 'What can I do?' And I said: 'Hell, don't ask me. If you
don't have enough guts to tell him to come to class first, and then come
to practice or get out, then you're never going to be successful as a
coach.'" Allert reminded him that every day he was going to have to face
"sixty or seventy other football players" ever watchful for such bell-
wethers. "He never stopped to consider what the other players thought
about him. It all boils down to R-E-S-P-E-C-T!"

Old-time coaches as a general rule were infinitely more assertive than
Allert's example, and were poured from many molds. Hoot Smith, for
example, remarked that each coach on his Hurst Bell staff took on a role
that suited his personality. In fact, they developed a chain of command to
deal with players who had problems, or ones who gave them trouble.
While each position coach would shepherd his own boys, Smith would
"father" them when they needed some extra attention. He sent trouble-
makers to Bill Bookout. "Bookout would get it done—he wore the black
hat, but the kids respected him. Now, [Kenneth] Potter was a 'good guy,'
but he swung the paddle. Rule was that the kid had to come to him and
say: 'Coach Potter, I need help.'" Some other coach would have already
meted out the sentence, so the player knew how much "help" he needed
beforehand. He also knew that afterward, he would be expected to shake
Potter's hand and thank him. "Sometimes a kid would be afraid, and
someone would take his licks for him. . . . We'd only use the board on

them for minor things, like disruptive behavior or bad grades. The bigger problems, you wouldn't use a board on them anyway."

Many coaches did not believe in using a paddle. Like Cotton Miles, they instead employed what coaches called "the eye" or "the look." A silent glance of disapproval, Miles declared, could speak volumes. Herb Allen swore by that technique. "Sometimes at halftime, I would fire up my team by just staring—glaring, really. . . . When I was at Klein, we were down 18-to-0 against West Columbia, and at the half I just stared them down without saying a word. We came back and won 21–18."

Other coaches projected a gentlemanly, almost scholarly image. Walt Parker, for instance, always used a calm voice, "even when I wanted to "scream and kick a bucket or something." Eventually, he laughed, "I developed ulcers because I bottled things up." Many considered Jewell Wallace to be among the game's finest gentlemen, and Wallace recalled Bill Stages of Corpus Christi Ray as a kindred soul. "When they went out of town, he'd make his players wear a suit and tie." Donald Jay recalled that Stages possessed panache as well: "He smoked cigarettes in a long holder, and even at practice he wore long, white pants." He also gave his players tests over their assignments and drilled them regularly to keep them alert.

No doubt the old-time coaches who strike the most familiar chord hearken the image of a man part drill instructor and part preacher. The intensity and sense of urgency that comes from commanding eleven moving pieces all at once normally elicits animation in even the most poised individuals. Carlos Berry, for example, learned that striking a balance between exhorting and cowering players required skill and sensitivity. "It's one of the hardest parts of the job, because every kid is different." When Berry was at Haskell, the prospect of facing Anson for the district basketball championship left the players even more anxious than usual. "When the game began, Perry Turnbow, a tremendous athlete, suffered a lapse that allowed the other team to score." As the game progressed, Berry realized "that Turnbow had been listening to me yell at him, rather than giving his full attention to what was going on on the court." At halftime Berry put his arm around the boy and said: "Don't look over at the bench. It's my nature to get excited, and I'm going to be yelling."

Chuck Curtis commented tongue-in-cheek that in large part "I became a coach because my father was in the related field of ministry." When he landed at Garland in 1963, the Owls had suffered several consecutive losses to rival Highland Park. Upon Curtis's first shot at them, they found themselves behind once more. "Boy, I mean to tell you we held a brush arbor revival at halftime, and we came back and won by two points." After the game, having talked to reporters and worked his way through the crowd, Curtis reached a silent dressing room. "Several players were down on one knee, and everybody had their head bowed down, praying, so I took my cowboy hat off and stood there. One of the captains, Ralph Weaver, asked me to lead them in a prayer. They all made a commitment right then and there to be the best team in Texas—bar none." The Owls went on to take the Class 4-A crown that year. And it was that very night, Curtis claimed, "I knew we'd win state."

Such pledges exacted tremendous burdens. Old coaches expected dedication from their players and never stopped to consider that they themselves would give anything less than a full commitment. "Coaching is not a sometime thing; you can't just call it a day at five o'clock and go home," said Richland's Hugh Hamm. Dan Anderegg at Fredericksburg patterned himself after his college coach, Bud Wilkinson of Oklahoma. "He was tops in his profession," Anderegg said. "He felt that you must work 365 days a year if you want to be on top. The ones who are successful work long hours and work hard."

Herb Allen recalled sleeping on the training table following home games and waiting for a local news crew to develop the game film. He would then take it home and begin reviewing it immediately. Preparing scouting reports was an all-night job, one that usually fell to assistants and junior high coaches climbing the professional ladder. The task required traveling to games out of town, after which the coach would prepare a report that was due the next morning. If a particularly big game lay ahead, he might follow another team almost all season in order to learn intimately its tendencies. Once, when a Haltom player asked Jack Atkins, who had scouted the Wichita Falls Coyotes all year, if he thought the Buffalos would be able to beat them, Atkins replied: "I don't know, I've never watched Haltom play."

Almost every old-time coach found the profession a consuming occupation. When asked if he had any hobbies, Joe Bob Tyler bellowed: "Hobbies? None!" John Hugh Smith said that for many years he turned his attention to nothing else because the job demanded all of his time. "Later, I played golf," he commented. Maurice Cook admitted to occasionally deer hunting or fishing so he could be outdoors. He didn't apologize either. "Bear Bryant said 'show me a coach that's a good golfer and I'll show you a guy that's not a good coach.' Of course, I understand he was a pretty good golfer himself," laughed Cook.

Joe Hedrick, who survived Iwo Jima, believed that "only war brings out the same type of camaraderie" as football. Donald Jay agreed. "There is a bond there that doesn't exist in other professions." Bob Harrell of Irving asserted: "Coaches are a tight-knit fraternity. They all think alike. They have the same pressures. The job life is confining. There's a common goal, and you struggle together to reach it. And if you lose, you're all under the same pressure. The pecking order was God, coaching, and family—in that order."

A Roller-Coaster Career

Even if the old coaches' behavior reflected the same priorities that Harrell so freely professed, they would not admit it. They would be quick to agree, however, that their careers provided "one hell of a roller coaster ride," as James Brewer proclaimed. The game, of course, is what every-body worked for—the coaches, the players, the fans, the band, the cheer-leaders, and the pep squad. And even though a team could field only eleven at a time, Friday nights held entire communities spellbound and made everyone feel a part.

When Joe Bob Tyler moved across town and became head coach at Wichita Falls Rider, he built his team around part-Indian Bub Deerinwater—a West Texas Jim Thorpe. With both Rider and Hoot Smith's Hurst Bell squad sporting 9–0 records, the two teams met for the 1965 district championship at Hurst's old Pennington Field. It was a time when only one team went to the play-offs. "Rider had posters up all over the place that said 'Rubba-dub-dub, We've Got Bub,' and things like that," Smith recalled. Then, in the second quarter Deerinwater left the game with an injured knee. "Bub refused to stay out," said Tyler, "so right before halftime was over, I went ahead and started wrapping it up."

With both teams already on the sidelines awaiting the second half, every eye remained focused on the dressing room's dimly lit doorway. The fate of the game, they knew, hinged on the big running back's condition. The facility was some distance away, in the shadows, well beyond a fence sur-rounding the track. Finally, with the referees becoming impatient and the crowd buzzing with anticipation, Tyler and Deerinwater emerged from the dressing room together, walking at first. The packed stadium fell silent. Then Rider's drummers started playing the Indian beat that Deerinwater had inspired: THUMP! thump, thump, thump, THUMP! thump, thump, thump. . . . Then, coach and player began jogging, through the gate and onto the field along the sidelines. The Rider fans "went absolutely berserk," recalled Smith. "We knew right then we were beaten."

Both Tyler and Smith said the same thing that almost every one of their colleagues echoed when recounting such memorable events: "If you weren't there, you just have no idea what it was like." Gene Mayfield experienced some big games and called the feeling "indescribable." Just a week before Rider and Bell squared off, his Permian Panthers hosted the state's number-one-ranked team, San Angelo. Mayfield's bunch had been picked before the season to finish dead last. "There was an electricity in the air," he asserted. "They told me several people left the stands with heart problems because there was so much at stake, and it was so close a game." When Permian scored a late touchdown to make the score 7–6, they faked the extra point kick. The boy holding the ball, however, did not tell the kicker, who "did a Charlie Brown." The ball holder then rolled out and hit a wide-open receiver in the end zone, and the Panthers gained a one-point edge. "It was a dogfight the rest of the way, but that's how it ended—8–7." The scene was "almost surreal," Mayfield recalled, and amid the excitement "were ambulance sirens blaring because of fans who had fainted and were being carried away."

Perhaps nothing could compare to the thrill of winning against seem-ingly impossible odds, which might happen only once or twice in a

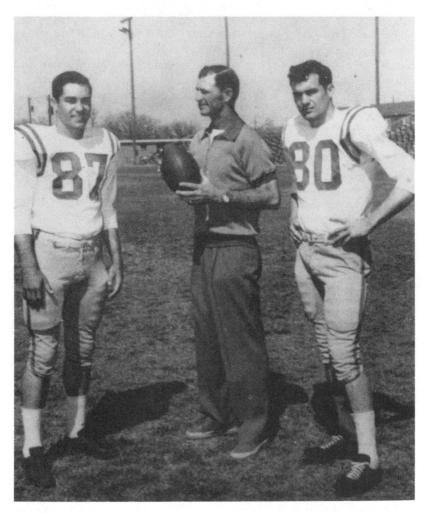

Hardin-Simmons co-captain Carlos Berry, left, poses with head coach Sammy Baugh and fellow co-captain Connie Baird. *Photograph courtesy Carlos Berry.*

coach's career. And if a coach was lucky, he only saw a winless season about as often. Darrell Tully, who began his career as an assistant coach of a very weak Crozier Tech, declared: "Unless you've had an 0-and-10 season, you've never coached." His players at that downtown Dallas school wore out their cleats walking more than a mile to practice at the city park, where the ground was uneven and glass and rocks lay strewn about.

Nevertheless, Tully insisted, the memory of that grim season grew sweet because Crozier Tech "never quit and never gave up. This bunch had no physical ability, and I remember thinking every week, 'This is the week they're going to collapse.'" But they never did. Theirs was the only team picture Tully ever put on his office wall, and for as long as he coached, wherever he moved, it was always the first thing that would go up on the wall.

Another high point on that roller coaster ride could be "the unexpected kindnesses of learning how much people cared for you," remarked Carlos Berry. After playing some semi-pro baseball, he began his coaching career at Hardin-Simmons under Hall of Fame quarterback Sammy Baugh. "As far as kids were concerned, I decided that I could do more at the high school level, so I took a job at Haskell." At that small West Texas school he was assistant coach of the football team and head coach of basketball and track, "plus, I did everything else necessary to support the athletic program." Like any other coach at a school that size, he swept the gym floor, and when it needed maintenance, he helped strip the wax and coat the floor with varnish. He also refereed junior high football games and worked concessions at baseball and basketball games. Then he accepted his first head football coach's job at Henrietta. "When we left, it seemed like everybody in the whole town was lined up along the road, honking and waving, and they all fell in line behind us and followed us until we got past the city limits."

The downside of that ride could be vicious. In ten years at Terrell, Leon Vinyard averaged ten victories a season, took his teams to twenty-three play-off games, and brought home two state championship trophies. In 1968 he did not think he would get his contract renewed, so instead of waiting to be fired, he announced his retirement. The incident that caused his troubles began over a parent—a man that Vinyard had counted among his friends since their college days—who wanted his son to go to the University of Texas and become an end. "The boy just wasn't fast enough, and I played him at tackle," explained the coach. The angry father became the "ringleader in a group that wanted me gone." Vinyard, understandably, was very resentful. "I had done right by those people and won a hundred games for them, and they edged me out."

Because only one team could win, coaches were guaranteed a bittersweet ride. In a bi-district contest at Texarkana, for example, Chuck Curtis found his Garland Owls behind by five points as they tried to keep Watty Meyers's Tigers out of the end zone very late in the game. "Seems like they had first and goal on the five," Curtis recalled, and "four times in a row, my middle linebacker, Gene Mayes, came through, and we stopped them on the one-yard line with a minute-and-a-half on the clock." Garland, he said, then moved the ball the length of the field to win the game. "Four times we faced fourth-and-ten, and we finally scored with about fifteen seconds to go." Afterward, Curtis and Watty Meyers fought through the crowd to shake hands. "'Chuck-a-Luck,' he told me, 'I came within one yard of whipping your ass.'" Meyers then turned around and walked away.

Poor Watty Meyers. Fate just never seemed to set him on the winning side of that razor-thin difference that so often separates winners and losers. When his name came up to Nacogdoches's Gordon Brown, he said: "Let me tell you about an old-time coach. It was twelve midnight on Friday in a restaurant in Marshall, Texas." Meyers, representing Texarkana, met there with Brown and the Lufkin coach to decide who would represent the district. "Each team had lost one game after having finished their schedule only a couple of hours earlier. The flip of a coin would decide the issue." All three of them pulled out a silver dollar and agreed that it had to hit the ceiling first, before hitting the floor. The coin that came up "odd" would be the winner. With the restaurant jam-packed and a radio announcer covering the event, the coaches flipped. "Here's what happened," stated Brown: on the first attempt, "the coins came down tails, tails, tails." A second time they flipped, and again, they "came down tails, tails, tails." After identifying their silver dollars, the coaches flipped a third time. "Two silver dollars came down tails, and the third began to roll around in a large circle. Finally it turned over heads, the only head out of nine flips, and Nacogdoches went into the play-offs." A very despondent Watty Meyers, Brown noted, left without a word. There was nothing to say.

For many coaches the ride was a rocky one. Some took a break from the game, and others got out prematurely. After heading up a good program at Masonic Home, Jack Whitley took a job at Polytechnic, a bigger school in Fort Worth. "Poly had some good kids," Whitley remarked, but they were slow and "not as well-honed" as those to which he had been accustomed. When his sophomore team beat crosstown rival Carter-Riverside, a spokesman asked Whitley "if they could be happy and do some celebrating. They didn't know how to react because they had never won a game!" Even in junior high, when the two Poly feeder schools played each other, they had tied. "This left me with a sickening feeling that I'd never known." Whitley was never able to make a winner out of them. Poly was a coach's graveyard, and it buried him. When Whitley retired from the profession, he remembered looking at the sports page and seeing that "everybody on the left column won, and everybody on the right lost—and I didn't have to care."

Whitley nevertheless admitted that coaching provided many great moments. He credited his own high school coach, in fact, for getting him out of that same Masonic Home orphanage where he eventually began his coaching career. And not until he was out of coaching did he realize what a truly uniqe profession it was. Observing from arms length all the changes that have affected coaching and football, he sees a different game today than the one that gave him his first job back in 1948. In fact, the old-time Texas football coach—part psychologist, part philosopher, part preacher, part military leader—represents a dying breed. "I had the privilege to coach at the greatest time," declared Waco's long-retired Truman Nix. His comments, upon being recently inducted into the Texas High School Coaches' Hall of Honor, spoke for a generation of his colleagues who helped shape one of the state's most important twentieth-century institutions. And they shaped it in their own image.

Part II

The Development of Coaching and Texas High School Football, 1890–1945

Chapter 2

Pioneers on a Hundred-Yard Long Frontier: Football in Texas, 1890–1930

Like most viruses, the pigskin fever that afflicted so many Texans during the twentieth century has nebulous origins. That it somehow reached the state by way of the eastern seaboard and the Midwest is almost certain. Some say that divinity graduates of Ivy League schools brought the bug with them to college campuses in the Lone Star State late in the 1880s. After football claimed scores of deaths as well as hundreds of serious injuries across the country during the early years of the new century, the game met with a storm of public protest and even provoked a normally plucky President Theodore Roosevelt to plead for reform.[1] Such dire grievances only fed the fever in young Texas males who fancied themselves products of a raw and rowdy frontier. Among those with leisure time, the game spread readily, and its participants seemed to revel in tallying up their black eyes and bloody noses as badges of honor in their pursuit of this rough-and-tumble fun.[2]

Football in Texas Emerges

For a game so closely identified with schoolboys in Texas, football did not reach very deeply into the high school ranks for almost two decades after the first recorded snap from center. That moment came in 1894 and involved Galveston Ball High School and some long-forgotten opponent. Galveston High's starting eleven, however, included mostly dock workers as well as doctoral students at the island's medical college.[3] Earlier, in 1891, the precursor to Houston's Sam Houston High School discontinued rugby, but revived the sport as "football" in 1896. Despite wearing advertisements on the backs of their jerseys, they failed to raise enough money to sustain a team. Perhaps it was just as well, since there was virtually nobody else to play against, and both parents and the school board discouraged what they regarded as a brutish pastime.[4]

In the first two years of the new century old "Dalhi"—later renamed Crozier Tech—and Waco fielded teams that at least managed to survive

West Texas football, Graham School, 1907. *Photograph courtesy John Miller Morris.*

after shaky beginnings. George Sargeant, Dalhi's captain in 1900 and later a Dallas mayor, encountered the same hostility that Sam Houston High had faced, as well as the indifference of the student body. "At our first game only two girls appeared," he lamented, and initially the "superintendent wouldn't let us practice on the school grounds." Still, the boys managed to kindle some interest by persuading their debating coach, Mr. Edwards, to add the football team to his coaching duties and by getting their mothers to sew uniforms. About the same time, a Waco student complained in his school's publication that "our team [has] no suits." Another editorialist later grumbled about "interest lagging" and mentioned that Waco had no coach, save for the team captain, Henry Lindsay.[5] Other struggling teams began carrying the names of their local schools, but they remained sparse and were confined to the cities. Future coaching great Pete Shotwell recalled playing "pickup games" in the Panhandle before going to Canyon Normal College in 1911, but remarked that "there wasn't much high school football going on anywhere."

The situation was different on college campuses. In fact, football made its inroads into Texas at education's top level by way of the country's most prestigious institutions of higher learning. As early as 1893 the University of Texas at Austin imitated its eastern counterparts by putting together a varsity team. When Texas A&M followed suit the next year, the pair inaugurated one of the nation's most heated rivalries. Almost immediately, pranksters from both schools tried to outdo each other. "Dutch" Hohn, member of an early A&M team, recalled the Aggies pulling into the depot at Austin and being mobbed by "Texas University boys" ripping at their banners and decorations before the train could even stop. Through the open windows of the coaches, "the A and M cadets would have to beat off the attacks . . . with the butt of their rifles— brought along, of course, for the parade."[6]

Other Texas colleges also followed the pattern of the nation's elite universities. Before the turn of the century, AddRan College—soon to be

Pete Shotwell of West Texas State Teachers College, c. 1915. *Photograph courtesy Texas Sports Hall of Fame, Waco.*

Texas Christian University—along with Baylor, Austin College, Trinity, and Simmons College (to which philanthropist John G. Hardin would later add his name)—began challenging each other, and occasionally they delighted in spoiling the clean records of the larger, state-sponsored schools. Football found a rabid following among student bodies eager to flaunt their sophistication while vicariously proving themselves the superior of rival institutions. Even those who never gave a thought to attending college became avid fans.[7]

Until the World War I years, however, football in Texas remained largely a sport for college kids and well-to-do young men. Into the 1910s the leisure time to practice and play games as well as marshaling the resources to outfit players prohibited all but the well heeled from organizing teams. In addition to colleges, local YMCAs and groups such as the Dallas Social Club scheduled their mighty elevens against the likes of Toby's Business College, Dodson Military Academy, or the reserves of college varsities.[8]

The scheduling of games among teams at different levels that relied upon casually assembled talent and dubious coaching often led to disastrous mismatches. In 1913, for example, Houston Sam Houston bulldozed its way to a 62–0 lead over Corpus Christi after only twenty minutes of the self-styled "Southwest Championship Game." Sam Houston afterward put together a more ambitious schedule and found itself on the short end of similar contests with abler opponents. In a game against a much heavier freshman squad at Rice Institute, Sam Houston lost players to broken arms and collarbones. In another contest, after "the only quarterback left on the Tiger squad ran into a goal post and split his head open," the school paper noted, "the athletic officials refused to allow . . . any more games that year."[9]

From sandlots and social clubs to high schools and universities, football in the early days was irregular and unsophisticated, involving only rudimentary strategies. Dutch Hohn declared: "Football as we played it at A and M in 1909 bore little resemblance to today's game." Before 1912, touchdowns brought variously four and five points, while field goals at times counted three points, and at others, four. Passing was illegal until 1906. Teams did not huddle either, and "when the ball snapped, the play started moving directly forward, right away," the former Aggie related.[10] No doubt, the phrase "three yards and a cloud of dust" is among the game's oldest expressions. Just after mid-decade, backs started throwing the ball, but their passes were limited to five yards; the new weapon was an uncertain innovation. Later, Texas A&M and University of Texas coach Dana X. Bible recalled that "you played with the shape of football that best suited the fancy of the home team"—at one place the ball might be slim and light, the next place more spherical, discouraging forward passes. During a brief interlude between 1906 and 1910, transverse lines every five yards overlapped the normal striping; the visual effect gave rise to the playing field's time-honored sobriquet, the "gridiron."[11]

In those early years brawn and courage served the participants better than agility and quick wits. Yet slowly the game grew more complex, and along with it, so did coaching as a profession. At first, little distinguished a team's captain from its coach at the club and town level; occasionally a coach was even known to draw howls of protest for coming off the bench to help his "high school" team win a close game. The college ranks, however, began hiring full-time coaches such as Dana X. Bible and A&M's

"Uncle Charlie" Moran, who saw the mechanics of the game as a matter of science. Yet just as often, said Canyon Normal's star running back Pete Shotwell, who played college ball between 1911 and 1916, "there would be some man teacher that would be coaching in addition to teaching." For a while physics and science teacher D. A. Shirley filled the role at Canyon Normal. By the time Shotwell became an upperclassman, however, the school had hired a man full-time to coach every sport, most often by himself, but occasionally with some help. Still, Shotwell insisted, coaches were just beginning to "pick up the game."

Education Provides New Opportunities

Because of athletics, institutions of higher learning began to open their doors to young men whose chief collegiate asset was their physical prowess. One of those men, Ed Varley, commented: "In those days, going to school was not a priority after one had learned to read and write." He credited football with getting him off the family's Bagwell farm in Northeast Texas. "I was a big ol' country boy, living out in the sticks," and Coach Bloodworth at Clarksville High School "invited me to play." An A&M graduate, Bloodworth had not been on the college team himself, but Varley felt that he knew something about the game and admired his coach's polished manners. "I wanted to be like him and began to toy with the idea of going to college and becoming a teacher and a coach. Impossible dreams for a farm boy in those days," Varley reminisced, "but I did go to college and I did become a coach!"

So did Rodney Kidd. Chatter Allen, who played for Kidd at Georgetown High School and later followed him into the profession, enjoyed telling how green his mentor had once been. Coach Lefty Edens at Southwestern University had recruited "Captain" Kidd in the 1910s, and told him that he would be staying at the "Phi house" (Phi Delta Theta), and to go there when he arrived. Kidd, without a family tradition of education, had never heard of a Greek fraternity. When he got off the train, he asked directions to the "fire" station, and there reported to a befuddled crew.

Once in college, both Varley and Kidd proved their ability in the classroom as well as on the field. And on their way up the educational ladder, both represented the masses who further developed the sport between the 1910s and the early 1930s, before high school football in Texas became a universal obsession. During this time the game reached slowly but steadily into all areas of the state at all socio-economic levels. Crowds remained small, and enthusiasm depended on the strength of their local teams and the interest of their readers. Radio, of course, burst into American homes in the 1920s, and even made its way into the backwashes of Texas, where batteries helped put rural folks in touch with the outside world. Yet beyond the cities and towns, most Texans were struggling to break out of nineteenth-century patterns of life, and for many of them Red Grange remained as much a stranger as Reddy Killowatt.

More than any other force, the politics of Texas Progressivism was most responsible for popularizing football—an unintentional byproduct of educational reform. During the 1910s the state began to provide free textbooks and pledged to match the tax revenues rural districts levied. Increasingly, glorified private secondary schools with pretentious names like Burleson College and Allen Academy disappeared, and high schools built with local and state funds that bore their towns' names became more commonplace. And while many farm families pulled their children out of school during harvest season, most of them complied with compulsory attendance regulations. Rural schools also found that pooling their resources helped them hire teachers and add the kinds of courses that until then were the privilege only of children in the cities. In the 1920s and 1930s, as roads improved and the legislature provided busing for country children, consolidations accelerated. Such an increasingly uniform system of education throughout the state begged outlets for interscholastic competition.[12]

About the same time that Progressives began to press their reforms, schools in cities and large towns in Central, West, and South Texas formed loose regional affiliations for playing football against one another.[13] But, as Pete Shotwell remarked, "the state did not have anything to do with it." In 1913, however, the official organization that governed debating clubs in Texas schools merged with a similar association founded several years earlier by some track-and-field coaches. The union resulted in the University Interscholastic League (UIL). The state-sanctioned organization clothed itself with almost omnipotent powers, regulating all aspects of interscholastic competition. From spelling bees and slide rule tournaments to one-act plays, music festivals, and contests in journalism, art, and athletics, the League dictated what it considered fair and ethical standards. In 1915, *The Lasso*, Fort Worth North Side's high school yearbook, recognized the new organization, but paid little attention to its broad sweep. It greeted the news instead, by proclaiming: "Since the new rules from the [UIL] have been adopted, there is a fine chance for all-round, clean high school football."[14]

North Side had a stake in assuring a "clean" game, free of grown men and ringers brought in from faraway places. During those formative years the Steers fielded a team of local boys that tested the state's best elevens. They included Matty Bell, who later coached SMU to a national championship, and future Centre College all-Americans Bo McMillan and James Weaver.[15] In 1915 the Steers fell to the Austin Maroons before two thousand fans in an unofficial championship game.[16] They also tied a Waco squad on which future TCU coach Dutch Meyer played alongside Ben Lee Boynton, who, in 1920, would lead the nation's colleges in rushing yards while gaining all-American honors at Williams College in Massachusetts. It was through North Side, in fact, that the country would first learn just how good the Texas-born talent really was. The core of the team in 1917 followed coach Robert L. Myers to tiny Centre College in

Round Rock Dragons, 1925; Chatter Allen, top row, second from right, standing next to coach. *Photograph courtesy Chatter Allen.*

Danville, Kentucky, where the "Praying Colonels" later broke Harvard's twenty-five-game winning streak. For forty-five thousand shocked and indignant fans of the game's architects, the defeat was a rude awakening to the fact that folks in other parts of the country were beginning to pick up the game.[17]

The University Interscholastic League proved a driving force in eventually leveling the playing field for Texas schoolboys. But as the UIL struggled to gain ascendancy in the late 1910s and 1920s, many schools whose football players packed shaving kits for road games held out; others reluctantly joined and tested the league's resolve. The new rules at first allowed men as old as twenty-one to play, but required that all participants be amateurs. The UIL also said that a player must have a three-month attendance record in the school he was representing, and that he had to be passing three courses.[18]

Chatter Allen, in the mid-1920s, attended Round Rock High School, one of the holdouts. "I played end at ninety-eight pounds and did not get to play very much as there were no UIL rules." This he clarified by adding: "Most of the players did not attend school and were past school age." In one road game he thankfully remained on the sidelines while his teammates fell to some very mature-looking Cameron boys, 62–6. Two weeks later at Round Rock the Dragons avenged the loss by a score of 68–0. "The big difference was that Round Rock recruited half the Southwestern University football team plus several Georgetown 'toughs' by the names of 'Hogeye' Lyons, 'Killer' Weeks, and 'Slime' Purl. In those days it was who could 'outringer' whom."

Even future all-American Darrell Tully found himself on the short end
of a mismatch when he was on an Eastland team looking forward to an
easy victory over Stephenville. Once the game started, he looked up to see
a big, menacing, unfamiliar kid with black curly hair and no headgear.
"We called pla᷃ ᷃rs who didn't have one of those old leather helmets a
showboater," he said; this one turned out to be a Tarleton Junior College
player. "That big fellow knocked out six of us and had no telling how
many limp-offs." Tully was among the unconscious. "I remember waking
up in the back seat of a car going back to Eastland and asking someone
what the score was."[19]

Ineligible players normally found more discreet ways to get around
UIL rules. Seldom did they try to skirt the attendance requirement, but a
particularly baby-faced player might doctor the family Bible to extend his
eligibility as far as a larcenous heart and youthful looks would take him.
For many young men with few economic opportunities, high school football well into the 1920s was not a boys' game; in communities that would
pay to build a winner, it was a way of making a living.[20]

In his effort to deliver high school football to the proper boys, UIL
Director Roy B. Henderson strove to inspire fair competition by coming
up with a way to crown an annual state champion. Texas, so vast and
demographically diverse, presented profound barriers. The task proved
even more formidable because of poor financing and an even poorer road
system. These difficulties, along with compliance problems, kept the UIL
from hosting its first state championship game until 1920. In that anticli-
mactic contest Cleburne and Houston Heights fought to a scoreless tie
on a muddy, rain-soaked Clark Field in Austin.[21] The league overcame
another obstacle two years later, in 1922. Until that time each of Texas's
254 counties boasted its own champion, which forced a league-supported
Bureau of Football Results to invite teams to play for postseason honors.
The UIL's solution was to organize the state into sixteen districts and
design a play-off system.[22] Suddenly, the race for an undisputable state
championship persuaded throngs of Texas high schools to gather under
the UIL umbrella.

The University Interscholastic League opened the door to high school
football at the same time that American sports in general entered a golden
age. Few Texans witnessed such great events of the day as the Tunney-
Dempsey fights or Man O'War's runs toward a Triple Crown; others
could only read Grantland Rice's praise of the Four Horsemen or hear the
crack of a Babe Ruth home run on the radio. Scattered numbers of
Texans, however, increasingly found themselves cheering for their local
football teams in person. Between its inception in 1914 and the 1930s,
the UIL grew from two hundred member schools to more than six thousand. Resolutely, the league enforced its rules, which increased interest
and participation in football all over the state. The league also demonstrated a flexibility in meeting changing conditions that would assure its
growth and make it a model for other states.[23]

Magnolia, 1921, one of a number of Oil Belt "outlaws" that challenged the UIL in the 1910s and 1920s. *Photograph courtesy Basil Clemons Photograph Collection, Special Collections Division, The University of Texas at Arlington Libraries.*

A Serious Business

The UIL's most formidable challenges came from maverick civic leaders and fans who wanted to use this schoolboy sport to magnify their town's prestige. If most city dwellers welcomed regulations that made the playing field more level, places in the oil patches of West Texas looked for ways to gain leverage. Towns such as Ranger, which grew from one thousand men and women in 1917, to mostly thirty thousand men by the end of 1918, saw nothing wrong with assuring that among those new souls were boys—and even a few grown men—with a talent for handling a football. Roughnecks and speculators with money to wager and appetites for manly, rugged outlets grew hungry for winning teams.[24] During the 1920s, towns in the "Oil Belt" found their fast and fleeting brand of football a perfect complement to their roughneck culture. Centered in an area where Ranger, Cisco, and Eastland lay only a few miles apart, the region included Breckenridge and Abilene to the west; Fort Worth to the east; and Wichita Falls, Electra, and Burkburnett to the north.

It was oil that brought future coach Brooks Conover from Indianapolis to Electra in 1916. After the nine-year-old boy and his two older brothers lost their father in a street car accident, the widow Conover decided to move to Texas, where she had a sister, the wife of a driller. Brooks's aunt had written that there was plenty of work in Electra for the boys. Shortly after the Conovers arrived, they settled in a shotgun shack on the outskirts of town, which was close to the football field. "Electra had a pretty good team," said Conover, even though it was coached by the superintendent. "He came to practice in the same suit that he wore to work." On game days the crowds were not very big, but since there were no

Between Hal- Breckenridge High vs B.P.O.E.lks.

bleachers, spectators packed the sidelines. "I had to elbow my way to the front to see the game," Conover remarked. Lucky was the person who got there early enough to pull up a car or wagon to the sidelines. Conover recalled arriving early for one game, where he tried to stake out a place with his bicycle, but someone pulled up a truck and crushed it. "That was the end of that bicycle," he moaned.

Electra was among the first big oil fields in the region. When other strikes brought waves of people and wealth to these erstwhile sleepy villages, the Oil Belt became legendary for recruiting football players. Early Abilene coach Jack Christian noted that even though powerhouses in the 1910s such as Oak Cliff, Waco, Cleburne, Amarillo, and Beaumont pioneered the practice of recruiting, none could rival the Oil Belt towns for providing good jobs for the fathers of promising prospects. A UIL residence rule required only that a player live in the school district on September 1 of the year that he played. All of the Oil Belt schools took full advantage of the loophole and lured families from all over the state, but when Cisco emerged on top of the heap in 1928, Eastland journalist Boyce House condemned his neighboring town by naming every player on its squad to his all-state team. Remarking that his Cisco selections represented Texas "more than any team I can find," House named a distant town of origin for all but one boy. For his similar role in luring talent to Ranger, coach Eck Curtis offered no apologies. In fact, after he took a job at the University of Texas, he attributed his recruiting success to "my experience along that line from 1925, until the league passed the one-year transfer rule in the thirties."[25]

Pete Shotwell coached for a while at Breckenridge, where he claimed oilman Jake Sandifer "was the guy behind the whole thing." When his Buckaroos were playing at Comanche, Sandifer walked up and pointed to a big, good-looking tackle on the other team and asked: "Do you want him?" A delighted Shotwell replied: "Of course." It turned out that the boy had four brothers. Shortly afterward, "Sandifer moved the whole family up to Breckenridge, and all five played," Shotwell said. "One of them was the best punter I've ever seen in my life—high school, pro, college, or anything." Boyce Magness was the player's name. Cooper Robbins, who later followed Shotwell as a Breckenridge coach, played

The Breckenridge Buckaroos lick their wounds and regroup at halftime of a game against lodge brothers of the local Elks Club, c. 1925. *Photograph courtesy Basil Clemons Photograph Collection, Special Collections Division, The University of Texas at Arlington Libraries.*

against Magness. He remarked that the punter "was supposed to be the best of the best; he convinced me." Shotwell recalled a game in which Breckenridge stopped Ranger inside the Buckaroos' ten yard line. After failing to get out of that hole, Magness backed up to his own goal line and punted; the ball went "at least sixty yards in the air" and it "rolled dead on the two."

Hugh Hamm, who grew up in North Texas, remembered hearing a story about a coach in his part of the state who tried the same thing as Pete Shotwell, but the ending was not as happy. In a community not far from the unlucky coach lived a poverty-stricken farming family with two lean and brawny twins who caught his eye. The coach persuaded some businessmen to create a good job for the boys' father, who was grateful for the seemingly unsolicited charity. When the man rolled into the town with his wife at his side and all their possessions bulging from the slats of their Model T pickup, there were some little children sitting atop the load, but the projected gridiron stars were nowhere to be seen. A citizens' group had assembled to greet them, and after some well-wishing a man asked tentatively: "Where are your sons?"—to which the father replied: "They didn't want to leave their friends, so they're gonna live with their grandparents."

Hamm asserted that however exaggerated or even apocryphal, the story at least speaks for the times. "Sports didn't mean much to that man," he remarked, nor, evidently, to his sons. The father of those twins never dreamed that someone would give him a job so his sons could play a schoolboys' game.

Yet Texans in the 1920s were beginning to take football seriously, and some places even wove it into the fabric of community life. While during the season attendance might be slight and composed mostly of home folks, the play-offs often would bring weekend games and chartered trains that left some places temporary ghost towns. Mayfield Workman recalled going to the Decatur station in 1927 to watch his play-off-bound brother and cousins board a special train that would take the Eagles to Graham. The nine-year-old was astonished to see "half the town had shown up to cheer them on." Even though Graham "won by a hair," the excitement that surrounded the

ing To Breckenridge vs Abline FootBall Game, Armistice Day,

Townspeople in Breckenridge line up to travel to the 1927 season's big game against Abilene.
Photograph courtesy Basil Clemons Photograph Collection, Special Collections Division, The
University of Texas at Arlington Libraries.

game piqued Workman's interest and made him want to be like the Decatur
coach, upon whom all the attention seemed to focus.

Had Mayfield Workman been able to make that trip, he might have
witnessed what stuck in future Columbus coach Bill Hartley's mind upon
seeing his first game. It was in the small West Central Texas town of San
Saba, and the ten-year-old was standing along the sidelines, close to the
action. Late in the game, with no chance to win, some of the hometown
players came off the field crying. The scene left a confused Hartley wondering what could make them behave like this, when they were playing a
game that was supposed to evoke the stoic characteristics of manhood.

A 1926 contest at Colorado City showed plainly the importance that
folks were beginning to attach to football. With Anson leading the home
team 21–14 and three minutes remaining, the heroic efforts of Huron
Gist put Colorado City on their opponent's twenty-yard line. When the
running back disappeared under a mountain of men, referee Y. P. Kuhn
signaled that Anson had recovered a fumble—even though Gist emerged
from the pile with the football. Colorado City fans immediately poured
onto the field and were persuaded to retire to the sidelines only after an
intense shoving match with the officials. When the gun sounded, ending
the game, the scene turned to bedlam. Law officers ringed around Kuhn
and battled their way to the nearby school building, leaving the other

officials to look for allies in hostile territory. Big Spring coach "Fat" Collins took up the referees' cause, turning in circles and swinging wildly, while head linesman Matt Dillingham dug in with a iron rod that he had been using to mark the scrimmage line.

Suddenly, boys on the Colorado City team began screaming: "We won! We won!" The referee, they asserted, had bet on the game. It turned out that Kuhn had taken a ride from Abilene with a man who began taking wagers on Anson as soon as they arrived. When law officers tried to force a statement out of the official, he convinced them that he knew nothing about it, and persuaded them to escort him to the city limits. In the wake of the game, accusations and finger-pointing led to bitterness as well as the removal of Colorado City's school superintendent and its Chamber of Commerce manager.[26]

Uneven Growth And Crude Conditions

Texans' interest in high school football during the 1920s and the early 1930s would grow with their schools' participation. A truly modern education system that reflected a popular priority on interscholastic competition, and football in particular, was still emerging. While educational standards at city schools in Texas were generally as good as any in the nation, too many of their rural counterparts were as poor and backward as in any other southern state. Often such places could not field enough players to scrimmage, and even when they competed, they might get embarrassed by much larger schools. Spur, for example, came to know both sides of humiliation during the 1930 season. After burying Lorenzo 186–0, the team found itself on the low side of another lopsided contest, this one to the Texas Tech varsity, 72–6.[27]

In "the old hardnose football as we knew it," remarked Jack Christian, "the tactics were 'anything goes'; you could be trampled under if you were not prepared." Chena Gilstrap insisted that it would almost "be an insult to the other team to take out your best players or move a lineman into the backfield." He also pointed out that a coach could not put substitutes in a game when his team was composed of only fifteen or so boys. Until 1926, when the UIL created two divisions, towns like Itasca, near Dallas, or Eagle Lake, outside of Houston, occasionally found themselves battling local giants in the big cities. Bob Cashion, just back from a forty-year high school reunion at Mexia, remarked that the passing of three-quarters of a century and two appearances in the state finals cannot entirely erase the sting that some old-timers at that place still felt about a 138–0 shellacking at the hands of Waco in 1921.

If this city game worked its way into the hearts of country towns in the Oil Belt during the 1920s, it seemed that folks in the Valley region of South Texas had not yet discovered it. According to one-time Rio Grande City coach Ralph E. Martin, South Texans might have occasionally enjoyed listening to Notre Dame or an Army-Navy game on the radio,

but the kids who hit the sandlots had "nothing but their imaginations" to recreate the experience. "They had no uniforms, no football fields, and no ball," declared Martin; and, because very few communities had local teams to follow, the game "seemed as foreign as cricket or lacrosse."

Even in the big cities across the state, crowds were nearly always small. Although the first state championship game in 1920 attracted over three thousand spectators, it drew only about 650 fans of the two teams who played in the contest. The others represented a vanguard of people who would travel from all over just to watch a good game.[28] Brooks Conover recalled that in the late teens and early twenties, the Texas League baseball park in Dallas swallowed up the tiny crowds that came to watch him and his North Dallas teammates play. Games normally were held on Friday afternoons, and in some places, if the principal caught kids skipping classes to watch their schoolmates play, they were expelled. "The crowds were small because everybody was at work," Ed Varley said, and also because "not too many people knew much about the game."

Ed Logan, who later coached at College Station and Haltom, recalled the childhood scene of his father taking him to a game, where they sat on a hillside to watch. Young Logan was used to baseball, which he understood; of football, however, he remarked: "I thought it was silly; just a mass of people moving around." Bill Shipman readily admitted that he was also among the great unwashed, but his immediate reaction differed from Logan's. "My first memory of football happened when I was about in the third grade," Shipman recalled. "Our local team was playing an afternoon game on Friday and the principal sent all the elementary students to the game free of charge, otherwise I could not have gone. I thought it was the

Action at the West Texas Fair Grounds, Abilene, c. 1922. *Photograph courtesy Basil Clemons Photograph Collection, Special Collections Division, The University of Texas at Arlington Libraries.*

most thrilling thing I had ever seen and was crushed when it was over. However, I had an immediate reprieve when I found that it was only half-time. From then on, I always had a football of some type."

The accommodations for fans did not keep up with the increased interest in the game. Most city high schools in the twenties constructed rickety bleachers, but certainly nothing that resembled a stadium. Brooks Conover remarked that few schools outside the larger towns had erected anything on which to sit. Many coaches echoed childhood recollections of fans having to follow the game from the sidelines. In fact, another of Bill Hartley's first recollections of football was trying to keep from getting trampled by men running up and down the sidelines to get closer to the action on the dirt fields at Eden and San Saba.

And not one of those fields ever had anything as cushy as turf. Chatter Allen humphed: "Today's football fields are like feather beds compared to the rock-strewn, sand burr-infested, sodless fields of the old day." Cotton Miles, who grew up in East Texas's Big Thicket, drew a vivid picture of Woodville's home field in a deceptively lush clearing surrounded by pine trees. Each year, he related, "on the first day of practice, players formed a line, and with a basket in our hands, we'd collect grass burrs, rocks, and sticks." For the rest of the season, however, the sandy loam constantly reminded them that they did not glean enough. Pete Shotwell said that when he arrived at Abilene in 1917, the Eagles—like most everybody else—played on the same field they practiced on. He told how coaches everywhere had to maintain their own fields and fill up holes "so kids wouldn't break a leg or something." Chatter Allen added that "after three or four games there wouldn't be a spot of green on them."

And at just about every place, it seemed, the flesh-nibbling lime that lined the fields on game days was crooked. Many old-timers, such as Robert Lowrance, winced at the memory of landing on the boundary lines with an open cut. "It would cause blisters and eat away at you," Lowrance recounted. Homer Johnson remarked that it would get into the hip pads and act with the sweat to produce a most chafing irritation. To counteract the lime burns, teams routinely carried bottles of vinegar in their medical bag.

Among other poor conditions were sloping fields and sand that could be ankle-deep in places. Lowrance remarked that at Lindale, in Northeast Texas, players could not move very quickly in the porous sugar sand, and when tackled they would come up with grass burrs on any part of their bodies that touched the ground. If "stickers" were the scourge of players in some parts of the state, Ralph Martin countered that the "goatheads" growing in the hardpacked ground of South Texas were much worse. Grass burrs might leave an annoying splinter, which could be easily picked out, but the thorny goatheads were hard, and "hurt just as much when you pulled them out as when they stuck in."

Perhaps nothing was as stifling to a game as a rainy field. Mud on these sodless surfaces slowed the pace of a game to a crawl. Particularly immobilizing was the thin band of rich, black, waxy gumbo soil that stretched from the Red River around Paris, down through Dallas and Waxahachie, and southward, east of Austin and San Antonio. With every step, more mud stuck to mud already there, which forced high-stepping players to trudge forward with huge blocks on their feet. These same Blacklands that could sink a mule up to its haunches made for many a scoreless tie.

Almost every early-day pigskinner could recall playing in a cow pasture or some other particularly crude field. Joe Hedrick told about the gridiron at Iola, where "half of it was an oat field, and the other half was gravel." The "town branch" also ran through one corner, creating a slope. "In one spot was a foot-deep ditch," he remarked, and "knowing that it was there was always in the back of your mind." Mayfield Workman explained how the football field at Bridgeport was almost downtown on a lot that was not quite large enough for it. "It had a wooden fence around it," he said, and the front of the end zone was "right up on the boards. If you got backed up, you'd have to borrow ten yards to punt."

Some other places were better. Jack Christian recalled that old Butler Field at Amarillo "was a converted baseball diamond" that "at least had grass on the infield." By the time Christian got to Abilene in the 1930s, the Eagles had three state championships under their belt and had moved to the West Texas Fair Grounds. The school had erected bleachers and even a grandstand for their considerable followers, but, like the old field, this one, too, was "full of burrs and had no grass."

Getting to those games could be an adventure in itself; money was scarce and roads were few and most often in poor condition. Ralph

UIL holdouts, the Rio Grande City Rattlers, 1931; nineteen-year-old Ralph Martin, top row, middle, player-coach. *Photograph courtesy Janice Perez.*

Martin remarked that his Rio Grande City Rattlers had no buses and never enjoyed anything like a pep rally before leaving for a game. He boarded the team unceremoniously onto borrowed trucks or got parents and merchants to drive the kids in cars. Once, when the team traveled to Weslaco in two old automobiles, the lead car broke down. Discovering they had no spare tire, Martin directed the starting eleven to climb into the remaining car with him, while the others walked into the next town. The teacher accompanying them did not have any money on him; however, he was a Mason and was able to persuade a fellow lodgeman to cash a check, and they made it to Weslaco by halftime.

On another occasion, after talking a local man out of his flatbed truck, Martin experienced generator problems on the way home from a game at Pharr. When he took advantage of a steep downgrade to gain some speed, the near-useless headlights gave short warning of a cattle herd crossing the road just ahead of him. "I zigzagged and threw off about half of the players and equipment," he laughed, "but I didn't hit a single cow!"

The equipment that players wore in the twenties and thirties was a perfect complement to their crude fields and spartan playing conditions. Whatever padding they used was mostly cotton, though the better players were sometimes outfitted in a precursor of shoulder pads that looked like horse collars. Ralph Martin recalled "the old 'moleskin' pants, fashioned out of tent-canvas material that would hurt your face if you were a tackler." Chatter Allen remarked that some of the gear "was so meager, ill-fitting and cumbersome that many players played without it. I never wore a headgear in high school or college, nor did I wear thigh guards." Jewell Wallace, who played high school ball between 1923 and 1927, told how he nailed oblong cleats onto his street shoes in a haphazard fashion. He also donned a flat headgear with floppy ears and wore thigh pads made of cardboard. Describing the style of

A cheerleader "fires 'em up" at Breckenridge, c. 1925; the man on the left is carrying a down marker. *Photograph courtesy Basil Clemons Photograph Collection, Special Collections Division, The University of Texas at Arlington Libraries.*

play, he said: "We didn't try to protect our faces, particularly, we just used our arms and legs more and ducked a lot."

Leather head protection seemed to be a particular curse. Robert Lowrance described his as an "aviator-type" helmet that "you could fold up and put in your back pocket." Some of them had "little ol' flimsy sticks in the top . . . for support," added Pete Shotwell. According to Chatter Allen, "most of those old headgears were always down in your face," and "you couldn't get one to fit you. He chose not to wear one, and as a result of countless tackles developed cauliflowered ears. "I got one of my ears nearly torn off playing San Marcos." They had a big running back named Zunker; "they'd ram him into the line," Allen recalled. "I got my ear hung on his pants . . . took Dr. Slaughter—isn't that a hell of a name?—something like twenty stitches to put it back together." At least Allen's decision to go without head protection was his own; Ralph Martin knew a Coach Kellum who "wouldn't issue you a helmet unless you were bleeding behind the ears." Bull Workman, who did wear one, said it was continually sliding down, and that every year his nose was "skinned solid" from fall to midwinter.

In those formative years, from the playing field to the bleachers, there was little sophistication to be found at a high school football game. Chronicler Harold Ratliff, who played at Hillsboro just after World War I, recalled a boy who "came in from the farm on Friday, couldn't find a jersey and just played in his blue work shirt."[29] To confuse opposing teams, Greenville's Henry Frnka outfitted his Lions in kaleidoscope colors that featured whirlpool designs on the helmets, pants legs of different colors, and vertical slashes on either side of their jersey numbers, giving the appearance of four digits. Once in motion the Lions would give the opposing teams fits and make a scout's job almost impossible.[30]

Game balls, too—normally the same ones the home team practiced with—were in as poor shape as any of the players' equipment. Joe Taylor, who played on some great Cisco teams in the late 1920s, asserted: "We only had one ball." Once, on a particularly windy day, teammate Buster Mills caused the suspension of play several times when he kept punting the ball out of the stadium. "He kicked it out where all the cars were parked, and they had to go look for it."

Old-time coaches agreed that poor officiating provided the crowning complement to the rudimentary conditions. Robert Lowrance claimed that "all you needed was a striped shirt and a whistle." A number of times during the mid-1920s, after being assessed a fifteen-yard penalty, Highland Park linemen would distract the other team by suckering the officials. The dumbfounded referee would fail to halt play while the Highlanders looked at each other with quizzical expressions and began debating: "Is that right? Fifteen yards for holding?" The cue prompted captain "Big'un" Rose to declare that his team was shortchanged. Commanding his center to hand him the ball, he would turn to the perplexed official, and say: "You owe us ten yards." As the opposing team relaxed to watch the argument, Rose would start stepping off the ten yards, and after clearing the defensive linemen, would scamper toward the goal for a touchdown. However unconventional, neither the outrage of the opposing team nor the referee's embarrassment could erase the fact that Highland Park had put the ball into play in a legal manner.[31] Poor officiating once upset a Teague lady so badly that when one referee wandered too close to the sidelines, she knocked him unconscious with a brick, which delayed the game until he could be revived.[32]

Manners on the sidelines were just as poor. Ratliff recalled how "the yell leader at my school would taunt the opposing team: 'They're yellow, every one of them. Take 'em out and put skirts on 'em.' And the girls would applaud." Chatter Allen added: "In the early days there was very little thought given to sportsmanship. . . . There were many fights and it seemed to be customary to badger the visiting team and rock their bus." He added that "about the only way the schools could combat this problem was to preach and practice sportsmanship." When he began coaching at La Grange in 1932, Allen recommended "such things as meeting the opponent's bus at the city limit with a group of cheerleaders and escorting them out the same way."

Allen certainly had an interest in fostering goodwill. In 1924 he had a brother who played on a Georgetown team that was hosting Giddings.

During the game, one of the hometown fans, Alvia Townley, began berating the visiting team's coach, "parading up and down behind the [Giddings] bench." When coach Toby Hausen asked him to move, Townley replied: "Let's see you move me!" And, said Allen, he did, "but good." When the humiliated Georgetown fan got up from the ground, he proclaimed: "I'll go get something I can whip you with." As the game was ending, Townley returned with a pistol and waited at the gate until he spotted Giddings mayor Charley Fields and his brother, John. Accosting the pair, he dropped the big hogleg down on the mayor and then pumped four shots into the sibling, fatally wounding him. "All this in full view of about a thousand horrified spectators." The gridiron murderer, Allen commented, was later executed at the state prison in Huntsville.[33]

The incident sounded more like something that would have escalated out of a nightmarish sandlot game, rather than a formally scheduled contest between the representatives of two towns. Townley's actions, significantly, stand virtually alone. Even on the field, fistfights became fewer as participants learned that poor sportsmanship was most often designed to take an opponent's mind off the task at hand. The bench-clearing brawls that plague all sports are rare in football; players on the gridiron no doubt learned early that contact "between the whistles" was enough to satisfy any violent urges.

One of the signs that football in Texas had come of age was that more and more players brought to the high school game some savvy and skills honed in countless pickup contests on the sandlot. Many early players did not have that kind of experience. Leon Vinyard, for example, insisted that in 1933 he played in the first football game he ever saw; in fact, he had never even seen a football until he went out for the team. After attending a rural grammar school in Van Zandt County, Vinyard entered high school at Canton. Some of the kids there had been playing football for four or five years, but Vinyard's backwoods country school had barely enough bodies to put a basketball team together.

Gordon Wood could relate to Vinyard, much to the regret of poor Gene Estes. When Wood entered the seventh grade, he explained: "I was big and the football team was small," and he started in the first football game he ever saw. Before the contest, the school kids held a pep rally, and young Wood took to heart the graphic oaths about what the other team had coming. "I took literally what they were saying," he insisted. Very early in the game, Wood found himself blocking Estes and "beat his face to a pulp" before someone pulled him off.

Too many times a "coach" would find himself possessing about as much knowledge of the game as his players. Very few places hired a man for his coaching ability. When Robert Lowrance was in school the principal would come out and "throw the ball out onto the field and say, 'y'all practice!'" At some places the school board considered football an activity that was better left to a townsman who had an interest in it. Chatter Allen played under Round Rock mailman Bob Carlson before moving to

Paul Tyson, Waco High School, c. 1925. *Photograph courtesy Texas Sports Hall of Fame, Waco.*

Georgetown. And at San Antonio, Ralph Martin worked for the city recreation department. Those employed by the school who took their added duty seriously would find themselves learning football at the same time as their players. Brooks Conover stated: "We played on nothing but natural ability because most coaches hadn't played themselves and really didn't know enough about fundamentals to pass on any advice." Conover, for instance, who had a natural talent for punting, had to find out for himself how far out to hold the ball to find the "sweet spot."

Coaching Becomes a Profession

As football developed, more coaches became students of the game, which enabled them to gain an edge on their opponents. Cotton Miles stated that in the early days, "football was all "6–2 defenses and single wings"—an offensive formation where the center snapped the ball directly to a player in the backfield. Jack Christian agreed. "We had one basic offense and one basic defense." Still, the coaches who placed a premium on learning the fundamentals of blocking and tackling won most of the time. Cotton Miles emphasized that the good ones would work to take advantage of training regimens and ask other coaches for plays and insights. Very often such a coach would be facing an opponent who had an "ag" or shop teacher at the helm, "so it was easy to beat them."

No Texas high school football coach gained a reputation for learning more about the game at an earlier date than did Waco's Paul Tyson. In 1904 his well-to-do parents sent him to Texas Christian University, while the school was still in Waco, intending for him to become a doctor. After

lettering in baseball and football, Tyson was offered a major league baseball contract, but instead chose to satisfy his parents by working on a master's degree in biology. When he took a break to teach high school science at Tyler, the kids recruited him to be their "football supervisor."
After teaching two more terms at Denison, Tyson decided that his destiny
lay with the emerging sport. In 1913, he returned to Waco High School,
where he remained the Tigers' coach for twenty-eight seasons.

A brilliant and imaginative man, Tyson understood the game like few
men did and possessed a talent for conveying that knowledge to his players. His success was rewarded with a small staff of assistants at a time
when almost every school employed only one coach. He took advantage
of this strength by developing a system to scout other teams. A great
innovator, Tyson developed an ancient version of the "wishbone" formation. He had more success, however, running a series of plays out of the
single wing, where one or both of the two backs receiving the snap would
spin and cross paths with the remaining backs and ends. During the
1920s the original and appropriately named "spinner" series brought a
flood of letters from coaches around the country, including Notre Dame's
Knute Rockne and Stanford's Pop Warner.[34]

Dr. W. L. Crosthwait, the Tigers' team physician, recalled that in 1927 a
hopeful Sherman team brought three trainloads of fans to Waco, bearing a
huge banner: "Stop that spin play." Upon forcing the Bearcats to punt
after the opening kickoff, Waco ran a spinner on its second play from
scrimmage, which resulted in a long touchdown. The doctor recalled: "I
don't think I've ever seen so many broken hearts in my life."[35]

Waco, under Tyson, dominated Texas high school football in the twenties. The near-invincible Tigers played in six straight championship games
between 1922 and 1927, losing only two games during that span and
scoring over a hundred points on nine occasions. Among Tyson's players
were future all-Americans and many who went on to become coaches,
including SMU's Dutch Meyer, and Jack Sisco, who brought a fleeting
prominence to North Texas State Teachers College.[36]

Tyson added to his considerable talent by traveling to clinics all over the
country and was regularly invited to college campuses to share insights
with the greatest coaching minds of his day. Frank Pulattie, who played for
Tyson in the thirties, visited his coach's home many times and saw stacks
of letters that Knute Rockne and other notable coaches had sent to the
Waco wizard, asking him to pick apart a play they had designed. For a
while Tyson helped run a summer clinic with Rockne, who once claimed
that his young protégé knew more about football than any man in
America. Tyson, in fact, was considering an assistant's job at Notre Dame
when the legendary Rockne perished in a plane crash in March 1931. That
autumn, Tyson took a sabbatical to work with Pop Warner.[37]

In 1927, the entire nation came to know the Waco Tigers. That year,
Tyson accepted an invitation to take his team to Ohio, where the Tigers
played a mythical national championship against Latin Cathedral High

"Boody" Johnson, Waco High, 1922, sporting the typical equipment of the times. *Photograph courtesy Texas Sports Hall of Fame, Waco.*

School of Cleveland. The 44–12 victory capped a year that saw Waco win fourteen games, rolling to an average of fifty-six points per contest—a record that would stand for forty-eight seasons—while giving up an average of only 2.4 points to their opponents.[38] Twice they scored more than a hundred points, once in a play-off game against Houston's Jefferson Davis High School. Jeff's coach, Roy Needham, said "Waco could have beaten a good college team" that day.[39]

Chatter Allen quarterbacked a Georgetown team that "played Waco in 1927 when Paul Tyson claimed the national championship . . . and clobbered a high school team from Ohio." Before the game Allen remembered sizing up the Waco bunch. Although they had a large squad,

Few in number but long on talent, Pete Shotwell's Abilene Eagles gather for a banquet at the home of Earl Guitar, a prominent fan, after defeating Paul Tyson's Waco Tigers 3–0 in the 1923 state championship game. *Photograph courtesy Texas Sports Hall of Fame, Waco.*

including a 210-pound tackle named Swift—"a 190-pounder was a giant in those days"—he nevertheless "figured we were just about as big as they were." As the two teams vacated the field after warming up, Allen was still wondering, "How good can they be?" He did not even have to wait until the game began to find out. "Boody" Johnson, alone, walked to the fifty-yard line with a football under each arm. From the middle of the field he drop-kicked one through one set of uprights—then situated on the goal line—and then turned around and duplicated the feat at the other end. Allen gaped. "I couldn't believe it." He thought to himself that Johnson could win the game just by kicking field goals. "But of course, they didn't even have to kick a field goal," he laughed; "they really put it on us."

For his part, the 125-pound Chatter Allen was named by the Waco *Tribune*'s Jinx Tucker to the Tigers' All-Opponent Team that year, mostly on the strength of running a kickoff back to the ten yard line as well as engineering a cutback play that went for forty-five yards. He admitted, however, the source of his motivation: "I was runnin' scared." In later years, Georgetown coach Rodney Kidd would tell about the time his team took on the mighty Tigers that year. When asked what the score was, he would chortle: "Waco 72-Georgetown $1,000!"

The name Paul Tyson still radiates in the hearts of Texans who take up his profession. He helped catapult the game into prominence, and his innovations inspired even more creativity. He also won on all the strengths that the best of his progeny would try to emulate. Rather than emphasizing winning, he focused on details, the little things that built a solid foundation for larger successes. For every former player who became a coach, there were others who grew up to be doctors, lawyers, professional men, and civic leaders. Tyson stressed character, scholarship, responsibility, pride, and a sense of team. He was part psychologist, part general, part father—and all coach. Bubba Nash, who played on some of the great Tyson teams of the twenties, recalled: "He knew football and he knew kids." He won his players' confidence and respect by sincerity and example, demanding that they comport themselves in a manner befitting their performance on the field. Although Nash said that Tyson "lived football twenty-four hours a day," the coach nevertheless found time to become a capable pianist and taught a Sunday School class as well. A confirmed bachelor, he lived "down at the YMCA," continued Nash, where "he would get the boys together and by shifting checkers around teach them football strategy and tactics." His players gravitated toward him, and in a day when the starting eleven played both offense and defense, Tyson sometimes suited up more than one hundred boys. In contrast, Pete Shotwell claimed that when his Abilene team split championships with Waco in 1922 and 1923, the Eagles fielded no more than twenty kids on either squad.[40]

Frank Pulattie agreed with Nash, and commented that Tyson "devoted all his time to us." He owned a big Packard that seemed always to be full of kids, continued the former all-state running back. Almost every night the coach would invite three or four players to his home and serve them steaks, a luxury that Pulattie rarely enjoyed in his mother's single-parent home. He recalled with a measure of amusement in his voice that after Tyson had finished his french fries, he would reach over and get more from whomever was sitting closest. Pulattie learned quickly that the napkin rack and condiment dispensers made a nice little wall that kept his coach's fingers at bay. With a more serious tone, he also recalled that Tyson's expensive shirts often found their way into the lockers of his poorer players rather than to the cleaners.

For Texans who think they know coaches, Paul Tyson towers above the stereotypical bully at the other end of the profession. The image of such a symbiotic pair indicates that these men, like those in most any group, are more complex than a superficial understanding might suggest. Not many of those who followed Tyson would learn to play the piano—their backgrounds did not lend themselves to such refinements—but legions of coaches would lead boys into manhood, often while filling the role of father. And, quite often, many coaches would find an appropriate Friday night analogy for relating to their Sunday School classes how Samson slew the Philistines with the jawbone of an ass.

Chapter 3

Growing up on Black-Eyed Peas and Football: Coaches' Childhoods, 1920s–1940s

igh school football in Texas grew into a popular pastime during the 1920s and 1930s, yet social barriers kept the sport from reaching into every corner of the state. In many cases players simply could not find the time to participate, and men and women found that the Friday afternoon games did not accommodate their work schedules. Yet the problem ran much deeper. The obstacles often were more serious than backward rural schools and the poor road system that connected them. For families like the one to which Bum Phillips belonged, football did not mean much when you "had a hard time eating." Too many Texans were facing that very predicament as the bumper years of World War I faded into an agricultural malaise that deeply affected the largely rural state. The roar that most Americans were supposed to have heard during the twenties sounded more like the same old grind to country folk in the Southwest, from whose ranks most of the old-time Texas coaches would hail.

Bill Carter, whose family settled near Littlefield in the mid-1920s, proved a woeful example. On a small farm outside of that Panhandle town, he and ten brothers and sisters helped their parents raise hogs. They bartered smoked hams for flour, sugar, and other necessities that they could not produce themselves. "Everybody had it tough," Carter remarked, but at least "we did have enough to eat, which is more than a lot of people." Nevertheless, "the way we got things done" in those changing times soon forced the family to look for more productive land in the countryside around Weatherford, as well as new ways to make ends meet. To the Carters and others who were just emerging from nineteenth-century patterns of life, technology frequently meant dislocation rather than freedom from drudgery.

A Rural, Working Class People

For most of those forced off the farm during the 1920s, life continued to possess a rural flavor. Even in Dallas, the Southwest's money capitol, the financial pulse beat more to the ups and downs of commodity prices than those of stocks and bonds. At booming port towns on the Gulf, men loaded cotton, corn, and other farm products onto outbound ships. In East Texas, lumber plants drew country folk to towns like Trinity, where Bob Barfield's father worked as a planing foreman, or to Diboll, where Herb Allen's father supervised a crew of loggers. Texans who looked for work in other industries found plenty of jobs at factories like the cotton mill in Waco that employed Frank Pulattie's mother, or at the Fort Worth stockyards, where Hugh Hamm's father labored. Hamm explained that his dad figured his family would be better off if he worked at slaughtering the cattle and hogs he had raised right up until he quit his land outside of Keller.

If coaches came from every walk of life, those who hailed from the upper strata of society were very rare indeed. Rather, it was the working class that produced most of those who played and later guided the sport between the mid-1930s and the mid-1960s—a time when football in Texas was truly king. Coaches' families typically represented a cross section of hardworking Texans with rural roots. Coaches' fathers cut hair, taught school, spread the Gospel, welded pipelines, and worked on automobiles. Many, many more tilled the soil and pulled cotton bolls—sometimes on their own land, but just as often on land owned by others. They also felled timber, broke horses, mined coal, labored on road crews and oil wells, and performed any odd job that would pay a day's wages.

While their fathers toiled from dawn to dusk, the coaches' mothers normally remained at home. And as they struggled to maintain their households, often without running water or electricity, mothers also provided the instruction that cinched tight the Bible Belt morals of their rural society. For every Catholic and Presbyterian coach, several others had been raised Baptist and Methodist. Still others had grown up in Pentecostal churches, the Assembly of God, or the Church of Christ. Only a generation or so earlier their forebears had brought to Texas the God-fearing folkways of places such as Arkansas, Louisiana, Mississippi, and Missouri. Like Joe Bob Tyler, whose mother's family made its way to Northwest Texas in a covered wagon by way of Alabama and Oklahoma, many of them heard from their parents how the oxen "just flat gave out" and "here's where we settled."

There were exceptions, to be sure. A few families, such as E. C. Lerma's, were originally from Mexico. Other coaches, like Chuck Moser, moved to the state after reaching adulthood. And if coaches such as Clarence McMichael and Elmer Redd shared the southernness of their peers, their experiences as African Americans set them apart.

In addition, many coaches came from single-parent homes. As children, John Reddell and Quin Eudy were abandoned by their fathers; Bill Hartley's and John Hugh Smith's fathers died unexpectedly. For dependent wives and mothers, life grew suddenly precarious, as they were forced into the homes of relatives or into low-paying jobs that sometimes meant their children went to bed hungry.

Despite such humble backgrounds, a few old coaches, such as Chatter Allen, nevertheless recalled dim childhood memories of prosperity. After World War I, Allen's father sold enough real estate between Round Rock and Georgetown to buy a comfortable home and a nice automobile. "We always had plenty of food on the table and nice clothes to wear," Allen boasted. Donald Jay, too, remembered feeling important, knowing that his hometown of Jayton had been named after kinfolk who had settled the community on the edge of the Croton Breaks. Just down the highway, Morris Southall was the son of the principal of Haskell High School, where his mother also taught. At Luling, Emory Bellard was one of twelve children, but they were no burden on their father. He was a geologist and driller who arrived in Central Texas in the late twenties to take part in the emerging oil boom.

The Great Depression and personal calamity, however, proved to be even greater social levelers. The Allens were left "land poor." The Depression also reminded folks in Jayton—never a very prosperous place to begin with—that the Croton Breaks was one of the stingiest places in already harsh West Texas. For the Southalls, being paid in scrip rather than hard currency provoked young Morris's father to take a job in Plainview with City Services; the gas company promptly folded as soon as they arrived. Tragedy for the Bellards came in the form of a rig's broken U-bolt, whose violent motion shattered the oilman's jaw and neck along with his family's prosperity.

At least for his family's reversal of fortunes, no trace of bitterness lingered in Donald Jay's voice as he recalled how his family went "from doing fairly well to eating red beans and black-eyed peas." He spoke for many others, in fact, when he commented: "We didn't know any better, because everybody else was eating the same thing."

Whatever their backgrounds, the boys who played football and became high school coaches in the sport's glory years were sons of economic depression and war. As men, they guided tens of thousands of Texas teenagers through rapidly changing times, yet their own values and philosophies drew from a more static society that was tearing loose from frontier traditions and drifting into a modern age. From whatever part of Texas they hailed, these sons of farmers, laborers, and jacks-of-all-trades embraced the hard-working, church-going folkways of their immediate ancestors. When they donned caps and hung whistles around their necks, old-time Texas coaches imprinted onto young, forward-looking minds the rigid, but certain, values and moral outlooks of an age that was slowly fading.

For Texans making a living in the country during the first three decades of the twentieth century, the new age emerged slowly as the mechanical revolution introduced more efficient farm machinery and replaced dirt trails with farm-to-market blacktops. Farm families still shared the work and labored at it from daylight to dark. Bob Barfield pointed out that wood-burning stoves, so fashionable and quaint today, were a mark of poverty in his childhood home. And, like so many others, his family's plumbing was supplied by an outdoor well. Rural Texans in the 1920s no doubt felt a closer affinity to their Populist counterparts of the 1890s than with the forward-looking city folk who were swept away by the Jazz Age and the new ideas of a material culture.

When Gordon Wood heard that another old coach claimed he had "come west on one of those wagon trains sometime in the 1800s," Texas's winningest coach laughed at the intended exaggeration. The man only missed the mark by a generation. Wood's father, in fact, did roll into West Texas in the back of a wagon. By the time Gordon Wood was born in 1914, his father had already sired seven other children. All of them, the coach remarked, helped their daddy farm cotton around Abilene "in the days before we used tractors, and let me tell you, it required hard work."

The image that Wood painted of his father was a painful depiction. Seeing his father work so hard and fail so often affected young Gordon. "He loved farming . . . he'd get out on that plow . . . and when he's turning that soil he'd be either whistling or singing at the top of his voice; he was just as happy as he could be." But grasshoppers, boll weevils, drought, and hail continually frustrated him. When he did get a good crop, plummeting cotton prices sunk him. "Seeing him work so hard and have such great expectations . . . made me want to find a way off that farm. . . . I just knew there must be a better way of life than that."

The elder Wood's farming operation always teetered on the brink of collapse, and the arrival of a young man just out of the penitentiary and his wife signaled the end. The guy "was down on his luck," Wood said, and so his father "sublet some land to him and also loaned him some tools. . . . And then the fellow wouldn't work, so he had to dismiss him."

A few days later the Woods' barn burned, killing their twelve mules and destroying all the tools that the family had accumulated. Wood's father always felt that the former convict had set the fire. The tragedy forced the family's patriarch to sell their remaining possessions just to survive. When a banker tried to extend him credit, Wood's father would not hear of it, and his family suffered terribly. "Dad had a peculiar attitude—wouldn't borrow a dime." On the day he died, he told his son, Gordon: "I don't believe I owe a man a penny, but if I do, would you pay him?"

For one more season Wood's mother tried to keep the farm afloat, but then the family's eldest son, Dick, broke his back. A doctor put him in a cast "from his knees to his armpits," and he remained like that for many months. Wood's mother pledged the year's crop as payment, and when it failed, she had to move into Abilene, where she ran a boardinghouse and took in laundry.

For folks who could hold a family farm, life was not always as dire. Young Joe Bob Tyler, for example, worked hard, but never went hungry. His parents and siblings raised chickens and a few cows, and they nurtured an orchard and pecan trees. They normally ate only what they grew,

Dan Anderegg on his family's Hill Country ranch. *Photograph courtesy Dan Anderegg.*

but hardly ever touched the eggs because they were a source of income. Pecans would fetch five or six cents a pound—money that the Tylers earmarked for clothes. Even during the Depression, Bailey Marshall's family broke from a tradition of sharecropping by saving enough money to buy some land near Jonah, east of Georgetown. Marshall's father provided the heavy labor while his mother kept the family books and sold butter and eggs. And the children, rather than draining the family income, made their own spending money by peddling the vegetables they raised.

Nevertheless, even the best situated rural families toiled to make the land produce. Dan Anderegg, for example, grew up on his family's seven-thousand-acre ranch near the Hill Country town of Doss. Yet despite his circumstances, young Dan was a far cry from a country squire. His father put him and his little brother to work "seven days a week" at ages five and eight years old, respectively. "We worked like dogs," Anderegg insisted, "and we grew up fast."

If you balance a map of Texas on a pin, the point would almost rest on a ranch near Brady, where Ray Akins's father worked. And if Ray's childhood was not exactly average, it at least typified the early experiences of coaches who grew up in ranching country. Akins remembered listening intently, yet somewhat stolidly, to the old foreman, Mr. Jay, tell stories about the cattle trails and the open range. "He had been orphaned up in Indian Territory, and the ranch owner picked him up when they were driving a herd of cattle to Kansas." To a young Ray Akins, however, the cowboy tales that Mr. Jay told did not seem like old times—"we were still living the same way that my dad and grandfather had lived."

The Akins' cabin, part of the wages-in-kind that the ranch owner supplied, had neither telephone, running water, nor electricity. What light they had was supplied by a kerosene lantern. Coach Akins remembered that when they got a new Coleman "we were in high cotton." They raised most of what they consumed, and when it was time to shell peas or grind corn, the entire family made the task a get-together. Chores such as producing their own soap in boiling vats, however, could not be made less onerous by any amount of togetherness. Only occasionally did they go into town for a barrel of flour or other necessities.

Before they became old enough to work for their father, Akins and his younger brother enjoyed hanging out at the stock pens, running errands, and fetching supplies for the cowboys just so they could be around them. Mr. Jay, especially, was ever inclined to delegate busywork to the boys. They looked forward to round up time, and the furious pace that accompanied dust-watered eyes, the sound of bawling calves, and the acrid smell of burning hair and hides. The boys knew that their reward would be a place at the campfire, where they could rub sore muscles and laugh at cowboy humor and "the jokes they pulled on each other to pass the time."

Akins recalled a routine that "began when I was about two years old," when the ranch hands gathered him up with some of the young animals and pretended they were going to brand him. "I yelled bloody murder." But he eventually learned that it was all in fun, and felt satisfaction for being included, even as the butt of a practical joke. Being one of the guys wore thin, however, when Akins occasionally found himself hovering over the stock pen well at the mercy of a laughing cowboy clutching him carelessly by the heels.

Such "fun" was fleeting. When they got a little older, a normal day began with the Akins brothers milking "eight or nine" cows. After that "we got the feed out and slopped around two hundred hogs." Then it was about 6:30 A.M., and time to round up their horses from the pasture and head for school. The boys owned only one change of clothes and carried beans and biscuits in a bucket for lunch. Leaving the ranch reminded them that elsewhere others had joined the twentieth century. "We always felt inferior because of the way we lived."

When the brothers returned home other chores awaited. They might bale hay, string fence, repair a windmill, or help cultivate their garden. Their father was actually the only family member employed by the ranch, but he was paid by the job, and delegating duties to his sons helped increase his income. The two brothers received fifty cents a day out of his wages, and every chance they got, they made extra money for buying clothing and other necessities by hunting varmints—skunks, opossums, raccoons, and ringtailed cats—and selling the hides.

When they became teenagers and gained some ranching experience, the Akins boys began breaking horses. They received the princely sum of between thirteen and twenty-one dollars per animal, depending on its intended use. "This is not as easy as it looks on TV, and it's dangerous,"

Akins asserted. One horse that he named Smokey, in fact, refused to be broken, and when the frustrated rancher gave up on it, he handed the animal over to the delighted teenager. "I had that horse for three years, and he pitched every time I got on," Akins declared, "but he was mine."

Like Ray Akins, Joe Hedrick grew up listening to the stories of old-timers. In the East Central Texas community of Wheelock, however, the old-timers were not cowboys, but former Confederate soldiers, who told young Joe woeful tales of how war had drained the male population of the once-promising farming center. Many of their brothers and cousins had never returned, which was why, they insisted, Wheelock never grew into much of a town. Along with a general store and post office, one of the few remaining buildings was the Union Church. But if anybody saw the irony, they did not comment about it. The name had nothing to do with Yankees, anyway; rather, "union" meant that every other Sunday the Methodists and the Baptists alternated services.

That Old-Time Religion

As life in Texas changed after World War I, religion became even more of a touchstone for families whose roots remained embedded in frontier ways and mores. For most, the church provided a social outlet. For others, especially farm families whose economic fortunes began to deteriorate even before the Great Depression settled in, the church offered hope in uncertain times. As a moral guide, the brimstone glowed brightly from the pulpit, lighting life's paths. The delivery was most often a pitch to the emotions, and many of the boys who grew up on it later imitated its evangelical style when they became coaches.

On their Red River Valley farm the Tylers were isolated and did not socialize much—"even working with other families was like a get-together," Joe Bob Tyler recalled. He looked forward to the weekends when their itinerant preacher stopped on his sporadic rounds to give a sermon under the brush arbor of tightly woven branches and leaves. Between services Tyler seemed to forget how long and boring the sermons could be. It was not really the message that he came to hear anyway, but the chance to get together with other children that evoked anticipation. Every once in a while he and other boys would slip away undetected to play at the creek, or to continue disagreements that teachers at his one-room country school had stopped.

Cotton Miles, too, recalled how "Brother Dean" would visit his Baptist congregation every fourth Sunday. Also, each summer, families would gather for a full week to sing, visit, relax, and hear the good reverend spread the Gospel. Just like their grandparents had, many arrived at the Big Thicket camp near Woodville in wagons, on horseback, and on foot, although the row of jalopies grew longer every year.

After suffering an injury at the local sawmill, Miles's father got a job driving the school bus on the condition that he provide a vehicle. The family's converted Model A pickup also came in handy at revival time. Miles's father also brought along his noisy Delco generator to the revival to recharge the batteries of folks lucky enough to own power-driven items such as radios and small appliances. For a people whom the New Deal's Rural Electrification Administration did not reach until 1938, these were rare luxuries. And "it didn't take much to have fun," Miles remembered. Everyone camped on the ground, and most of the time the men would sit on logs and rocks and talk, while the women prepared meals.

Well into the twentieth century, outdoor revivals remained a distinctive Bible Belt experience that Texans of all sections enjoyed. Like Cotton Miles, Joe Hedrick's family attended week-long services with three or four other families after their crops were "laid by" to await the harvest season. The mid-summer revivals "were more of a vacation than anything else," Hedrick recalled. "We got chewed on by mosquitoes" and everybody fished, set trotlines, and just generally savored the respite from hard work.

Increasingly, during the 1920s and 1930s, the paved roads that opened up the larger towns and cities seemed to run only one way. Many hamlets began disappearing, and with them, a nineteenth-century way of life. The old country preachers noticed that a decline of morality corresponded with the progress that spirited away members of their congregations. Quite naturally they lashed out at the agents of change. Automobiles were the target of much condemnation, and they singled out Hollywood in particular for glamorizing joyriding, drinking, dancing, and immodest dress.

A coach, whose mother became obsessed with a Pentecostal sermon condemning Tinseltown, told how she walked into a movie theater during a Saturday matinee and dragged him out by the collar. He still recalls the embarrassment he felt when she looked up at the screen and "gave ol' Satan the dickens." After being force-fed the preacher's Sunday sermons, the future coach sat on a curb with a young friend wishing they had never been born. "I remembered thinking that if what that son-of-a-bitch was saying was true, there was just no way we were going to make it to heaven."

If there were room, however, the typical mother would make sure that her boy would get there. Morris Southall spoke for most all of his peers when he insisted that his values "sprang from my daddy, but we got our morals from momma." She arranged all the family's social functions, which "revolved exclusively around the Baptist Church." Mrs. Southall "was almost a religious fanatic," her son laughed. "She taught the elderly women's Sunday School, and she would tithe before she'd spend money for food."

The mothers who raised future coaches insisted on regular church attendance and took seriously the Good Book and the preachers' admonitions. Bailey Marshall confessed that as a boy, he would use a curse word every now and then, and, every now and then, his mother would catch him and make him read passages from the Bible until he felt sufficiently contrite.

Marshall lost that influence just before he entered high school when his mother died suddenly. The tragedy occurred in the stream of larger events that found him equally powerless and left him just as profoundly affected. For a while it looked as if the former sharecropping family would hold fast against the currents of agricultural dislocation and the Great Depression. But for the Marshalls, like so many others, events swept them away just as the door to a better life seemed to be cracking open.

Rural folk were perennial optimists. When the people's choice for president in 1928 was campaigning, he declared: "We in America today . . . are nearer to the final triumph over poverty than ever before in the history of the land."[1] One East Texas couple was so inspired with his message of hope that they named their new son after him—Herbert Hoover Allen. By the time young Herb entered school, however, his family was living almost hand-to-mouth. Mr. Allen, a logging foreman for Temple Lumber Company, broke a foot and could no longer work. "If it had not been for us planning . . . raising a lot of vegetables, growing feed for our animals, well, I don't believe we would have made it," Herb Allen speculated.

At Quinlan in Northeast Texas, Bill Ellington's father enjoyed a decent living running a trucking company until the Texas Railroad Commission changed some rules that put him out of business. Afterward he chopped cotton for seventy-five cents a day. When some relatives in the Panhandle finally wrote that they could get him a job at a carbon plant, the Ellingtons paid a man $6.50 to take them as far as Canyon in his Model A Ford. From there they made it to Lefors, south of Pampa. "We were as poor as you can get," Ellington said, but "most people were in the same situation."

The Dust Bowl and Hard Times

Not long after they arrived in Lefors, the Ellingtons experienced one of the Panhandle's first great dust storms on a Sunday afternoon in March 1935. Erasing all the landscape in its path, the front "rolled forward like boiling fire." Just barely a teenager, Ellington naturally looked to adults for reassurance whenever uncertainty shook his confidence—and this was certainly one of those times. When a nearby man exclaimed: "The world is coming to an end!" Ellington frantically rushed home. Inside his family's little box house, a solitary light dangled from the ceiling, and "it got so dusty you couldn't see it!"

Bill Carter, just a year younger than Ellington, witnessed that same storm as it darkened the High Plains near Littlefield. He spotted what looked like a norther coming in, but noticed that it was darker than any he had ever seen. Everyone went into the cellar, thinking that it might be bringing hail, and when they came out "it was so dark you couldn't see your hand in front of your face." The local bootlegger, Carter chuckled, thought the world was coming to an end, and "busted all his bottles because he didn't want the Lord to catch him like that."

Bill Ellington commented that "after three or four you got used to it." Carrying out dust by the shovelful became routine for his mother. And

"Poor folks holiday," 1938. The Cashions stop outside of Roby on their way to pull cotton
bolls in West Texas. *Photograph courtesy Ty Cashion.*

when Ellington was in high school, football practice did not stop for a
light dust storm. Once, when his father's truck became stuck in deep sand
at a low-water crossing one evening, the elder Ellington simply walked
home and waited for daylight, hoping that a wind would free the vehicle
overnight. Sure enough, it did, and he drove home.

To a young Gene Mayfield the phenomenon symbolized the times.
One Saturday afternoon he had gone into Quitiquae for a haircut. The
little community was just under the Cap Rock and had not been as devas-
tated by the dust storms as towns on the High Plains. That day, however,
the sky grew so dark that the barber had to turn on the lights. "I wasn't
scared," he commented, "I was just overcome with despair." The storm
meant that their little farm house would be filled with dust, adding to the
woes of failing crops and plagues of insects. Sitting sullenly in the barber's
chair, "I just wondered: 'How much more can we take?'"

The Great Depression seared into young minds any number of agonizing images. Bob Barfield, who came from a family with nine children,
asserted that "there probably wasn't another family in Texas as poor as we
were." He and his siblings picked cotton "for twenty-five cents a hundred," and at one time his mother "worked at a dairy, milking cows for a
gallon of milk a day." Bill Shipman's family was actually homeless for a
while, living "sometimes in tents, sometimes in smokehouses—whatever
was available." His father was "totally against any kind of charity and we
never had a dime that we didn't earn." In some ways Allen Boren's family
was even worse off; in the mobile age that emerged in the 1930s, they did
not even own a car.

Bob Cashion remarked that "we'd have been better off if we hadn't
owned one." Induced by handbills that a relative collected, Cashion's
father left his job as groundskeeper at Ennis's country club and took his

family on a working vacation to West Texas to "pull bolls." When they made it atop the Cap Rock, young Bob fell ill after eating some fish that his mother had caught in a creek. "People thought if you drank milk with fish that it would bring on a fever. I had just had a big glass of milk. . . . " Hundreds of other people, of course, went west upon reading those same handbills, leaving hopeful pickers begging for jobs. What was supposed to have been a poor folks' holiday ended up a nightmare as the Cashions made their way back to Central Texas. "We stayed in an abandoned building for a few days when we ran out of money," the coach remarked. "Daddy walked into the town to get some work, so we could get some gas and something to eat." As it turned out, the building was also the lair of a mountain lion, "but it never showed up," Cashion smiled. "Maybe that panther knew how hungry we were."

Bill Hartley was also among those whose family's fortunes soured. In the West Texas town of Eden his father earned a good living working for a produce company. On the side, he and Mrs. Hartley ran an icehouse and sold turkeys and feed. "Then, in '33, my father died with a ruptured appendix," Hartley stated. At the hospital "they opened him up and when they found out what it was . . . they just sewed him back up and said: 'There's nothing we can do.'"

Hartley's father lingered for five days before leaving his family almost penniless and seeking the charity of kinfolk in San Saba, "seventy-five miles east of Eden." As the Depression deepened, they had to depend on "one old dairy cow" for their milk, and dinner was often "hog jowl bacon." They used the grease to fry bread, sometimes several days old, from which they first peeled off the moldy part and gave it to the cow. "It was not always this bad," Hartley declared. Many times they got together with his cousins and the kids played ball; they broke for ice cream and dinner, but always went back to their game.

Making the Most of a Bad Situation

Children, as Hartley suggested, can show remarkable resilience, even in the worst of times. Ed Logan's extended family resembled a real-life version of John Steinbeck's Joads in *The Grapes of Wrath.* Many of them, in fact, still live around Bakersfield, California. He declared, however, that not until he grew up and looked back on his childhood did he realize that his family had faced such dire times. "Hell, when everybody else is poor, you don't notice that you're poor, too."

Jap Jones summed up this happier side of the Great Depression: "We created our own fun." Living in a place where the Old South and the Wild West intersected meant that the Civil War and Custer's Last Stand could be reenacted over and over again, but this time by victorious rebels and cavalrymen. Bill Shipman professed to be a veteran of many a "mock war with BB guns and bean flips." He also "played lots of marbles, a lot of sandlot baseball and football," and he swam, fished, and "hunted during a

Bill Shipman, left, and a friend. The boys built the bicycle from scavenged parts and shared it. *Photograph courtesy Bill Shipman.*

lot of warm days when there wasn't work of some kind I could do." Shipman recalled: "On Saturdays, if I could make a quarter picking up pecans, selling junk, or mowing lawns, I saw a western movie, which cost ten cents, had a sack of popcorn, which cost a nickel, and afterward ate a hamburger for a nickel and drank a Double Cola for a nickel—a total of twenty-five cents."

Chatter Allen and his brother Henry skinning an opossum while their dog, Jack, rests after the hunt, 1922. *Photograph courtesy Chatter Allen.*

Almost everyone echoed Shipman with recollections of hustling spending money and of playing games like "Wolf Over the River," or of footraces, hunting birds with slingshots, gathering berries and pecans, exploring caves, and hunting Indian relics. Mayfield Workman "played a lot of tin can shinny," a form of hockey. "You'd swing as much at a kid's shins as at the can," he explained. Cotton Miles countered that "finding" a watermelon patch was infinitely more fun. And like many children who never owned a bicycle, Miles constructed a go-cart. His "Big Thicket Racer" was really nothing more than a pine tree with axles run through it, onto which he attached iron rims he had gathered from abandoned wheelbarrows.

Like Cotton Miles, Jap Jones and his brother took pieces of wood, wire, and tin and "made a car." They also wandered in the woods along Bear Creek, where the Dallas-Fort Worth Airport lies today. "Many times we had to hunt our food," Jones said. Even without a gun they could catch rabbits, opossums, and other small game. "Up on Grapevine Prairie we'd comb the bushes and find rabbits in their beds. We'd knock them down with rocks and cripple them so that they'd be easy to catch." Chatter Allen and his brother brought along a dog on their expeditions and used a trapline to snare varmints. "I was sent home from school several times because I smelled like a skunk," he laughed. "I still remember the old Funsten catalog; that's where we sent our hides."

Allen was also fortunate to know Bob Carlson, Round Rock's mailman and part-time coach. "His route was short, so he had lots of time to spend with not only his four boys but with all the neighborhood boys. His back yard was like a gym—an outdoor gym—even had a boxing ring. He taught us to box and we had 'fight day' once a week. During his vacation he took all the neighborhood kids on a weeklong camping trip on the Llano River."

But more than any other activity, it was the sport of the season that occupied the time of young boys. And most of the time it was football season. No matter how poor Allen Boren's family was, he always found time to play. One Christmas his parents rewarded his passion with a new plastic helmet at a time when leather was standard gear. "I can still smell it like it was when it was new," Boren said. Joe Washington's first memories of playing sandlot games at Rosenburg involved his best friend, James L. Simpson. The two wanted to continue playing football long after basketball season had begun, and "swaying kids one way or the other was almost like politics." Herb Allen said that in his little East Texas community, the kids were lucky to have one ball among them, yet they did not know enough about the sport to really play. So, they invented a game, "coming through," which meant simply that everybody went after the guy who had the ball. Allen remarked that "coming through" ended when a buddy, Ned Manor, led the group into the woods. "When we got back, there was no ball," Allen chuckled, and "our clothes were all torn up."

For older boys the hard times cut short whatever adolescence they had remaining. Bob Harrell, for example, was seventeen years old in 1932, when he began packing hot meat at a government canning factory in the Fort Worth stockyards. He worked seven days a week for fourteen dollars in a room that never dipped below 105 degrees. "Every night this little ol' girl would pass out . . . and I'd grab hold of her and run her outside and lay her on a bale . . . and then run back in and do both jobs until she came to," Harrell said. "She was from a real poor family, too."

The Great Depression, of course, was hard on almost everyone, but for the small number of African Americans who became coaches, their families actually fared somewhat better than their white counterparts. The kinds and numbers of lucrative and prestigious jobs held by upper class whites were normally barred to people of color. Today's black CEO, for example, might have been yesterday's logging foreman, like Herb Allen's father. More often, however, the cream of African American society owned small businesses or were teachers or ministers. Coaching provided one more welcome avenue into which they could funnel their brightest and most capable children.

Even though Jap Jones and Elmer Redd did not have it nearly as good as some, they both agreed that their fellow black coaches were generally better off than their white peers. While Jones and his brother "cut wood on the halves" to help their family make ends meet, others, he said, knew a measure of comfort. Joe Washington's father, for example, ran a funeral home and owned a dry cleaning business in Rosenburg. Clarence McMichael's father was the son of a Baptist preacher who founded several churches in East Texas, and his mother taught school. Although they worked hard, he remarked, they were nevertheless "in the upper echelon of the black economic community." Along with his eight brothers and sisters, McMichael helped his father run the family's productive farm outside of Nacogdoches, where they gained a reputation for breeding sturdy mules and horses. A young Clarence McMichael often delivered animals for his father, sometimes at distances of ten and fifteen miles before school. "As long as I got the ten cents a mile that he promised me, I didn't mind," he remarked.

Clarence McMichael decided very early what he wanted to do with his life. Recalling his grandfather, he remarked: "I idolized him for his work, but never thought seriously about becoming a minister." He did receive a calling, however, but "The Word" for McMichael was "Coach." At Nacogdoches, African Americans who came to watch Stephen F. Austin's Lumberjacks play football were not permitted to sit in the stands. Young boys like McMichael could hardly see through the crowd milling beyond the end zone, and so they would perch on the limbs of the tall pine trees that grew close to the field. When he looked down at the gridiron and let his mind wander, it was not to envision a breakaway run for the goal line or delivering a bone-crushing tackle; rather, his mind's eye focused on the anxious man pacing the sidelines. "I dreamed that one day that would be me coaching with the stands full of people."

That vision became a reality for Clarence McMichael, and one that paid rich dividends—and not just for himself, but for countless schoolboys who came into contact with him. For legions of others who became coaches, football would be the deciding factor that broke their family tradition of poverty, and in many cases, even illiteracy. Not many would see their future so clearly at such an early age as McMichael, in large part because such a position of authority, much less college, seemed far beyond their reach. From where most of these old coaches started, few avenues promised to lead to a better life until somewhere along the way their paths intersected with football. And that made all the difference.

Chapter 4

A Rough Sport for Tough Times: Football in the Great Depression

High school football in Texas did not suddenly bloom into the state's chosen pastime. By the mid-1930s, however, it had become such a ubiquitous part of community life that people regarded it as "Texan" as cattle and oil wells. Any number of conditions brought the sport to its adolescence. Continued school consolidations, better roads, and more widely available transportation opened up participation. New rules and improved playing conditions made the game safer, faster-paced, and fairer. And coaches continued to grow with the game, especially after they formed the Texas High School Football Coaches Association. Also, the seasonal rites became family traditions as schoolboys carried the torch handed to them by fathers, uncles, big brothers, and men about town. Football became more accommodating, too, as the game settled into a Friday night routine that crowned the work week.

As in football's earliest days, interest filtered down from the major college gridirons, generating a passion and excitement that every level below it tried to capture. In the 1920s, Southwest Conference coaches developed a wide-open style of play, which garnered little recognition beyond the state's borders. And after an autumn of cannibalizing each other, the blemishes on their won-loss records left few teams with a perfect season to turn the heads of those who bestowed national recognition. Still, rays of brilliance occasionally peeked out, as in 1927, when Texans dominated the East-West Shrine game in San Francisco, causing sportswriters to question their battered all-American picks. Or, in 1928, when the bright red-and-blue "Flying Circus" of Southern Methodist University dazzled the elite Military Academy with a bewildering array of pass formations and double and triple laterals. The Mustangs' brand of ball overshadowed the fact that the Black Knights beat them, although it took a Texan to produce Army's winning margin by kicking an extra point.[1]

Then, on October 6, 1934, Texas football leapt into the national spotlight when Rice and the University of Texas pulled shocking upsets against two of the country's elite powers. At Lafayette, Indiana, the Rice Owls beat a heavily favored Purdue team, while at South Bend the

Longhorns whipped a Notre Dame squad that was considered unbeatable. Although Texas teams caused few ripples in the decade's first three years, the 1930s nevertheless had a distinctively Southwestern flavor, capped by national championships in 1935, 1938, and 1939 for SMU, TCU, and Texas A&M, respectively. It was during this decade that the University of Texas also climbed near the top, and SMU's Ponies fell just short of winning a Rose Bowl bid. It showcased TCU's "Slingin' Sammy" Baugh and a small constellation of stars who made various all-American teams. Nearly every Southwest Conference school, in fact, boasted at least one all-American in those years, and some smaller colleges also fielded young men who gained national recognition. Elmer Tarbox, for example, led Texas Tech to a Cotton Bowl in 1939; even tiny East Texas State Teachers College could point to an all-American in Darrell Tully.[2]

The big universities packed the bleachers on Saturday afternoons and inspired a host of imitators who cheered on the smaller colleges. By the middle of the 1930s fan popularity was reflected in a formidable stadium for every Southwest Conference city. Scarcely a decade earlier, University of Texas fans had been overjoyed with their new forty thousand-seat structure; now they found the facility inadequate. Even at smaller places, crowds turned out like never before to watch such closely matched elevens as Hardin-Simmons and Howard Payne, or North Texas Agricultural College and Schreiner Institute.[3]

Brooks Conover remembered going to some games at the old wooden Fair Park Stadium just before the city of Dallas razed it to build the Cotton Bowl in 1930. Three or four big double entrance gates were each close enough to the field to provide the attendants a quick glimpse of the game's action. Whenever the anticipation of a big play took a gatekeeper from his post, boys and even grown men would hold up the sagging gate just high enough to allow their pals to crawl under it. Conover also saw folks occasionally lower ropes to their friends from the top row of seats, which extended past the gate. He recalled that one time the rope broke "with a guy about halfway up" and he "fell right on his keister."

At the high school level, too, fans became more involved in the fortunes of their local teams. School kids who did not play football formed bands, drill teams, and cheerleading squads. School pride and a dearth of other activities drew almost everybody else to support the football team, which also allowed parents and other community members a chance to be involved. City schools and large towns erected bleachers, and soon, lights, to accommodate the demand for Friday night games. Ed Varley, who in 1938 landed his first job at suburban Birdville High School outside of Fort Worth, was disappointed to find the Buffalos' little stadium so meager. Yet before the first game some local men imposed upon Texas Electric to donate four poles, which they raised and used to string up lights along one side of the field.

Lighting proved a luxury in Varley's loop. Traveling to Keller, Grapevine, and Handley, he related: "I didn't even see many bleachers."

At those places fans still walked the sidelines. Nevertheless, even at such agricultural centers, the crowds were growing. Although the autumn harvest diverted some talent from the gridiron to cotton fields and corn patches for a week or two, most of the season transpired after the crops were in. Men and women with spare time and some money in their pockets found the cooling weather inviting and looked forward to attending football games.

A New Era of Rules and Organization

This favorable environment was nurtured by the continued stewardship of the University Interscholastic League. Virtually every Texas high school in the 1930s had become a member and took for granted that the guiding institution called the shots. One story illustrating its high regard claimed that after a hotly contested game, an upset fan made a beeline for the head official and started to throw a punch. As he drew back, however, a more level-headed protester yelled: "If you hit him, the Interscholastic League will suspend our school." Taking the man's advice, the would-be assailant grabbed the referee's hand and sarcastically spit out: "Boy, you sure did call a good game."[4]

By the mid-1930s the league was firmly in the saddle. It had established residence rules and had defended them in court. It lowered the age limit of participants and banished adults to the stands. In addition, it banned recruiting as an insidious practice, and those suspected of violating the rule were viewed as outlaws. Like a benevolent dictator, the UIL guarded its ultimate power, but gained the fealty of its members by allowing district committees to settle disputes within their own regions. Schools welcomed the opportunity for local arbitrators to take swift action. Many times their decisions kept seasons going, when minor controversies might otherwise have left asterisks scattered in the record books.[5]

The league's unswerving commitment to enforcing its rules, however, sometimes provoked outcries from its members, yet nobody could argue with its consistency. In 1937, for example, Thomas Jefferson High School of Port Arthur fielded two teams because it anticipated suspension for taking advantage of a legislative act that allowed schools to add a twelfth grade. The school's action meant that its senior team would be in violation of a UIL attendance rule. While the league worked to adjust its policy to state law, it nevertheless held fast to its own rule book during the interim and declared T. J.'s seniors ineligible. And, after the Port Arthur school district sued and lost, it quietly fell back into line.[6]

Masonic Home's brush with the league was more heart-wrenching. In 1941 the Fort Worth institution for orphans and needy dependents of Masons was play-off-bound and appeared to be heading for a state title. Early in the season, in fact, Masonic Home had defeated eventual champion Wichita Falls and remained unbeaten throughout the regular schedule. As the district round came to a close, however, an inspection of substitute quarterback Louis Burress's birth certificate revealed that on his enrollment form his mother had mistakenly recorded the Mighty Mite as a year younger than he really was. The UIL felt it had no choice but to declare forfeits for the eight games that Burress had played in— several in which his only role was to hold the ball for extra points—thus robbing Masonic Home of a possible state crown. No doubt such firm action gave pause to any Texas school that thought of probing the league's rule book for soft spots.[7]

The UIL also followed the lead of major colleges and adopted some gradual changes that improved the sport and curbed its most dangerous aspects. Hash marks, for example, were an innovation of the early thirties; no longer did centers have to snap the ball into play a foot inside the out-of-bounds line. The league also eliminated a five-yard penalty for incomplete passes after a first down. Perhaps most welcome was a rule introduced in 1932 that made it illegal for a defender to strike an offensive player on the head, face, or neck. A player violating this rule could be ejected and his team assessed a penalty of half the distance to the goal. Other rules broadened the definition of clipping and prohibited such techniques as flying blocks. The UIL was also an avid proponent of adopting better protective equipment and assuring medical examinations. In 1940 it even designed an "Athletic Benefit Plan," which provided players with insurance policies.[8]

Coaches themselves, on Thanksgiving weekend in 1930, took steps to elevate the game by organizing their profession. A group of about thirty football coaches attending a teachers convention in Houston got together at the Rice Hotel to hear Corsicana's Johnny Pierce present his plan to form an association. The previous summer, at an SMU clinic, several coaches had encouraged him to develop the idea. Houston Davis's Roy Needham, who was at the November meeting, said "Johnny was a fireball-type person that could get things done." And he did. Pierce, in fact, was so sure that his fellow coaches would give the organization an enthusiastic reception that he showed up with a constitution and bylaws in hand. To that document a roomful of eager founding fathers signed their names and created the Texas High School Football Coaches Association.[9]

In a profession of "doers," Pierce's brainchild took off, although it struggled somewhat during the Great Depression. Among its first presidents were Henry Frnka, who guided Greenville to a state championship before he took Tulsa University to national prominence; Pete Shotwell, who won state crowns at Longview and Abilene; and three-time Amarillo titlist and University of Texas coach Blair Cherry. "I don't guess there was ever really any doubt that the organization would be a success," Needham commented.[10]

In 1933 the THSFCA recruited Dana X. Bible to inaugurate a coaching school at San Antonio that drew sixty-five coaches. Attendance got heavier in the following years as word got out and the benefits of the lectures bore obvious fruit. Gordon Wood attended his first coaching school in 1938

Johnny Pierce, founding father of the Texas High School Football Coaches Association. *Photograph courtesy Texas High School Coaches Association, Austin.*

because former Hardin-Simmons teammates F. O. Scroggins and Carroll Benson had bragged that they made every lecture the previous year. "I was afraid they'd get one up on me," Wood replied. Chatter Allen remarked that many coaches at first could not afford to attend the clinics; those who did, however, picked up some tips that gave them a distinct advantage over their competitors. When Allen was at LaGrange, for example, his arch-rival

First Texas High School Football Coaches Association coaching school, San Antonio, 1933. *Photograph courtesy Texas High School Coaches Association, Austin.*

at Schulenburg came back from one of the early coaching schools with a "trap" play designed to take care of hard-charging defensive linemen. Allen had such a player by the name of Jajovsky, whom he called "the best I have ever coached." Yet the Schulenburg coach, who had saved the play for the big game, "trapped him all night," Allen recalled. "Neither [Jajovsky] nor I knew what was going on." After the season was over, the two rivals got together and diagramed the play. Allen was also convinced to start attending the conventions. Before long, he added: "Coaching school expenses were included in most coaches' contracts."

At the 1935 convention, held on the SMU campus, the organization added an all-star game to crown its annual meeting. Darrell Tully, who later presided over the association in 1959, played for the North squad in that first game. What he remembered most about the experience, however, was just getting to Highland Park. Before leaving for Dallas, he stayed in Decatur with his high school coach, Red Petty, who persuaded an eastbound friend to drop the player off downtown. There Tully stood on a corner, holding his suitcase. "I had never been in any place that big and I had no idea where SMU was." There was very little traffic, since it was Sunday, but finally a policeman told him which streetcar to take. "So I went and sat down in the back, and we kept riding, and riding, and riding, and I kept thinking this guy knows I'm just a country boy and he's pulling a trick on me." After several more stops and starts, "I thought this is it,

I'm getting off at the next stop." Tully then moved to the door, and when the streetcar came to rest, the driver pointed toward a group of buildings on the near-barren prairie and said: "That's SMU right over there."

Two thousand fans showed up for the contest at Highlander Stadium, which the South won 3–0 under the direction of Princeton's Tad Wieman. Tully remarked that the training table made up for the disappointment of losing: "I'd never had meals like they gave us." And never again would he be on a field with so many stellar ballplayers. Among several all-staters and future college standouts on his squad was I. B. Hale, who lined up next to Tully. "The South rarely came our way," Tully remembered, even though Davey O'Brien quarterbacked the opposing team behind the blocking of Ki Aldrich. O'Brien and Aldrich joined Hale as all-Americans on TCU's national championship team in 1938, the year O'Brien became Texas's first Heisman Trophy winner.

The annual game as well as the chance to learn football's newest innovations from successful college coaches proved a strong pull. Nevertheless, the camaraderie surrounding these gatherings was also a powerful attraction. A Houston-area coach, recounting the 1939 coaching school "under the stands at old Rice Stadium," said that little pretension surrounded the event, and "the biggest names would mingle with the lowest high school assistants." The clinic featured TCU's Dutch Meyer at a time when he was at the peak of his career, coming off a Sugar Bowl victory and a national championship. At a hotel room where Meyer was staying, the Houstonian recounted seeing a group of college coaches shooting craps inside a larger ring of their colleagues. "Dutch was dressed in some longhandled drawers" and when he got down on his knees to take a turn "that flap would come wide open and show his bare ass. . . . I never will forget that."

Dutch Meyer already possessed a reputation for being as lucky at dice as he was with football. Brooks Conover told how at the 1936 school in Fort Worth, some coaches ended up in his room "and somebody pulled out the dice and started a big game." At about eleven o'clock Conover went to look for another bed to sleep in "because I didn't have the money to roll 'em." He remembered, however, that "Dutch Meyer was right in the middle of that thing; he had bills in his hand and was shaking those dice." The game broke up at about one-thirty or two o'clock in the morning, Conover remembered, but at breakfast, he looked over at the next table and there was Meyer. Pointing a fork at him, the TCU mentor leaned back in his chair and needled: "Hey, they've still got that game going on up there in your room!"

Gordon Brown recalled that Meyer's approach to football was marked with that same absorption and cocksureness. Several years later, when the coaching school returned to Fort Worth, he watched Meyer lecture on his famous spread formation. "There was no air conditioning, so he pulled off his shirt and here's this chubby little guy with his belly hanging over his belt, and he must have drawn two hundred plays on the chalkboard that morning." Brown recalled walking away "thinking I must be the dumbest coach in Texas. I learned afterward that it is not the system that makes you successful, but the perfection of a system"— and Meyer was a perfectionist.

Growing Pains

College coaches such as Meyer, insulated from such distractions as teaching and endowed with unlimited resources and a staff of assistants, were able to develop sophisticated programs because their institutions understood very clearly the recognition that football brought them. High school coaches, on the other hand, struggled under more burdensome conditions. When Jewell Wallace began his career in 1935, he was the coaching staff. He was also groundskeeper; there was no one else to water, cut, and line the field. "I hired the officials, made the schedule, and bought the equipment," Wallace commented, and "I had to teach four or five classes a day."

Wallace's experience was typical. Other coaches included among their duties driving the bus, washing uniforms, directing fundraisers, painting the field house, and coaching other sports. "To put it mildly," Chatter Allen remarked, "the coach was low man on the totem pole." And just as they took care of the football field, coaches also usually had to maintain the gymnasium as well, which included stripping and varnishing the floor once a year. When Ralph Martin arrived in Rio Grande City at the beginning of the decade, the school did not even have a football field, so he borrowed a ten-ton Caterpillar tractor, dug up the stumps, and graded one. "When I first marked it, I ended up with a parallelogram," Martin laughed. "It was still a hundred yards, but it kind of angled out at both ends."

For all of their duties, coaches received scant compensation. Being the lone man at the helm of the La Grange Leopards got Chatter Allen a five-dollar-a-month raise but no workload decrease in the classroom. But, he said: "I considered myself lucky because many school districts at that time were paying in scrip." Ironically, the man who would become Texas's winningest coach loved athletics, but in 1938 drifted into the position "because there were not many other jobs to be had." Gordon Wood had contracted with the Bynum Teaching Agency of Abilene to find him a job, and they placed him at Rule in a nine-hundred-dollar-a-year position. Out of that, the school district withheld a dollar a month for his retirement account, and the agency claimed five percent of his salary. Just married and fresh out of college, Ed Varley found that same nine hundred dollars "a handsome salary." Sizing up his situation "on the outskirts of the big city of Fort Worth," surrounded by "good teachers and great kids," he exclaimed: "Man, I had it made!"

Even though Ed Varley enjoyed better conditions than some surrounding schools, his equipment and facilities were "primitive" by today's standards. "I remember so well the first plastic headgear I saw—our kids and I went 'nuts,' thinking it was so grand." The boys, he said, did not have a trainer, and they could not even envision weight rooms or being able to review game films. And "these kids played both ways—many of them never coming out of a game once it started. Man, they had to be tough!"

Players had to be tough if they were to survive workouts. "We didn't fool around," Varley commented. Speaking for almost all of his peers, he described what a typical practice session was like in the 1930s. Grades seven through twelve were all out at the same time; they dressed in a classroom and walked half a mile to the public park and gathered under a shade tree until Varley had locked up the gym and joined them. "Then, I'd come out and blow the whistle, and we'd work out for two or three hours—'til about dark." Water breaks were unheard of, even during the dog days of summer when the season began. "Sometimes we'd line up twenty or thirty on one side of the line and the same on the other and do tackling and blocking drills. The kids never fussed or complained; they did what you said." Then, Varley continued, "after practice, dead tired and late in the day, we walked back up the hill to school."

To gain an edge on his opposition, Varley scouted other teams when his own squad was not playing, and he watched as much football as he could. "In 1937 they built Farrington Field and I got to play there some," he remarked. "It was a great high school stadium and every time North Side and Paschal played, it filled up." Texas Christian University was also just a short drive away, and Varley loved studying the Horned Frog's practices, where he watched some of the college game's best athletes display their skills.

The type of one-man operation that most schools employed was certainly limiting. Sherman's Verde Dickey felt very fortunate to have a volunteer. In the mid-1930s Dickey took the lead of college coaches and rigged up a phone so that he could get messages from the press box. When the Bearcats traveled, the assistant normally had to settle for a place on the top row of bleachers.[11] Future TCU coach Abe Martin occasionally got help too while at El Paso High, but suffered a great disadvantage because of the school's isolation. With a Blair Cherry-coached Amarillo team coming up on Martin's schedule, he complained about lacking the resources to scout them and wrote his colleague tongue-in-cheek that he would appreciate getting a playbook. To Martin's amazement, Cherry obliged. Nevertheless, Amarillo still won the game 87–0, to which Martin chided: "Blair, if you hadn't sent us those plays we sure would have been in for it!"[12]

While still rough around the edges, high school football in Texas had nevertheless come of age during the 1930s. Even in the Rio Grande Valley at places like Mission, where Ralph Martin's brother Robert would later coach a rangy young Tom Landry, and at Brownsville and McAllen, football had become just as integral to community life as in other regions. During the war years, in fact, Eagle Pass lured Robert Martin away from Mission with the astronomical salary of $5,000—making him at that time the highest paid high school coach in the nation. A great migration of Midwesterners into Valley cities had prompted an avid interest in the

E. C. Lerma. *Photograph courtesy Texas High School Coaches Association, Austin.*

game of their adopted state. In 1929, for example, the Screaming Eagles of Brownsville beat the Chicago city champions in an interstate game. The next year the Screaming Eagles rolled over Corpus Christi and San Antonio Brackenridge, each by more than sixty points, and were the odds-on favorites to win the state championship. Yet, like a curse that seemed always to befall the Valley's best elevens, its hopeful representative fell in the opening round of the play-offs.[13]

Ralph Martin recalled that most folks in the outlying areas regarded football as "a big city game" well into the 1930s. Yet, like the larger schools, rural places eventually fielded teams that captured enthusiastic followings. Martin insisted that isolation and a largely poor and Hispanic population kept rural schools in the Valley from adopting the sport as rapidly as country schools elsewhere in the state. He asserted, moreover, that the Hispanic culture was reluctant to let football interfere with the more popular pastime of baseball.

E. C. Lerma, on the other hand, insisted that racial prejudice was at least as responsible as culture for limiting Hispanic participation. Because most schools forbade the Spanish language, Tejano children fell behind in the classroom. Leon Vinyard, who coached at the Big Bend town of Alpine in 1940, claimed that "it usually took them about three years to get out of the first grade. If they remained in school long enough to graduate, they were often past the age limit and ineligible for football." In Lerma's case, athletics inspired him to make up for the two grades he had lost in elementary school. Upon reaching Kingsville High School in the early thirties, however, he dropped out after receiving a frosty reception from his would-be teammates. Then, as his senior year approached, he asked his best friend, Gerald Alvarez, to join him for tryouts. The two made the team, and their contribution to Kingsville's success melted the barriers against them. Lerma related that afterward other Tejanos felt less apprehensive about coming out for the team.

Other Valley coaches remarked that for whatever reason, Tejano participation was regrettably low. When Chatter Allen moved from the East Texas town of Overton to McAllen in the late thirties, he just assumed he would have many Tejanos on his team, but only one came out for two-a-days. "For some reason, I never knew why at the time," he reflected, "the Hispanics were not interested in football." Later, he figured that at the heart of the matter was a cloud of racial animosity that filtered down from the fans to the playing field.

Bob Barfield also expressed mystification at finding such a low Tejano turnout at Robstown, a predominately Hispanic town. When he got there, the superintendent told him not to expect many. "I had three or four try out, but they quit the team," he remarked. Barfield remained there only one year before he was drafted and "never knew what the story was," though he, too, suspected racism.

Other coaches claimed that prejudice was spotty. Barfield noted that even though his own Robstown bunch was all white, they were beaten by some opponents who found to their advantage that winning often rendered teams colorblind. And Jewell Wallace had no trouble at El Paso's Jim Bowie High School. In fact, he called the 1939 squad his "League of Nations" team; in addition to several Tejanos were boys of Jewish, Greek, and Scottish heritage.

Brooks Conover admitted that he did see evidence of tension when he coached at Brownsville High School in the late thirties, but avowed that it was directed more at class than race. He remembered that the wealthy Tejanos mixed freely with Anglos. He became good friends, in fact, with a ranch owner, Mr. Arturio, who took Conover deer hunting. He also recalled a player whose relatives ran a bull ring in Matamoros, who took him to see the fights and to show off the family's operation. Intermarriage, Conover asserted, blurred racial lines to the point where he had trouble discerning just what a Tejano really was. Recalling the two Anglo-looking sons of a white shrimp boat captain and his Hispanic wife—"I think their name was Jones," he said—"the only time you could see their Hispanic blood was when they began waving their arms and such." Even then, he remarked, "it was more a cultural thing than physical."

Tejanos in parts of the state where their presence was minimal met with mixed reactions at school. Lucky was the boy who could contribute to the local team in a society that clung fast to an otherwise clearly marked white-black color barrier. Of course, acceptance rarely extended past the football field, and even then, opposing teams could be quite unforgiving.

Such was the case of Fred Torres, who played for Ed Varley at Diamond Hill. Once, when the team traveled to Grandview, south of Fort Worth, they found a crowd that grew hostile when they saw "a Mexican boy" take the field for pregame warmups. "They only had one small set of bleachers, and the rest of them were walking the sidelines. . . . When [Torres] wasn't in there, they'd crowd in and push on him." Before long, he had to stand right next to Varley whenever he came out. When Diamond Hill won, the Grandview fans blocked their exit. "We didn't even make it to the locker room. They were trying to get at Torres, and so the players circled around him and took off their cleats and started swinging them at the crowd." More than anything, expressed Varley, poor Torres was greatly embarrassed by bringing the incident on his teammates.

Because of the climate of prejudice that pervaded the rigidly segregated Bible Belt, even Czech and German Texans were slow to discover the game. Before taking the job at Brownsville, Brooks Conover coached four years at the Central Texas town of Ennis. Several generations of Tex-Czechs had farmed the area's rich blacklands and held fast to their Old World customs, which had little to do with football. As Ennis grew into a railroad town, the traditional southerners and the ethnic whites developed an animosity toward each other. During Conover's first year, only one Czech youth came out for the team. "It took a while, but the rest of the kids finally accepted the boy." By the time Conover left Ennis, he said, the large and hardy Czechs had found the sport well-suited to their workhorse ways.

Chatter Allen experienced a similar lack of interest among Germans and Czechs in the largely ethnic town of La Grange, where he landed his first coaching job in 1932. He cultivated an interest in the sport, however, by integrating himself into the community during his six years there. Among other things, he became adept at the German card game skat, he attended countless Czech dances, and he even married one of the local girls. Still, getting these folks to accept football was a tough job. They believed that their sons should come home after school and tend crops or do household chores. "I visited many farm homes and worked in the fields alongside the fathers in an attempt to convince them that football would make their boys better workers," Allen commented. "I can recall one father that was so pleased with his son's work habits and attitude toward hard work after a year in the football program that he required his other two sons to play. . . . before I left La Grange, football had gained a good foothold in the community life." The town had erected bleachers, built a gym, and even allotted money for football in the school budget.

Still, an interest in football developed slowly at La Grange, which Allen illustrated with a story about a Czech boy named Kovar who "played in the first football game he had ever seen." He had only two weeks "to learn what it was all about before the season began," and "it was only natural for me to miss something," the coach remarked. In that first game La Grange received the opening kickoff and, partly on the strength of Kovar's blocking, marched down the field and scored. Then came time for the defense. Kovar "was charging across the line, but going too deep, so I had to get him out and give him some instruction." When a substitute tried to take his place, the referee called out: "Kovar off!" When the boy did not respond, the official looked at him and asked: "Are you Kovar?" The boy nodded, and again he was ordered to get off the field. "With that, he hung his head and trotted down behind the goal posts and sat down," Allen related. "Then it dawned on me that I had not told him about the substitution rule. I sent a player down to get him. He thought he had done something wrong and was ashamed." Kovar was a quick study, however, and the next year he made the all-district team." Adding a postscript to the times, Allen commented that "later he was drafted; he served in the Marines and was killed at Iwo Jima."

Alongside the mainstream of society, a strong current of African American interest in football arose. The sport did not develop as quickly among blacks as it did among whites, and its growing pains lasted much longer. Predictably, the equipment at black schools was very meager, and all but a handful of the coaches, professionally speaking, were behind the times. Joe Washington, who played for Rosenburg's tiny black community during the late 1930s, commented that he and his teammates played with equipment cast off by their white counterparts. He even coached the team himself before a teacher, Mr. Rigmaiden, took over. To compensate for his unfamiliarity with the game, Rigmaiden would bring a *Scholastic Coach* magazine to practice. As if following a book of instructions, he would look up, hold his finger on a marked place and say: "OK, boys, here's how we're gonna do it. . . . "

Born to Coach

As the sport matured, however, every community began producing generations of boys who grew up with the game. High school stars inspired imitators on countless sandlots, stirring visions of glory in young boys who yearned to play for the home team. Just before the war, John Hugh Smith got his first job at La Vega, in the Central Texas town of Bellmead, where he would sometimes watch "the little kids . . . play touch football on Saturdays and one of them would say: 'I'm going to be Bobby Brooks,'" or some other local high school star. At Burkburnett, Joe Bob Tyler wanted to be like Garth Landis, and when he got old enough to make the team, he wore his hero's number.

Age knew no limit for boys who fell in love with the game. Way out in the Trans-Pecos, the Jay family had moved to Mentone, seat of the nation's most sparsely populated county. Luckily for their son Donald, his father was a football fan who enjoyed taking him to games. The big rivalry between Wink and Pecos became an annual event for the pair, especially during the years when a Pecos boy, Joe Bob Kelton, made *Ripley's Believe It or Not!* for playing barefooted. Darrell Tully was not as fortunate: "I remember the time my daddy and uncle went off to see Cisco play Ranger . . . and left me on the front porch crying like a baby."[14]

James Brewer's father and uncles loved football, too, and took him to games "since before I can remember." And whenever he could, young James also listened to games on the radio. Once, when he was five years old and living at Quanah, the Brewers discovered that their son was missing. After searching frantically, they found him downtown at the hardware store listening to a play-off game in which the Wichita Falls Coyotes were beating up on some hapless and now-forgotten victim. When the youngster turned and saw his parents, he excitedly gave them an update on the game; he laughed, however, that "they were only interested in busting my butt!"

For many future coaches, football was much more than just a game to them, even at an early age. As the Great Depression began to unfold, fourth-grader Homer Johnson had to live at his grandmother's boarding-house in the North Texas town of Frisco because his father's job kept his parents out of town so much. Johnson, admittedly, "was always into some sort of mischief," and his family thought that one of the boarders, coach Don Helms, might provide a good influence for him. After inviting young Homer to room with him, the coach treated the boy like his own son and let him carry water for the team and work at the field house. The experience of being around the players and their coach affected Johnson. The following year his family reunited when his father found a more stable job in Teague, but Johnson declared that after his association with Don Helms "there was never any question about what I wanted to do with my life."

Eddie Joseph never questioned that he, too, would become a coach. His mother, widowed when Joseph was six years old, observed how much he enjoyed playing football and saw, too, that the game seemed to be helping him develop some character. With Mrs. Joseph's encouragement, her son played every chance he got and developed his talent. When he reached the fourth grade, in fact, the sparsely manned eighth-grade team invited him to play. The coaches at his Dallas school were only volunteers, and by the time Joseph reached the eighth grade himself, his teammates looked upon him as a player-coach. Even before he entered junior high, he had seen the film *Knute Rockne: All American*, and ever afterward aspired to emulate the Notre Dame icon. "I vaguely remember that after I saw the movie . . . I ended up being the only boy in a tap dancing class of girls." Rockne, related Joseph, "had taken his players and made them take dancing lessons because he thought it helped with their footwork."

By the time Eddie Joseph enrolled at Jesuit High School, Paul Tyson had left Waco and landed at the Dallas Catholic school. Promptly, he captured Joseph's heart. Tyson, of course, had known Rockne intimately, and was never wont to keep those memories to himself. Lavishing attention on his fatherless player came naturally to Tyson, and when Joseph broke a leg, the coach visited his hospital room every night. There he held the boy in rapture with stories about the great players he had coached during the golden twenties, about Rockne, and about coaching. Tyson left the next year, but Don Rossi, who eventually became general manager of the Kansas City Chiefs, took his place. Like Tyson, Rossi all but adopted Joseph, and whenever a father-son banquet came around, Joseph never worried about "the shame of having to stay at home."

John Reddell's coaching apprenticeship came more indirectly, but the experience was every bit as strong. As the Great Depression was ending, he was in the seventh grade and his family lived on a little farm outside of Oklahoma City. Then, Reddell's father left them. The lack of a male influence rendered him "underdeveloped emotionally," Reddell commented, but when his mother got a seamstress's job at Montgomery Ward they moved to the state capital and he began playing sports. Very quickly he developed a close relationship with the school's coach, former professional wrestler Choctaw Smith. "He was very outgoing," Reddell recalled, "but he could be mean, and if you disobeyed him, he'd slap you across the back." Choctaw Smith was also a military man, and after telling the boy he would teach him how to swim, he added to it another, unexpected, lesson. "He showed me I was capable of swimming through burning oil," Reddell recalled with a laugh.

If one moment stands out from John Reddell's youth, however, it was the feeling of satisfaction he got when he received a compliment from the minister of his Baptist church. Reddell was shining the preacher's shoes at the barber shop, trying to do an especially good job, when the man looked down and exclaimed: "Son!"—giving the boy a start—"I believe that's the finest shine I've ever had on these shoes!" To Reddell "that five-cent tip and the compliment really meant something." Afterward he attempted to recapture that feeling in everything he pursued, whether it was jerking sodas, working at a fruit stand, or ushering at the Mayflower Theater. Even as a delivery boy, he took pride "in getting that newspaper as close to the front door as I could."

Reddell noticed that he got the same feeling by performing well on the basketball court and on the football field. Becoming an all-state roundballer on a state-championship team at Classen High School produced thrills that he was unwilling to let go of. After playing football for the legendary Bud Wilkinson at the University of Oklahoma, Reddell made a career of athletics for the "thrills and natural highs." Coaching, he asserted, "gave you respect, appreciation, and admiration, but most of all it made you feel great and gave you a chance to make other kids feel that way, too."

Perhaps no group of kids ever strove more diligently to walk that same path as the boys of Fort Worth's Masonic Home. Football gave the orphans and dependents of widows a chance to shine, and their success made them the darlings of fans everywhere. Newspapers regularly ran

Thirteen-year-old John Reddell, 1943. *Photograph courtesy John Reddell.*

stories about the outmanned and outnumbered boys, and, in 1941, *Collier's* magazine even ran a feature on them.[15] Other teams always outweighed them, sometimes thirty-five pounds to the man, and in few seasons did the Mighty Mites even field enough players to hold full scrimmages. In 1932, the year that they made a drive to the state finals, Coach Rusty Russell had only a single substitute and never played him. Upon being asked why, he reportedly avowed: "He's too valuable, we can't take a chance of putting him in and getting him injured."[16]

The tiny school's Davidic image guaranteed a rich gate and assured that they would play a great, if unenviable, schedule against some of the state's best teams. The Mighty Mites were able to compete against the bigger schools because they played an imaginative style of ball and practiced year-round, but most important, because they formed close bonds with both their teammates and a succession of surrogate fathers who coached them. Talking about his strategy, Russell once explained that "we thinned the defenses out and made 'em cover us from sideline to sideline and end zone to end zone. And when they left the gate open, we'd throw." In an age of one-dimensional offenses, their playbook was so thick that opposing teams seldom bothered to scout them. Highland Park's Floyd Hightower remarked: "They have new plays for every game, plays you've never seen before."[17]

During a four-season stretch from 1930 to 1933, Masonic Home lost only one game—to a junior college. In 1930 and 1931 the Mighty Mites participated in a classification that played only to the regional level; the next year, however, the big schools in their district voted to move them up despite "the Home's" small enrollment. The team took advantage of the opportunity by going all the way to the state finals and tied Corsicana 0–0. It would be as close as Masonic Home would ever get to an outright state championship. Over twelve thousand fans crowded into the Tigers' stadium, even though it was designed for only eight thousand. Officials delayed the game three times to clear the overflow from the field and some temporary bleachers became so overcrowded that they collapsed. The fiercely fought defensive game turned into a punting duel that favored the Tigers. The valiant orphans were obviously outmatched, but they managed to stop five Corsicana drives deep in the Mighty Mites' territory, shutting down the last one on the six-inch line as time expired.[18]

Ten-year-old Jack Whitley, typical of the boys who resided there, enrolled at Masonic Home that year. Until his father died, the Whitleys had lived in the East Texas town of Palestine. Afterward, Whitley's mother moved to Houston, where she bought a cigar stand at a hotel. The boy was often alone at night, and when his grades began to suffer and he started to get into trouble, she sent him to Masonic Home. He grew into adolescence at the institute and later in the decade played on some other great Mighty Mites teams. And, like Paul Smith, who played on the state finalist squad, Whitley returned as coach after graduating from college.

For Whitley and other children, the institution provided a bittersweet environment. It was not like having a mother and father, of course, but during the dark days of the 1930s the school provided a comfortable haven that contrasted with the situations most of them had faced before arriving. And for that reason, as Whitley remarked: "This Great Depression really didn't affect me so greatly." In fact, for boys and girls who had known trouble and broken families, "the Home was a grand place." Despite a tight regimen and strict rules, the kids found plenty of time to play along Sycamore Creek, and, when they got a little older, to spend weekend days in Fort Worth. Regular stops included the Poly Theater and the Will Rogers Memorial Coliseum, and when the rodeo or Golden Gloves came to town it was a special time.

Like most Masonic Home boys, Jack Whitley made football his passion. Squads were formed by size, rather than by age, and he began his career on the "one-hundred-pound team." Whitley recalled that their opponents often laughed at the little ones because they played barefooted and wore overalls instead of uniforms. Still, "we didn't pay any attention to the city boys riding us"—no doubt because the team always seemed to win. "Football was everything," Whitley declared; "we felt like we were the best at what we did, and that was very important." Far from feeling insecure, the Mighty Mites were even "a little bit cocky." On game days they would roll into Sycamore Park on a flatbed truck with staked sides, confidently returning the gazes of the crowd. If the repetition of constant practice made them precision perfect, their situation gave them a strong sense of unity. "Everybody was the same, and we all pulled for each other," Whitley said; "the other team was the enemy, and even though you didn't know them, you didn't like them."

Football at Masonic Home was a year-round pursuit, even though the season officially began in August. And once they started in earnest, they practiced every day, "even on Sundays after Sunday School," Whitley said. Former players would come out and scrimmage with them, and since there was no restriction on training rules, spring practices would begin on the second day of the new semester. One year, Whitley recalled, the pads had not even dried out from the semifinal game against Amarillo that had ended the previous year's campaign. But, he noted: "We'd take three weeks off for track season." The steady diet of practice made them a remarkably synchronized team, and nobody produced players with sounder fundamentals. Some days the Mighty Mites would do nothing but work on perfecting their blocking and tackling and catching passes. The boys did not know anything else, and so this routine to them was a "way of life."

Whitley described the discipline the boys received as strict, but loving. He asserted that when the teachers swung a paddle, "you always knew why you were getting it." Once, he recalled, the home's superintendent had to kick out a popular boy and the administrator wondered aloud why the other kids were not mad. Whitley later told him it was because they all accepted the way they were disciplined. The boy had broken the rules and he had to pay the price.

For Jack Whitley, it all paid off when he made the varsity team. Both at Fort Worth and at faraway venues, fans regarded a Masonic Home game as an event. The boys did not field a band, but the Shriners' fez-and-tassled drum and bugle corps filled in admirably and performed at all their games. At home the Masons often played at LaGrave Field, which the city overlooked from a bluff, and on more than one occasion the police had to

"Mr. Russell," coach of the Masonic Home team, gives advice to his Mighty Mites, 1941.
Photograph courtesy Fort Worth Star-Telegram *Photograph Collection, Special Collections
Division, The University of Texas at Arlington Libraries.*

shuttle the Mighty Mites from the courthouse to the stadium because
game traffic had produced gridlock. The Masons grew accustomed to
packed stadiums, and even when they traveled, the opponents' fans often
cheered them on, no matter how badly the home team was being
whipped. In 1938, after the tattered Mighty Mites advanced in a tied
play-off game at Highland Park, for example, the admiring Scottie's fans
bought them new uniforms for the next round.

Even the players on opposing teams held them in high regard in an age
when competing gridders rarely fraternized. In 1941, the year the UIL
suspended the school, the eventual state champions from Wichita Falls
paid them homage; the orphans, of course, had produced the only blemish on the Coyotes' otherwise perfect record. In a letter addressed to
Mighty Mite star Gordy Brown, the Wichita Falls boys commiserated: "In
our eyes, you're the true champions."[19]

Before Whitley moved up to the varsity, he admired some of the older
players and those who had gone on to TCU and other colleges. "We did-
n't know what a role model was, but we wanted to be like them," he
remarked. He particularly looked up to Paul Smith, who later became the
able successor of the paternal Rusty Russell. Yet however much he admired
and looked up to Smith and the older players, it was Whitley's coach—
called "Mr. Russell" by all of his charges—who had the greatest influence
on him. "He was never really buddy-buddy with you," Whitley recalled,
"but you just respected and liked him." Russell taught history in addition
to his coaching duties, and Whitley asserted that in both vocations the

coach demanded the same attention to detail. One semester Russell confis-
cated a rubber band gun that a boy had made, and rather than punish the
student, the coach used it himself. If the answers to his questions came too
slowly, "he'd be popping you on the back with it until you told him,"
Whitley chuckled.

On the practice field, however, Russell did not resort to such methods.
"He never chewed you out . . . he would just look at you until you felt
you could just crawl into a hole," Whitley said. The "eye"—that silent
means of communicating—could also convey approbation, which the
boys craved, and Russell seemed always to know which buttons to push.
Years after he graduated, Paul Smith said of his coach that "his players
would and still will fight a buzz saw for Mr. Russell."[20]

Whitley, upon coming back to fill the position that Rusty Russell and
Paul Smith had held, recalled one last shining moment after the Mighty
Mites' glory days had faded. In the season opener at Hillcrest, the Dallas
team showed its disdain by not even bothering to break out their new
game jerseys. Hillcrest was about to move up to the state's highest classification, Whitley recalled, and "Masonic Home was not even expected to
stay on the field with them." Before the game an official, killing some
time, remarked to Whitley: "Those Mighty Mites used to really be able
to hit." Peeved, the coach retorted: "They still do." Whitley then
stomped toward the dressing room and called on some old ghosts, and
that night, like so many others in the past, the game belonged to
Masonic Home.

In life, as in sport, self-confidence and a sense of purpose inspired success. For Mighty Mites who advanced to college and on to professional
careers in medicine, law, business, and even football, self-esteem came
wrapped in pigskin. Athletic ability gave many others living in humble
conditions that same measure of self-worth and determination, and it
earned them wide respect from schoolmates and townspeople alike. Many
future coaches were lucky to have parents who, although poor, nevertheless saw the significance of sports clearly enough to nurture their sons' talents. Ed Logan recalled the close relationship he enjoyed with his father
and remembered him saying once: "I never saw a kid get into trouble
who was hunting, fishing, or on the practice field." At Lamesa, athletics
was second only to church in Carlos Berry's family. His father bought
baseball gloves so that he and his son could practice together, and often,
when a long row of cotton still needed hoeing, Berry's father would "let
me go off and play ball and take up my slack."

On the other hand, many future coaches had great difficulty getting
their parents to understand just how much athletics meant to them. Most
of their fathers had no background in sports, and, as Robert Lowrance
commented, they "attached no importance to it." After Ray Akins took
up football, his father wondered what all the excitement was about, so he
rode his horse into Brady to see firsthand. He peeked through the boxing
planks that surrounded the field, but did not come inside. Only years

later, after the elder Akins had died, did Ray learn that his father had seen him play, if only so briefly.

Many coaches' parents could not understand why their sons would become so deeply involved in such a frivolous game when they could be doing something more worthwhile. Dan Anderegg commented that his mother enjoyed watching him play, but his father "didn't see much sense in football." He expected his son to tend to his ranching chores at five in the morning, even after a game the previous night. Joe Washington lamented that his mother never came to a football game, and when some teammates brought him home with a sprained ankle, he tried unsuccessfully to hide it from her. He just knew that would be the end of his career, but after some pleading to remain on the team, Washington said, she gave in, and "I breathed easier."

Where the imagination was strong and the game remained unseen, mothers and fathers rightfully worried about their sons. The parents of Oak Cliff great, Roy "Father" Lumpkin, for example, were so afraid their tall, rangy boy might suffer an injury that they gave him fifty dollars to quit. When Lumpkin returned the money along with some tickets, they decided to go watch him play. Afterward they again gave their son the fifty dollars—this time extracting from him the promise that he would not hurt anybody on the other team.[21]

Bob Harrell's parents were in no position either to nurture or discourage him. When the elder Harrell became too ill to work, he left his wife and son in Fort Worth and moved in with his own mother in Arlington, who had volunteered to take care of him so her daughter-in-law could take a job. Afterward, Harrell had to make it largely on his own, and at times he and his mother had only one meal a day—"usually grits." In spite of his desperate situation, Harrrell remained as determined as ever that hard times would not rob him of his promising football career, the one thing that made him feel equal to anyone. When his coach at Polytechnic High School, Wesley Bradshaw, learned about the boy's predicament, the coach invited Harrell to move in with him.

Bradshaw was no stranger to adversity, and knew what could lay ahead for his player if he persevered. The coach had earned sixteen athletic letters at Baylor, and later played professional football on the same team with Jim Thorpe. While Harrell was living with Bradshaw, the Carlisle legend visited and stayed with them for a couple of days. "I got to sit down and talk to him at night, and boy was I thrilled—a high school kid talking to Jim Thorpe!" Thorpe told Harrell some great stories "about playing ball, about tough playing conditions in the rain, the mud, and the snow." He also told him that to stay in shape, he ran everywhere he went. But what stuck with Harrell the most was Thorpe's admonition to "never give up." Relating his own misfortunes, the great athlete confided to the high schooler his sorrow over the incident that cost him his Olympic medals. For a while Thorpe turned his back on everything, but "he told me that he finally realized that he could not let people down, especially kids, who looked to him as a role model."

Bob Harrell, head coach, Lamesa. *Photograph courtesy Bob Harrell.*

Even before Thorpe departed, Harrell began running everywhere he went and developed the attitude that "I might not beat you, but I'm going to be in better shape." Then later, with Coach Bradshaw's encouragement, he tried out for a scholarship at Texas Christian University in 1934. "I had a dime in my pocket and what I had on; I didn't even have any clothes. . . . And I 'highwayed it' out there because I wanted to save that dime." After two months at the training table, "I went from a hundred and forty-five pounds up to one-eighty."

To Bob Harrell, both he and Wesley Bradshaw represented "what football was all about" to the kinds of players who would find in the game a path to a better life. Harrell was among many future coaches who found themselves in similar situations. And even if football was still developing in the years before World War II, one aspect of the game had already reached maturity. For many players who later became coaches, it affirmed character in those whose situations made them suspect their mettle, and for some, football also extended the opportunity to fulfill a richer destiny.

Chapter 5

Down at the Stadium and Other Theaters of War: Football in the 1940s

A s the century approached its halfway point, Texans had come to enjoy their high school football. During the war years, especially, coaches, players, and fans alike immersed themselves in the game, briefly insulating themselves from distant events beyond their control. Folks who had a difficult time sorting out what was going on in the Philippines or North Africa could more readily understand the battles waged between the chalk lines at any of hundreds of places where schoolboys girded for Friday night combat. In an age when Americans did not question their country's greatness, football's proponents claimed that the sport called upon the characteristic virtues of the times. Mexia's Ty Bain, who served on an aircraft carrier bombarded by kamikazes, cataloged among them "courage, self-sacrifice, loyalty, self-discipline, and determination."

Texans gearing up for World War II could feel that they were becoming a more industrialized people. In places like San Saba, where dogs still slept in the street and where the night watchman who checked the doors of every business never reported a break-in, the transition was not readily evident. But, commented Bill Hartley, "you could sense suburban life emerging even back then. Every time we went to San Antonio it seemed to be creeping a little closer to San Saba." For Ed Varley, who moved into the suburbs beyond Fort Worth in 1938 after spending his college years in Paris, Waxahachie, and Denton, the stark contrast between the static country life and the bustle of the city left a vivid impression. In the emerging working-class bedroom community, "people were coming and going . . . nobody had much money, but most fathers had jobs." They worked "at the packing houses in Fort Worth, at the stockyards or the oil refineries, and later at the defense plants."

Each autumn in Texas communities, whether city, town, or village, football normally dominated talk about local affairs and helped keep folks' minds off the larger and more troubling events of the day. And when the work week ended, people increasingly turned out for the game, even when some distant opponent hosted the event. John Hugh Smith vowed

The Odessa Bronchos corral Kyle Rote Sr. of San Antonio Jefferson before a crowd of thirty-eight thousand at Austin's Memorial Stadium, 1946. *Photograph courtesy Texas-Dallas History and Archives Division, Dallas Public Library.*

that at La Vega during the 1940s every home game was a sellout. "Nothing competed with football for the town's attention," he said. "Not a single group met on Fridays; they knew nobody would show up." When the team traveled, caravans would follow the school bus to places like MacGregor, Gatesville, Mexia, and Groesbeck. "The old story about the last one leaving town turning out the lights was true," Smith insisted.

In this age before television and a wide interest in professional football, the mobile society that was awakening from the Great Depression ached for some excitement. That desire was reflected in new attendance records set during the 1945 season, a year when arriving veterans filled the air with a sense of perpetual homecoming. Six play-off games alone drew more than twenty thousand fans apiece. And at the state championship game in Dallas, 45,790 fans overflowed the forty-five-thousand-seat Cotton Bowl to watch Highland Park and Waco battle to a 7–7 tie.[1]

James Brewer, who played and later coached at Fort Worth North Side, claimed that eight or nine thousand fans at Farrington Field was a small crowd during the 1940s. When he played against Paschal during the 1945 and 1946 seasons, in fact, each contest drew more than twenty-five thousand people. The rivalry between the two Fort Worth schools extended back to the early 1910s, when Paschal was old Central High School. About four times as many townspeople as students showed up for North Side's pep rallies. Brewer's teammate and future coach Doyle Reynolds remarked that famous exes traveled from all over the state to attend rallies for the more important games. Once, former Centre College all-American Bo McMillan, who had become head coach at the University of Indiana before taking the helm of the Detroit Lions, flew into town to exhort his alma mater to victory. Another time, when arch-rival Paschal was ranked number one in the state, Texas legislator and North Side graduate Salty Hull gave a speech extolling the great 1912 team that included SMU's Matty Bell. He brought many fans in the bleachers to tears, and the emotional lift helped North Side pull off a 14–0 upset.

Economic conditions, of course, did not magically improve. In many small towns patterns of life remained largely unaffected by budding mod-erninity. Morris Southall said that in most rural areas during the 1940s farmers still needed all the help they could get during harvest season. When he was at the West Central Texas town of Winters, the school "let out for two weeks when it was time to pick cotton." The buses did not run then, either, and after practice, Lion's Club members volunteered to take players home. Occasionally parents "could not afford to do without their kids and I had to give them the two weeks off and played without them."

And just after the war, Masonic Home's Jack Whitley took his Mighty Mites to Boyd, where the fans—just like before the war—enjoyed neither bleachers nor a scoreboard. The field, however, was ringed with cars, and when Boyd made a touchdown and went ahead by a couple of points late in the game, the din of honking horns was almost unbearable. Taking possession after the kickoff, Mighty Mite quarterback Jackie Evans lined up the team and barked out his signals amid the tune of sporadic beeping. Taking the ball from center, he stood up and lobbed a long pass that James Young caught on a dead run. When the fleet Masonic Home end carried the ball over the goal line, a few horns were still honking hollowly as the referee's gun signaled the end of the game.

African Americans, whose public schools and sports programs devel-oped in the shadow of white society, were also slow to catch up. The Prairie View Interscholastic League, the black counterpart of the UIL, remained only a bright idea in the minds of its eventual founders until the end of the 1930s, and not until 1940 did it hold a state championship contest. A. C. Williams of Greenville Booker T. Washington remarked that for a long time the league's umbrella was only large enough to shelter schools in the cities and large towns. A year after that first PVIL game, Williams' Golden Tigers won the self-styled Class A championship against Athens. "But we weren't part of the league then," he said. "It took sever-al years for them to find us out here in the sticks."

As Williams suggested, the PVIL spread its power slowly and unevenly, but it did grow and eventually made great strides in assuring a fair game. Like the UIL in an earlier time, teams that recruited and played grown men challenged the league's authority. A white coach recalled seeing a contest in the early 1940s in which the home team was behind at half-time, yet when the referee called the players out of their dressing rooms for the third quarter, the home team fielded an almost entirely different group—and one that was obviously larger and more experienced.

Houston Yates' Pat Patterson, one of the PVIL's founding fathers, declared that until the league established itself: "There were a lot of black schools using players that were twenty-five years old." He insisted that even some boys up to age eighteen were too young and small to make the team. Many times, he continued, "players worked all day, went to practice in the afternoon and played in the games, never going to school."[2]

Creating a level playing field, even in an unlevel society, created a fan interest that knew no racial boundaries. Jap Jones, who starred for Booker T. Washington High of Dallas, produced the only blemish on the record of Fort Worth I. M. Terrell, the inaugural champion. Jones found the thrill of kicking the winning extra point in a near-packed Cotton Bowl almost indescribable. "Booker T." had fought back from a six-point deficit, which meant that he had to line up for the point-after-touchdown before a sea of anxious faces in the bleachers, both black and white, who all but fell silent in anticipation. When the ball split the uprights, he remembered, one side of the stadium sparked into wild celebration and the other drooped into a heap.

Similar scenes were repeated countless times in stadiums all across Texas, and that kind of excitement made high school football the state's unrivaled passion. Most every schoolboy, of course, yearned to be a part of it. Gordon Brown, who played at Groesbeck during the 1940s, asserted: "The importance of making the football team, of becoming a starter, of getting mentioned in the local paper, and especially of your team winning a game over a close rival was unbelievable during this era." As a freshman, however, he found himself in a big game before he was actually ready. A first-teamer's equipment failure meant that he had to line up on the Goats' kickoff receiving team—one of many they fielded that night. "The kicker looked like Goliath," Brown recalled. The ball fortunately skipped out of bounds, and the Groesbeck starter was able to return to the game before the next kickoff. "Was I ever glad to get off the field and away from the massacre."

Waco great Frank Pulattie said that the spotlight could be "as scary as it was thrilling." During the 1939 season his hometown sportswriter Jinx Tucker wrote: "As Pulattie goes, so goes Waco." And it did, right into the state championship game against Lubbock, where Pulattie said he played most of the game like a punch drunk after getting his "bell rung." It was Paul Tyson's bid for one last title, and when it fell short, the coach's chiding reference to one of Pulattie's few long gainers let him know that everything was all right. Placing a hand on the boy's shoulder, Tyson winked: "I knew there was something wrong with you, Frank; you ran it right for the first time."

A lot of money changed hands that day. Making wagers on high school games, in fact, was both routine and a serious business. Former Hurst Bell coach Hoot Smith knew of coaches who either lost or kept their jobs on point spreads rather than on won-loss records. "Coach Snow at North

Side didn't score many points, but he was making the play-offs," said James Brewer. Yet, "the team was not beating the point spread and some folks started clamoring for his scalp."

Moon Mullins also noticed "plenty of gambling going on." He often spotted men with "rolls of money" in the stands before home games at Crane and later at Anson, and in the lobbies of hotels when the team traveled. "These people followed the teams just like they followed horses," he said. Garland coach Homer Johnson recalled traveling to a game at Breckenridge where he had to fend off a professional gambler who rode up to the practice field in a big black Cadillac demanding to get the inside scoop on the point spread.

In 1949, the smell of money became so irresistible to a Mexia man watching the first Class 1-A state championship game that he made his way to the sidelines in a desperate effort to convince coach Ty Bain to close the spread with a last-minute field goal. The Blackcats were on the short end of a 14–0 shutout and inside the Littlefield twenty yard line with the clock ticking away the inevitable defeat. "Coach," the gambler frantically pleaded, "you ain't gonna win, but if you beat the point spread, we can take $50,000 back to Mexia with us!" Bain grabbed the man by the back of his collar and the seat of his pants and promptly "helped" him over the chain link fence that surrounded the field.

Ty Bain, like virtually every other coach, felt that gambling quite simply had no place in the sport. When the subject came up at a Lion's Club meeting at San Angelo, Jewell Wallace admonished: "I don't want any of you to ever ask me about points on a game. . . . These are young kids and you don't have any business trying to bet on what they're going to do."

A Formative Experience

Moving to loftier subjects, Wallace told his Lion's Club audience: "Football is not a game, it's a way of life." Even before the 1940s the profession had evolved to a point where coaches saw their livelihood as a mission that transcended anything akin to an eight-to-five routine. They were in charge of the community's most precious resource, and the large majority made that responsibility their chief commitment above all others. Yet they were also expected to take the town's name into battle and represent it well. To accomplish both goals, coaches drew upon their own backgrounds and experiences to evoke the kind of mentality that would make their athletes both accomplished players and successful young men.

Very largely, the men who became coaches at mid-century, and who came to dominate the profession, were hard-working poor folks and first generation college graduates. They carried with them personal values grounded in old-time religion and the Great Depression. As World War II came and went, they added a military regimentation to their code.

Football in the years leading to mid-century had established itself as an avenue that helped poor boys better themselves economically. Gene

Mayfield represented many who took that route. His parents were share-croppers, and he worked in the fields alongside them. As a gradeschooler Mayfield walked five miles to class and wore shirts that his mother had fashioned from flour sacks. At a time when others were benefiting from the New Deal, such attire was the Mayfields' way of announcing that they were getting by on their own. Nevertheless, the experience con-vinced the family's son that "I was not going to be a farmer." So, in 1945, the 155-pound quarterback of Quitaque's six-man football team borrowed a leather suitcase and headed for Canyon, where he tried out for the college team and won a scholarship.

The path was not always marked so clearly. Walt Parker remarked: "I didn't even play football in high school because I was always working." When the Great Depression forced the Texas and Pacific Railroad to lay off workers, Parker's father received a pink slip. Afterward the switchman was unable to find regular work. For eleven-to-fifteen-year-old boys, however, there were always ten-cents-an-hour odd jobs. Young Parker mowed lawns, bagged groceries, and performed tedious chores for two of Fort Worth's big department stores, the Leonard Brothers' and Striplings. Even after he graduated, Parker worked six days a week for two years at Montgomery Ward in a twelve-hour-a-day shift. "I was a porter—what they called janitors during those days."

Out of his $12.50-a-week salary, Parker saved enough to enter North Texas State Teachers College at Denton. Accustomed to a never-ending routine, he did not know what to do with all the free time he had at school. One day "I walked by the football field and I asked a fellow: 'How do you get to do that?'" An assistant coach, Choc Sportsman, told him: "We'll let you come out, but you don't have much of a chance because you haven't played ball." Parker, in fact, had never even been to a game. Sizing him up, head coach Jack Sisco told him: "You look like a guard," and so they placed him in the line along with some other freshmen "for cannon fodder." Parker estimated that when he went out for the team he was five feet, eight inches and 165 pounds, but "I was wound pretty tight, because I had grown up tough." The next year he worked his way to end, and the next year to halfback. By the time he graduated, he had grown into a six-feet, one-inch, 205-pound bruiser with two varsity letters.

Even though Sisco's regimen bordered on being oppressive, Parker insisted that it was nevertheless "easier than working"—a casual statement that belied a more profound truth. Teammate Leon Vinyard agreed, and added that playing ball was infinitely more interesting as well. When the last semester of his high school days at Canton came around, Vinyard learned that he would still be under the UIL's cutoff age of nineteen when school began the next fall. So he decided to drop a course in order to enjoy another football season in that East Texas community. Graduation meant only that he would have to go to work in the cotton fields full time. After finally receiving his diploma, that is exactly what he did.

Toward the end of the summer, however, Vinyard was having serious doubts about his future. Then, one afternoon, he looked up from his plow and spotted a fellow Canton graduate walking down the road with a suitcase. Vinyard said that when he asked the boy what he was doing, he replied: "I'm going up to Denton to North Texas; they're having tryouts and will let you go to school for free if you make the team." Impulsively, Vinyard replied: "Wait a minute, I'll go with you." Right there, he tied up his mules and just walked out of the pasture and into a new life. Until he actually won a spot on the team, he had to come home every weekend. He hitchhiked through Dallas and caught another ride going east, always making the last few miles on foot, dragging his suitcase through the woods and across that field which, by then, had become a happy reminder of his decisive moment.

More often, high school players from poor families found their way to college just like Bob Harrell did. They played under men who knew that higher education was more accessible than it seemed. For example, Bill Ellington's coach knew that he was smart enough to attend college and talented enough to play ball, but not many recruiters made it to the small Panhandle town of Lefors. The coach had a friend, however, at Sul Ross College, who agreed to give Ellington a scholarship just on the coach's word. The two of them loaded the boy's things into an automobile and together they drove five hundred miles to Alpine, where Ellington played until the war forced the school to suspend its program. From there Ellington went on to McMurry, in Abilene, where he completed an education that others in his family had never even envisioned.

As more and more first-generation college graduates made their way into the profession, coaches increasingly found themselves around boys with whom they shared the same background. Even before Gordon Wood buried his father under the patch of farm land that had defeated him, he was loath to accept the same way of life. Once in school, Wood looked to education as a way out. His parents, with only nine years of schooling between them, at first balked at their son's vision. "Daddy told me that if you have an education, you become a teacher or a preacher, and you starve." Persistence and achievement eventually earned their support, but success came in a long series of little victories.

Wood's first memorable academic experience came in the seventh grade when he met debate coach Comer Clay. "He was the first person to ever impress upon me the importance of an education," Wood recalled. Yet after a miserable showing in his first contest, "Clay told me that I was the greenest, dumbest, country debater in the world." The teacher nevertheless encouraged his pupil to keep trying, and he did; in fact, he became quite proficient.

Gordon Wood found that he possessed some athletic ability as well. In the late 1920s, when it came time to go to high school, he enrolled at Abilene, which was then an annual contender for the state crown. Wood's father tried to discourage him, and insisted that his son's routine on the farm would not change. Almost every day the team practiced until dark, and even then a long walk awaited young Gordon after the bus dropped him off. When he got home, he had cows to milk and other chores to do. After eight weeks the regimen overwhelmed the boy and he gave up. The next spring, he enrolled in his little country school and went out for track. It took three successful years in the classroom and on the track as well as all the debating talents that Wood could muster to convince his father that his future lay in the field of education. And, when Hardin-Simmons came knocking with a scholarship in hand, Wood's father gave the boy his blessing.

However misplaced the priorities of society were, it was not debating enthusiasts who put Wood through college. Rather, it was a stadium and gym full of football and basketball fans willing to pay to see him play who ponied up the money for his scholarship, and it was sports that allowed Wood to open that same door to scores of other boys like himself. A few former players who might have otherwise accepted far less, instead worked their way into courtrooms, hospitals, and even the halls of Congress, in part because their coach made them believe "they could be somebody."

Not long after Gordon Wood got into the profession, he encountered Curtis Johnson, a big kid in bib overalls, the son of a poor Jones County farmer. When the coach looked into the boy's eyes, he saw himself. Wood quickly learned that Johnson was both smart and talented, and before the boy's senior year, he encouraged him to set his sights on college. His family, however, did not want any part of it. "They threw a fit and said college people grew up to be crooks," Wood recalled the boy telling him. When he persisted, his father kicked him out of the house and told him not to come back until he had cleared those notions from his head. For a while Johnson's mother hid him in the barn and fed him. Finally the boy disavowed the idea of going to college, and his father welcomed him back.

Wood related, however, that after the season ended Curtis Johnson brought the subject up again. The father and son then volleyed their arguments: "We can't pay tuition"—"Well, I get that free." "You don't have a place to stay"—"They're going to let me stay in the dormitory for free." "We don't have money for books"—"They're going to furnish my books." "How are you going to eat?"—"I get my board, too." Exasperated, Mr. Johnson finally barked: "That's what's wrong with this country—we work day and night and they're going to let you go to school just to play!" Unlike Wood's father, Mr. Johnson never did give Curtis his blessing, and when the boy accepted a scholarship, the man disowned him. The young man made the most of the situation, however. While he never won anything like all-American honors, he did receive a solid education and eventually led all Austin-area traders in selling stocks and bonds. He also contributed to many worthy causes. Upon dedicating a sound system to his church, in fact, he put up a plaque that read: "To my high school coach Gordon Wood who is responsible for any and all successes that I've ever had."

The coaching profession attracted many young men whose life-shaping experiences with their own mentors made them want to become part of the fraternity. At Groesbeck, for example, Charles Lawrence had a tremendous influence on Gordon Brown, who would later adopt his mentor's approach to the game. "Many coaches, as mine, became a role model for players, teaching us how to win as an individual and a team, and in so doing taught us how to be successful in life," Brown remarked. "The indoctrination made us believe we could win and we believed strongly in our coach." Seldom did the Goats ever beat their nearby rivals, the Mexia Blackcats, but "Coach Lawrence made us believe we could, and we did, three years in a row."

Lessons like the ones Gordon Brown described were often formed on a more personal level. After Bailey Marshall's mother died, his father was often too busy with the daylight-to-dark demands of running a farm to keep track of his son. Once, when Marshall had a broken leg, Georgetown coach Bernald Birkelback observed him negotiating the stadium steps on crutches. When he asked what Marshall was doing, the injured player told him he was planning on sleeping in the stands that night so he could be at school in the morning when his Future Farmers of America group headed to a show in Dallas. Birkelback took Marshall home that evening, and afterward he made sure that his player never wanted for guidance and attention. Marshall reciprocated after college by making sports his career, and every Father's Day he thanked Birkelback with a card.

A Spartan Ethic

Such tenderness contrasted with football coaches' rough exteriors. Charles Qualls holds warm memories of Hillsboro's P. T. Galiga, yet his initial brush with the coach was anything but genial. On the first day of school one year, Qualls found himself in Galiga's health class, and when "I got smart with him" he "beat me with a rolled up calendar." Bobby Meeks, who played for Bull Bates at Fort Worth I. M. Terrell, said the coach "stayed on my butt"; however, Meeks also declared: "I probably never would have finished school if it wasn't for Big Man." Once, when a receiver beat Meeks on a pass play in practice, Bates gave him the standard punishment for "loafers": twenty laps around the track.[3]

A steady diet of hard work, discipline, and accountability was part of the game, and most players accepted the spartan ethic without question. Clarence McMichael insisted that contact was the order of the day. "We had grueling workouts" that lasted the better part of the afternoon—"one-on-one, two- and three-on-one, and five yards apart tackling drills." Arm padding was rare equipment, and teams never saw a trainer in those days. About the only medication was ammonium for groggy players and flesh-staining mercoruchrome to disinfect wounds. Once, when a teammate broke Frank Pulattie's nose in practice, the Waco running back plugged cotton in his nostrils and did not hit the showers until the rest of the team was finished. "It was a tough practice after a loss, and I wanted to be counted among the men," he said.

Even Bernard Birkelback, whose gentle nature so deeply affected Bailey Marshall, was a taskmaster on the practice field. Until well after the war, many schools held football camps before the season began, and often invited another team to board locally so that the two squads could scrimmage under game conditions. The Georgetown team on which Marshall played boarded outside of Mexia in the barracks that German prisoners of war had recently vacated. "The Geneva Convention would probably have condemned us if they could have seen what we went through," the coach remarked. The Georgetown players slept on cots and worked out three times a day; water, of course, was forbidden in practice. They scrimmaged against other nearby schools like Groesbeck and Marlin, but normally they were shackled to the Blackcats. "Actually," Marshall insisted, "the experience was quite fun." Although the grueling workouts did not leave much time for the boys to go into town, they nevertheless strengthened ties among their own teammates and developed lasting friendships with the opponents they scrimmaged against. After his sophomore season, for instance, Marshall and some of the Georgetown boys followed Mexia when the Blackcats advanced to the play-offs and cheered for them.

Discipline came from within as well as from without. Many coaches declared that during high school they never touched a carbonated beverage because folks at the time believed "it cut your wind." Few recalled ever having tasted water during practice—"But you did get lots of salt pills," laughed John Reddell. The prevailing wisdom held that drinking water showed weakness, but that replacing the vital mineral was essential. "You'd get cotton mouth and just have to go on," Reddell added. At North Side, the players themselves administered the punishment for failing grades. James Brewer recalled that paddle-wielding letterman issued five licks for each "F." "The fathers would show up to watch, and they would clap and egg 'em on," he stated. And, when the boys got home, they'd get it again—"It was traditional."

Bailey Marshall commented that players routinely hid both pain and emotion—"This was mostly as a display of self-discipline." Three days before the 1948 state semifinal game between Waco and Port Arthur, for example, Waco quarterback Claude Kincannon suffered a dislocated shoulder. It had rained all week and turned the field into a mess for runners, and the Tigers, Kincannon knew, hoped to ride his passing arm to victory. When coach Carl Price went to visit his quarterback at the hospital, he found Kincannon at the foot of his bed, swinging his arm. "Coach," he said, "I am going to play Saturday." And he did; in fact, the Tigers won 13–6 on the strength of Kincannon's forty-one passes.[4]

However manly their gridiron actions may have seemed, kids will be kids; smoking and drinking occurred from time to time, and the consequences were predictable. Late in the 1940s, for example, after the football season had ended, sophomore Allen Boren made Carthage's varsity basketball team. The seniors on the squad felt like their sports careers were all but over, so during a tournament they decided to celebrate at a Sabine River cabin. They invited Boren to come along, and when he got there he was alarmed to find everybody drunk. With two promising football seasons ahead of him, he had never even thought about drinking and knew that if his coach caught them, there would be hell to pay. "The next day we got strummed by Elysian Fields, and sure enough Coach Tatum found out and called a team meeting." He ended a terse speech by telling them they could still have a trophy. "Y'all can set a beer bottle on the mantel," he barked. The coach then made the entire team run twenty-five miles over a four-day period. Even though Boren had not taken part in the bender, he ran with his teammates. "If the coach told you to do something, you did it without question."

College ball presented a different type of experience. Until veterans of World War II began playing, new recruits were freshmen right out of high school who mustered for two-a-days before the rest of the student body ever arrived on campus. All strangers to each other, they had to compete among themselves for a limited number of scholarships. Making the squad at this level required talent as well as heart, and not many coaches could afford the luxury of keeping a player who did not possess equal measures of both. The experience could be eye-opening.

Bob Barfield, for example, enrolled at Jacksonville's Lon Morris College to play under former A&M great Puny Wilson. In a scrimmage during two-a-days, Barfield was quarterbacking when the coach turned his wrath upon a running back who could do nothing to please him. At the end of each play, he hollered: "Run him again, Bob!" After countless repetitions, the runner was knocked semiconscious, and Wilson yelled: "If he can't go, drag him off!"

Barfield, admittedly, was afraid of Puny Wilson. He saw no action in the season opener, but in the next contest, against Stephen F. Austin, the coach "put me in the game in the second quarter and the first pass I threw in college was for a touchdown—but it was to the other team!" At halftime the Lon Morris squad regrouped at the far end of the field, where Wilson singled out Rosey Langford, a player whose family the coach had known most of his life. "I can't use all the words Puny said," Barfield remarked, "but he went something like this: 'Rosey, you son of a bitch you! You haven't done a damn thing; you're from my own home town, and if you don't like what I'm saying, I'll whip your ass right here!'" Then, Barfield continued, "he looked over at this old boy from Crockett, Dog Dawson" and screamed: "Dog—you! You stand out there and holler 'come around my end, come around my end.' And what do they do? They run six-foot-six-inches right up your long gangly ass!" Barfield concluded: "The game's over and we get beat 6–0 thanks to my pass. On the way home, he says: 'Fellas, we'll hit the field at four o'clock in the morning.' Well, I woke up at six o'clock and it was just me left in the dormitory. . . . I packed my suitcase right there and left for Huntsville and then got into Sam Houston."

Stoney Phillips, who coached at Pasadena and hired Bob Barfield upon moving up to the athletic director's post, also played for Puny Wilson, and commented: "He could have stayed there." Barfield was only seventeen years old at the time. "It was like your daddy," said Phillips; "you have to grow up before you appreciate your daddy." Wilson was tough on the practice field, Phillips conceded, but "when you crossed that line off that field it was a different story; he was your buddy then." Barfield indeed learned later that when the running back had gone down in practice, Wilson had been the first one to the hospital—"he hadn't even taken a shower."

Barfield also came to understand that Puny Wilson's experience at Texas A&M during the 1920s shaped his coaching style. Everyone at the all-male school was part of the Corps, and the rituals could be brutal. "The hazing was tough," recalled Brooks Conover; in fact, "it was unnecessary." Conover, who played at A&M right after Wilson graduated, described what it was like to be an Aggie in those days. "When you went in as a freshman, one of them would single you out and say: 'O.K., fish, you're my fish, you come up and clean my room and make my bed every morning.'" Part of the routine included regular paddlings. "These were no little boards," Conover said, "I saw many a butt that was black and blue." Every corpsman "had a board that you could hold with both hands. They could walk into your room at any time, and if you didn't jump to attention, they'd take the board to you." Once, the team was covering Conover's punts, and he was having an especially good day. In the dressing room after practice he was sitting naked on a bench, and some of the upper classmen came up and said: "Look here, Freshman; next time D. X. [Bible] calls you over to do that punting, don't you kick it so damn far—our tongues are about hanging out chasing those damn things." Punctuating their demand, they ordered: "Bend over!" One of them produced a split and taped fungo bat, a long, skinny baseball bat that coaches use for hitting flies and grounders in practice, and "whacked me about three times as hard as that guy could swing it."

Like Puny Wilson, Jack Sisco of North Texas State Teachers College was another hard-nosed coach, yet he tempered his field marshal's approach with verbal admonitions that a tough regimen would make his players better men. Standing six feet, four inches and weighing somewhat more than the 230 pounds that he carried while earning all-Southwest Conference honors at Baylor in the 1920s, Sisco towered over most of his charges. He inspired them by revealing just how far they could push themselves. Young men found such personal revelations a practical resource in the days of economic depression and war. Leon Vinyard commented that Sisco helped him form the philosophy that hard work and

Prairie View A&M coaching staff, 1949, left to right: William Nicks, Fred "Pop" Long, Wister Lee, and Jimmie Stevens. *Photograph courtesy Coleman Library, Prairie View A&M University.*

self-sacrifice produced character. "I was taught that way in football," he declared, "and I followed through with it all the years that I coached." So did many others who played under Sisco; scores of them, in fact, attest that many believed his approach was a valid one.

Both Vinyard and teammate Walt Parker recalled Sisco's workouts as torturous. Sisco believed that the team that hit hardest and possessed the greatest mental toughness would win most of the time. "He felt like you didn't need water if you were in shape," remarked Parker. Yet Vinyard told how every now and then they were still able to enjoy a few precious mouthfuls. The practice field adjoined a golf course, and on each corner was a green. "They fertilized at North Texas with sheep manure," Vinyard chuckled, and as the team ran laps "we'd bend over and scoop a little of that water up off of that fertilized golf green and get a sip of it."

Not all college coaches, of course, were made from the same mold. As in high school, there were all types, and they used any number of approaches. They developed programs partly out of imitation and settled on styles that suited their personalities. Whether taskmaster or nurturer, none stood taller than Fred "Pop" Long of black schools Paul Quinn, Wylie, Prairie View, and Texas College, whose passion for the game and love for young men inspired dozens of players to enter the profession. Among his most successful protégés was Joe Washington, who vowed: "I could coach five hundred years and never be a Pop Long." Though almost invisible to white society, those who knew Long pointed to his four national championships and dozens of awards and honors, and insisted that he belonged in the same class as some of the college game's most eminent coaches.

Jap Jones, whose high school teammates at Dallas's Booker T. Washington had nicknamed him "Plank Foot," commented that his high school coach Raymond Hollie thought he had a future in football. "He said that youngsters who had big feet usually grew to be pretty good sized individuals." After Jones's senior year, Pop Long "came up in the summer and said he saw me walk across the street and couldn't help but notice the size of my feet *and* hands." Jones deadpanned that he had always known Hollie was among the best, but right then he knew that Pop must be a great one.

"As I grew older," commented Joe Washington, "I realized that Pop was way ahead of his time." But more than that, Washington continued, "he was a great person from head to toe." Elmer Redd, longtime Lufkin Dunbar coach, said that Long "took me under his wing like a son." Both Redd and Jap Jones remarked that everybody enjoyed being around him, and that his players actually looked forward to the normally boring "skull sessions," as they called team meetings.

Washington proclaimed: "I would always feel in a light and airy mood around Pop because he was just different." Long was a big man, and "his mannerism was such that it would hold your attention." He was also gruff. With a laugh, Washington affected Pop Long's deep voice and muttered: "Let's go son, move your butt down the field." Turning somewhat more serious, he added that Long "could raise as much hell as he wanted to" yet he "never made me mad or irritated me." His loud bark and mild bite could be almost comical at times. Long always came to practice in everyday clothes—"he wore a dress hat; if it was cold, a civilian jacket; street shoes, thin socks rolled up and turned down." Contrasting Long's style with that of assistant coach Jimmy Stevens, Washington remarked: "We could see [Stevens's] car coming a mile and a half off, and anybody that was sitting on their butt would jump up. Now, we didn't do that with Pop," but "we still gave him everything we had."

Bob Harrell commented that coaches went into the profession either because some personal experience steered them that way, or because a great college career made them want to remain close to the game. For him, it was both. On the first day of practice at Texas Christian University, the former high school quarterback "went out there a little bit early and watched Sam Baugh work out." The freshman coach, "old Howard Grubbs, says: 'What do you play Robert?'; I said: 'Halfback!'"

Although Bob Harrell graduated the year before Dutch Meyer and the Horned Frogs captured the national title, he nevertheless started in the first Cotton Bowl game in 1937, in which TCU beat Marquette 16–6. The previous year, when Harrell was a second-string sophomore, a single touchdown kept them from taking the Rose Bowl bid from SMU. The Frogs took consolation, however, in winning the Sugar Bowl 3–2 in a driving rain storm. When the starting halfback went down with an injury in the first series, Harrell recalled, "I went in and played the rest of the game." After that, he enjoyed two years as a starter on a team that contended for both conference and national crowns.

World War II

Just after Bob Harrell graduated and began coaching at the West Central Texas town of DeLeon, World War II interrupted his career. The experience, however, did not change him—"I was already a man and knew right from wrong"; it was the Great Depression, he said, that shaped his personal outlook and values. As America readied itself for the conflict, Sergeant Harrell found himself at Camp Wolters outside of Mineral Wells in charge of sixty men—"I managed them just like I had my football team." In fact, Harrell even formed a squad out of his best recruits and arranged some games against other outfits, but the army shipped out his entire unit before they had a chance to play.

For many other coaches the experiences of combat, of encountering people of different backgrounds, and of seeing what lay beyond the borders of Texas profoundly influenced the way they looked at themselves and the sport that was, or would become, their life's work. Joe Hedrick, recalling the lessons of his youth, remarked: "Nobody is fully educated until they go through depression and war." Growing up in Central Texas was sometimes a hand-to-mouth experience; as a Marine, Hedrick was wounded at Iwo Jima. What he remembered most about hitting the beach at Iwo was that "there was nowhere to go; I was scared to death." More than anything else, he learned: "Combat is survival, football is not; one is competitive, the other is survival." Still, he added: "War did make you tougher, and that did carry over into football."

Recalling the hard times, Bill Hartley declared: "You wouldn't take a million dollars for the experience, but you wouldn't want to do it again." Like Hedrick, he also served in the Pacific theater and repaired airplanes at Guadalcanal after U.S. troops secured the island. "We met all kinds of people, sorry ones and good ones, and you learn to make a better judgment about people," Hartley said. "I would talk to these guys who had aircraft shot out from under them, and . . . some of them were really mean. I often wondered why—what has shaped everybody; but they might have been mean . . . or not had many scruples . . . before they ever got into the service." One acquaintance, a young man from Arkansas, had barely finished the third grade—"in fact, I helped him write his letters home to his wife; it would take him all day if he did it." But, Hartley declared: "He could play poker and make those dice do anything he wanted them to." Hartley never considered the man dumb or corrupt, rather, "it was just the environment he came out of." Reading people was a quality that came in handy when Hartley began to make his living as a coach.

The lessons of war did not immediately sink in for those who were too young to go off and fight. Charles Qualls was eleven years old on December 7, 1941. He and some school friends were spending that Sunday at a vacant lot playing ball, when his father drove up and interrupted them with the news of the Japanese attack on Pearl Harbor. The boys fell silent, listening intently, trying to fathom the significance of the moment. A very solemn Mr. Qualls then climbed back into his car and departed, leaving behind a small cluster of concerned faces. Charles Qualls remembered them watching as his father drove away—then, someone knocked the ball out of his hands, and they went back to their game as if nothing had happened.

Joe Washington, also eleven years old at the time, declared that at first it was just a matter of going from "playing cowboys and Indians to playing war." Bob Cashion remembered regular hikes down to the railroad tracks to see the troop trains pass. Until he learned what the "victory sign" was, he returned their greetings with rocks—"I thought they were giving me the finger or something."

For young Allen Boren, the gravity of having four stars in his family's window—one for each of his older brothers who was fighting—made the war more immediate. Recalling the intensity of the times, Robert Lowrance remarked that a "division of attention" developed between what was going on within the community and what went on in Europe and Asia. The situation made men and women long for activities into which they could retreat. Eddie Joseph believed that football was a primary diversion; it "helped draw communities together," he insisted. The backdrop of World War II also added a measure of innocence to the game and evoked a sense of continuity with more normal times. "In college you didn't know who was going to be playing from one day to the next because of the war," said Bob Harrell. At the high school level, however, it was as if football provided a final and glorious moment of youth for boys who might soon find that manhood meant facing a more deadly contest.

Still, the war affected the high school game. Many schools economized by suspending their junior high programs. Some smaller places, like Quitaque, dropped sports all together. Gene Mayfield felt very fortunate when that Panhandle community at least joined the state's six-man league during his junior year. Jewell Wallace recalled that gas rationing made it difficult for fans to follow his El Paso team, but by pooling their stamps, they started the happy tradition of traveling to games together. At the other end of the state Grand Saline cut back on many extracurricular activities, but townspeople considered football a sacred cow. Hoot Smith, who played on the team during the war declared: "Every week was like homecoming." The school arranged its schedule to coincide with holidays, which allowed folks to close down the town and stage big parades. A game with their arch-rival, the Van Vandals, Smith insisted, would virtually empty the visiting team's town.

In 1941 and 1942, Texas high school football even became a diplomatic tool for President Franklin D. Roosevelt's Good Neighbor Policy. To help cultivate ties with Mexico, Jewell Wallace agreed to take his El Paso Tigers to play in Mexico City. The first year he, his wife, and three other adults chaperoned 250 kids on an eleven-day adventure. The round-trip ticket cost only $21, and for a dollar a day they received room and board at the posh Imperial Hotel. "Kids didn't get into a whole lot of trouble back then," Wallace noted, "but when we stopped at Chihuahua, I caught a boy with a beer." After alerting the student's parents, "I sent him packing on the next El Paso-bound train." When the group reached the outskirts of the capital, Mexican officials stopped them and ushered aboard three mariachi bands, which entertained the kids until they reached town. Mounted policemen, with an American flag draped over one arm and a Mexican flag over the other, escorted the boys and girls everywhere they went. The surprised children enjoyed a parade and barbecue in their honor, and, after the game, a dance.

Wallace remembered less about that first contest against Mexico City's YMCA than the larger experience itself. Many players on the opposing team were "grown men, some as old as twenty-five." The arena had hosted a horse show just before the game, and rather than clean the field, groundskeepers simply shoveled sawdust over the manure. Wallace's wife, in charge of the drill team, had a brief scare when some intemperate Mexicans slipped under the bleachers and began squeezing every bare thigh within reach. When the game was over, there was no shortage of chivalrous young El Paso gridders willing to escort the girls from the field. Despite the minor annoyances, the affair proved so successful that the next year 385 boys and girls returned to take part in a match with Mexico City Polytechnic.

Perhaps no incident during the war years brought the importance of high school football into focus more clearly than the controversy surrounding the Lufkin Panthers' run at the state championship in 1943. The San Angelo Bobcats won the crown that year amid the protests of Lufkin fans who believed the University Interscholastic League had unfairly singled them out in an effort to affirm its amateur rule.[5]

Panther boosters at the end of the 1942 season had rewarded all-state quarterback Jitter McKinney with a grant of $45 so he could purchase a new suit. McKinney's father, crippled in a farming accident, was barely surviving off the wages he made as a night watchman, and certainly could not afford such an extravagance. Somehow men in Henderson and Jacksonville learned about the gift and lodged a protest with the UIL's district committee, which suspended McKinney just before the 1943 season. The Lufkin *Daily News* indignantly pointed out that such gifts were commonplace, and that by this standard "there were few eligible players in East Texas." Indeed, two other Panther players had received small favors for their efforts during the 1942 season, but the cash involved did not exceed UIL limits and they were cleared to play. McKinney returned his money to everyone whom he could locate and formally apologized to the committee. The body, however, refused to overturn its ruling. As the season unfolded the matter consumed sportswriters and editorialists statewide. Lufkin citizens even burned district committee chairman Bonner Frizzel in effigy.

With the controversy raging, a Lufkin citizen wrote to the editor of the local newspaper to complain that high school football was commanding

Game program, Graham vs. Fort Worth North Side, opening day, September 14, 1945.
Courtesy James Brewer.

too much attention at a time when the country was involved in a war. A hurricane, he pointed out, was also at that moment heading for the Texas shore. Another reader followed the jeremiad with a poem:

There's a war going on as some of us surely know
But to read the Lufkin *Daily News* you'd never think so.
The headlines of the paper say the Panthers just must win,
And in a small corner it says the war is such a sin.
Now I don't dislike football, I think the game is fun;
But why go crazy over it when the war is not yet won?

Jitter McKinney can't play, he's been disqualified;
A mother's son can't fight again—he, for our country died.
"All out for war" is the slogan that's heard the world around,
"All out for the game today" most certainly fits this town."

The *Daily News* responded with a poem of its own:

On far-flung battle fields today death faces boys we know;
In letters home to us they say "Keep those Panthers on the go."
As they risk all that you and I may have our freedom great;
Their minds to Panther Stadium fly, as they weigh their Panther's fate.

War, as the angst-ridden critics noted, did present a higher duty, and
scores of coaches took part. Many who had earned exemptions left their
coaching posts to join the armed forces; others, either right out of high
school or enrolled in college, volunteered or were drafted. Bum Phillips,
who saw action at Guadalcanal and New Georgia as a member of the U.S.
Marines' "Raider Division," said that war was "something that we felt we
had to do." He remarked that before volunteering, "I just couldn't
believe that they could win it without me, and after I got in, I felt they
couldn't win it because of me!"

Wichita Falls's Joe Golding related that those already in the profession,
like himself, Bob Harrell, and Morris Southall, were "ticketed" for athletic
training because of their backgrounds. Golding, for example, was in charge
of a field program that included setting up an obstacle course as well as
physical training and testing regimens for non-commissioned officers.
Ironically—or, then again, perhaps not—he was assigned to Sheppard Air
Force Base at Wichita Falls.

Walt Parker started out the war at San Antonio, as assistant coach of
the "Randolph Field Ramblers." The squad played a creditable schedule
against other service teams and also battled such college teams as SMU,
Texas, and Southwestern. The Ramblers, Parker asserted, beat the college
boys badly because they were able to supplement their lineup with grown
men. A clean record earned them a Cotton Bowl berth in 1944, where
they tied Texas 7–7. Later on Parker was transferred to March Field in
California, where he was a running back on an all-star team that challenged the Washington Redskins.

The war ended for Walt Parker, however, on the South Pacific island of
Tenian. On that eleven-mile-long, four-mile-wide island, he served in the
Air Force's 113th bomber group—"the wing that dropped the A-Bomb."
At the time he was unaware that he was helping support an event that
would change the world. When he learned what had happened, he was
"just relieved that we were going home." The "severity didn't sink in
until later on," Parker reflected.

World War II provided a leveling experience for future coaches Jap
Jones and Clarence McMichael, who served in the 777th Field Artillery
unit. Upon being drafted, the group in which Jones was mustered into
service gathered at Tyler, where they pinned on him the nickname that

followed him ever afterward. Scouting for a place to eat, someone spotted the "Jap Jones Cafe," which had not expected such a large crowd. "They were just about to run out of food when I got served," recalled Jones, and the guys "accused me of eating it all up."

One of the few black combat outfits in Europe, the 777th was composed largely of young college men from Texas and the South. Their responsibility was sighting targets several miles away. "We zeroed in on cities, towns, enemy headquarters, et cetera," Jones related. Their gun, "a 4.5," was supposed to require some intelligence to operate—"it didn't," laughed Jones—but it did lob shells eleven miles, and the men who used it proved very effective.

Yet Clarence McMichael related that among the white combat soldiers black inferiority was almost taken for granted. Once, he remembered, a white captain and former Aggie Corpsman recently assigned to the 777th was sitting down, observing a firing mission. "I was sending down commands to the gun, and he jumped up and hollered: 'Cease fire! Cease fire!,' and we all looked up and wondered what was going on." The captain had realized the group was about to shoot and insisted on checking the calculations himself before he allowed the firing to proceed. Later he confided to McMichael that when he was put in charge of the group, other white officers had given him a hard time—"You mean, you're going over to that dumb outfit? . . . You're going to be killed!" He also admitted being afraid. "I didn't think you people could learn," he told McMichael. The group, however, did so well that the 777th gained the reputation of being among the European theater's most proficient outfits.

While at Brownsville, Brooks Conover had coached Alfredo Patraca— "such a poor student that he failed Spanish." Nevertheless, the boy was "well-liked, a good kid, and a good football player." Shortly before World War II, Conover took a job farther up the coast at Orange, and, sometime after America had entered the conflagration, he learned that Patraca was among those captured at Corregidor and subjected to the infamous death march that followed. Turning to his wife, Nell, he remarked: "Ol' Patraca wouldn't hurt a fly." Right then he was inspired to avenge his former player in the war effort. Conover joined the Naval Air Corps and eventually participated in the invasion of Okinawa, where he shuttled Marines onto a one-hundred-and-fifty-yard stretch of sand called "Blue Beach One." By that time the Japanese had already retreated to the island's interior, but every evening "about six o'clock" the kamikazes came in. The sight was etched indelibly into Conover's mind. "It's really something to have one of those [planes] drop over your head," he remarked; of the return fire, he added: "It looked like you could walk up the tracers."

Ray Akins was aboard one of those transports at Okinawa. The terrible conditions, he asserted, matched the life-threatening situation. Digging in after a thirty-inch rain, he remembered seeing "some boys—actually grown men—just give up after not eating for two or three days." During combat he also saw dead bodies and craters everywhere; drivers maneuvering their amphibious landing craft, of course, could only discern if soldiers were alive if they were moving. Yet Akins declared that occasionally some soldiers would simply lie down and allow the vehicles to roll right over them. It was there, he insisted, that he developed his coaching instincts. "Somehow I survived . . . and I learned that when you think you can't go any farther, you can go farther."

Few coaches experienced what Joe Bob Tyler endured. Captured at the Battle of the Bulge, enemy soldiers marched his group out of France, through the eastern part of Belgium, and across the Siegfreid Line to a rail center in Germany. From there they were herded into a prisoner of war camp. For four or five days during the forced march he and his fellow captives did not eat. Finally they were turned loose in a turnip patch beside a railroad track while the Nazis waited for the boxcars that would take the Americans to Gorlitz, near the Polish border. Tyler remembered hearing Russian guns on February 14—"Valentine's Day," he recalled thinking at the time—and saw on the horizon that evening the glow of exploding bombs. Until that moment he had thought the Germans were winning the war, but his elation quickly faded when the frantic Nazis forced them to begin another march, this time one hundred and twenty-five miles to Leipzig, and then north into Germany's coal mining region. The soldiers worked under horrific conditions, and Tyler grew so weak that "I had to have help just to unbutton my trousers." Once, he and another prisoner labored all day just to move two sacks of concrete, one lying behind pushing it and the other lying in front pulling.

Before they were captured Joe Bob Tyler had been a squad leader, and when his former gunner caught a turkey during that second march, the prisoners planned a feast. "We put it in a sack, and we were so weak that it took three of us to carry it," he recalled. That night the guards confined them in a barn, and in a pile of hay the Americans dug a hole and skinned the bird, then ate some of it raw. They placed the remains back into the sack to eat later, knowing that the cold weather would keep it from spoiling. They saved the leftovers, in fact, until they were able to persuade some British prisoners of war to cook it for them. The Germans did not allow the U.S. soldiers to build fires, but found it more difficult to deny that right to English prisoners for brewing tea. Together, the allies enjoyed a rare treat.

When he became a coach, Tyler understood the physical sacrifices that the game demanded of his players. "Football is ninety percent mental," he asserted. "If you could get over the mental part, the physical part was easy." After the war, it was a lesson that Tyler and many of his peers carried with them onto practice fields across the state.

Most of those who returned from Europe and Asia felt that war had changed them; they found that Texas had changed, too. Bill Carter's story summed it up. Before World War II, all he had ever known was poverty, and, like Leon Vinyard, all that awaited him after high school was a life behind the plow. As a senior at Weatherford in 1938, Carter's schoolmates elected him class president. And since he, like Vinyard, would be under the UIL age limit the following autumn, he decided to drop a course so that he could return for a second senior year. Once more, he laughed, "they made me president."

Instead of becoming a farmer or going to college, however, Bill Carter joined the Army. He was at Normandy on D-Day and saw action in other battles. The experience, he remarked, "changed my entire outlook on life." In combat he saw men die, and as he struggled to survive, he found a resolve to live that surprised him. He also learned the value of charity from a nurse at a Red Cross station in Scotland. The woman was passing out coffee and doughnuts, and Carter explained to her that he had been at sea aboard the *Duchess of Bedford* for the past twenty-one days, and had "not eaten good" in that time. "If you'll give me two of those doughnuts, I'll contribute to the Red Cross for the rest of my life," he begged. She did, and he kept the promise.

After the war Bill Carter enrolled at Abilene Christian College on the GI Bill and saw another side of life. "Depression had given me a gloomy outlook," he remarked, "now there was hope." Cotton Miles, who had entered college in 1940, and again in 1946 after a stint in the Navy, added that the second time he enrolled "I had the GI Bill and associated with people who experienced war; these were different people than the old farmer boy." Veterans, he continued, were more "seasoned" and serious about school and life. "When you played football in 1940, you lined up beside another nineteen-year-old boy; in 1946 he might be twenty-four or twenty-five."

In 1946 Gene Mayfield was that nineteen-year-old farm boy. Both he and Joe Washington joined the service to get the GI Bill. Mayfield could see that returning veterans would take the scholarship he had won as a freshman at Canyon Normal. Washington, on the other hand, had grown to idolize soldiers and decided to become one himself. While in the service, both of them played football on military teams.

Mayfield, in fact, made the Korean all-stars, who traveled to Japan and took the "Rice Bowl" in 1947. Their reward was spending "R&R" at a Japanese resort, where many of his teammates attempted to ice skate. "I had never seen such a thing; I can still see the rink and all the lumbering southern kids falling all over themselves." Washington, for his part, turned some heads playing pick-up games against some seasoned college athletes, but the service team in Honolulu was reluctant to allow a black man on the team. One day in a scrimmage, however, "I had my helmet in front of me and the coach said: 'Give me a guy who knows how to block.'" Washington jumped up and started onto the field so hastily that he forgot his helmet, but once in the game, he became a regular. In large part, military ball steeled the two Texans' resolves to return to college and continue their playing days until they could get on the other side of that whistle.

Quoting Arthur Wellesley, Ed Logan waxed eloquently: "The battle of Waterloo was won on the playing fields of Eton." Logan believed that, too, but added that if the Duke of Wellington had not said it, some high school football coach would have likened war to the conflicts that unfolded on the playing fields of some small Texas towns. The difference between the two, however, is that while Wellesley was looking backward, Texas coaches projected the analogy forward and gave their boys a taste of trench warfare waged with forearms and headgears. Perhaps the experience made the former football players who faced North Koreans or the Viet Cong better prepared for the struggle. Yet even those who never received an insincere greeting from Uncle Sam still had to prepare themselves for Friday night battles with Indians, Vikings, and Vandals, and even Gobblers, Porcupines, and Pied Pipers.

Part III

The Golden Age of Texas High School Football, 1945–1970

Chapter 6

The Last Days of the Iron Man: Texas High School Football at its Peak

At the same time that Texans adjusted to postwar conditions, high school football entered its glory years. Economic prosperity and an abundance of leisure time generated a surge of popular interest in the game. And football, like no other endeavor, reinforced the values of young manhood and created a rabid following in towns where gridiron success stamped an identity on the community. Everyone, it seemed, was pulling in the same direction. Crew-cut boys who compliantly accepted instruction from parents and figures of authority expressed pride in their uniformity. School spirit reached beyond the playing fields into classrooms and homes. Bands, cheerleaders, drill teams, pep squads, student cheering sections, boosters, and fans were ubiquitous appendages of local teams. School districts, moreover, possessed the resources and the support of parents and administrators to build better public school facilities, and a well-outfitted football team was the typical crown jewel of every town. For a generation—from just before the 1950s through the early years of the 1960s—high school football was the state's unrivaled pastime, unfettered by the distractions of depression and global war.

The late world war and the economic surge that followed it cast the first glowing rays of Sunbelt prosperity upon a predominantly agrarian state. Stoney Phillips, who had reached maturity among the sleepy strawberry farms surrounding the village of Pasadena, returned home a few years after the war as the coach of a budding Houston suburb. He described the Pasadena High of his youth as "a little ol' school. We weren't even in a district, we just played independent football. We barely had enough to make a team every year. I lettered four years and I didn't weigh but a hundred and ten pounds or so." Phillips graduated in 1933 in a class of twenty-nine kids. Yet even before the war, Sinclair, Crown, Shell, and Phillips petroleum companies built area refineries and Champion Paper entered the area as well. By the time Stoney Phillips returned to Pasadena in 1950, eight hundred students walked the halls of the new high school.

While places like Spring Branch, closer to downtown Houston, attracted a new class of managers, technicians, and scientists, Pasadena grew into

141

Stoney Phillips. *Photograph courtesy Texas High School Coaches Association, Austin.*

a rough-and-tumble blue-collar suburb. "When the chemical industries took off, families came from all over, and Pasadena became a big union town," remarked Phillips. The recent arrivals brought varied backgrounds with them. "My best quarterback came from North Carolina where there was that paper mill, and they transferred down." High school all-American Bert Coan moved with his family from a small town near Henderson. "He was six-foot-four and weighed about 190 pounds, and he could run like hell!" Phillips recalled. Coan proved it during the 1957 track season by anchoring the 440-yard and mile relay teams as well as winning state in both the 100- and 220-yard dashes.

The phenomenon that Stoney Phillips witnessed repeated itself all over Texas. Just down the road at Deer Park, for example, row upon row of neat little tract houses began popping up in the shadow of the San Jacinto Monument in the years following the war. By 1952, the burgeoning little town with a brand new high school came within a touchdown of winning the Class 1-A state championship. Suburbs emerged outside of other Texas cities as well. Many former "wide spots" situated along new highways or atop natural resources also enjoyed a newfound prominence as outsiders began to pour into Texas.

In other places the rural-to-urban transformation made faint inroads; and, of course, there were places that modernity scarcely touched. Bill Ellington recalled that folks in the West Central Texas town of Winters got together with citizens from several nearby farming communities for an annual rabbit drive. "They made it a social event with dinner on the ground and such. People would line up across the fields and run those rabbits into a net. Then, they'd club them to death." Children, especially,

"Picture day" at Mexia High School, 1950. *Photograph courtesy Ty Cashion.*

anticipated the event, and their parents would pressure teachers into giving them excused absences. Before long, however, chemists invented poisons that proved more humane and efficient than clubs, and the practice was discontinued and forgotten.

Ways of life were certainly changing; conspicuously in some places, subtly in others. Among the more obvious manifestations of progress was a more literate and educated population. Whether former GIs or blue-collar workers looking to improve themselves, grown men who had the good fortune to attend college came to prize diplomas more highly than athletic accolades. On the other hand, as college enrollments increased and schools began handing out more scholarships, high school ball became more important for schoolboys who wanted to continue their gridiron careers. At the university level returning veterans became fewer, and high school seniors could look forward to playing college ball without having to line up across from twenty-five-year-old veterans.

Chena Gilstrap, who left Cleburne High School for the head coaching position at Paris Junior College shortly after the war, made light of the contrast. Upon noticing that some of his players were chewing tobacco, he called the team together and scolded them for breaking training. When he demanded they abstain, future Athens coach Joe Murphy, who picked up the habit at Guadalcanal, told Gilstrap that the rule would give him problems. "I chew four or five pouches of Beechnut when I go fishing on the weekends," Murphy complained. "That afternoon," said

Gilstrap, "I revised the rules and said ' . . . unless you have been in the service.'" After practice Bobby Jack Floyd, just out of Paris High School, complained that some of the veterans had gotten him hooked on the stuff and made his own appeal. "The next day I amended the rule again, and said ' . . . veterans, or those who hang out with veterans!'"

The Path to a Coaching Career

A sprinkling of ex-soldiers continued to fill out the college ranks into the 1950s, yet such scenes as the one Gilstrap recalled became rare as the lure of jobs made returning veterans more anxious to get an education that would enable them to climb aboard the money-go-round. By the early years of the decade the last Depression-era children ended their playing careers and became coaches. Like those who preceded him, Chuck Curtis declared: "Many of us did pretty good in college and had such great experiences that we wanted to make a living out of it." Yet their career paths in the booming post-war economy often turned on any number of life-shaping decisions. Curtis's first was "just realizing that I might be able to get a scholarship, because it looked like that was the only way I was going to get to go to college." His father, a near-indigent evangelist, was kept constantly on the move. During his son's senior year the minister moved to Taylor but allowed the boy to remain at Gainesville in a garage apartment in order to keep his eligibility.

Curtis thought he had enjoyed a good season, but became alarmed when recruiters ignored him. Then he met TCU's Abe Martin. "He came up and gave me a scholarship when no one else had even looked at me." With summer coming on, Oklahoma's Bud Wilkinson finally became interested in Curtis and even offered him a gravy train job as extra man for an oil company drilling deep holes near Lake Texoma. "Being an extra, I would be able to work as many towers as I could handle and get all the time-and-a-half I wanted," Curtis explained. When Curtis called Martin about his dilemma, the TCU coach did not see any problem at all. "Shoot, laddie," Curtis remembered Martin saying, "I'd just take that job; that's the best one in the country, because you've already told me where you're going to school." Curtis took the advice, but eventually he felt obligated to Oklahoma because of the easy money, and he called Martin to tell him he had a change of heart. "He told me: 'Don't say anything else, I'm driving up!'" As soon as he got there, the two sat down on an old swing in front of the garage apartment. "He told me: 'Now laddie, the last time I was here, we were on this same swing, and what did you tell me?' And I said: 'I told you I was going to TCU.' And he said: 'That's good enough for me,' and he got up and drove off. That tied the knot. I went to TCU."

Abe Martin developed a fatherly interest in Chuck Curtis, and the young man found the coach's quiet manner and country yarns endearing. "For a while I took commercial art courses, but the longer I was around Abe, the more I decided that I'd just stick with football," he said. Curtis related that nothing he had found in life could impart the emotional peaks and valleys of a hard, close football game. "Every once in a while you'll get into a situation where it's root hog or die, and everything hinges on that one play. If you make it, it's the penthouse; if you don't, it's the outhouse." Once, for example, against a great Baylor team that boasted Doyle Traylor, Dale Shofner, and Bill Glass, quarterback Curtis was facing third and fifteen inside TCU's own five yard line. "Here comes Ray Taylor into the huddle, and he goes: 'Coach said to punt.' And I said: 'Did he say when?' And Ray said: 'No.' So I said: 'Well, shoot, we'll just give you a little elbow room, then.' When we came out of the huddle and lined up for a run, I could hear Abe yelling, 'Shist o' Pot!' all the way down to the end zone. . . . And so I handed off to Jim Swink, and he made sixteen yards and a first down." After several more long gainers, Swink took a pitchout the remaining length of the field. After the extra point "I just eased over on the sideline, and here comes Coach Martin, and he put his arm around me. 'Chuck, my boy, your momma's sitting up there in the stands thinking I'm bragging on you right now, but if y'all hadn't scored that touchdown, I'd'a kicked y'ore ass!' And he just walked off and never said another word about it."

Curtis's "valley" came amid the last furious gasps of a hurricane as it petered out over College Station's Kyle Field. The A&M team featured future NFL Hall-of-Famer Jack Pardee and Heisman Trophy winner John David Crow. "Going into the wind, we got a first and goal and took a shot from the one yard line with Swink trying to bang it in. . . . The wind was blowing, I don't know, fifty, sixty miles an hour, and it was hailing. Light poles were bending. We couldn't even hear the signals because of the hail hitting our headgears." In the huddle Curtis called the same play, but as the Horned Frogs lined up, "I tried to holler to Swink that I was going to fake and bootleg it, but he couldn't hear me, so I went ahead and handed off to him again. They stacked it up, and they beat us 7–6. And as I glanced to my right after I handed off to Swink, there was no one covering the boot, and all these years I've kicked myself in the ass. I could have walked in."

Before joining the high school coaching ranks, Chuck Curtis played professional ball for the New York Giants. His achievements fell short of the success he enjoyed at TCU, yet as an aspiring coach it worked to his advantage. Both Vince Lombardi and Tom Landry were assistants on the staff, and "I absorbed some football knowledge from those men. They spent a lot of time with me because I was in a backup role, and every week I had to copy our opponents' stuff. . . . I got to know so many other offenses and defenses." After his brief career, Curtis landed at Holliday, in Northwest Texas, where he used many of the innovations he had learned.

Other men found that new opportunities abounded after the war and settled into coaching only after finding more lucrative careers unsatisfying. John Hugh Smith, a Texan who had played ball at LSU, became a high-paid lease hound for Gulf Oil. Yet he gladly abandoned the promising business career when his fiancée's father helped him land the head

John Hugh Smith, who played college ball at LSU, while coach at La Vega, 1948. *Photograph courtesy Mrs. John Hugh Smith.*

Future UIL director Bailey Marshall while coach at White Oak, 1963. *Photograph courtesy Texas High School Coaches Association, Austin.*

coaching job at La Vega. In Nacogdoches, Bailey Marshall was on the fast track with the Northern Indiana Brass Company when he went into the president's office to tell him he was quitting to become a coach. "He told me, if you want money, stay with the brass company, but your happiness is most important, and I won't try to talk you out of it."

Others were not so resolute. After college Ed Logan played a year of semi-pro baseball for the House of David. The "Whiskered Wizards" were sponsored by a group of Mormons from Benton Harbor, Michigan, whose descendants broke from the church when Brigham Young decided to move the congregation to Utah. The army claimed Logan between 1952 and 1954 and trained him as a surveyor. Afterward, Shell Oil tempted him with an offer of twenty-five thousand dollars for a year-and-a-half's work in Ecuador. Before it came time for him to leave, however, he met a girl and fell in love. "I also learned why Shell was paying so much," he stated. Headhunters of the Jivaro tribe, he had heard, were active in the area, and the company had lost a few men.[1] Through his brother, Logan learned about an assistant coach's job at A&M Consolidated. The $3,600-a-year job was considerably less than the petroleum company had offered, "But," he said, "I ended up with the girl, and I didn't have to worry about losing my head."

The postwar years, of course, did not extend open-ended opportunities without their own unique perils. Being drafted into the armed services remained a potential fact of life for all young men. Like their World War II counterparts, those of the Korean War era faced uncertain futures. Many coaches served in Korea and learned that lesson firsthand. Herb Allen, in combat for over thirty months, endured trials as arduous as any

World War II veteran. He once dodged a mortar that an enemy threw at him, and another time he jumped aside in time to avoid a booby trap just as it detonated. Watching the way different soldiers reacted to war taught him a lesson that he took into coaching with him—"I didn't coach a sport, I coached young men, and every one is different." He also learned that "disciplined teams win, whether in war or in football." He put it into practice, too. One year Allen boasted a team that was called offsides only once during the entire season.

Homer Johnson found himself in Korea after he had already begun his coaching career at Garland. Like so many soldiers, war reinforced his concept of manhood, yet his most pressing concern was just surviving the experience with as little discomfort as possible. As a coach in limbo, he figured that he would use his knowledge to make an insufferable situation more tolerable. "We were going on patrols across the line, and I had blisters all over my feet," Johnson remarked. So he wrote to sporting goods salesman Frank Stevens and asked him to send a bottle of Tuff Skin. "In a few days I got a letter from him that said: 'Homer, Tuff Skin costs three dollars and sixty cents a gallon, and there's a good chance you'll get killed up there, and you're going to have to send me three dollars and sixty cents before I send you the Tuff Skin.' Boy, I was hot! The next day, though, I got the Tuff Skin; he was only kidding."

What the Korean War era taught Bill Patrick was that he wanted to make coaching his life's work. "I had gone to Stephen F. Austin on a basketball scholarship, and when the war broke out, I enlisted in the Air Force instead of waiting to be drafted." Patrick never left the United States, and spent his entire stretch at Langley Air Force Base in Virginia. "I played a lot of ball there, and it helped me keep my sanity. When I got out, I went back to college knowing what I wanted to do with my life."

The same natural athleticism that Patrick possessed provided a natural conduit for transforming many players into coaches. Cotton Miles stayed with the game out of a love for competition. "I played every sport in high school, and after the war, I did the same thing at Stephen F.," he declared. "I got into coaching because I loved the arena." As if there were no other options, Buzz Allert remarked, "I just got into it." In college Allert majored in physical education, and after graduating and playing for the Detroit Lions and Toronto Argonauts, he stepped naturally into a coaching career in 1958. Bob Cashion echoed the sentiments of many others when he professed: "I just never thought I'd do anything else. I knew that I'd received so much help from coaches, that I wanted to give something back." Upon Cashion's graduation from college in 1955, his former high school coach, Ty Bain, invited him to join his staff at Kilgore.

A New Era Emerges

Landing a job was not difficult because school districts were expanding and adding assistants. "It was a good time to get into coaching," contended

Bob Harrell, "because after the war football just took off, and there weren't enough coaches to go around." And because so many young coaches had never known anything better, the mere prospect of stability and a steady paycheck in a familiar environment was alluring. "Football was not instant riches by any means, but it was a way of life," insisted Chena Gilstrap.

Bill Hartley agreed. Having grown up in abject poverty, he set his sights on teaching and coaching. Hartley's opportunity developed after he befriended "Pop" Giddens, the custodian at his Southwestern College dormitory. Unbeknownst to Hartley, the man's son was the superintendent of the Columbus School District. When the younger Giddens came to visit his father shortly before Hartley's graduation in 1949, Pop brought him to his young friend's room. "Here I am, sitting there in my underwear interviewing for a job!" Hartley recalled. Shortly afterward, Hartley hitchhiked to Columbus and signed a three-thousand-dollar contract that gave him a full load of teaching and required that he coach all sports.

The same year that Hartley entered the profession, the Texas legislature enacted the Gilmer-Aiken Law, which reorganized the public school system and raised teachers' base salaries to $2,400 for a nine-month year. Many school districts sweetened the pot by adding a premium for such extracurricular duties as coaching. Zac Henderson had followed the bill's development, and as soon as it passed, the recently graduated Texas Tech star called Chicago and declined the offer to continue his playing career with the Bears. "After Gilmer-Aiken you could actually make more money coaching than playing professional ball," he laughed. So, "I went down to TCU and got my teacher's certificate in one semester, and at midterm one of the old Tech bunch that had played under Pete Cawthorn offered me a job at Slaton."

"Some people think they were born to be in coaching," remarked Bum Phillips; "maybe so . . . I kind of fell into it that way." Fresh out of the service, he took a job at the Magnolia refinery in Beaumont. "I felt that I'd do like everybody else, I'd just stay there until I retired." After about half a year, however, a slip of paper came around asking all employees to authorize a deduction for the Red Cross. Phillips refused, saying: "Well, I'll tell you what I'll do; I'll give it to the Salvation Army but I'm not giving to the Red Cross." When his boss tried to convince him, Phillips related how overseas one of the charity's representatives had tried to sell him the goods they were supposed to be giving away to soldiers. Unimpressed upon hearing the story, the president of company then called him "into a big mahogany office" and tried to coerce him into signing the pledge. Phillips quit on the spot, demanding: "Have my check ready, because I'm leaving."

Phillips related: "There I am, twenty-one years old with a wife and no job and no future." He started for his home in Orange, but when he reached a fork, he turned toward Port Arthur instead. "I'm driving down the road, and I see these guys practicing football . . . I didn't have anything else to do, so I pulled over." It did not take long for him to learn that it was Lamar Junior College working out, because their coach, Ted

Ty Bain, foreground, and his Kilgore staff relax before beginning the 1957 campaign. *Photograph courtesy Ty Cashion.*

Jeffries, became curious. Approaching Phillips's truck, he asked: "'What are you doing?' I said: 'Just watching.' He said: 'Are you a football player?' and I said: 'Used to be before the war.' And he said: 'Do you want to try out for a scholarship?' And I said: 'I don't know, what's a scholarship?'" Phillips soon found out. "And that's what led me into coaching. . . . Just to show you how everything falls into place, it happened to be about one-thirty; had it been four o'clock in the afternoon or ten o'clock in the morning, hell, I wouldn't have been a coach. . . . Some things are just supposed to be, I guess."

Phillips's relationship with Jeffries blossomed. In fact, when the coach shortly afterward took the head job at Stephen F. Austin, Phillips followed him, and there he graduated. Jeffries was well known in football circles. He had taken Wichita Falls to its first state championship in 1941, and he knew the game well. Jeffries, moreover, "was a real, real good 'people coach,'" remarked Phillips. His skills and manner piqued his protégé's interest in the mechanics and psychology of the game and helped him realize what he wanted to do with his life.

Bum Phillips, like so many other young coaches, joined the profession's veterans at a time when the game was reaching its zenith. "By the 1950s," declared Joe Bob Tyler, "high school football had really come of age in Texas." An ever-improving highway system and fleets of "yellow dogs," as school buses were called, facilitated the competition. By the end of the decade, said Stoney Phillips, "some of the big schools would fly so that they could match up with the best regional schools in non-district. . . . You'd pay your own way and they'd get the gate, and then the next year

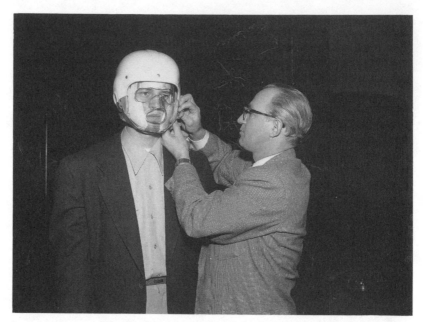

A player tries on an experimental facemask, c. 1951. *Photograph courtesy the Texas-Dallas History and Archives Division, Dallas Public Library.*

you'd switch." His Pasadena Eagles, in fact, initiated a home-and-home series with Hayden Fry's Odessa Bronchos, six hundred miles distant.

On playing fields across the state, patchwork progress came in the form of more knowledgeable coaches, improved officiating, the construction of new stadiums, and better protective equipment. Just before the decade began, plastic headgears had become standard issue, although face masks were still a few years away. Not until the mid-1950s did most players begin wearing a single semi-circled bar. And for good reason—it was not until 1957 that grabbing a face mask carried a penalty. Also slow in coming was two-platoon football. Just as teams began to exploit a 1941 rule that liberalized substitutions, the rules committee decided in 1953 that it was leading to offensive and defensive specialists, and abolished it. While perhaps unwise in the long run, the decision nevertheless assured that the 1950s would be remembered as the last days of the "iron man" who played both ways. Other rules made more sense. In 1952, clipping was defined as any block from behind, and the rules committee had enough sense to restore the fair catch in 1951 after abolishing it prior to the 1950 season.

Football had become more sophisticated, too. Jewell Wallace explained the difference between the war years and the generation that followed. While at San Angelo in 1943, "we won the state championship with only eight plays in our playbook." In just a few years, he continued, coaches had devised completely new formations and adopted complex

San Angelo's Jewell Wallace looks over his starting lineup for the 1944 season. *Photograph courtesy Jewell Wallace.*

terminologies to explain the game's intricacies. Very few teams clung to the old three-yards-and-a-cloud-of dust single wing, favoring instead any number of offenses that opened up the passing game, which produced a steady stream of strong-armed quarterbacks and fleet receivers. Coaches also added more assistants to their staffs and brought junior high coaches into their orbit. And while weight training was still a few years off, some staffs nevertheless developed off-season programs to gain an edge over their competition.

Coaching school, more than anything else, asserted John Hugh Smith, elevated high school football in Texas to another level. "It gave everybody a chance to see rivals in a friendly atmosphere. Coaches from big colleges would come in and talk about their programs," he said. "It was the kind of place," agreed Bum Phillips, "where an average guy, if he applied himself, could learn a lot of football. You could network for jobs, listen to good speakers, and talk football. Then it was small enough where anybody could ask questions."

When coaches returned home, many were fortunate to be equipped with the kinds of facilities that bred success. Field houses constructed of cinder blocks adjoining manicured practice fields became the norm in large schools. Where once the head coaching job had included the extra tasks of janitor, maintenance man, groundskeeper, trainer, and business manager, the typical head coach of the 1950s shared some of the more onerous duties with a growing staff of assistant coaches.

Whether a team resided in a field house or remained within the dank catacombs under rickety bleachers, the practice facility became the staff's home away from home. Few of these spartan quarters enjoyed anything akin to a woman's touch. Normally unadorned except for homemade motivational posters and perhaps the team's name and a crude painting of its mascot on the wall, locker rooms possessed ubiquitous sights, sounds, and smells. In most field houses the windows, situated close to the ceiling, were designed for ventilation, rather than for the view. Covered by wire grates, they discouraged natural lighting as well as thieves and peeping Toms. Along the walls, players' equipment and personal effects bulged out from rows of open lockers. And in every room, the concrete floors, usually smooth and sometimes painted, sloped gently toward drains in the center. The typical facility also housed an equipment room with Dutch doors that allowed managers to dole out towels and supplies. A row of urinals and toilets lay exposed, their only measure of privacy afforded by their placement off to the side of "the showers." Routinely large and open, the tiled shower facility was usually the only room that was finished.

Rounding out the average field house was a coaches' office, always cluttered with papers and cans of game film. Here the staff could smoke cigarettes, relax, pore over film, and talk football. In fact, coaches spent far more waking hours with each other than with their families. Donald Jay remarked: "My kids thought my name was 'bye-bye' because every time they saw me I was heading for the field house."

"There's nothing like the smell of a locker room," insisted Ed Logan. "Every one of them's the same." The air, heavy with sweat-soaked cotton socks, jocks, and jerseys, "got ripe in a hurry . . . we used to wear those moleskin pants that could go a whole season without being washed," Logan recalled. Jerseys, after several practices, would harden into salt-reinforced shells. "And it was a badge of honor to have blood on your clothes," Logan added. The echo of dripping showers, the whir of Laundromat-sized fans, the clattering of metal-tipped cleats, and the ripping of tape complemented the pungent smell, as did youthful voices and the admonitions of coaches who walked briskly through the locker room hollering and clapping their hands to hurry up any laggards.

In some places improvements were slow in coming. Early in his career, O. W. Follis's Lamesa team was still traveling to games in the automobiles of school administrators. Of their equipment, Follis said: "We didn't have much, but what we did have was good." Nevertheless, "the school didn't get tax money for it, and we were always running out of things." Walt Parker, who faced the same situation at Denton, reluctantly scheduled a tough Amarillo squad that he knew his Broncos could not beat. Sure enough, the Sandies won, 70–6, but the gate balanced Denton's budget. Echoing Rodney Kidd's "Waco 72–Georgetown $1,000!" rejoinder following his lopsided loss in 1927, Parker commented: "The only consolation I had was thinking I'm able to pay for some of the bills; our kids would have better uniforms, and things of that order, and that's what I did it for."

Katy coach Gordon Brown surveys equipment, 1959. *Photograph courtesy Gordon Brown.*

Black schools, especially, lagged behind. In 1948, Hallsville's Galilee High did not even have a team until African American community leaders in the East Texas town asked recent Wylie graduate Jap Jones to come and start a program. "In these days there were not too many good professional jobs for us, and I was married and had a child to feed," explained Jones. Having enjoyed success as a college athlete, Jones was a natural for the job. "When I went there to check out the facilities, there was no gym, no football field, and no track." In addition to coaching, Jones became the vice principal. The less prestigious duties of driving the bus and cutting firewood to heat the school also fell to him. The principal, a former athlete himself, helped Jones carve a football field out of a stand of pine trees. "A gracious white man who owned a tractor graded a track for us," Jones said. It took them the early part of the football season to clear the field and burn the stumps. Nevertheless, Galilee High School began its schedule in the middle of October, played three games, and won two.

Rural white schools often fared badly as well. In 1959, for example, twenty-seven-year-old Allen Boren landed his first head coaching job at Bellville, a Class 2-A school between Houston and Austin. As an assistant coach for three years at Wharton and Sweeny, he had been on the short end of twenty-four games in twenty-nine outings. "Luckily, the hurricane in 1958 canceled the Angleton game, or it would have been twenty-five," he said. Bellville Superintendent Otto Longlois offered Boren less money, a morning bus run, and other duties and "I must say, all of his promises were fulfilled," Boren said. Still, a shabby office in an old gymnasium and a three-showerhead dressing room converted from an old army barracks did little to dampen Boren's enthusiasm. As Longlois showed him the nearby junior high, Boren commented that he did not see any shoes, to which the superintendent replied: "Our kids think they can run faster barefooted." Finally they arrived at O'Bryant Field, a three-block walk from the high school's dressing room, where Boren found the conditions somewhat better. He surveyed some solid bleachers with a good capacity, a good fence surrounding the field, and a crow's nest on one light pole from which he could film. "I also noticed that the goats grazing on the field had grown fat . . . but it hit me that there were not any restrooms." Longlois told him: "Oh, Mr. Boren, don't worry about that. All the home folks go to Charlie Deere's house across the street and the visitors soon learn to stop before they get to the game." After some arm-twisting, Boren finally persuaded Longlois to let him build some facilities—literally. Along with "Mark, the maintenance man" he laid the plumbing, poured the cement, and put up cinder blocks and a roof.

When Walt Parker arrived at Denton in 1951, conditions were even worse. Not only did he suffer a disadvantage in enrollment—"we had four hundred students as opposed to a thousand at Highland Park"—but he also had one of the "lousiest" facilities in North Texas. "We had an old stadium with flimsy wooden bleachers, and underneath it was our dressing room; it was dilapidated—small shower space, and cramped. . . . We painted it and fixed it up, but there was no masking the fact that they should have condemned it," Parker said. After practice one day, "one of the kids asked me: 'Coach, what do we have to do to get a new dressing room?'" Without giving it much thought, "I shrugged my shoulders and said: 'I guess it would just have to burn up or something.' . . . That night I got a call about three-thirty in the morning from the fire chief and they said: 'Mr. Parker, you better get down here, your football stadium's on fire.'" Shortly afterward the school district built Denton a new field house.

Pigskin Mania

It did not take much cajoling to convince the school board to construct new facilities. Parker related that Denton, the home of North Texas State, was a college town and composed of "different people" than he had known at previous stops in Palestine and Farmersville. "But their common ground was that everybody was in the stands on Friday night." It was a scene repeated across the state.

Even if the home folks at Lamesa "couldn't bear to watch the slaughter" when the Odessa Bronchos came to town in 1953, they at least remained close to their radios, "just in case." Odessa was heavily favored—"It was the year they went to state," recounted O. W. Follis. Almost always outmanned, Follis suited up only eighteen Golden Tornadoes, yet somehow they managed to get ahead of their more powerful opponent. Follis laughed upon recalling how, when the whistle sounded the end of the second quarter, he headed toward the dressing room and Lamesa's stands were only half filled. "They always opened the gates at halftime and let

Fort Worth fans queue up at the Hotel Texas to buy tickets for the city championship game, 1948. *Photograph courtesy Fort Worth* Star-Telegram *Photograph Collection, Special Collections Division, The University of Texas at Arlington Libraries.*

people in for free, and when the second half began, the stands were full." Lamesa lost the game, but for three years afterward they blacked out radio for home games.

Back then "everybody loved football," declared Bum Phillips. Crane's Dan Anderegg added: "Two hundred people might show up for a practice. . . . Every once in a while, we'd have to ask people to move off of the practice field so the boys would have enough room to work out." Townspeople just expected kids to contribute to the common cause. "Everybody in the school had a part, whether it was the band or the drill team or whatever," continued Anderegg. "A small school like ours needed every kid to compete in order to do well." Bum Phillips remembered that in Nederland during the 1950s, "a good-looking kid, about 160 pounds, walked into the barber shop, and one of the men asked: 'Say, you're not out for football?' The kid said: 'No.' And the man said: 'What's a matter, you yellow?'" As Richland's Hugh Hamm maintained: "If you were a male and had any ability at all, folks just expected you to play."

At Garland, where Homer Johnson consistently turned out winners between 1948 and 1962, "little kids worshiped the players. . . . Most of the town's fathers and uncles had played there, and their children's ambitions were to be Garland Owls. Many times on Friday nights the town would be all but empty when the Owls played away games. . . . To get season tickets in 'Section B' [the fifty-yard line] someone would have to die to create the vacancy."

Johnson claimed that once, before a district-deciding match with Highland Park, he had to stop at the old administration building on his way to Sunday School. "Tickets went on sale on Tuesday morning, and there were already people lined up to buy them." For two weeks in a row, first at the Cotton Bowl, where the Owls played Amarillo Tascosa, then at Rice Stadium versus Galena Park, "Garland outdrew SMU, TCU, Rice, and the Dallas Cowboys," he declared.

Across the state ticket sales for big games brought all other activity to a halt. Brownwood, for example, had beaten arch-rival Breckenridge only once in the school's history before Gordon Wood arrived in 1960. "That first year he beat them and won district," declared Wood assistant Morris Southall. Brownwood was scheduled to host the bi-district game in its rickety old stadium, a facility that held about three thousand people. At the local Weekly-Watson Hardware Store, where tickets went on sale, "the line stretched down the block more than a day before the box office opened. The first guy in line bought sixteen tickets. The second guy in line said: 'I'll take the rest of them.' After that, they had to suspend sales, and then they reopened with the rule that nobody could buy more than four."

"Nothing brings a community together like winning," added James Brewer; "everybody from the bands to the fans feels like a part of the winner." Bull Workman asserted that "back when we had only one high school," the sport brought Arlington together during difficult times. Once, when the city council split over a touchy issue, "football gave them an 'all for one' attitude, and they patched up their differences." Joe Hedrick, who coached many winners during his thirty-nine-year career at Franklin, commented: "We've got a big school district, 413 square miles, and the kids come from half a dozen communities, and football's a very unifying thing." Cotton Miles said, "at White Oak, everybody was a booster." His East Texas town was a big oil producer composed of "the Mobil Camp, Humble Camp, and Tidewater Camp, where people lived in company houses. . . . This, along with the Emmanuel Baptist Church and the school, was the society." Yet football, he asserted, provided the glue that held the town together.

As always, interest in high school football extended into the betting community as well. Corpus Christi High's Chatter Allen, for example, speaking to boosters at a Monday night "quarterback club," fielded a question that left him scratching his head. The inquisitor's motivation quickly became evident. "A member asked me why I did not run on fourth down, leading 13–0, with the ball on the fifty yard line and only two yards to go. Before I could answer the question, the 'big cheese,' Knox Coulton stood up and said: 'Coach, before you answer the question I have a counter question for the member: Did you bet on the game?' 'Yes,' he said, 'I bet on all the games.' 'How many points did you give?' Knox asked him. 'I gave fourteen points,' he said. And Knox told him: 'Well you just gave too damn many points. Sit down and keep your mouth shut.' And he did, for Knox was a powerful man and my friend."

In West Texas, especially, gambling was a popular pastime among men in the oil patches. Zac Henderson recalled that "people would meet at

Katy fans get ready to depart for the Class 1-A state championship game against Sundown, 1959. *Photograph courtesy Gordon Brown.*

the old hotel in downtown Wichita Falls and lay bets before the games." O. W. Follis said that at Breckenridge, gamblers made little effort to conceal their illegal business. His Lamesa squad always stayed at the Birch Hotel when they played there, "and if those gamblers didn't know who you were, they'd just come up and ask you if you wanted to bet on the game. The first time we saw it, we were just flabbergasted." Homer Johnson said the bettors were so bold that while a group of Garland and Breckenridge coaches were visiting the week of their play-off game, they had the gall to approach them for a point spread. "When that big 'ol black Cadillac drove up, the Breckenridge coach turned and ran like someone was going to shoot him. . . . He didn't want any part of it."

The "wildcatting" nature of the oil business bred an easy-come-easy-go attitude, which lent itself to speculation and gambling. Dan Anderegg, who at Crane saw booms flower in 1954 and 1960, believed also that vestiges of frontier life reinforced the practice—that, and oil companies' loose expense accounts. When, in 1955, some gamblers had the audacity to call him "wanting to know the line," Anderegg intimated by his silence that his Golden Cranes were "going to blow the other team away." Indeed, after three quick touchdowns it looked like they would. But then, Anderegg pulled the first team and kept the game close, no doubt causing the gamblers to pay up.

Denver City was another town that enjoyed a big oil boom about that time. In 1960 it fielded a team that crowned its good fortune. Led by the Gravitt brothers—Bert, calling the snaps, and Bill, anchoring the line—the Mustangs advanced to the Class 2-A championship game at San

Coach Allen Boren with Joe Ed Lynn, Bellville, 1960. *Photograph courtesy Texas High School Coaches Association, Austin.*

Angelo against Bellville. Both teams brought perfect 14–0 records, yet Denver City was clearly the favorite. Only two teams in Texas schoolboy history had scored more points. "Their quarterback alone had more points than we had made all year," remarked Bellville coach Allen Boren.

The week of the game two prominent West Texas bettors wearing Stetsons and boots rolled into Bellville and emerged—once again—from "a big black Cadillac," and lingered just long enough to let it be known that they were "giving twenty-one points and covering all bets." At nearby Sealy, contended Boren, the normally busy auction barn sold only about forty animals that week because everybody had tied their money up betting on the game. Inside the barn's vault, in fact, lay six thousand dollars in bets.

When Friday finally came, San Angelo's population swelled when the *Brahma Express* from Bellville pulled into the train station, and more than a hundred private airplanes landed at the airport. Boren remembered hearing a cryptic announcement over the P.A. system, gathering that it was a veiled message "for anyone wanting to put down a bet, that they'd better come behind the stands because it was their last chance." Some more brazen Denver City boosters then walked onto the field, waving wads of cash at the Bellville side of the stadium, which brought many Brahma supporters out of the stands.

As predicted, Denver City won the game. But the 26–21 score was much closer than the West Texas bettors had figured. Late that afternoon the joyous losers returned to Bellville with about fifty thousand dollars. When Allen Boren returned home, he found his wife crying. "She saw how happy everybody was and thought they'd bet against their own team. I had to explain to her how the spread worked," laughed Boren.[2]

Not every place, of course, glowed white hot for autumn's ritual. For a number of reasons some communities never developed a passion for football; in other places the ardor might have lasted until the first loss, or interest might wax and wane with the local eleven's success. Ed Logan remarked that if the team in a good football town lost, "the coach and kids might lay low and not even go into town." In the early 1960s Logan took a job at Haltom, which, he learned, had gained the reputation of being a basketball town. When he bemoaned the football team's low attendance to a Port Arthur Jefferson coach, he was told: "Hell, we have as many come out and watch practice as y'all do for a game."

Individuals, of course, had their own priorities. At Winters in the early 1950s, Bill Ellington coached two great backs who had been "running wild." Just before an important game, a big tackle named Brademeyer told him that he had to take a calf to the Fat Stock Show in Fort Worth. "You can't do that," Ellington told him, "We've got to have you . . . if you don't play this game I don't know what we're going to do with you later on down the road! . . . Next day his daddy—he was about six-five and two-fifty—was standing by the barber shop. I didn't know yet who he was, until another man walked up and said: 'Hello Mr. Brademeyer. What are you talking to the coach about?' Then, Brademeyer said: 'I'm just talking to him to see if he's going to try to whip me or not.'" Ellington quickly assured the man it would be all right if the boy went to the Fat Stock Show. "I wished him well, in fact."

Notwithstanding the vagaries of football-dispassionate people and populaces, Morris Southall declared: "The entire self-perception of a town

PVIL action: Dallas Lincoln vs. Merrill. *Photograph courtesy the Texas-Dallas History and Archives Division, Dallas Public Library.*

could revolve around winning or losing. Whenever Brownwood people traveled, they usually found some way of letting people know where they were from." The herculean effort of stringing together seven state titles in a pigskin-mad state assured they would not have to make many acquaintances before they got a response. Beyond the state's borders, especially, Brownwood citizens "delighted in hearing people exclaim how they had heard of the football team."

For the state's African American population, football provided a means of identity that evoked community pride. The wide-open style of play drew large mixed crowds who delighted in watching both talent and showmanship. While at Galveston Ball, Darrell Tully regularly followed the island's all-black Central High School. When Charlton-Pollard came to town, the stadium would normally be filled. The Beaumont school's linemen, he remarked, "would break the huddle and do somersaults and come up to the line, shaking their hips and pointing a finger at the defense." Some of the visiting team's players wore ribbons on their helmets as well. The referees, Tully continued, carried long red flags in their back pockets that hung almost to the ground, and when they indicated penalties, their calls were often accompanied by exaggerated gestures.

Joe Washington, who coached at Bay City Hilliard from 1951 through 1964, did not countenance such histrionics, yet he contended that "when white coaches went to see black kids play, what they saw were kids in a more natural atmosphere without all the fundamental coaching and teaching and training. They saw kids playing on natural ability. . . . And you saw coaches with limited staffs and limited facilities doing the best job of improvising." Like white coaches of an earlier era, many black coaches had not played football themselves. "A lot of them were agricultural teachers who were equipped with all of the tools that they could get from a liberal arts college. They came and used their best teaching abilities to get those kids to utilize their best athletic abilities." African American coaches, Washington believed, "used a lot of things that a person with a large staff and knowledge of the game didn't use. We appealed to the innermost part in youngsters—discipline, psychology, and the best mental tools we had."

Joe Washington, however, possessed a good background in coaching, which he cultivated by attending clinics. His knowledge helped Hilliard compete against some of the Prairie View Interscholastic League's larger schools. Some other black coaches, such as Elmer Redd, Jap Jones, and Clarence McMichael, were former standout athletes who took advantage of available resources to fashion top teams. After winning a state championship at Arp Industrial in 1952, Redd was invited to head up Lufkin Dunbar's program, where he built a perennial powerhouse. At one point, riding a string of thirty-nine victories, "we felt like we couldn't lose." That night, however, Nacogdoches's E. J. Campbell, under Clarence McMichael, ended the streak 6–0 in a game that produced a graver tragedy for the Lufkin school. The excitement, it was said, was too much for the homecoming queen's father, who died of a heart attack.

Lacking the funds and resources of its UIL counterpart, the PVIL nevertheless fostered intense rivalries between teams that often played each other twice a season, and sometimes again during the play-offs. Houston schools Yates and Wheatley played a Thanksgiving Day classic that dated back to 1927. During the 1961 season, a record crowd of 31,877 turned out to watch the two undefeated teams contend for the District III championship.[3]

On game days, white communities gladly shared their facilities with the PVIL schools for the privilege of watching them play. And to underscore the importance of high school football, many towns and cities began building stadiums worthy of their football squads. Texans with agrarian and blue-collar heritages seldom engaged in debates about balancing their priorities between sports and academics. The needs in many communities seemed obvious because football was perceived as something from which everyone could draw benefits. In an age when the professional game was still in its infancy and college ball was not always easily accessible, few questioned whether such expenditures were appropriate.

In 1955 town fathers in San Angelo recognized the need for a new facility when Bob Harrell returned the Bobcats to their winning ways. The old field was referred to derisively as "Ugh Stadium," Harrell recalled. "In Amarillo there was a stadium similar to the one they wanted in San Angelo. We were up there playing, and after the game we sat down on a motel floor and started drawing up our own plans." Shortly after Harrell returned home, he was out riding with San Angelo Superintendent G. B. Wazdeck. Pointing to an empty spot in a vast vacant lot, the administrator said: "'There's where we need to build our stadium.' . . . He called me back later and said 'I think we can get that land.' There was a lawyer on the school board who was a big football fan and the land was tied up in an estate. So he had it condemned and the school district bought it." The superintendent told Harrell: "'If you can go downtown and raise a hundred thousand dollars, I'll match it; we're due a-hundred-and-fifty from the government for Goodfellow Field.' . . . I went downtown to a friend of mine, and he said: 'Well, I'll get that in two weeks.' He got it in one." When Harrell told Wazdeck about his success, the school board promptly approved the plan. To raise some additional cash, they sold seat options. "Later," asserted Harrell, "this was copied by many communities."

While Brownwood was among the towns that copied Harrell's plan, it did not complete its new stadium until 1972. Morris Southall contended that a decade earlier a bond issue for a new stadium failed only because "it also called for three or four other buildings; it was seven or eight million dollars in all." The old facility, where the Lions fielded five state champions, "was the worst stadium in Texas for a school this size." Naturally, their opponents hated playing there. O. W. Follis recalled that the dressing room was so poor that at halftime he shepherded his Lamesa bunch into a "cubby hole" under the stands. Right before it was time to take the field for the second half, "My quarterback, Jerry Millsap, jumped up and hit his head on the metal frame holding up the bleachers, and it knocked him out. It made us late getting onto the field, and so we had to start the third quarter with a penalty for being late," Follis said.

During Wood's first year at Brownwood, the Lions beat Snyder in a Saturday bi-district game. The Monahans coaches, whose team had won the previous evening, entered the press box and stated that their kids wanted to play at home and had voted to chance the site of the next round on the flip of a coin. Southall remembered Wood pointing to the chewed-up field, "full of sand burrs, and weeds, and everything else." Wood reminded the other coach "that there's a fifty-fifty chance we'll play right out there in that sand, and I'll tell you, we're pretty tough out there." As it turned out, Brownwood won the flip, and they also won the game, 27–16.

Playing conditions at many other schools, of course, were just as slow to improve. Joe Bob Tyler told about teams playing in West Texas stadiums that doubled as rodeo arenas. "They made for some terrible fields," he said. Homer Johnson recalled playing in near darkness at Denison, a railroad town where the stand's undergirding was made of crossties. When all but one strand of lights went out, he met the other coach at midfield, and they decided to go ahead and finish the game. Even with a full complement of lights on playing fields in the smaller classifications, a towering punt could push the ball beyond the range of their overgrown telephone poles. And long into the 1950s, at some of "the little country towns," recalled Bob Barfield, "there weren't many bleachers." He remembered traveling to places where "groups of men running up and down the sidelines" often got in the way. Once, at Alto, he recalled: "I'm on the sidelines and these guys were just running over me, and the sheriff's there, and I'm trying to coach, and I said something to him, and he wouldn't do a thing to them. I just had to put up with it; they did what they wanted to."

"What they wanted to do" was win. Very often crowds could become menacing when the game did not turn out like they had planned. Many places, in fact, gained a reputation for intimidating their opponents. Recalling his biennial trips to Galveston Island while at Pasadena, Bob Barfield asserted: "We always took a bunch of cops with us when we went down there to play them, [and] when you parked your bus over there at the stadium, it was in a very poor spot, and you had to leave someone there with it all the time. Kids would come right out of those old houses there by the stadium and tear up your bus." Some years the Pasadena team could not even sit outside the dressing room before the game because of the abusive fans, who occasionally threw more than insults. "They could get up pretty close to the dressing room, and you'd have to go back inside to keep from getting hit." Afterward, "they'd chase us out of town and throw stuff at our bus." Mercifully, the police customarily followed the Eagles all the way across the bridge and onto the mainland.

Allen Boren's most harrowing experience came after his Bellville team defeated heavily favored Needville with a field goal just as time expired on a play set up by two consecutive offsides calls. As the kicker lined up, Boren commanded his boys to get ready to run. "It was a two-hundred-yard race to the gymnasium with the Needville fans right on our heels," he recalled. Once the team reached safety, someone outside turned off the lights, and in the pitch darkness Boren told his boys: "Get your clothes on, we'll shower when we get back." Somehow the bus driver maneuvered the vehicle through the angry fans, who were hollering that the referees had thrown the game. With the bus pulled up almost flush to the door, the team climbed inside. "Looking back, it was more frightening than threatening," Boren laughed. "But I wouldn't want to do it again."

Just about any coach could tell a similar story. Joe Bob Tyler, coach at Burkburnett, recalled that on the way out of town after a close come-from-behind victory, the Bulldogs' school bus cut through a hill, where "a bunch of folks in pickups" greeted it with rocks and bottles. The projectiles reverberated against the bus, and sent kids scrambling underneath the seats to avoid the shattering windows.

Memories Of A Golden Age

When he moved down the road to Wichita Falls, Tyler landed at a place that had gained a reputation for the surly crowd that ringed its stadium, nicknamed "Coyote Canyon." The nickname itself appropriately suggested bushwackings and last stands. Gene Mayfield declared: "This was the worst place in the world to play." Few coaches whose boys ever sat on the visitors' bench would disagree. Arlington's Bull Workman asserted that the bench "sat right up against the fence, and there was only about three or four yards of sideline." The stands were elevated, perhaps six feet off the ground, remarked Breckenridge's Emory Bellard. Between the fence and the first row, "six or seven guys were allowed to sit behind the opponents' bench on little stepladders. . . . Over the years I got acquainted with those guys." During some games the crowd would grow in both numbers and meanness. Bob Harrell called the rowdy group "barflies," and said, "they'd get up against that fence talking that trash." The stadium site itself was "kind of down in a hole," remarked Coyote assistant coach Zac Henderson, and, he conceded, "there were not many good sports behind that fence." Fellow assistant Bill Carter admitted that the windows in the visitors' dressing room were full of holes, through which fans threw things. "Playing there gave us a two-touchdown advantage," he asserted. Once, when an Arlington assistant coach reached over the fence and grabbed one of the Coyote fans, Bull Workman had to pull him off, telling him: "We've got more than enough to handle out here on the field."

Whether at home or away, during the glory years the Wichita Falls team was always a handful for its opponents. While almost every other team in the state had abandoned the old single wing by the time Joe Golding retired in 1960, he continued to ride the archaic offense to victory. Six times in his twenty-one-year career his Coyotes reached the state championship game. "Getting our kids ready to defense it was tough," said Workman. Spinning backs who hid the ball and pulling linemen who crossed in every direction gave defenses fits. "Most teams really didn't have much of a chance," Workman continued. "Those kids had been running that offense since the fourth grade."

Gene Mayfield, one of the state's most successful coaches, nevertheless regretted that both of his shots at the Coyotes fell ever so short. Before he arrived at the oil field town of Borger in 1958, the Bulldogs had been the doormat of the district. When he took them to the play-offs in his first year, the town went wild with excitement. "They had never won a championship," he commented, and when a coin flip gave Borger the home field advantage for its bi-district game with Wichita Falls, a very rowdy line immediately developed outside the ticket booth. "Fistfights and such broke out because people were cutting in line," Mayfield recalled. A standing-room-only crowd went home disappointed in a 12–6 loss, but was nevertheless proud of closely battling a Coyote squad that eventually went all the way and buried Pasadena 48–6 in the state final. In 1961, Mayfield's Bulldogs again narrowly lost the bi-district game to Golding's bunch, this time as the visiting team. Mayfield lamented: "I always wanted to go back to 'The Canyon' and win, but didn't ever get the chance."

It was a sentiment that many coaches shared, both white and black. Just as Joe Golding's Coyotes sent so many opponents home disappointed, so

Wichita Falls coach Joe Golding kicks back following his Coyotes' 14–13 victory over Austin High for the 1949 Class 2-A state title. *Photograph courtesy Fort Worth* Star Telegram *Photograph Collection, Special Collections Division, The University of Texas at Arlington Libraries.*

too did Irving Garnett, at Wichita Falls's "other school," Booker T. Washington. The black team always seemed to be contending for the Prairie View Interscholastic League's crown. In 1966, however, Elmer Redd became one of the few opposing coaches who emerged from Wichita Falls victorious. His Lufkin Dunbar team traveled there to play the 1966 PVIL state championship game on a day when a howling blue norther dropped the temperature to seventeen degrees. The stands nevertheless filled up; about half of the fans were white, Redd recalled. The Wichita Falls team had counted on the weather being an ally, but just before the game, Redd told his team: "If they can stay out here a lifetime, we can stand it for two-and-a-half hours!"

"Booker T.," Redd recalled, had a tremendous team that featured "Reginald Robinson and Roosevelt Fly and all that crew." Several of them, he contended, ran "better than ten-flat hundreds." As usual, the hecklers were crowded right up against the fence, behind Dunbar's bench. "They were telling us to go back to East Texas, that we couldn't play . . . and they just hounded us to death." But Redd got the last laugh. All week long he had stressed a ball control strategy that "would run the clock off." With just over seven minutes left in the game and Dunbar ahead, the East Texans took over the ball. Once the game was safely in the bag, Redd turned around and gave the men behind the fence "some of their own medicine. And when the game was over, there wasn't a single one of them back there."

Texas's golden age of high school football produced countless teams whose moments of glory grew to legendary proportions in the memories of their followers, some of which enjoyed a longer run than others. At Abilene, for example, Chuck Moser led his storied Eagles to a short-lived national record, winning forty-nine consecutive games—three of them state championship contests. Powerhouses that aroused fear and envy in their opponents emerged in every section of the state and in every classification, yet few won so consistently that others in their districts surrendered their dreams of making the play-offs as each season approached. Rivalries flowered, engendering participation among schoolboys and the rabid devotion of fans. Fantastic upsets occurred just often enough that even the most lopsided matches were able to evoke faint hopes that the local team would defy all odds and win the big game.

It happened to Kilgore in 1959, when the Bulldogs traveled to Nacogdoches and beat a heavily favored Dragon team 14–13. Bob Cashion, then a young Kilgore assistant coach, recalled: "Our linemen averaged 152 pounds from end-to-end, and they got pushed around all night, but they hung in there, and about in the middle of the fourth quarter the people began to realize that we might win, and there was this anticipation that you just can't describe." When Nacogdoches rallied and marched almost the length of the field, it appeared that the Bulldogs' luck had run out. A valiant last stand, however, stopped the Dragons at the Kilgore fifteen-yard line, and forced Nacogdoches to try a field goal. "There was less than thirty seconds left, and from our sideline it was impossible to see whether it was good or not. When the referees signaled that it was wide left, the Kilgore people just went crazy," Cashion recalled. "There must have been around fifteen hundred or two thousand Kilgore fans on the field, and they carried the coaches and players around the field on their shoulders. You know, Kilgore was an oil-rich town, but that night everybody became one, no matter how rich or poor. Probably the most unusual sight I ever saw was our superintendent, Mr. Newsome, and Mr. Adams, the custodian, hugging each other and jumping up and down like ten-year-olds, just laughing and yelling."

No team and community manifested the state's football culture more spectacularly than Breckenridge, which reached the Class 3-A finals five times in the 1950s and won all but one, which they tied. Until Gordon Wood's Brownwood Lions eclipsed them in 1960, the Buckaroos were the scourge of West Texas.

Breckenridge's winning tradition reached back to the Oil Belt era. Joe Kerbel, who coached there between 1952 and 1954, related that after some long-forgotten early-day contest the school superintendent had written an article saying their kids had "played like Buckaroos, and the name stuck." In 1929 Pete Shotwell took the team to the finals, where the Buckaroos tied Port Arthur 0–0 in a foot of snow in Waco. Very early Breckenridge had developed a tradition of playing some of the largest schools in West Central Texas. As the oil boom faded, Breckenridge's population declined while the other towns continued to grow, yet the

Breckenridge coaches Emory Bellard and Murry Holdich. *Photograph courtesy Texas High School Coaches Association, Austin.*

schools still maintained their rivalries. Of the days when he was coach, Kerbel said: "Wichita Falls at that time, I think, had about a hundred thousand people, and we had six thousand people."[4] The Coyotes beat the Buckaroos 13–0 his first year, but it was the only game his team lost on a schedule that also included the comparative metopolises of Big Spring, San Angelo, and Abilene. The next two years Breckenridge avenged the loss to Wichita Falls, 13–7 and 41–13.

Breckenridge was one of the few teams to emerge victorious from Coyote Canyon. In 1958, in fact, one of those wins represented the only blemish on the Coyote's Class 4-A championship season. The Buckaroos claimed the Class 3-A crown that year. Emory Bellard, the winning coach, remarked: "We played in Wichita Falls all five years while I was there; they won two, we won two, and we tied one. . . . In all my years of coaching . . . those were the toughest, most physical games I ever saw, two schools that would just mortally get after one another."[5] Bellard said when his team got off the bus, "I'd tell my players: 'Don't you say one word until we get into that dressing room.' Because you'd have to walk the length of the stadium underneath the stands. Man, people lined up there, and, well, they'd be talking rather harshly," he smiled. The fourteen thousand or so people who turned out for each of those contests witnessed some of the best high school ball Texas had to offer. "Every time we played them," said Bellard, "we went home with cleat marks on our hairline."[6]

The Buckaroos' mystique ran deep. Dressed head to foot in green—green helmets, green jerseys, green pants—their appearance gave them "a tremendous psychological advantage," said Kerbel. "Everybody was afraid of the green suits in those days. You just run on the field in those green suits and people dropped dead. They didn't believe they could defeat them. Some of those teams hadn't beaten them in forty years." To enhance their image, none of the boys on the sidelines ever sat down during a game, and nobody in the stands ever saw a Buckaroo take so much as a swallow of water while they were on the field.

Like Masonic Home of an earlier generation, the Buckaroos' Davidic reputation left larger opponents consternated, and every team they played was larger. Several times their enrollment would have relegated them to Class 2-A had fellow district members not "voted them up." Cooper Robbins, who preceded Kerbel, said that each year the team normally suited up only about "twenty-three or twenty-four players. . . . We were lucky if we had fifteen or sixteen boys that we could play, but they stayed in such fine shape and trained so well that they felt like a game was a holiday. . . . Other teams would come for a state championship game with maybe sixty-five boys suited up and look across the field and see only nineteen or twenty Buckaroos. . . . We only had a total of 375 students at school . . . counting girls . . . and we were playing against schools very often with fifteen hundred students." When Emory Bellard held the reins between 1955 and 1959, Breckenridge remained the smallest 3-A school in Texas—"in by half a student" every year, he laughed.

"The town just lived their football, and as a result the boys did, too," said Cooper Robbins, the Buckaroos' coach between 1945 and 1951. Emory Bellard remarked: "You could drive around town, and you might not see many basketball hoops, but on every vacant lot, there would be a touch football game going on. Some of the players were men in their forties . . . it wasn't a game, it was their way of life."[7] Joe Kerbel declared that even during the summer adults seemed oblivious to the baseball games—even while they were watching them. "Men would approach the boys and ask them how much they were weighing and if they'd been running and working out and about the games that would come up the next year. 'How much do you weigh?' 'How tall are you?' 'You're going to be playing tackle this coming year, so you better be ready, now; you're going to have to run a lot.'" During the season, continued Robbins, "it was three nights of football a week." On Wednesdays the coaching staff refereed elementary school games; the junior high and B-team played on Thursdays; and each Friday, when Breckenridge was host, Kerbel commented, townspeople would get together for meals and cocktails before the game. Then, said Robbins: "About six or seven o'clock on football night, the band would march down through town, and everybody would just close up and follow the band to the football stadium." Afterward folks would sit around and talk football, sometimes until the wee hours of the morning. After the occasional loss, remarked Robbins, the armchair "quarterbacks would meet down at the drugstore on Saturday morning and decide what was wrong, ya' know, and that would be the end of it. By Tuesday they'd be back on the bandwagon, ready to go."

Legions of Breckenridge fans followed the team everywhere it played. "Even at scrimmages they would have a pretty good crowd," said Joe Kerbel. Some of the town's oil and gas elite would fly to distant games in their Cessnas and Beechcrafts. Those who could not attend out-of-town contests went to the drive-in theater, where the games were broadcast, and pent-up fans would get out of their cars and lead yells, Kerbel recalled.

Breckenridge won consistently in large part because the school hired coaches who knew what they were doing. When Cooper Robbins landed there, he found "a small town, completely different from what I'd been used to. But they made it so attractive that I did accept the job and stayed there in Breckenridge for seven years." His was a long tenure. Not many Buckaroo coaches lasted for more than a few seasons, because others recognized their talent and lured them away with more lucrative offers. Among them was charter Hall of Honor coach Pete Shotwell, who won championships in Longview and Abilene after he left Breckenridge. Eck Curtis, who followed later, went on to the University of Texas in 1945. The three coaches who succeeded him—Joe Kerbel, Cooper Robbins, and Emory Bellard—remained for a total of fifteen years, and all won state championships. Bellard, who developed an early version of the wishbone formation while at Breckenridge, went on to perfect the offense at the University of Texas; later, Kerbel briefly made West Texas State a powerhouse.

Coaching and High School Football Reach Maturity

Other communities besides Breckenridge also began to recognize that they could not rely solely on talent to field a competitive team. The wellspring of consistent success, they came to understand, flowed from savvy coaching. "I think Texas high school football is as good as there is," said Emory Bellard, in part, "because the coaches are very professional. They spend a lot of time developing themselves and having a good understanding of the game." As town fathers across Texas came to appreciate that fact, the state's most successful strategists found communities beckoning them with promises of more money and better conditions. Wichita Falls, for example, whom Tugboat Jones shut down with an obviously inferior Electra squad in 1943, made their conqueror head coach the very next year. The raise was only two hundred dollars—"The car wash downtown was making more money than we were"—yet the support of townspeople, a larger school, and a superior working environment made the decision to move an easy one. Later, Midland came calling, this time with a salary to match. Not long after building a winner there, Jones accepted an even sweeter offer from Highland Park, where he rewarded boosters by producing a state championship in 1957.

John Reddell asserted that giving priority to football programs assured the growth and success of high school ball in Texas. After receiving some on-the-job training as a University of Oklahoma assistant his senior year in college, he found a head coaching position at DeKalb, in Northeast Texas. After a couple of seasons he returned to his home state for a job at Classen, an Oklahoma City suburb. "I thought it would be a good career move," he stated. "Classen had the second largest enrollment in the state and had good athletes." Reddell went 9–2 his first year, but the Classen job brought with it a full teaching load, something that DeKalb had not asked of him. "I also took a nine-hundred-dollar pay cut." As soon as he could, Reddell crossed the Red River once more—this time for good.

John Reddell recognized something that many other coaches already took pride in: Football in Texas had grown into a unique institution. Compared to any other place, "it was as different as night and day," Reddell declared. When Palo Duro High School opened in Amarillo in 1955, he became its first head coach and enjoyed a $6,500 annual salary—almost three thousand dollars more than Classen had paid him. He found the competition that faced his Class 3-A Palo Duro Dons "better than anything in Oklahoma." In fact, his only win that first season came against Enid, a team from the Sooner State.

Zac Henderson, who spent part of his childhood in Healdton, Oklahoma before he moved across the river, remarked: "Sports were not that big there; but, when we moved to Quanah, it was." In the mid-1950s, after Henderson began coaching, he moved to Jena, Louisiana, a town that had never enjoyed a district champion. In his three seasons there, he earned a district crown every year. In retrospect, Henderson asserted that he was able to win in Louisiana because his coaching background in Texas gave him an edge over his opponents.

Joe Kerbel asserted that the Texans' brand of football was superior because everyone—from the smallest children to the adults—took the sport so seriously. Before beginning his reign at Breckenridge, Kerbel had coached at the Oklahoma oil town of Bartlesville, home of Phillips Petroleum, where he produced some outstanding teams, in part, he said, because the town possessed the typical pool of roughnecks' sons. But the company was always transferring its employees, which caused the team occasionally to lose some of its best players. At Bartlesville it was business first.

In contrast, fans at the company's namesake town in the Texas Panhandle made certain that the talent pipeline did not leak. In fact, some of Phillips's best players had been born in Bartlesville. Boosters also hedged their bets by assuring that their boys would be well coached. For eighteen seasons, from 1939 to 1956, Chesty Walker—"The Grey Fox"—made the town's name synonymous with championship football. Walker ended his career at the University of Washington, where he helped lead the Huskies to two Rose Bowls.

Texan Frank Pulattie, who spent two seasons at Lincoln High School near San Francisco, California, compared football in the two big states. He found that the scant pay added to coaches' salaries in California did little to breed commitment. "I had a good assistant quit, who said: 'Coach, I'd like to work with you, but I can make more money in my off time bottle hunting.' . . . It was a nine-to-five job with a lot of them. In Texas we just outworked these other guys." But coaching wasn't the only difference. Upon arriving at Lincoln, Pulattie checked his equipment. When he opened a big cabinet and saw it lined with Voit rubber balls, he turned to a player and asked: "What are we doing in the athletic department with these P.E. balls?" The boy replied: "That's what we play with, coach." Pulattie remarked that "there were a lot of little things that I had to get adjusted to." Before games, for example, they had to wait for the junior varsity to play, which made many of the fans flag before the main event ever began. And, Pulattie asserted: "Once the season was over, it was over. Period. They didn't play to a state championship. Can you imagine that in Texas?"

Franklin's Joe Hedrick recalled that former Texas A&M coach Ray George also had coached in California. "He said that the talent was just coming out the cars, but [football] wasn't important at all. It was just sort of like P.E. class. It was played in the afternoon. People weren't especially interested in it. Maybe that's the way it should be handled, I don't know—but Ray didn't think so," Hedrick laughed.

Bailey Marshall, former coach and head of the University Interscholastic League, pointed out that one of the reasons high school football became so important in Texas was that it developed when the state was overwhelmingly rural. Like a tie that binds, the sport lashed the different regions together with a statewide play-off system and helped Texans overcome the vast distances that separated them. Eddie Joseph, Marshall's counterpart at the Texas High School Coaches Association, added that "in no other state was it as important as early as it was here." Very often, "it was the only game in town, and people scheduled their social events around it, like chicken cookouts and melon festivals." Clarence McMichael underscored Joseph's remark by proclaiming: "In Texas, a man first wants a son, and then he wants to see him in a uniform."

"Football is an activity," Bailey Marshall continued, "where not only do you have your football players, you have your cheerleaders, you have your drill teams, you have your bands—you have all these youngsters that were actively involved. And that also involved all those parents." He also believed that football became a sophisticated endeavor because competition "bumped us up to a higher level. Our communities have supported good programs and wanted good teams and good coaches." Trumpeting his own organization, Marshall also noted that the UIL responded to changing times by adopting and enforcing rules regarding age, eligibility, and grades to fit new conditions.

In the mid 1960s, Texas proved the superiority of its football culture to the nation. Over a period of four years, 1964–1967, Texas sent all-star teams to Hershey, Pennsylvania, where University of Texas-ex and NFL Hall-of-Famer Bobby Layne coached them in what was called the "Big 33," after the thirty-three graduating high school seniors that each state fielded. Prior to the short-lived series, Pennsylvania had soundly defeated some adjoining states in similar match-ups. No team, in fact, had ever scored a touchdown against the brutish sons of Pennsylvania's coal mining and steel mill towns, a feat that had stirred Pennsylvanians to proclaim that their players were the best in the land. Several other states protested, but none more loudly nor indignantly than Texas. The Hershey Foundation, sponsor of Pennsylvania's interstate all-star games, felt that the prideful Texans would make ideal opponents.[8]

The first year the Keystone State won the contest, 12–6, prompting *Sports Illustrated* to announce that the "extraordinary bone bruiser" had indeed erased any doubts about who possessed the toughest teenagers in the land.[9] What the gloating fans in Hershey did not learn until later was that back in Fort Worth more prominent Texas schoolboys, such as Warren McVea, Linus Baer, and Ronnie Pipes, had played the following evening in Texas's annual North-South game.

The Texas High School Coaches Association had forbidden its North-South players to participate in any other all-star game prior to its own contest. Yet the sting of losing the Big 33 provoked the THSCA to make sure that any subsequent match-ups with the Pennsylvanians would fall after the intrastate game. The Northerners' coach, Syracuse's Lefty James, discounted "as a lot of baloney" the rumblings that he had faced a "second string squad" in that first contest. In 1965, however, the Lone Star State exacted revenge, 26–10. *Sports Illustrated* again ran an article, this time titled "Texas Teeners Strike Back," in which correspondent John Underwood described vividly how the visiting all-stars outmatched their opponents. The linemen drove the "heavier Pennsylvanians back a yard before they could react," he noted, and the Northerners' defensive backs moved "as if they were wearing Army boots."[10]

Twice more Texas won by wide margins—34–2 in 1966, and 45–14 in 1967, which forced the Pennsylvanians to cry "calf rope." Future Grapevine High School coach Gary Mullins, who quarterbacked the last

The 1965 Big 33 squad visits with U.S. Congressman Jack Brooks of Texas on the steps of the U.S. Capitol. *Photograph courtesy Fred Cervelli.*

all-star team to victory, commented that by 1967 a tradition was beginning to develop. He said fellow Texans not only expected them to win, but to "dominate" as well. "This was an extension," he declared, "of how we played Texas football." After that last drubbing, the series fell apart. First, the Hershey Foundation balked at paying some players' medical and dental claims, and then bristled when a Texas attorney threatened to sue. They also refused to entertain overtures for a home-and-home series, or to consider giving Texas a share in the charity's proceeds. The final straw came when the foundation fired Texas director Fred Cervelli, sports editor of the Orange *Leader*. The ensuing discord gave the Pennsylvanians an excuse to back out and still save face.

Even after Texas's iron-man era had passed, many observers believed that the state continued to produce the best programs in the nation. Many coaches pointed to the rosters of top college teams of the present day, noting that it would be difficult to find one that did not possess at least a Texan or two. Donald Jay insisted that "Texas football is the envy of the country. Nobody is as organized, none have as good off-season programs, none have the fan interest. Texas has the largest clinic and the largest membership of any high school coaches' association in the United

States. Ohio has several clinics and California has regional ones, but none have the one big one that we do."

Walt Parker remarked: "Having traveled all over the United States with the National Football League, I've met up with players that played in every state in the union. They generally agree that Texas is the best. Texas has the most organized setup of any state in the union. They go to the state championship in every division; most states don't do that."

Said Emory Bellard: "Now, there's a lot of states that have great football players and some great teams. I just don't think they have as many great teams as does Texas. . . . You can go over into Louisiana and get some teams that can play with the good teams in Texas. But there's a bunch of teams over there that can't play with them." Bum Phillips proclaimed: "Texas high school football is the very best football of all. And I've been around enough to say that."[11]

Many no doubt would challenge whether Texas indeed continues to produce the best football in the land. What cannot be disputed, however, is that the state's football tradition was built on wide participation and a dedicated following at all levels. Indeed, part of the identity that Texas projects to the rest of the nation rests on the peculiar attraction that has so long compelled men and women across the Lone Star State to seek the lights of local stadiums on autumn Friday evenings.

Chapter 7

A Glorious and Bittersweet Career: Coaching in the Golden Age

ootball, as an occupation, always had defined coaches. The profession, in fact, was not very old when something of a stereotype emerged that superficially reflected all the gruff, manly ways of the coaches' character. To that length the image was largely accurate. Theirs was a rough sport, one that required its participants to be rugged and aggressive, and the man at the top had to provide a fitting example. But certainly, coaches were not without feelings. The code of masculinity nevertheless demanded that they stop short of putting their emotions on display—at least those that betrayed weakness, pain, disappointment, and, sometimes, even mercy. At the same time, the coaches' devotion to shaping young manhood coincided with the child-centered society that had emerged in the generation following World War II. Coaches reinforced such prevailing ideas as obeying authority, following rules, and conforming to social expectations, yet they did so by shepherding their charges the same way they had been coached. In Texas, at least, coaches drew upon values that reflected an older, bygone era. And even if the next Great Depression or World War III never came around, their boys would still be prepared to "root hog or die."

Making Men out of Boys

Wherever coaches and players gathered, life's lessons—at least those that mattered to the man who blew the whistle—were being taught. Back then, declared Bull Workman: "Kids came into the program already knowing what was expected of them. . . . The players, the community, the family, and the coaches were all on the same channel." And coaches, insisted Bill Ellington, used their own experience as a model. A child of the Dust Bowl and a World War II veteran, he stated: "When we got out of the army, we were used to strong discipline. If you were told to do something, you didn't question it, you did it. As all that group started coaching, they followed up."

Walt Parker asserted that coaches employed "the same system that's used at West Point and the Air Force Academy and the officers' training school when I went through. You did everything in the world to them, and you didn't allow them to respond; they have to do what they're told to do, and then, when the time comes to produce, they can produce." He believed that a football player "might not like it while he's running laps and doing the various drills and so forth, but later on they can see that you were only trying to get them to perform more capably than they thought they could."

While coaching at Edna, Allen Boren tried to impress that lesson on tackle Calvin Hunt, who later played for the Philadelphia Eagles. Hunt was having trouble performing a technique that required some finesse, and in his frustration, he blurted out: "This just ain't gonna work!" Grabbing the young giant under the shoulder pads, Boren started shaking him, and hollered: "Son, if I point at a chicken and say it dips snuff, you'd better look under his wing!" That Friday night, the coach said, Hunt's block sprung the play for a seventy-yard gain, and as the big young tackle passed the bench he looked over at Boren and yelled: "Coach! That chicken's dippin' snuff!"

Any number of coaches related that many times former players would come back and tell them that all the drudgery and hard work had, in retrospect, provided a positive life experience. "After they get through it," remarked Bill Patrick, "they realize that all we were asking them to do, was what was right and what was good for them."

Nevertheless, said Ace Prescott, some kids were receptive to the message, and others were not. Prescott, who in the 1950s coached under an old Hardin-Simmons roommate for six years at Falfurrias, admitted that he was never quite able to identify why. "You couldn't run a kid off at Falfurrias. You might take his uniform up, and the next day he'd bribe the manager, and he'd be back out there at calisthenics." When Prescott took over the reins at nearby Raymondville, he found that "they just didn't want to play. . . . We were the same size school, and we had thirty-three out and [Falfurrias] had ninety-some-odd. I don't know . . . just different type people."

Chatter Allen learned that no amount of smoke and mirrors and jawboning would bear fruit if the kids themselves did not want to produce. In 1949 he became head coach of the Beaumont Royal Purple, which had lost twenty-three games in a row before he arrived. "The first thing I set out to do was to get everyone to think positive—'We can win, we are going to win.' I had most everyone convinced—even myself—because I had scheduled the first home game with Jefferson Davis." The Houston team had not only gone winless the previous season, but also had failed to score even a single touchdown. "At the half they had us down 26–0," Allen deadpanned. "Unfortunately, the band director prepared a halftime show called 'The Old Way, the New Way, the Winning Way,' and there we were getting the hell beat out of us . . . it was most embarrassing."

In the next game Beaumont faced Texas City, a team that featured the soon-to-be Baylor star "Long Gone" Dupree. "They beat the stuffings out of us," said Allen. In the next game "Baytown whipped us soundly." Before each of the three losses, continued Allen, "I gave my best pregame pep talk and a 'fire and fight' halftime talk, but to no avail." With Lufkin, the season's toughest opponent, coming up, he thought: "How do you motivate a team that has had the stuffings beaten out of them three times in a row? I knew my team was not that bad; they just needed to relax and forget the pressure. So, I took an entirely different approach. I told them that football was a fun game: 'So go out and play the game and enjoy yourself. And, if it ceases to be fun, then come to the sideline, and I will send in a replacement. If you win, fine; if you lose, it's not the end of the world. Now get out there and have fun.'" To Allen's surprise, the Royal Purple "played a flawless game and won by a wide margin." They also went on to win the next five games "having fun," only to fall short of the district championship in the final game of the season.

Most coaches, however, professed that satisfaction, rather than fun, was more enduring. And such an end, they believed, could only come through hard work and dedication. During Chuck Moser's string of forty-nine consecutive victories in the 1950s, assistant coach Ray Overton recalled him saying: "There are three things required for a state championship: you've got to be physically tough, you've got to be mentally tough, and you've got to have poise."

Football tested those qualities like few other endeavors by giving boys a chance to see what they were made of, and how far they could push themselves. Longtime East Texas-area coach Maurice Cook declared: "Football is special to me. I think it teaches a lot of things that some other sports don't. I've always told my players football is a game that brings you face-to-face with your courage factor. 'You're going to get to know yourself, son, because you're going to see what you do when you're scared.' When you line up against a guy that outweighs you by twenty, or thirty, or forty pounds, you're going to know in your heart—'What do I do when I'm scared?'" That, he proclaimed, was a lesson in character building that made the drudgery of football worthwhile.

In this period of prolonged prosperity and federally funded social safety nets, coaches believed that the manly shibboleth of surviving football could cultivate the same kinds of inner qualities that day-to-day life had at one time forced upon them. Stocky Lamberson, from the town of Panhandle, commented: "We've never been very large. I can count the players we've had over two hundred pounds on one hand. So over a period of time we've developed this thing about being ornery and mean. Some of these boys have gotten by on that mental toughness."[1] Allen Boren added: "So many kids grow up today and never even have a bloody nose. Once you've been stung, you realize it's not all that bad."

Jack Whitley, at Masonic Home in the late 1940s and early 1950s, took that kind of mental toughness for granted. The Mighty Mites, he said, had not changed much since he had played on the team himself. Whitley recalled the "boot tough" attitude of one player in particular, Quin Eudy, who later followed him into the coaching profession. As they were getting ready to play, the boy told Whitley that he had developed a boil on his shoulder, so the coach fashioned a "doughnut" to cover it, and then told him: "'Now, Eudy, hit somebody right at the first of the game real hard, and that'll get that core out.' And boy, he popped one, and he came running over to the sideline, and he said: 'I think I got it.' And we went into the dressing room, and cleaned him up, and put him back in. Ol' Eudy never even winced."

No matter what adversities coaches themselves had faced, they all seemed to be able to point to a particular athlete who taught them something about overcoming personal limitations. For Bum Phillips it was Leon Fuller. When the 110-pound freshman came out for the team at Nederland, the equipment manager had trouble finding pads small enough for him, yet the boy started all four years. Once, during a track meet, Phillips recalled, Fuller had lost the 440-yard run to future Detroit Lion Billy Pavliska "by fifteen yards." But, when it came time for the final event, the mile relay, the district championship was on the line. "Leon is anchor, and Billy Pavliska is anchor, and whoever wins, wins the track meet," Phillips remarked. Receiving the baton "fifteen yards behind Pavliska, Fuller caught him on the last curve, and "coming toward home, shoulder-to-shoulder, Leon beat him by about six inches at the finish line. That's the kind of kid he was."

Yet, when it came time for college, no one even bothered to look at the 135-pound Nederland graduate, so Phillips convinced Floyd Wagstaff at Tyler Junior College to give him a scholarship, and Fuller promptly became the team's most valuable player. A couple of years later, when Bear Bryant called from Alabama to ask Phillips if he knew any good junior college talent, he told him: "I only know one guy that I guarantee can help you." Bryant then told Phillips: "Well tell him he's got a scholarship, and put him on the bus." When Fuller arrived, the Alabama coach probably thought Phillips was playing a joke on him. Yet during his first year Fuller made the all-Southeast Conference team at safety, and during his senior year he made the all-star team on both offense and defense and served as team captain.

The fitting crowns of recognition that belong to winners, however, were not always necessary to prove that individuals, or even entire teams, had achieved something worthwhile. Bailey Marshall, like many coaches, believed that even in losing, the fruits of hard work and dedication paid off. In the mid-1950s, at a time when his White Oak team was struggling, the Roughnecks faced a New London squad that was winning games by forty- and fifty-point margins. The handicap of losing his best running back and linebacker to a season-ending injury did not improve his prospects. "Before this, I never went into a game thinking we didn't have a chance to win," Marshall admitted. Yet when he entered the dressing room right before kickoff, "I saw all these kids with tears in their eyes, all tensed up, and they were so emotional. And I realized that they thought they could still win."

In the first half the Roughnecks never even allowed New London to cross the fifty-yard line. In the second half, however, White Oak lost the runner who had filled in for their star, and after some turnovers they lost 6–0. Still, "they fought to the bitter end and gave it all they had." Marshall said that when his team walked off the field, they did so unashamed, with their heads high. "It was a very maturing experience."

A manly attitude went hand-in-hand with the qualities that football imparted. Bill Hartley remarked: "If you got hurt out there on the field, don't you crawl back to the huddle, you walk back to the huddle, and then you can get down; but don't you let that guy know that he got the best of you. That sounds kind of brutal, but there are times when you get to feeling sorry for yourself, and you're tired, and you want to give in, but you've got to keep going." Against Navasota in 1954, he said, "we had a little ol' five-foot-eight, 185-pound fireplug for a fullback, and he broke through the line at full speed," where Navasota's safety met him head-on. "They butted like two rams and fell back on their butts," Hartley recalled. Then, he said, "they just got up and pranced off." Hartley knew that both of them must have felt like falling into a sobbing fit, yet "they had both been taught the same way—you don't show pain."

An anecdote that Darrell Tully told about himself illustrated how deeply ingrained that attitude was. Tully had developed a drill where a coach would stand on the sidelines with an air dummy and try to knock the running backs out of bounds. The players, in turn, would have to lower their shoulders and deliver a hard blow to remain on the field. "So I'm watching my backfield coach Joe Taylor, and I didn't think he was hitting the kids hard enough, so I said: 'Let me have that dummy.' And it just happened that the biggest back we had was the next one up; and, of course, when I got that dummy, he knew I was going to try and lay him out of bounds. How he got past that air dummy, I'll never know, but somehow he got up under that thing and hit me in the chest and knocked me clear over backwards, and I made a complete somersault. Thank goodness, about that time, the whistle blew to change drills, and boy, my chest was hurting. But I jumped up and said: 'All right, that's the way to do it, now go to the next drill!' I didn't tell the coaches, and I surely didn't tell the kids, but when the workout was over, I got away from the field house and went straight over to our athletic doctor. I swore him to secrecy, and he X-rayed it, and sure enough, it was a partially collapsed lung. I wouldn't let him tell anybody about it, and it was years before I ever let anybody even know."

Being tough, however, did not mean that coaches were insensitive. Chatter Allen recalled a boy named Giese, the son of a good friend. "I wanted very much to make a football player out of him, but he was not a 'hitter,' he was a 'grabber.'" When Allen put Giese on the punting team, he noticed that most of the time the boy "would fall down and try to grab the ball carrier's foot or just stick out an arm or even overrun the punt returner—anything to keep from hitting." Finally Allen confronted him: "What's wrong with you?" he asked; to which the boy replied: "Coach, my problem is that I just don't have no guts." Right there, Allen said: "I told him that he didn't have any business playing football, but because of his love for the game and being so honest, I made him 'team manager,' and he made a good one. He went on to college and became a team manager there and earned a scholarship."

And neither did being tough mean that coaches had to remain devoid of humor and emotion. Leon Vinyard, for example, performed a "victory dance" he had developed from the tap lessons he took as a boy. At Terrell pep rallies, students would chant: "Victory dance! victory dance!" until Vinyard took center stage. "Sometimes, I'd spice it up with the Charleston," he laughed. The exhibition did nothing to lessen the team's respect for him. After Terrell won the 1957 state championship game the boys could not bring themselves to throw him into the shower, said Vinyard, because "they didn't have the grit."

In ten seasons at Terrell, Vinyard's players had come to know him as a serious-minded taskmaster on the practice field. And, like most coaches, if his motivational messages seemed somewhat evangelical, it was not by accident. Coaches clung to the things that inspired them, and football—in its broadest dimensions—had always seemed something akin to the "fire and brimstone" on which they had grown up. In most programs, coaches led their players in prayer before every game, and, after every game, they would pray again—often huddled with their opponents in the middle of the field. Coaches encouraged their boys to be active churchgoers and sponsored clubs, such as the Fellowship of Christian Athletes, that grounded them more closely to Christianity. In 1963, in fact, the congregation at Charles Qualls's McKinney church sent him to Japan and Taiwan to "witness" for the "New Life" movement. Talking through an interpreter, he told schoolchildren there about his Christian values, and how they had affected his life. The kids, he said, "would sit on the gym floor, and you could hear a pin drop. Everywhere we went, people told us how pleased they were."

Religious faith, coaches insisted, bolstered the dogged persistence that football required. Carlos Berry recalled an example in Tommy McClure, a 165-pound lineman who played for him at Henrietta. The boy was certainly serious about football. Before games, Berry remarked, "I knew we were ready whenever I noticed McClure 'dry heaving.'" Very late in a contest against Bowie, a team they had not defeated in several years, Henrietta found itself behind by less than a touchdown with a last chance to block a Bowie punt. As the rest of the Bearcat defense huddled, Berry saw McClure standing off to one side. Sure enough, the coach said, when his team lined up to rush the punter, "we blocked it and ran it back for a touchdown." Later, when he quizzed McClure, the boy told him that he was "making a deal with the Lord. He said that if they won, he would rededicate his life." That Sunday, he made good on his word. Although McClure was a Methodist, most of the other boys on the team were

Baptists. So it was at the First Baptist Church that McClure walked up the aisle, followed first by the player who blocked the punt—a boy whose father owned the liquor store—then many others. "I really believe that it was Tommy McClure, and not that play, that gave us the spark to go on and have a successful season," Berry concluded.

There was something about having grown up on old-time religion and red beans and black-eyed peas and of having to face the prospect of going off to war that evoked in coaches a singular view of their larger purpose. Most of them felt that developing maturity in their players was an incumbent responsibility. Qualities such as mercy and forgiveness and lessons such as the Golden Rule were things that society once taught naturally, they believed. What they had to instill was the kind of mental toughness that was necessary to succeed on the football field. Later, the coaches hoped, when life confronted their players with obstacles, such lessons would carry over.

Ed Logan emphasized that in the present age of such casual domestic violence, "it's easy to forget that used to, you had to develop that killer instinct." But, he added, football players knew enough "to leave all that on the field." It was quite common for coaches to nurture violent behavior; however, "instead of beating up somebody on the street," players were encouraged to do so "down at the football stadium, and to the tune of the band and the yells of the cheerleaders," said Logan. The larger lesson was competition, continued Carlos Berry. "Football teaches kids how to take a blow and how to develop healthy minds. What is more brutal than people in society raping and murdering each other? That is certainly not what football teaches. Competition is good, and if things come easy, then kids will never have to search themselves." That, according to Ed Logan, was something that General MacArthur knew. "He said once that if all things were even between two men, he would take the athlete, because he was already trained to react."

Herb Allen also believed that football players were intelligent enough to distinguish when "to turn it on, and turn it off." Nevertheless, he conceded that sometimes those lessons "did not always take." Once Allen had a good quarterback at Diboll's Temple High School, a smart kid who overcame his thin, gawky frame with a "mean attitude. . . . He was a street fighter," Allen remarked. "I played to that part of his personality, because on the field it helped him compete." He recalled that against Grapeland his team was down by a point late in the game. Backed up against his own end zone, the quarterback called time out, and only later did the coach learn from a referee what went on in the huddle. "He pointed toward the other goal line and told them: 'I'm going that way, if you want to come along, let's go.' The next play he made it to the forty-one; the next play to the six; on the next play he scored." After graduating, Allen said, the young man got married and moved to Oklahoma City with his wife. "He slapped her around a lot, and finally she had enough and killed him with a gun. . . . He had been a good leader, but never learned to leave his mean streak on the football field."

Reflecting on what went wrong, Herb Allen simply concluded that "some kids are just bullies." The lessons of mental toughness that he and other coaches tried to impress upon their players concentrated on trying to help them develop self-discipline and a good work ethic. They exhorted kids to maintain their momentum when things were going well, and to persevere in the face of adversity. The "killer instinct" that coaches talked so much about did not advocate opportunism or taking advantage of the weak. Rather, coaches preached a creed of commitment to duty and good sportsmanship that sought to strike a healthy balance between the seemingly contradictory messages.

With rare exceptions coaches inculcated those lessons with clichés by the score. The maxim-spewing coach, of course, is one of the profession's most familiar caricatures. Herb Allen had one for every occasion. In fact, fellow coach Howard Clark made that very observation and encouraged Allen to begin collecting them. "I've got four-hundred-and-nine of them," he laughed. A sample of "Allenisms" illustrates the kinds of messages that coaches tried to convey: "Everybody wants to go to heaven, but nobody wants to die"; "The only way to avoid criticism is to say nothing, do nothing, want nothing, and be nothing"; "Dancing is a contact sport, football is a collision sport"; "You have to live with yourself—see to it that you always have good company"; "Success is a matter of luck—ask any failure"; "Tough times never last, but tough people do"; "You cannot get lost on a straight road"; "The worst use of success is to boast of it"; "Opportunities always look bigger going than coming"; "There are some defeats more triumphant than victories"; "You are never a loser until you quit trying"; "The trouble with self-made men is that they worship their creator."[2]

Such clichés could be found in any locker room. John Reddell believed that the sayings fostered a positive attitude, which is why coaches found them very effective. "I always stressed that character was more important than natural ability," he said, so he hung signs around the locker room that reinforced that belief—"'Do it with class,' and 'Be a Champion Off the Field,' that sort of thing," he said. In big letters over the entrance to Pasadena's locker room, Bob Barfield posted "DID YOU GIVE YOUR BEST TODAY?" Although some of his players might have appeared to disregard it, or even to make fun of it, he insisted that at one time or another every kid on the team at least had some private moment where he had to reconcile with it.

Bill Shipman remarked fondly: "I used locker room clichés to the extent that when I see former players now, they yell them at me!" Eddie Joseph, a former English major, echoed: "I collected reams and reams of them." In fact, he kept a bulletin board labeled "Thought for the Day" that showcased an appropriate saying. Such phrases, Joseph believed, "were trite, but true." The clichés that coaches used "were words of wisdom that have withstood the test of time. Kids like something that's simple and concise, and those little axioms fit the bill."

So many times people misinterpreted the manly ways and attitudes that coaches tried to cultivate as simply some barbaric expression of virility. Bob Cashion made that point by telling the story of a car dealer who longed to be associated with him and the rest of the Kilgore staff. Arriving in one of his new automobiles, the car dealer chauffeured the coaches to a Henderson country club and treated them to a round of golf. When the man hit two balls into a water hazard lying to the right of a fairway, "we told him, that's all right, just set it up in the 'frog hair' in front of the green." When he shanked the chip shot into the water as well, the car dealer began cursing and stomping, and he picked up his bag and threw it in, too. Then, Cashion remembered, the man "looked at that caddy and said: 'Boy, how'd you like a brand new set of clubs?' And he said: 'Shoot, yeah.' So that son-of-a-bitch picked the kid up and tossed him right into that pond, about where he threw those clubs." Shortly afterward, the man "walked off that golf course, and as far as I know, he's never played another round of golf again."

Cashion recalled that the coaching staff just stood there in disbelief. The caddy, of course, was humiliated, and the coaches strived mightily to console him. They also insisted, against the car dealer's second thoughts, that the boy keep the clubs. "I guess that's how that guy thought we'd have acted, but he was dead wrong. We'd have never treated a kid like that." And although Cashion admitted that later they all enjoyed telling the story, he also insisted that "it took us a long time to see the humor in it."

Prestige and Pressure

Like the car dealer, many others wanted to count coaches among their friends. According to Herb Allen: "Boys and girls and adults alike looked up to you and were always happy to be in your company. The coach was where the action was, and they wanted to be near the excitement." The importance of football in Texas imparted to members of the profession a certain measure of distinction. Joe Washington declared that in every town in Texas the coach was a familiar figure who commanded considerable prestige. "Although I did not realize it at first," he said, "if you believe otherwise, you're missing the beat." In John Reddell's estimation, "they deserved it." Coaches performed their job in front of the entire town, he asserted, and they were evaluated every week. And if they did not post consistently passing grades, they might not last long. "The community expected the coach to be a model citizen, active in the church and civic clubs" as well, said Homer Johnson. "In places where they produced winning teams," Morris Southall insisted, the coach "was the most revered, best-known, and highest profile figure in town. If he wins, he could be mayor if he wanted."

The gentlemanly Walt Parker, in fact—Scout leader, Sunday School teacher, and head coach at Denton—rode his recognition into the state

Gene Mayfield and his family Christmas shopping, 1956, courtesy of the Littlefield Booster Club. *Photograph courtesy Gene Mayfield.*

legislature. Men and women in Denton and Cooke counties had come to know him as one who would stand firm in his decisions without regard to personal feelings, and time and again they sent him to Austin unopposed. Eventually his interests drifted more toward legislation and business than football, yet he could not stay away from the game completely. At the college and professional level, coaches came to respect him as a referee who could empathize with them. Eventually Parker earned the distinction of having officiated Super Bowls III and VIII.

By the 1950s, showering gifts on coaches became a more prosaic and routine way for fans to express their appreciation. "Very often," Buzz Allert commented, "booster clubs gave the coaches $500 at banquets, and merchants often donated gift certificates." Typical was Gene Mayfield's experience at Littlefield, a Panhandle town that he took to the quarterfinals in his first season. Around Christmastime downtown merchants invited him to visit their stores, where they lavished gifts on him as well as his wife and young daughter. Arlington's Bull Workman contended that the practice had begun in an earlier age to make up for the slight pay coaches received. "Aw, they'd gripe that 'all Workman knows is those pitchouts.' But the other side of the coin is that twice they gave me a new car." After taking Kilgore to its first-ever district championship in 1953, Ty Bain received a station wagon at a time when he was already driving an almost-new Ford, so he sold the car and divided the money among some very happy assistant coaches.

As a way to say "keep up the good work," boosters at San Angelo similarly feted Bob Harrell three games into a good season. "I always held

John Hugh Smith, second from left, picks up a 1958 Buick Special donated by appreciative boosters at Belton. *Photograph courtesy Mrs. John Hugh Smith.*

closed workouts," he remarked. "They all knew that, but right in the middle of practice, I look up and here comes all these people through the gate. I yelled at a student manager to lock it, but then I saw my wife and the superintendent, too, at the head of the crowd. And then came this brand new Pontiac rolling up."

Then, "somewhere around 1960," remarked Carlos Berry, "the UIL set limits on gifts because it got to where booster clubs bought and fired coaches more than the school boards." As Berry suggested, such emoluments did not come without high expectations. Being head coach, of course, brought with it tremendous responsibilities. While an assistant coach at Victoria under Gordon Wood, Eddie Joseph marveled at the respect that his mentor commanded from the community, yet he also perceived the weighty burdens that Wood carried.

Said Buzz Allert: "When you're an assistant, all you have to do is worry about your position and show up for the booster club meeting. Once you become head coach, you're the one up there showing the game film and answering all the questions. . . . When the word came that I was going to be head coach, it really hit me that I would be responsible for the whole team, plus ten assistants as well as the junior high programs." The thought "'What am I going to do?' hit me. There were so many more bases to touch, so many more people to deal with." Being head coach, Allert realized, would require "a lot of organization and communication."

The Pasadena Rotary Club presents a Stetson to Bob Barfield. *Photograph courtesy Bob Barfield.*

When Carlos Berry started out at the small West Texas town of Haskell in 1957, he did not feel such pressures. "We did pretty good, and I thought, 'There's not much to this winning.' . . . Later I realized that I had just had some pretty good athletes." At some other places he found the talent average and the competition fierce. Commenting on the day when victories did not come as easily, he said simply: "I felt humbled."

Several coaches looked back with amusement at their naiveté when recalling their first days as helmsmen. Donald Jay, for example, recalled: "My first year as head coach [at Kingsville], I was going to be so organized, and I got all ready, but when it came time to hit the field, I realized that we had forgotten to air up the footballs."

Bill Hartley, a one-man staff at Columbus in 1950, admitted that he had to learn from the kids. "We spent all of two-a-days working on fundamentals. Just before kickoff [in the first game] a second-string guard came to me and said: 'Coach, we don't have a reverse, and we don't have a counter play.' So we diagrammed them right there, and, without ever having practiced it, we ran the reverse in the first quarter and went eighty yards for a touchdown." Hartley had some intelligent players, and since he did not have any assistants, he remarked: "I learned right there to allow my kids to have input."

Gene Mayfield, too, made light of his callowness. After four successful years directing Littlefield's program, he had earned a good reputation, "but I didn't realize it at the time," he said. When Class 4-A jobs opened up at Pampa and Borger, he visited both places. At Borger the kids were in off-season practice, and he got to observe them. "I noticed how big-legged they were compared to my kids at Littlefield. After I took over the program these two or three quit, and I felt foolish for making the decision based on how good the kids looked."

Similarly, Bill Bookout did not find many road signs on his path to the head coach's office, and when he got there, the job was nothing like he had envisioned. Something of a "phenom" as a player, nature had not blessed him with great talent, but it more than compensated by endowing him with uncommon grit and determination. Doyle Reynolds, who later coached with him, recalled that even before the two met, he knew Bookout by reputation. Fresh out of Wichita Falls, said Reynolds, Bookout "hitchhiked to Norman and told the freshman coach [at the University of Oklahoma]: 'I want a uniform.' When he said: 'You're too small.' Bill told him: 'I'm as tough as anything you've got.'" In the first practice, when a defensive back was injured, Bookout grabbed a pullover and got into the scrimmage. Then, when all-American halfback Billy Vessels tried to run over him, "Bookout hit him in the sternum and he fumbled." Later, when the freshman team scrimmaged the varsity, Bookout went "about eighty yards" on the first play. The next day, Reynolds remarked, Bookout walked onto the practice field as a scholarship athlete.

Passed over again by the pros, Bookout traveled to Green Bay, where he beat out all-pro cornerback Clarence Self, a former Wisconsin all-American. "I didn't know that pro ball was any big deal," Bookout remarked. "We were pretty poor, and I never even had a TV." Recently married, and with a child on the way, he decided to get into something more stable and accepted his first "real job" as Pug Gabriel's "B-team" coach at El Paso Austin.

After the season, the school district announced that a new high school, Burgess, would open across town the next year. Thinking he was ready for the helm, Bookout campaigned for the job and got it. At twenty-four-years old, he became the youngest head coach in the state's highest classification. "Boy, it was a gut check, let me tell you! I only thought I knew something about football. I found out pretty quick that before, I had been surrounded by some good athletes, and it only made me look good." Right away, Bookout continued: "The booster club approached me, and the band, and the principal, and everybody else wanting to know what I wanted them to do. Man, I was lost! Coaching is more than a game. The coach has to deal with so many other things." Two seasons later, Bookout was an assistant coach on the staff at L. D. Bell in Hurst. It was several more years before he felt ready to move up again.

At a time when schools were endowing programs with larger staffs, head coaches began to rise more commonly from the ranks of proven assistants. That is where Garland supporters found their new coach, Homer Johnson, after Bill Ellington took a job at Amarillo Tascosa. Even though Johnson had grown up in the emerging Dallas suburb, the job was not without pressure, since Garland's population growth had moved it into the state's highest classification just as he took the reins. The day that Ellington handed the keys over to him, Johnson recalled: "He was

Homer B. Johnson, posing at the Garland I.S.D. stadium that bears his name. *Photograph courtesy Homer Johnson.*

walking away, and then he stopped and turned around and said: 'Homer, I just want to tell you something, son. If people like you, you sure are hard to fire.'"

Ellington knew better than Johnson what lay ahead. The first season Garland lost a close game to Highland Park in a district-deciding contest; the same thing happened the next year. "The third year they told me if I lost again, I would be gone. . . . We scored with six seconds left to go in the game, which tied it, and we won the district championship," Johnson commented.

Johnson attributed at least part of his survival and success to being a risk taker. When he was playing center for Jerry Sellers' Owls in high school, the coach let him call the plays in the huddle. "I was always passing when we should have been running short, et cetera, and that just always gave Coach Sellers fits." As a coach Johnson again demonstrated his gambling nature against a strong Grand Prairie team by taking chances on fourth and one six times. "Each time we made the first down, and we won the game." Sellers, said Johnson, always came to watch the Owls, but never came around afterward until that night. "He liked to shake my hand off. . . . He said: 'Homer, I just want to congratulate you. I found out tonight you'd gamble with your own damn job as bad as you would mine!'"

Johnson spent his entire career at Garland and eventually handed his keys over to another young coach. He enjoyed many successes and even though he felt some "heat," he insisted "I never gave a thought to being fired." Yet no coach ever won so consistently that he became immune to community pressure if his team's fortunes turned south. "What other business could you get into where every week only half the people can be successful?" asked Cotton Miles. "People have a short memory about winning."

Even Joe Golding, on the heels of a 1949 state crown, found himself hung in effigy the next year after losing four consecutive non-district games in a season that eventually produced another state champion. And Paul Tyson, considered by many to be Texas's best high school coach, saw his career at Waco end ignominiously when he was fired in 1941. Frank Pulattie, who two years earlier had led Tyson's Tigers into the state finals, learned that some school board members had come to dislike the once-popular coach and worked to bring him down. Not long afterward, when Pulattie was playing at SMU, Tyson visited him at the dormitory. "I have this picture of him in my mind standing in the doorway in his overcoat, and he looked pathetic. Here he was earlier, with his chest sticking out and all that, and that [his firing] just crushed him."

Nothing could engender petty vindictiveness more quickly than falling short of a community's expectations. Charles Qualls told of a friend, Rusty Talbot, who took Nocona to the play-offs one season and suffered only two losses the following year. Nevertheless, "the next year he had a bad season, and they asked him to leave." Bob Harrell could commiserate. After rebuilding San Angelo's team from scratch, he stumbled one season, and the school board decided not to renew his contract. "All coaches go from being a hero one season to a goat the next," he commented. After a 4–6 season at Hooks in 1959, once-friendly fans became angry and started calling for their coaches' scalps. When a group confronting the staff justified their rancor by pointing out that the boys had gone undefeated in junior high, head coach Ben Burton could only vent his frustration by shooting back: "They probably still can!"

Coaching at Stamford in 1955, Gordon Wood witnessed a more serious incident when his Bulldogs traveled deep into East Texas for a play-off game against New London. Preoccupied with getting past Phillips and Breckenridge—both ranked number one at the time that Stamford played them—Wood had not paid New London much attention. After the well-prepared East Texans jumped out in front of Stamford 12–0, Wood's bunch came back with three unanswered touchdowns and won 21–12. After the game he and the New London coach, John Ramseur—"a big, dark German, a perfect gentleman"—were exchanging their respects on the field. Off to one side, Wood noticed a Texas A&M student in a corps uniform. "When we quit talking, he called that kid over there and told him: 'Son, don't let your daddy come around the dressing room, I can't put up with him today.'" As the two coaches walked off the field, Wood watched as the agitated father approached Ramseur. "I'll teach this S.O.B.," Wood recalled the man saying, "and he tapped him [Ramseur] on the back, and I don't know what he said, but John hit him in the jaw and broke it on both sides." The parent went to the hospital; Ramseur went before the school board, which fired him.

The incident illustrated what Joe Washington came to learn in his long career at Port Arthur Lincoln: "There are three things people can do better—build a fire, run a hotel, and coach!" After retiring from Pasadena

High School, Stoney Phillips fell privy to such "bettering." He was always aware that "shift workers at those refineries up and down the ship channel would all get together at night and complain about their coaches. . . . One day I was sitting there [at a lodge] listening to all the bullshit—'how to run this play and that,' and I said: 'How many of you played college football?' And not a damn one of them did because they were working at these plants; a few of them played high school. I said: 'How in the hell can you be so damn critical of a game if you've never really played it?' . . . I said: 'You don't have to be a star, but you've got to love football, and you've got to be with it to understand it.'" Tongue-in-cheek, Phillips ended by telling them: "The only mistake I ever made when I was coaching at Pasadena was that I was too poor to join one of these clubs, because I know damn well that if I had been a member right here, with all the wealth of football knowledge that I've learned today, I would have won the state championship."

Stoney Phillips was frank, and he admired that same quality in others. He laughed upon recalling that a fan "came up to me one day and shook my hand and said: 'Stoney I like you, but I never did think you could coach worth a tinker's damn, but you're my buddy.'" Turning more serious, Phillips commented: "He wasn't my buddy, but he was." Phillips knew that there was always going to be some grumbling, which he understood and accepted. Too many times, however, grumbling grew into action, and in places with active booster clubs, there seemed to be inflated expectations. Experience taught that in good times adoring eyes were nevertheless watchful, and in bad times they were almost always critical.

At Campbell High School in Nacogdoches, Clarence McMichael enjoyed the approbation of a strong booster club. He also coached winning teams year after year. When a Henderson coach, already under pressure, visited him to ask about organizing his own booster club, McMichael's advice was short and to the point: "You're better off without one!"

"The trouble with booster clubs," remarked Carlos Berry, "is that they would get their tentacles into you by giving you things and obligating you. After a while, they felt they could influence your decisions." Any maverick ideas that did not "pan out" were sure to invite negative consequences. "Towns are full of Monday morning quarterbacks," remarked Homer Johnson. "When a coach is winning, everybody is his friend; but when a coach is losing, he can have more enemies than Carter has liver pills."

Ed Logan, who joined John Hugh Smith's staff at Haltom City in the early 1960s, discussed the consequences of their backers' deflated hopes. During a question-and-answer session at the first booster club meeting an optimistic fan asked Smith: "Did you ever notice how many times a new coach goes undefeated in his new job?" To which the coach responded: "Well, I've noticed how seldom he was undefeated in his old job." Smith's teams at Haltom never got close to an undefeated season; in fact, he never produced a winner there, and his tenure was a short one. "I remember reading John Hugh's record when we came to Haltom High School," Logan remarked. "He had been coaching actively seventeen years. He had won fifteen district championships, played in the state finals twice, and didn't remember how many times he had been to the quarter-finals. . . . Now, that's fifteen out of seventeen times he won. Yet he gets up here, and he's a bad coach. I just can't see it that way."

In a game that is often decided on breaks, so too, were careers made and destroyed on the narrowest of margins. Coaches knew that too many close defeats, too close together, could produce a groundswell of discontent that could turn insurmountable. Such was the luck of Longview coach Ty Bain in 1966.

As if the season, marked by two ties and a couple of close losses, was not already going badly enough, the disgruntled father of a junior varsity player interrupted practice one day to rail at the boy's coach, Eddie Cannon, for making his son run laps. The coach tried to make the man understand that the player had skipped practice to attend the Gregg County Fair, and at the very least he needed the running to make up for the conditioning he had missed. The father—"a real big man . . . [who was on mind-affecting] medication"—did not see it that way, said Bain assistant Bob Cashion. When Bain looked across the practice field and saw what was going on, he got the man aside. "C'mon," Cashion remembered Bain saying, "let's go into the field house and talk about it." As they walked away, Cashion heard the man muttering some curses at the coach, and, knowing Bain's volatile temper, thought he had better follow them. "Somewhere along there, he called Ty an S.O.B., and Ty told him: 'Don't call me that again.' So the guy said: 'Let me put it this way—you're a goddamned son-of-a-bitch'—and Ty hit him right between the eyes."

By the time Cashion reached them, Bain and the father had gone inside the field house, where the assistant coach saw them exchanging blows. When the angry father began throttling the much smaller Bain, the coach somehow broke free and threw a punch that sent the man reeling into a heap. Then, when Bain walked over and extended a hand to the man, "he grabbed Ty by the face and the back of the neck and pulled himself up and raked several inches of meat off of him. . . . Blood was dripping down off his chin like a leaky faucet." With that, Bain put "a hammer lock on him and started popping him on the head, and the whole time this guy was swinging Ty around like a rag doll." When Cashion finally separated them, he pushed Bain into a pile of dummies and positioned himself between the tired pair. "I finally convinced the man that the best thing for him to do was to leave."

When it was all over, Bain walked back out to the practice field with a bloody towel wrapped around his neck. As a quizzical bunch of boys gathered around him, he announced: "If any of you are thinking about getting into coaching as a career, you'd better think hard; it can be a tough-ass job!" At the time he did not realize just how right he was. Some boosters seized on the incident to feed an already seething discontent over Bain's record. He had spent four seasons building a program, and the year it was supposed to come together, *Dave Campbell's Texas Football* magazine ranked Longview in the preseason top ten. Upon losing several heartbreakers, however, the Lobos won only half of the games on their schedule. In the wake of the fight and the disappointing season, school board members decided not to renew Bain's contract. The next year Bain had to read about a very capable Tommy Hudspeth taking the Lobos to the play-offs with a 10–0 record.

In 1953, Bob Harrell arrived at San Angelo to replace a man who had been cashiered just as Bain would be in 1966. The community was ten years removed from a state championship and was eager to find someone who could return the team to its former glory. After one meeting with Harrell, the community believed that it had found someone who would take whatever steps were necessary to lay a solid foundation under the team.

Harrell's first action seemed to justify San Angelo's judgment. "As soon as I got there, I asked the superintendent if he could have a town meeting—everybody in town was invited to the auditorium." Not only had the team lost nineteen straight games, Harrell remarked, but he had also learned that some of the kids had been getting drunk and were smoking. At the gathering, he announced: "If I can get your help and some backing, and you start coming out and liking what you see, that's all I ask, but we're going to win with or without you."

The following day he convinced the principal to call an all-school assembly. "I walked out on the stage, and they were all sitting down and I screamed through that microphone and said: 'Get your heads up! You're not going to get beaten around anymore!' I really laid it on 'em, boy. I said: 'Get behind this team, because we are going to win.' They had lost nineteen straight ball games, what can you expect?" He then asked the teachers to support him by making the football players more responsible students and to give the coaches "a good word." The entire town, he felt, helped him rebuild the team, and for a while San Angelo again enjoyed a winner. For Harrell, his success lasted until boosters felt that he was not winning enough. Unfortunately, San Angelo was in the same district with Abilene, and Harrell's tenure there overlapped the years that Chuck Moser's Eagles were flying high.

Charles Qualls expressed that "every coach has to deal with the disappointments, the 'what if's,' the one that got away." Ed Logan recalled a head coach, who, in the heat of a close game stalked frantically along the bench calling for a player who had graduated two years earlier. "I didn't want to end up like that, and I got into administration." The mercurial profession drove many coaches into other careers, whether they were fired or simply burned out, or because they found the pay too modest or other opportunities too alluring. Very often, after many years at the helm, coaches accepted posts as athletic directors or principals and gladly turned their programs over to younger men. Still others found that they could not find contentment in any other field and returned to coaching after testing other waters.

Doyle Reynolds, for example, established a successful dry cleaning business, yet he quickly sold it. "I couldn't stand being away from the game," he commented. Even after retiring, Joe Bob Tyler quit a good-paying part-time job as a salesman to volunteer his expertise at Midwestern University. "Getting into retail made me realize what a great life I'd had," he said. "A job becomes so much more than a job when you like what you do." Oday Williams, no doubt, would have agreed. In the late 1950s, after suffering some poor seasons, he purchased a Texaco station in Graham, yet "he damn near walked off and left it" when Chuck Curtis offered him a job after being hired to replace Homer Johnson. "I saw his shoes sticking out from under a car," remarked Curtis, "and I said: 'Oday, get your greasy ass out from under there, and let's go to Garland.'"

The Coach-Player Relationship

For many men who found their niche in coaching, it was not just the profession itself that attracted them, but also shepherding high school boys in particular that made the game so rewarding. "At the high school level," said Walt Parker, "you love the kids and feel like you're shaping their lives." Many others believed that at no other level could they achieve the same results. Nobody stated that point more clearly than Woodrow Wilson's Cotton Miles, who did some scouting for the Dallas Cowboys in the late 1960s and early 1970s. Traveling with the team to a game in Washington, D.C., Dallas sports columnist Blackie Sherrod asked him if he were interested in a job that had just opened up at Arlington State. Miles told him: "No. I don't coach football, I coach boys." That, Miles insisted, "is the difference between high school and college."

Many successful schoolboy coaches had to learn that lesson the hard way. Gene Mayfield, for example, never could adjust to coaching at the college level because he was not willing to make the compromises that he felt were necessary to build a winner. In a stellar high school career, Mayfield had developed an aloof, but effective, coaching style that fit his reserved personality. Among his staff and players he commanded unwavering respect. He also possessed a kind of presence, a "look," that allowed him to express with a mere glance tacit approval or abject dissatisfaction. While encouraging his position coaches to develop warm, fatherly ties with their players, Mayfield himself remained somewhat enigmatic, a manner that mightily awed the impressionable high school boys.

At Borger High, Mayfield related, he imposed a curfew, which one of the players violated by fifteen minutes. The boy became convinced that Mayfield had found out, and worried about it for two days before finally confessing. "It wasn't that he was afraid of being punished," the coach remarked, but simply "because he did not want me to think any less of him." That shade of omnipotence revealed itself in another way at his

Haskell coaching staff, 1957: A. J. Virtell, left, head coach Ray Overton, and Carlos Berry. *Photograph courtesy Carlos Berry.*

next stop, Odessa Permian. When the threat of lightning forced Mayfield to end practice early, he retired to his office. Players and assistant coaches alike milled about the locker room, enjoying the unexpected respite. Then, one of the boys, Red Woodward, positioned himself in front of the door and imitated Mayfield commanding the storm to abate—just as the coach emerged from his office. Woodward's frozen expression of embarrassment evoked raucous laughter, recalled Mayfield, yet "until right then, I didn't fully realize how they felt about me."

Then, in 1970, Mayfield became head coach at West Texas State University, where he found that the "look," which had commanded so much respect from his high school players, often met with defiance. "My coaches and I always felt strongly about some basic things," he remarked. For example: "My players always had short hair. Then, in college, we've got these kids with hair down to the middle of their back. I tried to fight that for a while and lost the battle." At previous stops, he continued: "I always had coached highly motivated, dedicated kids who walked the line. And they were good students. If they don't pass, they're in study hall." Then, at West Texas State, "we get to a situation where students are having grade problems, and the attitude was such a change." Many of them, he knew, had accepted their coaches' leadership in high school. Once in college, however, they were not as willing to be led. They came to view themselves as young adults, and "they began to stray, and their priorities became confused." Mayfield felt helpless. "I remember just about every kid that played for me in high school; a lot of the kids that played for me in college, I don't remember that well."

Mayfield also expressed that "you take what you've got in high school and do the best you can." At that level, he believed, coaches could get so much more out of their players, because the boys were malleable and willing to take instruction. At the high school level, moreover, the relationship between coaches and kids extended well beyond the practice field. Clarence McMichael said that "the coach was looked at as the father of all his players." All year long they came over to his house "and just hung around," said McMichael, a comment echoed by many others.

Carlos Berry recalled that on autumn Saturdays when he was at Haskell, kids would pass the time by riding around in their cars, listening to sports announcer Kern Tipps call the play-by-play of the Southwest Conference games. "He was very descriptive, and he'd get you all keyed up." Often, boys would see Berry working in the yard and stopped in front of his house, where together they would listen to most of a game.

Bill Hartley, much closer to the SWC action, said that at Columbus he took players to Houston and College Station, where they watched Rice and Texas A&M play home games. "It would always be a family atmosphere. Sometimes they would take dates and all that. We'd just load up in a bus and go."

And at Arlington, during summers in the late 1940s and early 1950s, Mayfield Workman and his wife played music at an upstairs room at city hall, which became a place where all the community's teenagers gathered. "They'd come down there and dance, and if they smoked, they'd go outside. They didn't drink at all, at least as far as I knew, and there were certainly no drugs," Workman recalled.

Buzz Allert contended that "back then people respected coaches and placed high expectations on them not only to win, but also to guide their children." Very often, he said, when kids complained about the coach, their parents stood by him because they knew the coach had the children's best interest at heart. Carlos Berry related what happened one time when a player told his parents that he did not like the way the coaches were doing their job. "The dad told him: 'Shut up! You don't have to play football, and if you don't like the way you're being coached, then quit!'"

Once, when a player did quit Buzz Allert's team at Lamar Consolidated, the boy's mother stepped in. "Unlike many kids who just wanted some spending money, this young man had no father, and his mother worked two jobs. She told him that if he quit just because football was a little hard, that he had no guts. I told him that his mother was the one with guts because she was working two jobs so that he could play football and make something of himself." Allert finished his speech by saying: "Stay with it and help yourself and your mother." Still, the boy wanted to quit, but that night his mother convinced him that the coach was right. "About midnight I heard a knock at my door, and found the boy in tears. He had been agonizing over his decision, but decided to go ahead and play. Later he got a scholarship, and today he's doing very well."

Buzz Allert. *Photograph courtesy Texas High School Coaches Association, Austin.*

Frank Pulattie, 1968. *Photograph courtesy Frank Pulattie.*

Many times there were no parents around at all, and so coaches filled in. Frank Pulattie, who, as a fatherless boy was shepherded by Paul Tyson, found it easy to coach some orphans who played for him at Itasca. "They adopted me," he smiled. Pulattie, just like his old mentor, took the boys places, and he and his wife regularly fed them at his home, where the boys sat on crates and ate with plates on their laps. "For Christmas one year they made me a big table so they could all come over and eat on it." And once, he remembered, when a former player in the service got a furlough, he came back and stayed with the Pulatties because he had no other family.

"Just about every coach at one time or another did things for kids that the UIL would have probably busted them for," declared Bob Harrell. Buzz Allert said that finding summer jobs for players was routine, but coaches also sent boys with bad teeth to dentists who were boosters, and they got glasses for others the same way. "I even got one kid a glass eye," Allert remarked. When a player on Harrell's San Angelo team did not have the white shirt that complemented the boys' cashmere letter jackets, he got one for him. "That was pretty typical," Harrell said. "There were poor kids in every town; that one lived right down on the edge of the dump ground."

Coaches' jobs, of course, were not all pressure and social work. Being around high school boys, in fact, provided far more light and carefree moments than ones filled with tension. And dealing with boys, they always had to expect the unpredictable. John Hugh Smith related: "Every once in a while, I'd have a kid that was a good player, but not the type of kid who was committed. So, I'd go to the team leader and had them try to encourage the boy that was sloughing off; help him get in line, you know." Many times, Smith remarked, his strategy worked. One time at Belton, however, "it worked the other way around!" Off the field the team's leader was not as popular as the other boy. "The lazy kid had a great social life, and my captain liked the way he was living, and he let him drag him into it!"

Coaches suffered many practical jokes. Bob Barfield's experience at Cedar Bayou was more memorable, and no doubt more galling, than most. The superintendent there owned a Brahma bull that he grazed on the football field during the off-season. "We had a little dressing room at the far corner of the football stadium, and to this day they talk about it at the reunions, but I still don't know who put it in there. Anyway, they put that bull in there, and you talk about bullshit! He messed that office up like you wouldn't believe. I started trying to find out who it was. I was young and had a lot of fire, and I was really mad. You'd think that bull hadn't taken a crap in a month."

Coaches themselves were not beneath pulling some sort of mischief if it helped their cause. In 1967, Needville faced a Sweeny squad that had won the state championship the previous season, and the coaches believed that they would have to whip their boys into a frenzy if they were to stand a chance. So, Roland Conrad and his assistant coach, Quin Eudy, bought several dozen powder blue pom-poms—Needville's colors—and drove to Sweeny, where they placed the pom-poms in the mail. "We got them a couple of days before the game," remarked Eudy, "but we didn't let our boys open the box until the pep rally. . . . When they saw that Sweeny postmark, they were really hot!" The ruse, Eudy believed, helped give his players the edge that inspired Needville to victory.

Cotton Miles related a very peculiar episode that would have seemed like a conspiracy to someone not familiar with Texas high school football. It occurred during the play-offs, when his Woodrow Wilson team had to go to West Texas for a semifinal contest. Miles remembered being pleasantly surprised when his opponent agreed to let his team hold a closed practice. Then, just as the workout began, a telephone truck rolled up, ostensibly to hook up the sideline phones. Sometime later, Miles saw a baffled custodian walk up to the truck and ask the "foreman" of the crew: "Coach, what'chall doin' all dressed up in them telephone uniforms?" Then, once the Wilson High team settled in at the motel on the night before the big game, an intermittent parade of cars serenaded the players and coaches with blaring horns. When Miles summoned the highway patrol, the officers apologized, but said there was nothing they could do. "It was private property," they told the skeptical coach. Miles expressed that he would have been more forgiving if the game had not ended on such a sour note. Behind by eight points very late in the game, Wilson scored a touchdown that was called back by a questionable penalty.

Coaching School

Such incidents were familiar to every high school coach. Their ranks indeed provided something of a fraternity, its members initiated in common experiences, aspirations, and pressures. Almost all of them had played ball, and at one time most had possessed some athletic ability. And many, whether in high school or college, had even played alongside or against one another. Long before they met, then, coaches knew each other by reputation as players or fellow members of the guild. Very few looked across the gridiron and saw a complete stranger directing the team on the other sideline. At the very least, if the two got together, they could exchange stories about common friends and rivals.

Each year coaches got an opportunity to make new acquaintances and reaffirm old ones when they gathered for their annual meeting late in the summer. The Texas High School Football Coaches Association, born during the Great Depression and nurtured by its most accomplished and distinguished members, drew a large and loyal following. College coaches, anxious to establish ties with the men who supplied them talent, were eager to lend support as well by lecturing about their programs and innovations. Although it dropped "Football" from its title in 1941 and embraced coaches from all sports, the THSCA nevertheless remained predominately a fraternity of gridiron coaches. As the broker of ideas, jobs, and professional ties, "coaching school" grew into a distinctively Texan rite that bound its membership more tightly. It also provided coaches a common arena to integrate themselves into a unique culture.

"Coaching school was a social thing," remarked James Brewer. "Your lectures were good, but you learned more getting together with six or eight coaches in a room and talking and drinking beer, and playing poker. That way you'd get to rub elbows with guys like Jerry Sadler and Watty Meyers and Charles Churchill—guys that were veteran coaches when I first started. . . . At coaching school you got to know everybody else. You stayed within a couple of blocks of everybody and went to the same hangouts. And afterward you'd all congregate at one place to eat. That way you'd meet every coach in Texas."

With four months of football ahead, said Maurice Cook, "it was like a soldier just before he was going off to war." Gordon Brown believed that it "was a good time for the children to visit their grandparents. . . . Coaching school became the biggest event of the year," he continued. "Your expenses were paid for, and that was good. . . . You got to see many of your coaching friends and have a good time. You met famous coaches like Bear Bryant and Darrell Royal, and you wanted to hear everything each speaker said, for if you didn't, your opponents would use it on you and beat you with it. . . . The last night of coaching school was often reserved to 'eat big' at a famous restaurant. You would save some of your expense money for this special night and spend it all."

"I attended my first coaching school in Lubbock in 1956, and I haven't missed one since," said Allen Boren. "It was a great conference. . . . The mayor came in and told everybody to have fun and not to worry about parking tickets—'The town is yours!' We'd get up every morning and hear people like Jess Neeley, Henry Frnka, Wally Butts, and other college

Coaching school, c. 1965. *Photograph courtesy Texas High School Coaches Association, Austin.*

coaches speak; at night it was poker." By the 1960s, Fort Worth, Dallas, San Antonio, and Houston rotated as host towns, yet earlier venues included Abilene, El Paso, Austin, Corpus Christi, Wichita Falls, and Beaumont.

When Hardin-Simmons hosted the clinic in 1948, said Cotton Miles, "it was hot as hell, and we slept in the dorms. Of course, there were no air conditioners, . . . and every night at midnight we'd pull our mattresses out onto the sidewalk; and then at dawn, we'd have to go back in, because we were all in our underwear."

The only time the clinic ever met in El Paso was in 1947. Bob Harrell remarked: "It was different than any other one, because it was so far out there. A lot of guys just said 'to heck with it' and had a good time. There were a lot of crap games going on in those hotels." Nobody traveled farther than O. W. Follis, who was living in Texarkana at the time. He wisely took the train, and at every stop, it seemed, another coach or two would get on board. Predictably, he said, "we spent the time telling stories and talking football."

The long, monotonous drive and trips to Juarez remained as prominent in most coaches' memories as the school itself. Robert Lowrance asserted that once across the Trans-Pecos "the roads got narrow and the cars got tenuous." Somewhere along there, a bus stopped for James Brewer, then a high school senior-to-be, and a friend, Red Wood, who were hitchhiking in the 110-degree desert. Settling in the back of the bus, they met fellow high schoolers and future coaches Hayden Fry and Pug Gabriel of

Odessa, with whom Brewer established lasting relationships. Chena Gilstrap, who traveled with the North Texas Agricultural College staff (later the University of Texas at Arlington), said: "We drove at night because we still had wartime tires, and we were afraid they would explode during the day." On one stretch that paralleled a railroad track, NTAC's head coach was trying to get some sleep in the back seat. "And this engine was coming along, and it whistled real loud. And one of the assistant coaches said: 'My God, don't hit that thing!' and the head coach came up out of that back seat. It woke him up for a while, I'm sure," Gilstrap chortled.

For men who spent most of their public life being scrutinized, coaching school gave them a chance to unwind. Those who worked in rural towns enjoyed a respite in the big city all the more. Many wives came along, too. In fact, Gordon Brown declared that "some of the coaches called the week 'wives school,' because so many of them attended with their husbands, and for them, it was a week of shopping." Coaches such as Homer Johnson made it a family vacation. Most high schools, he said, would give everybody on their coaching staff a hundred dollars apiece, and their wives would try to match it with money they had put back for the occasion. In the late 1950s the coaches' wives organized and planned their own daytime activities while their husbands were busy at meetings.

Coaches, as a general rule, were not a very worldly and sophisticated lot, and for those who attended the clinic by themselves, their entertainment settled into earthy routines. Many of them, as James Brewer remarked, simply enjoyed talking football in their hotel rooms over beer and poker. Others asserted that just as many enjoyed conversation and games without drinking. At the same time, Cotton Miles said, "a lot of the young, single coaches went girl hunting." Darrell Tully, at a San Antonio school in the 1960s, was well aware of his companions' virility and worried about taking his sixteen-year-old daughter to the conference, but counted on his high regard as a past president of the association to keep the wolves at bay. Once in their room, he told her: "Now honey, there's going to be lots of coaches here, and the young ones might get flirty with you. If they do, you just tell them that you're Darrell Tully's kid." Sure enough, the girl told her father that the admonition kept the young ones away from her, but, she said: "You didn't tell me how to keep the old coaches away!"

Upon hearing about all the fun some of their peers were having, assistant coaches Bill Shipman and Max Goldsmith once decided they would go to a strip joint "and see what it was all about." They knew that their head coach would not approve, so they waited until they were sure that he was attending an evening lecture before slipping away. "When we got into that girlie show, we got up to the runway as close as possible," said Shipman. "Then, to our horror, we saw our head coach living it up at a table with a bunch of his friends on the other side of the runway." Terrified, the two assistant coaches crouched down and duck-waddled behind the row of seats. Once outside they "breathed a sigh of relief," and then fell down laughing. "The next day," remarked Shipman, "we received some very brief answers when we asked Coach about the lecture he attended."

The Longview staff did not walk so lightly around Ty Bain. In fact, every year the coach hosted a night on the town for his assistants, paid for with his "dead cow money." Bain owned a few acres in Central Texas on which he ran some cattle; his wife, Eileen, kept the books and managed the family budget. Bain, afraid that his wife would not approve of such frivolous spending, would come to her every summer with the bad news that he had "lost another cow."

When coaching school met in Dallas in the early 1960s, the Longview staff gathered with friendly rivals at a club called the "It'll Do," where they partied until the departed cow had given up all its milk. The next week, when they returned to begin two-a-day workouts for the fall campaign, Bain gave the Lobos his annual speech admonishing them to work hard and keep in training. He knew that many of the players had spent a considerable number of summer evenings cruising a Longview drive-in restaurant called "The Golden Point." Yet, when it came time to address that issue, he blurted out: "You won't make this team if you spend all your time hanging out at the It'll Do!" The players exchanged quizzical glances as they wondered what he was talking about, and why the rest of the staff was bursting with laughter.

Learning something about the game, of course, was the purpose of coaching school. And while members found the clinics fun, most of them also found out that football was much more complicated than they had ever dreamed. Charles Qualls, as a young Kingsville assistant, looked forward to his first conference, but came away feeling overwhelmed. "It was at Houston, and when I got down there I thought, man, there's more football to learn than I could ever think about teaching. I thought that coaching school would be all fun and time to goose around a little," which he did. "We were staying at the Rice Hotel. Across the street was the 'S&Q Oyster Bar.' I'd never had oysters, so I talked Donald Jay into going there with me, and afterwards we went to the movies, and dancing, and all the things you weren't supposed to do." His mentor, Russ Holland, had warned him: "Now Charlie, you do what you want to, but there's a difference between coaching and playing." It took Qualls three weeks into the season to understand what Holland had tried to tell him. "I had made a terrible mistake," he said. "I decided that from then on, I was going to take notes and pay very close attention, because I didn't know very much at all about the coaching profession."

Coaches who did not take the school seriously, Qualls said, did not last long. Moon Mullins, who felt that he was typical of his colleagues, attended most of the lectures and felt privileged to see the Southwest's most prominent college coaches. "I took down every word," he claimed. Once, he said, when he was quizzing Bear Bryant about the defense he

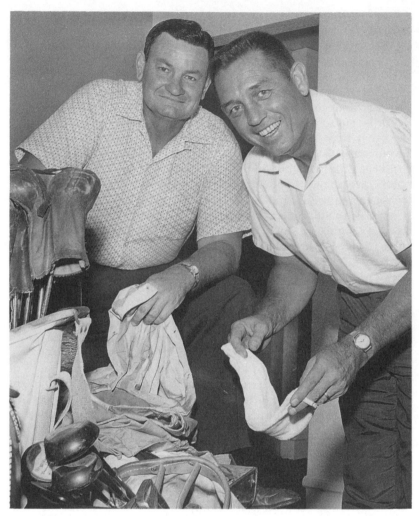

John Garrison, left, and Darrell Tully get ready for coaching school. *Photograph courtesy Texas High School Coaches Association, Austin.*

had just lectured on, the coach invited him up to his room to talk about it at length. "He was very cordial and treated me like a peer."

"Lots of football was learned in those hotel rooms," declared Bob Barfield. As Ray Overton remarked: "You have to remember that we are a professional people. Everything coaches do, they borrowed it in some way from someone else, and they're good at sharing it." Chuck Curtis agreed. "The best way to learn was to get a bunch of napkins and a six-pack and go to the bull sessions, where the older coaches were." Sporting goods salesmen such as Wichita Falls's Bobby Evans, he said, "used to show up and fill bathtubs with ice and beer." Charles Qualls said coaches also developed their own circles of friends who stayed up all night talking football. "We were always calling down to get chalkboards at the hotels; we used to run them crazy keeping us in chalk. We finally just decided that we'd take our own. That was always one of the staples that we'd take to coaching school—a couple of chalkboards and a whole box of chalk. And I'm sure we messed up a whole lot of hotel towels wiping off those boards."

Hardly any coach that regularly attended the clinic failed to end up in Bum Phillips's room at one time or another. Bob Barfield remembered as many as forty and fifty coaches on occasion packed into Phillips's room exchanging ideas. And it was not as if Phillips alone was disseminating wisdom; on the contrary, he was absorbing everything that his colleagues told him. "I think this is one of the things that made him such a great coach," Barfield commented. Phillips himself recalled the setting as "very informal." His down-home manner and quick wit just naturally attracted a crowd. Even college coaches such as Darrell Royal, Frank Broyles, and Bear Bryant joined the crowd. Hugh Hamm, then a young assistant coach at Carrolton Turner, recalled asking Phillips a question, and "next thing I knew he was handing *me* the chalk and wanted to know what *I* thought."

Many times the "X's and O's" would come alive on the floors of hotel rooms. When there were not enough coaches to provide a proper formation, chairs and coffee tables and any loose piece of furniture might suffer some physical demonstration. At the Austin clinic in 1950, Ray Akins recalled Michigan State's "Biggie" Munn exhibiting some defensive techniques. "Several coaches in succession barreled at him, and he shucked them all—nobody could budge him."

James Brewer remembered a more ignoble scene involving a bunch of coaches watching Spring Branch's Darrell Tully and Temple's Alan Winters engaged in a heated discussion over the "split-four." It was then the hottest new defensive innovation, and Winters appeared sold on it. "Now, if I'm a defensive lineman, that guard can't block me when I'm in a three-technique," he recalled Winters saying. "And Tully said: 'The hell he can't; I'll just show you.' Both of them had been drinking a little bit, and Alan weighed 150 pounds," commented Brewer. With everybody anticipating how the mismatched coach would handle the former all-American, one of them called the signals. "About half a count before they snapped the ball, Alan jumped about nine feet straight left; Tully couldn't have touched him with a ten-foot pole. That was the kind of crap that would go on."

Clearly, coaching school exuded a sense of fraternity that lent itself to practical jokes. An occasional incident would become part of the lore that coaches enjoyed telling wherever they gathered. One evening, after they listened to the University of Kentucky's Adolph Rupp, many of them gathered afterward in one of the hotel rooms. There, the legendary roundball coach regaled them with stories of his experiences. After every anecdote, said Gordon Wood, the Texans were literally

Gene Mayfield, 1965. *Photograph courtesy*
Texas High School Coaches Association,
Austin.

bursting in tears of laughter. Rupp, notorious for his overinflated ego,
appeared delighted that his audience found him so amusing. Behind
him, however, was Brownwood assistant coach Mike Brum, who had
fashioned a giant placard that read "BULLSHIT." Each time a punch
line came up, Brum raised the card, evoking hysterical laughter.

Then Rupp turned serious, remembered Wood. Sharing his secrets
for molding team unity, he reviewed a litany of requirements that had
the team "sleeping 'X' number of hours, and spending 'X' number of
hours together studying and eating and practicing." All the while,
Brum was taking notes. Jerking his head up with a quizzical look, he
caught the attention of the room and cut Rupp short: "Excuse me,
coach, I'm not real good at math, but you've got these kids tied up for
twenty-five hours, and you haven't even given them time to shit, shave,
or shine up." Turning around to face the impudent Brum, Rupp
looked down and saw the big sign, and suddenly it all became clear.
Grabbing his hat, he pushed through the howling coaches and
stomped out of the room.

The event that crowned the week was the annual North-South all-
star game that pitted Texas's best graduating high school seniors
against each other. Until 1957 two college coaches headed each squad.
Beginning in 1957, however, Texas high school coaches in both
regions began the tradition of choosing representatives from among
themselves. Coaches who were selected saw it as an honor for their
entire program. Gene Mayfield, whom his colleagues selected twice,
claimed: "What we did was pretty vanilla; our skill was in motivating
our kids and teaching them fundamentals. We were pretty worried
about going to coaching school and being in front of all our peers."
His concerns, however, were no doubt misplaced. A check of the
record shows that he won both contests.

One of the highlights in Charles Qualls's career came when his McKinney staff got to coach the North all-stars at Fort Worth before a record crowd in 1964. "I was so excited when I got the call," he said. "I couldn't wait to tell my other coaches, because it was such a great honor for them, too." Corsicana's Jim Akree oversaw the South squad. "They had all the big names like Warren McVea and Linus Baer," said Qualls. "All the write-ups all week were about the South and how strong they were, and what a great team they assembled." When it was all over, however, the North won, 23–14. "Our kids just gave a super effort; it was one of my greatest thrills in coaching," Qualls said.

A decade later Lewisville's Bill Shipman coached the North all-stars to victory on the last play of the game at the Astrodome. Ironically, it came against a South team that was headed by the same Uvalde coach whose Coyotes had beaten Shipman's Farmers on the last play of the Class 3-A state championship game the previous season. What Shipman remembered most about the all-star experience was the thrill it gave the kids who played. Nobody, he said, was more elated than Hugh Veale, who was chosen for the game as alternate from tiny Class B school Van Alstyne. "When Hugh got the news that he was moving up, he was at home plowing a field, and he just jumped off the tractor and sprinted to the house and got his stuff ready and came down," Shipman related. Everybody had told the coach: "You probably won't be able to play these Class B boys much," but Veale ended up starting for him at guard and played almost the entire contest. "Hugh was full of life," Shipman recalled, and his country ways made him a favorite among his teammates. They also enjoyed "getting his goat." When some of them locked him out of his room one evening, Veale violently pulled the knob right off the door. "Hugh was conscience-stricken, and he came down and told me what he'd done. I chewed him out and made him pay for it." But, Shipman continued, "I got the knob and the connecting rod from the hotel manager, and when I got home I took it down and had it made into a trophy and sent it to him. The last time I talked to him, he said he's still got it sitting on his desk."

That desk was in a coach's office in Sherman, Texas, where Veale landed a job after he graduated from Austin College. And, like Shipman used to do, the former all-star began making the rounds at coaching school every year. In many ways it is a different crowd that gathers for the annual conventions. Chances are that Hugh Veale, more than most, would have fit right in with some of the older coaches at those beer and poker marathons. A small-town boy, his adolescence unfolded in the early 1970s, when, in the old coaches' vernacular, football players in Van Alstyne still "toed the line." Yet conditions both on and off the field had already changed all around him. No doubt his all-star teammates found him "a favorite," as Shipman said, in part because he reminded them of what football players used to be like. Veale no doubt found that the boys he began to encounter as a coach had to be reached in different ways. He and his colleagues, most who never developed a taste for red beans and black-eyed peas, and whose only good wars were waged on the gridiron, nevertheless try to achieve many of the same results as their old-time counterparts. They have to do so, however, under far different circumstances. Not long ago, Shipman related, he and fellow coach Max Goldsmith were talking about that very subject. "He told me: 'You know, Bill, we got to coach through the good part.'"

Chapter 8

Autumn Widows and Other Dependents: The Coaches and Their Families

In many respects, coaches as family men were like any other people with demanding and time-consuming jobs that kept them in the public eye. Among them were faithful husbands and good fathers, and, of course, there were others who were not model patriarchs, which could only be expected from such a wide sample. Many helmsmen in the group regarded their families as part of the team: Wives headed up all types of clubs, sons played for their fathers, and daughters cheered from the edges of the field, megaphones in hand. Yet the spotlight that glowed on so many coaches' families could just as likely cast long shadows over others. Almost any wife who attended games regularly had to digest the bitter bile of critical fans. Sons who played football certainly endured pressures and expectations beyond the normal ken of their teammates. And for daughters and sons alike, just having their father at school placed them in awkward social positions. Many coaches handled the dual role well and claimed that the intersection of career and family life provided their most treasured moments. Others, so very certain about most aspects of their life, expressed regrets and remarked that their roles as husbands, and especially fathers, left them unsure of themselves.

As members of a group used to a regimented life, almost every coach predictably headed a traditional, nuclear family household where husbands and wives took on typical roles. Donald Jay remarked: "My wife made the minor decisions, like making sure the rent got paid, if the kids could get braces on their teeth, if we could afford new shoes for them, and that kind of thing. I decided things like whether we should let Red China into the U.N.—all the important decisions." Jay's comment reflected, for men, the expectations of the times. And like most males of the postwar generation, he no doubt stepped into his role quite comfortably without giving it much thought.

The legacy of the Great Depression naturally weighed heavily on how coaches' families approached their finances. The experience of Ray Akins, and his wife, Virginia, was representative. Appropriately, the couple had met at a football game while he was playing at Southwest Texas State. At the Bobcats' home field, he had noticed her sitting in the front row of the student section, and once, while the team was relaxing before a game, he approached her. "Later, I sought her out and asked her for a date. The rest is history," Akins laughed. His first coaching job at Rosebud paid $150 a month, out of which he insisted they save fifteen dollars. Except for their house, they bought nothing on credit. "If we couldn't pay for it, we didn't buy it." Later, Akins insisted, "I loosened up," but evidently not much. His comments revealed a rigid pattern of work habits that belied the comfortable living he eventually enjoyed. For example, he remarked that he routinely kept cars and trucks for ten years and performed all the maintenance work himself. During the summer break, in addition to getting ready for football season, he worked every spare moment.

Again, Akins was a typical case. The coach who simply took off during the summer break was virtually nonexistent. Whether performing the manual labor jobs that had been so familiar in their youth, or taking advantage of newfound connections, coaches added to their income any way they could. Across the state they worked on construction sites, baled hay, and mowed yards; others sold insurance or worked in offices. In East Texas some of them became forest rangers or lake patrol officers. Others in West Texas and on the Gulf Coast worked in the oil field. Bob Harrell asserted: "There were times I made more money in three months on one of those rigs than in nine months coaching." Another summer he drove a furniture truck back and forth between Texas and California. Most often, though, coaches headed recreation programs and taught summer school and driver's education.

Allen Boren fondly recalled a summer in Edna during the early 1960s when the school district hired him and some fellow coaches to paint and maintain the physical plant. It was the same summer that controversial Dallas stripper Candy Barr—a former Edna resident—found herself on probation after being locked up for possessing a small amount of marijuana. One of the conditions of Barr's release was that she had to return to her hometown and could not leave Jackson County. While in town she stayed with her younger sister, who lived across the street from one of the elementary schools. "Let me tell you," said Boren, "that school was the cleanest, most well-maintained building in town."

Just after the war, when Bull Workman got into the coaching profession, he spent his summers working at a filling station. The man who would later have a school named for him commented that it didn't bother him to be "top man" for nine months and pump gas for three because of his Depression experience. Playing football and manual labor was all many coaches of his generation had ever known, so when it came time to make ends meet it was not unusual for coaches to fall into familiar routines.

The old coaches' backgrounds also made them value education. Because the vast majority were first-generation college students, they certainly appreciated the importance of a degree, and most of them made sure that their accomplishment became a family tradition. Coaches, in fact, pointed with great pride to the number of coaches' sons and daughters who became doctors, lawyers, Ph.D.'s, and professionals, including many teachers and coaches.

"They say that a coach doesn't believe in education?" asked Elmer Redd rhetorically. "I answer it like this: All three of my daughters finished Lufkin High School with honors. One of them is a medical doctor in Tyler, another is home economics instructor at Barbara Jordan High School in Houston and teaches at a night college there. The other owns her own company in Houston; she represents professional athletes."

Coaches' Wives

While coaching families normally planned their futures and made other major decisions jointly, wives almost always took over the household from the time their husbands returned from coaching school in late July until early winter, when the season ended. "They understand that during football season nothing is going to get done around the house," said Joe Hedrick. "If the hinges would fall off the door, she knew she'd better fix it herself." On the other hand, he asserted: "My wife was always very supportive, and I think she would have argued very strongly with anyone who would have kept her own children from playing."

"The vast majority of coaches I know coached as a family with all members invaluable to the cause," echoed Gordon Brown. "But I also know of families who suffered because there was not a husband and father in the house, due to the commitment of time they gave to coaching." Donald Jay added: "The hours are incredible . . . when your job is your hobby, you can lose track of time."

Even in the best of situations, Jay asserted, wives from time to time would express their resentment. When his own wife once tested him, declaring: "You love football more than you do me"—he deflected it by retorting: "That's OK, honey, I love you more than I love basketball!" More dramatic, he recalled, was a coach's wife who laid down behind the family car to keep her husband from pulling out of the driveway. Looking up, she protested: "Every time you get into this car, you're going down to the field house, and I don't see you for the rest of the day!"

Nevertheless, most coaches' wives persevered. "A wife would have to be very unselfish and understanding to survive in many cases," remarked Gordon Brown. "If she was expecting an eight-to-five workday, she would certainly have some adjustment problems." Added James Brewer: "Coaches' wives are a different breed. Hell, they have to be." To an extent, the same pressures that in part made coaches such an animated bunch tested the mettle of their spouses as well. Being unable to do much to influence their situation made it all the more frustrating. The tenuous stability that rested on winning and losing, for example, uprooted many a football family after a poor season. Even a successful season that brought an offer promising to better a coach's career might compel his wife to call the moving company.

THE **OL' COACH**®

CAP... *TO COVER HAIR THAT HAS BEEN PULLED OUT*

EAR PLUGS... *FOR SHUTTING OUT CRITICISM OF SECOND GUESSERS*

FOR WHISTLING WHILE HE WORKS

FOR POPPING *AFTER UNDEFEATED SEASON*

TAPE FOR MOUTH... *SURE CURE FOR NOT CRITICIZING OFFICIALS*

TRICK BUZZER... *FOR GREETING SPORTING GOODS SALESMEN*

STOMACH PUMP... *FOR BANQUET CIRCUIT*

CUFF... *FOR SPEAKING OFF OF*

WRIST WATCH... *INSTRUMENT FOR LETTING HIM KNOW WHEN TO TAKE ULCER PILLS*

PERSUADING DEVICE *HE'S ACCUSED OF USING BY PLAYERS AND PARENTS*

TO HELP HIM REMEMBER *WHAT FAMILY LOOKS LIKE*

TOWEL ... *FOR CRYING ON OR THROWING IN*

NOTICE TO ASSISTANTS... *STAB HERE*

BABY BOTTLE... *FOR PLAYING NURSEMAID TO STAR PLAYERS*

STATE COACHING DIRECTORY... *FOR KEEPING TRACK OF BUDDIES WHO MIGHT GIVE HIM A JOB*

BUTTER CHURN... *FOR BUTTERING UP IMPORTANT SCHOOL OFFICIALS*

TO REMIND HIM THERE'S *"ALWAYS NEXT YEAR"*

HOE... *FOR THAT ROUGH ROAD*

SPRING... *FOR BOUNCING BACK AFTER BAD YEAR*

HAVE BAG WILL TRAVEL

DUNCE CAP *DONATED BY OTHER MEMBERS OF FACULTY*

INSTANT EFFIGY... *FOR FANS' CONVENIENCE*

Courtesy Ray Franks Publishing Ranch, Copyright 1967, P.O. Box 7068, Amarillo, Texas 79114.

It was in the bleachers, however, where coach's wives suffered their greatest pains. Walt Parker lamented the hard times his wife, Mildred, endured, especially when his teams traveled. "A couple of times I know she was in tears when people knew who she was, and they kept it up anyway." Bill Shipman related that during one game: "My father-in-law and my wife were sitting there, and a disgruntled fan in the stands kept yelling slurring remarks down toward the field. Finally, someone nearby said: 'Hush. That's the coach's wife sitting there.' So, the fan said: 'Coach? Coach? Hell, we ain't got no coach!'" And poor Jewell Wallace's wife. While watching Wallace's El Paso team roll up a 56–0 score against Albuquerque by running "student body right" and "student body left" all night, a man complained to her: "That lousy husband of yours only

MRS. OL' COACH

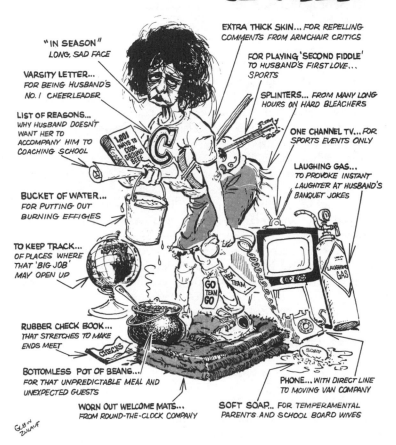

"IN SEASON" LONG, SAD FACE

VARSITY LETTER... FOR BEING HUSBAND'S NO. 1 CHEERLEADER

LIST OF REASONS... WHY HUSBAND DOESN'T WANT HER TO ACCOMPANY HIM TO COACHING SCHOOL

BUCKET OF WATER... FOR PUTTING OUT BURNING EFFIGIES

TO KEEP TRACK... OF PLACES WHERE THAT 'BIG JOB' MAY OPEN UP

RUBBER CHECK BOOK... THAT STRETCHES TO MAKE ENDS MEET

BOTTOMLESS POT OF BEANS... FOR THAT UNPREDICTABLE MEAL AND UNEXPECTED GUESTS

WORN OUT WELCOME MATS... FROM ROUND-THE-CLOCK COMPANY

EXTRA THICK SKIN... FOR REPELLING COMMENTS FROM ARMCHAIR CRITICS

FOR PLAYING 'SECOND FIDDLE' TO HUSBAND'S FIRST LOVE... SPORTS

SPLINTERS... FROM MANY LONG HOURS ON HARD BLEACHERS

ONE CHANNEL TV... FOR SPORTS EVENTS ONLY

LAUGHING GAS... TO PROVOKE INSTANT LAUGHTER AT HUSBAND'S BANQUET JOKES

PHONE... WITH DIRECT LINE TO MOVING VAN COMPANY

SOFT SOAP... FOR TEMPERAMENTAL PARENTS AND SCHOOL BOARD WIVES

Courtesy Ray Franks Publishing Ranch, Copyright 1967, P.O. Box 7068, Amarillo, Texas 79114.

knows two darn plays!" Wallace winked and added: "Now, keep in mind this was same man who drew up a play and gave it to me, but it took about thirteen players to run it."

Many coaches tried to shield their wives from carping fans. Even though Joe Washington believed that his wife, a schoolteacher's daughter, already was acclimated to critics, he made sure that all the staff spouses at Port Arthur got seats in the press box. James Brewer encouraged his wife to "sit off by yourself," or, at a packed game, "find a spot in the visitors' stands." Otherwise, he told her, "you'd be exposed to some things you don't need to hear."

Still other coaches' wives, cut from the same cloth as their husbands, gave back as good as they got. Gordon Brown recounted: "My first game in a new coaching job found my wife sitting by a man who early in the game said: 'This new coach they hired is more ignorant than the last.' My wife said to him: 'My name is Mrs. Brown, the coach's wife, I haven't met you yet.' Shortly thereafter the man went to the concession stand and never returned."

Eddie Joseph actually got to enjoy the moment when his own wife had enough. It came the year after he retired, and the couple was unable to enjoy watching their son, who was playing for Austin Westlake, because of the constant taunting of a particularly crude and vocal man. Making her way through the crowd, Mrs. Joseph confronted him: "I've put up with this for twenty-odd years, and I don't have to put up with it anymore. Now, shut up and sit down!" The scene evoked a standing ovation from everyone within earshot.

Even less subtle was Bill Patrick's wife, who watched fans turn rabid one year when Galena Park's season went south. "Some of the fans had made little pickets with 'Fire [head coach] Sadler' on them." Storming down the aisle, she grabbed the placard from one of the more vocal fans and "ripped it up and then hit him so hard with the little stick that it broke over his head."

Because the nature of the profession limited coaches and their wives socially, laying a firm bedrock for their relationship was of paramount importance. "The only people outside of coaching who can understand the coach is the coach's wife," claimed Maurice Cook. Even so, he continued, "young coaches especially have tended to suffer some heartbreak, and many of them have had to leave coaching because their wives couldn't adapt to the demands on their time and the paltry salary." Cook noted that as he got older, he increasingly found himself counseling younger colleagues. He told about one young couple that had separated. "Finally, I just got them both together, and I promised her I'd get him home earlier, and it worked out."

During Donald Jay's tenure as executive director of the Texas High School Coaches Association, he occasionally spoke to college physical education classes in which the students were in part composed of aspiring coaches. Citing the countless hours they would be spending in practice and in the field house, he admonished them to consider the strains that would burden their families. "Before you get married, you need to take your prospective bride back to your hometown or her hometown, and talk to the coach's wife." Only in that way, Jay said, could they both "truly appreciate the sacrifices they would have to make."

It helped if they shared some common ground. While attending Hardin-Simmons, Carlos Berry's future wife became interested in the Baptist school's missionary program. But her mother, said the coach, "convinced her that she could do just as much good right here at home as a coach's wife if she took an active part," which she did. At Henrietta, for example, the Berrys noticed that after games, kids had a lot of pent-up energy and no place to wind down. So, the Berrys organized slumber parties at the gymnasium, where they allowed the kids to run amok all night. "After a while the churches caught on and started throwing their own after-game parties," Berry said.

Knowing that Moon Mullins was going into the coaching profession actually appealed to his girlfriend, whom he married when they were seniors at Hardin-Simmons College. "She had always wanted to marry a coach. She was born in Wichita Falls, and her dad was a great Coyotes fan." John Hugh Smith remarked: "My wife usually taught at one of the elementary schools where I coached. If they are teachers they understand better." O. W. Follis called his spouse "the best coach's wife I've ever seen." The couple taught together at Lamesa High School for thirty-seven years and retired at the same time. An English teacher, "she also sponsored the cheerleaders for, I think, twenty-five years, so she was close to a lot of the girls."

Others grew into the relationship. "My wife, Marjorie, thought she knew what she was getting into, but she didn't," said Herb Allen. When the college sweethearts from Prairie View became serious, Allen warned her that the career for which he was preparing would require him to be away from home much of the time. While at Hearne, in about the third year of their marriage, Marjorie learned just how lonely those long stretches could be. She began complaining how her friends were playing cards with their husbands and socializing together while she was sitting at home. "I knew this was going to come up," Allen recalled telling her. "I told you before we got married that I would have to provide for you and this is how I intend to do it."

Not long afterward, Marjorie Allen left home and returned to her parents. "Marjorie's mother set her straight," Herb Allen recalled. "It took about three months, but she called and told me to come get her." Afterward Mrs. Allen became a top booster at every place the couple lived, and she regularly involved other coaches' wives in activities during the football season.

Organizing groups was a practice that many coaches' wives initiated. "At Brownwood," said Morris Southall, "they had a 'Mothers' Club' for all the football players' moms, and a lot of the wives would be active in that." Several other coaches drew similar examples. Such relationships worked, asserted Herb Allen, only because their wives realized that without football their husbands would not be the same men, and they could not excel at their jobs without putting in the time.

"What I did to meet her part of the way was to try and take the losses and frustrations out on myself," Allen continued. James Brewer, too, commented that he "did not bring much home" because his wife would read more into his problems than he wanted. "Women are much more sensitive than their men and they tend to see things differently."

The game, of course, absorbed coaches, and rare were individuals who could leave behind their emotions at the field house when the long day ended. Especially when football season rolled around, wives clearly noticed a "Dr. Jekyll and Coach Hyde" transformation in their husbands, and a small dose of "Coach Hyde" went a long way. In that respect, many coaches believed that their wives were almost grateful for their prolonged absences during football season, especially on any Friday night after a loss.

For example, an East Texas coach's wife and her elementary-school-aged daughter and son waited up until after midnight one bleak season to console the man whose team had lost "the big one" by a narrow margin in front of the home crowd. His mighty eleven, down by less than a touchdown with under two minutes to go, was marching down the field for what would surely be the season's finest hour. Deep in their opponents' territory, the quarterback raised up to throw the ball out of bounds and stop the clock. Only he did not throw it far enough, and the visitors' tall cornerback picked it out of the air and sailed eighty-some-odd yards down the sideline to preserve the victory.

At long last, the wife and kids heard the family car ease into the garage. In the utility room they met the crestfallen coach; his children sidled up and hugged him around the legs. Searching for some soothing words, the coach's wife shrugged: "Well, honey, you can't win 'em all." Letting go of their daddy's legs, the siblings shot worried glances at each other and stepped out of the way. Something primordial, guttural, and unintelligible exploded from the coach's lips. Looking around for something to throw or smash, he finally just hit the wall, sinking his fist in so deeply that it bulged out on the other side. As he pulled his arm out, white flakes of sheetrock and dust flew everywhere. While the kids headed for cover in the kitchen, the coach's wife never flinched. Without a word she stoically brushed the debris from her nightgown, and the next day a year-old calendar hung over the hole.

A Wonderful Life

"Fortunately there were seasons of the year that were less demanding," asserted Gordon Brown. "I decided early on that I would not let the game keep me from my church and my family. It was rare, if ever, that I missed church to work on football. . . .[And] I made time to play, hunt with the kids, and do other family things. . . . It is probable that my family felt I did not do enough of this . . . . Although some of my successful friends who were coaches prided themselves on working all night or all weekend, I always felt it counterproductive to success. I felt my staff and players needed the break away from the sport in order to come back fresh. It took great planning to accomplish what had to be done in preparation for the game. . . . I now strongly recommend this practice to all young coaches."

Brown was not alone in his approach to the game, and he took it farther than most of his peers. Then again, the life he carved out also depended on involving other family members in football. "In my case," Brown continued, "my wife was a teacher, my son played under me, . . . and my daughter was a cheerleader. . . . I understand the risk I was taking, but—and I might be biased—fortunately it was a great experience for all."

It was a sentiment that many coaches echoed. Donald Jay recalled Doctor Campbell, the family's practitioner at West Orange, once telling him: "Donald, I envy you coaches. I can go in and perform a great operation and save someone's life, and my kid never sees it. Your kids see your work every Friday night."

For daughters, however, watching was as close to the game as they could get, and involving them was often difficult. Men such as Gordon Brown, or Robert Lowrance, who raised two cheerleaders, considered themselves fortunate to have daughters who were involved with football, even if in a peripheral way. Little girls who were the pampered apples of their daddy's eye had many counterparts who were neglected because their fathers were away from home so much or did not know how to treat them. While the young sons of coaches were fixtures around the field house, daughters often became invisible.

Coaches who fashioned good relationships with their daughters often had to venture beyond the football field. Gordon Wood, for example, made time for his daughter by regularly borrowing a couple of ponies from a rancher friend at Stamford and taking rides with her. During the summer he ran the municipal swimming pool and spent a lot of time in the water with both his daughter and son.

Many coaches told similar stories, but perhaps none of them formed a more unique bond with his daughter than Zac Henderson. At the family's brief stay at Jena, Louisiana, he got into the routine of asking his three-and-a-half-year-old daughter for predictions. "Before the game, I'd say: 'Carol, is daddy's team going to win?' And she'd say: 'Yes,' and sure enough we'd win. . . . She kept going and going all that year, and she'd predict the losers, too." The next season young Carol got them all right again and kept the string intact the following year—even the time before one game, when she said neither team would actually "win." Henderson had asked: "'Is daddy's team going to win?' And she says: 'No.' 'Well, is the other team going to win?' 'No.' 'Is any team going to win?' 'No.' And I thought: 'What in the devil?' . . . What happened was that we got out there on the football field and the other team didn't show up."

For three straight years at Jena, Carol called them all correctly. The Hendersons then moved to Cisco in the old West Texas Oil Belt, where she continued her accurate predictions. Their second year there, into the play-offs, she still had the string going. With highly ranked Cisco playing number-one-ranked Stamford, a nervous Henderson knelt in front of his little daughter and put his hands lightly on her shoulders, awaiting the word. When she crowed: "Daddy's team's gonna win!" the overjoyed coach jumped up—"Awright!" On the scoreboard, however, Stamford came out ahead and the next week again defended its top ranking against Brady. But after the Brady game the UIL declared that Stamford had been fielding an ineligible player

Young Mark Smith sizes up a full-sized "J–5V" held by his father, Hoot Smith, 1961. *Photograph courtesy Hoot Smith.*

and awarded forfeits for several of the previous games—including the Stamford contest with Cisco.

"The psychology class at Hardin-Simmons wanted to interview her and a lot of other hoopla," remarked Henderson, but the big fuss unsettled the girl. "The next season, before the first game, I asked her, and she said: 'Daddy, I'm getting too old to do this.'" So the reluctant coach relented, and Carol Henderson retired her crystal ball, her perfect record intact.

Coaches' Sons

Where sons were involved, standing aside was not so easy. What coaches had lived and taught to their players often went double at home. These sons of the Great Depression and World War II worried whether their material and social gains might make their sons go soft. Coaches were the kinds of men who taught their boys to love Jesus and show respect for women, yet at the same time admonished them never to forget that, when push comes to shove, the guy who throws the first punch wins most of the fights. Southern men have been trying to reconcile this contradiction since "y'all sic 'em," and Texas high school coaches were certainly products of their environment. Some handled the dilemma better than others, but in general they were among the most ardent defenders of this perception of spirituality, chivalry, and manliness.

On a social level the coach-player association blurred the lines between father and son when the two stepped onto the same football field. Many relationships worked out well, but others developed strains. Coaches tended to overreact and either placed additional pressure on their sons to succeed or bent over backward to avoid charges of favoritism, often without even realizing it. Sons, already in the awkward teenage years, also found themselves trying to conform to their fathers' values while struggling to fit in socially with their classmates, which many found a difficult task.

Maurice Cook likened the experience of coaching his own son, Mike, to "that sweet and sour" food. Recalling their days at Pine Tree, outside of Longview, he commented: "We had a lot of tremendous times together, a lot of mountain tops. And, boy, we had some valleys." As the team's quarterback, Mike found himself in a slump during his senior year. "He tried too hard, and I was trying to get him straightened out, and the more we [coaches] tried, the more frustrated he got." The fans, of course, placed even more pressure on the staff, and for a while the coaches played another quarterback for the sake of appearances. "It's tempting to listen to the stands and try things out of desperation instead of going by what you know is right," remarked Cook. Eventually he reinstalled Mike and the boy had a good season.

But at home, Cook continued, it was Susan—the coach's wife and quarterback's mother—who was caught in the middle. "Any problems that a young man has, he ought to be able to go talk to his daddy about it. But Mike really didn't have a dad, he had a coach. I tried to be a dad, and we tried not to talk football, but it was such a big part of both of our lives, it was like avoiding that elephant in the room." As for the role of "daddy," he said: "My wife had to fill those shoes for a long time. . . . She didn't pity him, but she listened, [and] if there was something that she felt I was wrong about, we would discuss it where he never knew it. I listened to her wisdom, and she helped me see things as they really were. . . . She helped me get my priorities back together."

Mike Cook suffered in another way, too. Like most coaches' sons, there remained that element that separated him ever so slightly from the pack. "A coach's son is not just one of the players," asserted his father, "because anything that's said about the coach is about his dad. So, as a result, the normal locker room conversation, or down at the local Dairy Queen, or wherever kids assemble, he's left out a little bit, because he can't hear everything that's said. And if he does, he's in the position—'Do I defend my dad, or do I just try to be a team member?'"

At Nacogdoches, Clarence McMichael's son was in that very spot during one spring training, when the other black members of his ninth-grade team quit to protest a cheerleading election. The McMichaels lived only a few blocks from the school, which enabled them to eat lunch together.

On the day after the ill-fated election the coach walked into the den and found his son crying. Some of his teammates had told him they would understand if he did not join them because of his father. Looking up at the coach, he said: "How would you feel if you were the only black kid that showed up for practice?" McMichael pledged to support his son no matter what he decided, but also told him he would have to make that decision himself. When the black players met that afternoon in the locker room, young McMichael told them he had chosen to be loyal to his father. One of the leaders in the group then said that he could not let McMichael show up alone. While about fifteen players did sit out that spring, three others also decided to come back.

On the field, especially, coaches and their sons could not escape the fact of their relationship. "Most coaches faced a time when their own kids were playing," Carlos Berry said, and "you can really lose your perspective, because you love your son, but you also have a strong sense of duty and don't want to be accused of favoritism." Berry continued: "Every once in a while, a coach will get fired for putting his son on the depth chart in front of some other kid who an important person thinks is better. There's a lot of jealousy involved. That paternal instinct takes over almost every time."

Drawing his own example, Berry professed that he knew what it was like to be a parent. His oldest son, Dusty, was trying out for the Little League all-star team in Haskell. Berry had to leave momentarily in the middle of the selection process and did not hear whether the boy had made the cut. "I got back, and there he and some other kid were, sitting there in center field on the scaffolding of the scoreboard. I thought to myself: 'Surely Dusty was chosen, after all, he was a good player.' The more I thought about, the more I stewed over it." After a while Berry's son came up and begged a quarter. Apprehensively, the coach asked him if he had made the team. "He just kind of walked off and said yes, and I realized right there that to the parents it could be a lot bigger deal than to the kids."

Even so, players got jealous, and on the practice field coaches were routinely tougher on their sons than anyone else. Bill Shipman professed: "I enjoyed coaching my own son, Walter; however, in an effort not to show favoritism, I was probably harder on him than any other player. His teammates often spoke up in his defense, which pleased me." Bum Phillips, long proud that he had treated his son, Wade, like everybody else, learned the unpleasant truth years later. While on the staff of the San Francisco 49ers, he visited with Mike Simpson, whom he had also coached at Port Neches when Wade was playing. "We were talking about it, and he told me: 'If I'd been Wade, I couldn't have played for you, because you were so hard on him.'"

Darrell Tully commented: "I think I did my own son a big disservice by not coaching him more. I let the other coaches coach him, and I should have done it myself, at least more than I did, for the simple reason that I was afraid I'd be too tough on him." It was a realization born of a particular incident. "When he was on the sophomore team, the varsity would scrimmage the JV, and I'd use him sometime as the opponents' 'best man.' When we were playing Bellaire in the play-offs, they had a good end, and we were going to put a double-team on him and knock him down, and not let him off the line of scrimmage. That was the job my son got, and he still complains about it!"

At the East Texas high school where Steve McCarty coached, the sons of several coaches on his staff had played quarterback. "It became kind of a tradition," McCarty recalled. The coach and his son, Ty, both felt some anxiety because "his abilities just weren't as big as his heart." Before it got too far, however, the boy fell from a ladder while painting the house and injured his knee so badly that he could no longer play football. "Really, it was a blessing," McCarty said. "Both of us could feel that the pressure was off."

Some coaches avoided having to coach their sons and sent them to other schools or encouraged them to go out for other sports. After Charles Qualls's youngest son saw the hell his big brother went through, he decided that basketball was the sport for him, and by the time he came of age, his father gave him his blessing. "I knew I'd be too hard on my son," asserted Paschal's James Brewer, "so I sent him to Richland." Frank Pulattie did the same thing, but only after he had brought his son up to scrimmage against the varsity while he was still in junior high. "I couldn't control my patience with him a couple of times and didn't want to repeat the mistake." Sending a talented son to Dallas's Bryan Adams "really hurt" Woodrow Wilson's Cotton Miles. In fact, after both teams won district, father and son squared off at the old P. C. Cobb Stadium before a sellout crowd of twenty-two thousand people. "The week of the game we didn't talk about it much, but it sure made my wife nervous," Miles laughed. Due in part to his son's play, Bryan Adams squeaked by, 21–17, and the next week Cotton Miles was up in the press box helping his son's coaches.

Despite the touchy situation, many helmsmen professed that they coached their own sons with no apparent problems. "I heard of coaches who did not want the burden of coaching their own sons, but I wanted the best for them, and that was me!" exclaimed Morris Southall. "Nobody had their better interests at heart than their daddy." Eddie Joseph coached three sons and had no problems. "I enjoyed the experience. As a rule we never talked about football at home because we spent so much time on it at school." At practice, Joseph conceded, he probably yelled at them more than some other boys, "but it just wasn't fair to subject them to any pressure at home."

Rusty Workman, who played during his father's last two years in the profession, provided the coach one of his most treasured moments the night he led Arlington to a tight 10–0 win over a great Grand Prairie team. Amid the jubilant crowd, the coach's wife made her way onto the field, where she embraced both her husband and their son. "Rusty made it easy because he was such a good athlete. The other players

Mayfield Workman, Arlington High,
1969. *Photograph courtesy Texas High
School Coaches Association, Austin.*

selected him as MVP of his peers, and he made all-district at fullback
and went on to the University of Texas on a scholarship." Even so, during the boy's junior year, Workman had to be scolded by another member of the team's staff before he regularly installed his son into the starting lineup.

Sons who inherited their fathers' athletic prowess certainly were more
likely to avoid the pitfalls that the relationship could bring. Coaches such
as Zac Henderson, Joe Washington, Ray Akins, Moon Mullins, and John
Reddell enjoyed coaching sons who, once in college, either matched or
overshadowed their fathers' considerable accomplishments. Bob Barfield,
too, had a pair of sons who performed well in high school. His youngest,
Gary, went largely unnoticed because of his near-invisible position as center, but the other, Danny, played quarterback and earned all-state honors
for leading Pasadena deep into the play-offs in 1961.

"Let me tell you about a great moment that we got to experience
together," said Barfield. "It will let you know just how special coaching
your own son can be." The occasion came against Texas City during that
1961 season, when Pasadena had gone from elation—after going ahead
with two minutes to go—to utter dejection, when Texas City answered
with its own go-ahead score with under half a minute left on the clock.
"We received the kickoff, and just to show you how lucky you can be, on
the next snap, Danny threw a pass right down the middle and the kid miss-
es it. If he catches it, he gets tackled [and the game's over]. But on the last
play of the game he throws it in the end zone and we won the ball game."

For coaches' sons whose experiences were good ones, growing up with
football made them set their sights on a career in the profession. Maurice
Cook, Eddie Joseph, Quin Eudy, Carlos Berry, Clarence McMichael, Bum
Phillips, E. C. Lerma, Bill Patrick, Hugh Hamm, Moon Mullins, and
Morris Southall all had sons to whom they passed the torch. Yet for these
coaches' sons and other kindred souls who grew up in a locker room, the

game has changed. Whether because they became disillusioned or because they developed new interests, some have dropped out of the coaching ranks. Still others have adjusted and perpetuated their fathers' legacy.

"How I got to here from where I came, I can't believe it," stated Moon Mullins. "From an old dumb farm boy that had never been out of Rusk County, and being able to go to college, and to meet my wife there and see my kids grow up the way they have . . . " his voice trailed. "I had four boys, and all of them had college scholarships. Football is my life, and it's been my family's life." And for one son, at least, it continues to be. Just recently, Moon Mullins was able to enjoy vicariously Grapevine's 1996 Class 4-A state championship through his son Gary, a former all-state quarterback at San Angelo who, as Mike Sneed's quarterback coach, molded an all-stater of his own. "It's been a wonderful experience," Moon Mullins concluded. "I'd hate to think where our family would be—or even if I'd have a family—if it weren't for football."

Part IV

An Era of Change and Crisis: The 1960s and Beyond

Chapter 9

Falling out of Step: Coaches and Changing Values

ometime during the 1960s all of the changes that marked post-war society began forcing Texas high school coaches from the center of the cultural mainstream. The more observant men in the profession began to reexamine their roles and values and how their methods and philosophies fit into cultural currents. As early as the 1950s some of them recognized that society was outgrowing their Depression-centered view of the world. More important, by the 1960s, coaches recognized that the players they shepherded were beginning to hear a drummer whose tune most adults could not discern. They lamented that more and more boys who had traditionally come out for the football team were finding other activities more appealing. Educators, too, began developing new ideas that transcended "reading and writing and 'rithmatic" as well as the "hickory stick" that had so long accompanied established practices. And during the era of integration and Vietnam, Texans, like all Americans, grew suspicious of one another and distrustful of authority figures. Increasingly, progressive-minded men and women came to take football less seriously, and the values the new generation advocated were often at odds with those of the old-time coaches. As their ranks began thinning during the 1960s and 1970s, the coaching veterans who remained in the profession found that changing conditions forced them to adjust their methods, even if their goals remained the same.

Rise of the Suburbs

The economic explosion that swept Texas into an industrial age fostered new social conditions that also changed the character and composition of the state. One noticeable manifestation of economic growth was a swelling population that occupied new suburbs and stretched enrollments in outlying schools. Stoney Phillips, who described how the chemical industries had transformed Pasadena, added that the postwar boom was only one wave in an open-ended growth curve. If Pasadena High School seemed large with about eight hundred students in 1950, when Phillips became head coach there, he scarcely recognized the school system from which he retired as athletic director in the 1970s. And now, he exclaimed: "Pasadena's district has four high schools with about twenty-five-hundred kids apiece!" The entire area between Houston and the Gulf Coast, in fact, seemed filled with new people and new schools. When he began coaching, Phillips said: "There wasn't anything where NASA is, and over at Clear Creek, there was a school, Webster. We played them, it was about our size, but there wasn't a Clear Lake. Now it's got three high schools."

Burgeoning suburbs and former crossroads towns accumulated large pools of talent from which to draw athletes, and in places lucky enough to sustain or establish a tradition, football reached a new kind of prominence, less inclusive to be sure, but more polished and sophisticated. All over the state, whether in the suburbs or in small cities, as new schools emerged, some of those that had once commanded respect shrank into mediocrity alongside their more upwardly mobile competitors. At places like Odessa and Galena Park, new powerhouses emerged with appendages such as Permian and North Shore. Other erstwhile contenders such as Garland, along with new crosstown rivals as South Garland, North Garland, and others that opened later, seldom rose above the shuffle of so many sister schools.

John Reddell, the first coach at Amarillo's new Palo Duro High School, remarked that when it opened, "we were kind of the 'step school' to Amarillo High." The established institution enjoyed a trophy case full of weathered footballs, including three that represented consecutive state championships during the 1930s. Each of those teams was led by Blair Cherry, who moved on to greater fame coaching at the University of Texas. Consequently, "we had to build our own tradition," Reddell said. "When we started playing Amarillo High, we were the 'school across town,' and it was quite a few years before we got to where we could really compete with them." Nevertheless, he insisted, for those attached to schools like Palo Duro, "your part of town was very, very strong for you."

Expansion schools were at a disadvantage in their first few years, not only because they lacked traditions, but also because they suffered from low enrollments and a reluctance on the part of athletes to be the pioneers in new programs. Very quickly, however, the new schools with their gleaming facilities, fed by growing neighborhoods, began eclipsing places on the "old side of town" that suffered the kinds of social problems from which well-to-do families wanted to escape.

On the Houston Ship Channel, Galena Park assistant Bill Patrick had enjoyed being part of teams that came within a touchdown of winning a state championship in 1961 and 1964. When the town added North Shore High School in 1964, Patrick said, "it watered down the talent, but everyone expected us to keep on winning, even after it became obvious that North Shore was getting the better kids." Patrick remained with the Yellowjackets until the entire staff was fired after an 0–10 season in 1980. Places like Galena Park became "coaches' graveyards," remarked Patrick, "where people finishing their careers ended up."

Many of the old-time coaches did not wait that long. In fifteen years at the helm of Wichita Falls, Joe Golding never suffered a losing season. With Rider High opening the year after he brought home the class 4-A crown in 1961, the old coach called it quits—"It was quite obvious that there was only one thing for me to do." Nevertheless, over the next decade the Coyotes would make two more appearances in state championship games. In fact, Rider coach Joe Bob Tyler eventually left town in frustration after the school district's purported gerrymandering kept sending the best players to Wichita Falls High.

Such cases were rare. At Odessa, where its two white high schools had openings for a head coach in 1964, Gene Mayfield ultimately set his sights on fledgling Permian, even though the tradition and facilities at the older school seemed superior. Just like players at Amarillo, boys at Odessa High had once sported letter jackets with state champion patches on their sleeves. "Both of those [Odessa] schools looked just great," Mayfield recalled, and with the decision presenting a dilemma, he turned to the advice of longtime friend and former Odessa coach Jack Brewer. "He wrestled with it for a long time himself, and he finally told me: 'Coach, I believe you'd be better off if you'd go to Permian.' So I did, and I never looked back."

Placed in charge of the "feeder schools and all the hiring and firing," Mayfield took a young program with almost no past and laid the foundation for a modern-day high school dynasty. "We went to work with the belief that quickness and speed were going to 'do it' for us as opposed to size," he said. Permian, which had gone 4–6 the previous year, lost its first game at Lubbock to Monterrey High, itself a recently created crosstown rival to yet another former state champion. "But then, the kids were kind of catching on to what we wanted to do, and we turned it around and won the next twelve games, including the state championship.

"I don't remember exactly when," Mayfield continued, "but it was either that year or the following year that the 'Mojo thing' got started. . . . The story that the players told me is that we were playing in Abilene, and some of the college kids who had gone to Permian were in the stands there and singing part of some old song—'We don't want no mo' Joe'— and it caught on. First thing you know they were using it as a rallying cry, and of course it worked, because we were doing a lot of winning."

Whether winning or struggling, conditions in suburban schools produced different kids than the ones most coaches were accustomed to. Franklin's Joe Hedrick commented: "Quite often, in the small schools, coaches are dealing with fifty percent of the male students. At places like Conroe High School before they split up you're dealing with what? One percent? And that's a different ball game." Hedrick recalled that at a coaching school in the early 1960s he ran into old Brenham rival Owen Erickson, who had taken over a Houston-area program. "He was just absolutely shocked at the difference in kids' attitudes. The things that had worked for him in Brenham didn't work for him there. And he didn't stay very long."

John Hugh Smith, who moved from Belton to the newly created
Cypress-Fairbanks High School outside of Houston in the late 1950s,
echoed Hedrick. "The game was more important in the smaller towns
than larger ones. At Cy-Fair it wasn't that important because it was a suburb. There were other distractions. Cy-Fair was growing so fast that it
wasn't stable as far as fan support and interest. There were more people
from other places than from the original communities themselves."

The sense of rootlessness that kids often felt in growing schools composed largely of outsiders, as well as the deteriorating environment in
overburdened inner-city schools, left many former athletes walking the
halls instead of working out on the practice field. Moreover, a UIL rule
designed to discourage recruiting relegated non-senior move-ins to a year
on the B-team. Faced with that prospect, many of these students decided
not to play at all. Kids began to feel lost in such environments, and the
coaches increasingly were unable to touch young lives.

Ray Overton declared: "You should never let a school get over a thousand students." For some kids, "it's as important for them to get recognition as it is to eat the noonday meal. If they can't do it in a positive way,
they'll do it in a negative way. . . . A school has to be small enough for
everybody to find a niche where they can be important. . . . You get as big
as schools are today, and you have a lot of kids who either can't compete
or have the feeling that they can't compete."

At one time, declared Bob Barfield, he was able to keep "a lot of the
borderline kids out for football," yet gradually coaches were left with fewer
avenues. Going to the homes of players and their families used to be a typical custom, he contended, but when he arrived at Pasadena he found that
busy parents in the rapidly growing community had little time for him, and
he had to discontinue the practice. Clarence McMichael said the same
thing, and added that new burdens on coaches such as evaluating film,
supervising weight training, and running off-season programs "got to
where it took up much of their 'team time.'" Consequently, coaches "lost
some kids" who might have benefited from that extra attention.

Social Changes Affect Youth

As the 1960s unfolded, coaches noticed that young people were losing
the measure of social innocence that seemed to have marked earlier generations. Despite the weighty challenges that had always confronted them,
school kids had nevertheless found security and a touchstone of values at
school. Football, too, had an insulating effect on communities and provided a diversion into which fans could briefly retreat from events that
unfolded beyond the stadium gates. Yet increasingly, the divisive forces
that rent American culture in the 1960s did not spare any element of society—school and football included.

For Kingsville's Donald Jay, his experience during the week of
President John F. Kennedy's assassination brought home the realization

that times had changed. "It happened the week we were playing Roy Miller High School [of Corpus Christi] for the district championship. I got back to school about one o'clock that day from dinner, and [assistant coach] Ray Gomez and the principal met me on the steps and said: 'The president's been shot in Dallas.'" Jay and Gomez then hurried to the field house and turned on the radio only to hear the national anthem. "Ray said: 'He's dead,' and I said: 'No, he can't be dead,' but sure enough they came on and said he was."

The two coaches then met the principal and the superintendent to see if they could postpone the game, "but the district champion had to be certified by twelve o'clock Saturday." Officials at both schools agreed to go ahead and play the game, instead of deciding the district championship on the flip of a coin. "And I guarantee you, that game is just as vivid now as it was then," Jay recalled. "It was just like a nightmare. I bet we had fifteen thousand people in the stands, but they were silent. It was like a dream. The people were there, the stands were full, but everyone was still in a state of shock. No excitement; no jubilation; no nothing. In fact, we scored a touchdown, but we couldn't even tell until a kid came to the sidelines and said: 'Coach, we need a tee to kick the extra point.' . . . That game really put things into perspective."

Even though football remained a cornerstone in communities statewide, social changes began to weaken the sport and to undermine the coaches' influence. Coaches contended that at places where administrators purposely subordinated the role of football in campus life, there seemed to be a corresponding loss of school discipline as well. Buzz Allert found himself in such a spot when he became the B-team coach at suburban Smiley High School outside of Houston in 1961. "There I am, a young coach in a very, very rough situation. . . . The first day of school, thirty minutes before the bell, a student got shot, and the principal got whipped—got hit in the nose. He comes running down the hall, white shirt, blood just streaming . . . I'm on one end of a hall that's about fifty yards long, lockers all the way down. I'm standing there, some students are at the other end, and all of a sudden, a whiskey bottle they threw from one end of the hall to the other came to rest at my feet. That's the first day of school!"

Not long afterward some administrators interrupted Allert during P.E. to inform him: "We have a problem with a senior history class. You're going to have to take it." The coach objected, commenting, "I'm not even qualified in history." The fact that Allert was just three years out of professional football and weighed two hundred and twenty pounds seemed to overshadow the fact that he did not possess a social studies certificate. "They said: 'Look, they've already—literally—run two teachers out of there. You are going to take that class.'"

It was a demanding situation, Allert conceded. Yet even though he eventually prevailed in the classroom and on the football field, the experience at Smiley would prove "my greatest disappointment in life"— because the administration did not share Allert's belief that athletics provided an appropriate avenue for "turning everything around." That first year, while the varsity lost every game, Allert's freshmen and sopho- mores went 8–2. "The varsity was horrible, they were a bunch of unrulies," and the coaches, he said, "did nothing to discipline those kids; they were just trying to survive from week to week." At the end of the season the school board fired the entire staff, except for Allert, and asked him to take over the program. "We're in a 4-A district with Baytown, Pasadena, Brazosport, Galveston Ball . . . four of those teams are ranked in the top ten in the state when the 1962 season begins. . . . We start with eighty-five kids, and boy, we worked them out; we play our first game, and we're down to eighteen kids."

When that year's campaign was over, Smiley had won one, tied one, and lost the other eight. "But those eighteen kids started something. Those kids never missed one day of school, one day of practice, were never any problem whatsoever; great, great attitude." The next spring that core of eighteen varsity players grew to about ninety, but Allert knew that he needed to gain some material support to succeed. "We had so many kids wanting to play that we had to work out in shifts. . . . A group of kids would actually work out in a set of uniforms; they would leave, and another group would come in and get in those same dirty, sweaty uniforms."

When Allert took his proposal to the school superintendent, "Mr. Scarborough sits there with his hand on his chin, and lets me go for about thirty minutes or so. Then, he said: 'Buzz, if you go to the board with this program, I'm going to fire you.'" That night, at about eleven o'clock, Allert went before the board anyway and asked for more coaches, more equipment, and some additional funds. "At 1:15 they fired me. . . . That was the biggest disappointment I ever had in my life. Not so much for me, because I was going to get another job . . . but for those eighteen kids who worked their butts off and never, ever, got any payback from the board of education at Smiley High School."

The episode made Allert realize that people's priorities were changing. Just a few years earlier, at San Angelo, Bob Harrell had appealed success- fully to every level of the school's administration as well as to the town itself for the moral support to rebuild its team, while Allert met frustra- tion at every turn. If football was still king in Texas, it was becoming evi- dent that the kingdom had taken on some definable borders.

Even Gordon Wood recognized the insurmountable task that confront- ed him at coastal Victoria in the early 1960s after a long and successful reign at Stamford. "The general run of kids had partying things to do," declared Wood's assistant Morris Southall. At Victoria, he asserted, "there was a caste system. . . . We had good athletes down there, but the upper- class white kids just never got the idea that they had to get out there and bust their butt to get ready for a ball game, and then to give all they had when they got there. . . . Of course, we just stayed down there two years, and then we got back to West Texas as quick as we could.

"The change started 'down there,' but it was moving," Southall continued. "Even out here [in Brownwood] we started getting kids that would not come out for any form of extracurricular activity." Buzz Allert echoed that ever since he could remember, "football was 'it.' If you were healthy and didn't play, there was something wrong with you." When his career began, Allert enjoyed a "situation where there were around three hundred kids, [grades] nine-through-twelve out for football." Then, "when the economy heated up and kids needed material goods, they started falling off."

Long before the youth counterculture began separating boys from the pack, players began quitting football for any number of reasons. Some of them wanted to get jobs so they could buy cars and kill time; in larger places, growing enrollments left the athletically marginal boys reluctant to try out for the team, and still others began to see little point in making the sacrifices that football required.

Carlos Berry remarked that "when it comes time to flesh out the depth chart, you're going to get some hurt feelings; it's unavoidable." Some just accepted it, he remarked, and others tried harder, but increasingly many of them would quit. John Reddell believed that being a part of the team never lost its importance, but, like Berry, he eventually found it more difficult to keep players interested if they did not become starters. To recognize boys on the "scout team," Reddell regularly handed out awards for their contribution. "Used to, they'd stay out as a blocking dummy, but not anymore."

In Fort Worth, Jack Whitley noticed a disheartening pattern emerge among his mostly blue-collar players at Poly High School. Most of their classmates had part-time jobs, and frequently, when players began "going steady" with girls, they would quit the team in order to make enough spending money for dates. Too often Whitley would hear how the students would then get behind on car payments, which forced them to take full-time jobs. "One thing led to another," and soon they would be married and locked into a rut of undereducation and underemployment.

Cars, many coaches agreed, became very important to kids, and with mobility came other temptations. Clarence McMichael remarked that "back then, you had to do everything on foot. Kids got to where they could cover a lot of ground in an automobile, and their parents couldn't keep up with them." Upon learning that a Brownwood sophomore had won several events at a track meet, Gordon Wood was anxious to know what kind of gridiron potential the boy possessed. Yet the track coach responded: "You can write him off—his dad just bought him an Olds 98." The track coach predicted: "Watch him, you'll see his shoulders get narrower and his butt get bigger." And, asserted Wood, "that's just what happened."

Very often parents would not allow their sons to quit the team for such superfluous reasons. Once, when Joe Hedrick had to suspend a player, "he told me he'd never darken the door of the locker room again. But his dad brought him back. This is important—the dad brought him back. Parents today sometimes can't control their kids and they don't want anybody else to, either. In the old days . . . any adult who saw a kid on the street after 11 P.M. could tell a kid to go home and they usually would."

Until the mid-to-late sixties, insisted Ray Overton, "the worse thing they'd do is smoke a cigarette or drink a beer." When Overton was growing up, "the whole community knew what my parents expected of me, and if I did anything out of line, I couldn't turn and run and get home before the news got home. And my parents had already had the trial and set the punishment, and when I got there, they administered it. But I never did resent that, because I knew those people cared for me." Eventually, however, kids became more anonymous, Overton continued. "They go out and do things and nobody knows who they are, and if they do, too many people say: 'I don't want to get involved.'"

Drugs, of course, were added to the list of problems that coaches faced. Gordon Wood called the late 1960s "my roughest time," because of drugs. In balancing his personal ledger, he felt that "losing" several kids cast something of a pall over the three state championships he won during that half-decade. "I lost some good ones in junior high." Among others, he said, "were a lawyer's son, a doctor's son, a banker's son, and a college coach's son."

New Rules and Innovations

While kids became more worldly, high school football reached new plateaus. "These are changes that I've seen, mostly since I quit coaching, that have made football a different game than it was before," said Ed Varley, whose last season was at Fort Worth's Diamond Hill in 1964: "Two-platoon football. Weight training—both the facilities and professional trainers. Wonderful protective equipment—even uniforms. Training rooms and knowledgeable trainers—taping, whirlpools and special pads, et cetera. More coaches—used to, there'd be one coach; now there are special coaches for each position. Better referees and officials— highly trained. And films, films, films!"

As soon as video cameras debuted, coaches were among the first to make use of them. When the Haltom staff got one of the new gadgets in 1973, Joe Bob Tyler instructed the team managers to mount it on the band director's platform. Accustomed to the silent 16mm projectors, the managers had no idea that these new models picked up sound as well as sight. The three-hour practice was narrated, then, by a group of unknowing sixteen- and seventeen-year-old analysts who used the full range of their vocabulary to color the play-by-play, mimicking both coaches and players. The next day, laughed Tyler, "there were some red-faced managers that thought we were going to kick them off the team."

In some respects the changes made the game faster paced and more exciting. In other ways, new conditions left coaches and fans longing for the "good ol' days." James Brewer remarked: "Used to, people didn't specialize. I sometimes wonder if all these weight programs and things don't hurt athletics in a way. Of course, it makes the kids stronger and better, but you can't compete in two or three or four sports like you used to. I never lifted a weight—nobody did. But the day football season was over, I went to basketball, and the day basketball was over, I went to track and baseball. We competed year-round and worked manual labor jobs in the summer."

Nevertheless, contended Eddie Joseph, "football today is a much, much better game than it was in the forties and fifties." Because of nutrition and body building, players today "obviously are stronger, bigger, faster, and they're better coordinated." Joseph underscored his assessment by commenting on a roster he looked over at a recent game. "They had kids 250, 260, 270, and 280, and I can remember many, many teams I coached—and pretty good football teams—that did not have one youngster over two hundred pounds."

Beginning in the late fifties, asserted John Reddell, "people began to really concentrate on strength-building, nutrition, improving speed." Yet weight training, according to most old-time coaches, was slow in coming because of a general belief that it was counterproductive. As Reddell proclaimed, "most folks thought that if you lifted, you'd get muscle-bound and couldn't move." Joe Bob Tyler recalled that in the early 1960s Irving High School was among the first to initiate such a regimen, but his fellow coaches in Wichita Falls did not put much stock in it. "Seemed like we beat them by fifty points just about any time we played them," remarked Tyler. "This was just one reason we scorned weight lifting. Our kids worked in the oil fields and in construction, and they felt that it made them strong enough and tough enough."

Spring Branch's Darrell Tully, whose limited experience with weights had left him similarly unimpressed, became "a believer" after he watched his linemen being manhandled by boys on Bill Stages' Corpus Christi Ray team. "Bill was the first coach I ever knew to have a weight program," Tully recalled. Upon reviewing the game film, Tully noticed that "we would block their kids and move them a yard or two off the line of scrimmage, and they were strong enough in their upper bodies and legs to throw us off and be back in the hole by the time our ball carrier got there." As soon as that football season ended, grunts and huffs and the clang of metal became common sounds at the field house in Spring Branch.

At Holliday, just down the road from Wichita Falls, Bill Carter instituted a weight training program in 1957. He had read an article about lifting that year in *Texas Coach* magazine, and at coaching school he had heard some of the Texas A&M staff endorse the practice and became sold on the idea. So, when football season ended that year, Carter filled a few old buckets with cement and attached them to some oil field pipes, "and those were our weight facilities," he chuckled.

John Reddell did the same thing at Palo Duro—minus the oil field pipes. Yet such homemade equipment, fashioned out of coffee cans and

closet rods, he asserted, became standard issue in programs throughout the
state. Another fad that Reddell identified was "exergenies." The device
looked like a shock absorber with a doubled-over rope strung through it;
the ends terminated onto a harness. Anchored onto a goal post or gym
wall, it worked on resistance and could be set at any level of difficulty.

During football season, of course, teams concentrated on the next
week's opponent, and the long, laborious workouts in full pads left no
room for any other type of exercise. Increasingly, though, remarked
Eddie Joseph, coaches inaugurated off-season programs to develop the
kinds of complementary skills that the more dedicated athletes had previously gained by enrolling in tap and ballet classes. By the 1960s, the three
weeks of spring training proved insufficient to maintain the edge that a
higher level of competition required. Across the state, players spent
countless afternoons after football season learning their position assignments and techniques. At any given school an observer might find linemen honing their blocking skills by following footsteps that coaches had
taped to the gym floor; alongside them, ends and backs would be practicing ball-handling exercises; and, outside, quarterbacks would be tossing
footballs through the hole in a swinging tire, while punters and kickers
were busy perfecting high, lazy arcs and directing short punches at highway cones set on the sidelines.

Boys certainly fell into such a routine at L. D. Bell High School, where
Hoot Smith was suddenly thrust into the head coaching position in 1962.
The promotion followed the tragic death of his mentor, Fred
Pennington, who was electrocuted by a lamp that fell into his swimming
pool. Bell, in suburban Hurst, was a rapidly growing community between
Fort Worth and Dallas. "When I got there in 1960 we had just moved up
from Class 2-A . . . and I never saw so many good-looking athletes in all
my life. . . . And they were 'hungry' for football." Aware of changing conditions and the job pressure that was sure to follow, Smith and assistant
coach Bill Bookout "sat down and started talking about how to get a program started." They ended up with a system that included boys from
kindergarten through high school. Pointing out the window of
Pennington Field's press box, Smith broke from his interview to remark:
"See those Swedish gym sets out there? Bookout and I got one of those
in 1963 for every elementary school." They also launched intramural programs for the grade schoolers as well as one of the state's first summer
track programs for boys of all ages.

At high schools and even junior highs, coaches conceived activities that
taught boys the value of teamwork, how to be more aggressive, and how
to play smarter. Traditional endeavors such as boxing and wrestling, however, actually were quite rare. Coaches preferred "mat drills" and even
more imaginative outlets such as "roughhouse basketball," where the
only rule was that putting the ball through the hoop counted two points.
For a while a form of volleyball played with a gigantic canvas-covered
bladder became popular. The game pitted two teams who tried to guide

the sphere through the goalposts. The only problem was that the ball was larger and heavier than the players, and too often, when individuals found themselves under the ball, it would snap arms and leave necks and shoulders severely strained. Word spread rapidly among coaches, and the game faded as quickly as it had arisen.

Arlington's Bull Workman remarked that using pugil sticks—"just like in the army"—was a more common practice. Resembling giant Q-Tips, the homemade sticks were fashioned out of broom handles to which coaches taped thick, compressed foam. The object of the game was to wrest the stick away from your opponent. "Whapping somebody upside the head" with the butt ends would be a good way to loosen a grip, if such a move could be maneuvered, Workman commented. The more improvisational boys developed techniques such as rolling backward and flipping their opponents over the top with their feet.

Charles Qualls, who relied on such mat drills, recalled an often comic exercise—a form of tug-of-war—designed to teach players to "fire out low and hard and keep your feet moving." He had learned about it at coaching school, where all sorts of ideas were traded back and forth. The drill involved tying two long ropes to an inner tube. At the end of each rope was a shoulder harness—usually salvaged from discarded exergenies. On the command of a coach's " . . . set, hut!" two players standing back-to-back would sprint in opposite directions. The inner tube would soften the point where the ropes ran out of slack, after which the contestants would try to drag each other over a line. The exercise also demonstrated a very convincing lesson on the principle of leverage, for occasionally a boy would reach the end of the rope with his center of gravity too high, which allowed his opponent to propel him backward and headlong with nothing but sky between his feet.

However much off-season programs honed players' skills, coaches nevertheless expressed that the laborious routine compelled many boys to develop second thoughts about playing football. During spring training one year at Nederland, Bum Phillips and his staff were meeting after practice when he answered a knock at the door. Standing before him was a glum-faced Don Chambers, an all-state selection the previous autumn. "He said: 'Coach, I'm going to quit football.' And I said: 'Nope,' and shut the door." After some mental reconnoitering, Phillips went out and asked the boy why such a gifted athlete would want to give up the game. "He said: 'Coach, it's just not fun anymore.' And I said: 'What do you mean it's not fun? It's fun when we win, but you've got to pay the price in the off-season to be able to win in the fall—that's when you get your fun.'" Yet Chambers insisted that the ex-Marine's training program had become simply intolerable.

"So, I went back in and told the staff about it." The long meeting that followed brought them to the conclusion that: "We had everything organized so doggone well that we had organized the fun out of football. . . . Every second of every practice was 'taken.' [The players] didn't have time

to joke or talk or do anything. . . . We had timers going and whistles blowing and people sprinting from one area to another." The next afternoon
the coaches introduced Chambers and his teammates to a revamped program. They relaxed the regimen and gave the boys plenty of breaks as well
as opportunities to become more familiar with the coaches. They also suspended some particularly onerous activities such as tackling drills and
butting each other off of a board. "We just tried to put the fun back in it—
and we did. . . . If you let them, they will enjoy it," Phillips concluded.

The fresh approach was as much an innovation as the "veer" offense or
any other technique or scheme designed to make the program more successful. And to win in Texas, staffs had to "keep up with the Coach
Joneses." Ed Logan believed that "high school football evolved because
people wanted it to." Communities demanded winners, he said, and winning required skill and strategy. And the best teams were well coached
teams. Ray Overton mused: "Most people like me, you started out and
took a job where you had to line the field and sweep the gym floor, and
do all the extra things besides coaching. And everybody had to coach all
sports, and most of us had to coach junior high kids as well as the older
kids." Yet eventually, coaches, like their players, began specializing in one
aspect of the game. Sometime in the 1940s and 1950s coaches began
concentrating on either backs or linemen, and by the 1960s and 1970s
they began specializing on directing backs and linemen on just one side of
the ball, whether offense or defense.

In many respects, asserted Jewell Wallace, "coaches have taken the
game away from the players." Blocking backs in the old single wing,
and quarterbacks afterward, used to call plays in the huddle. Eventually,
free substitution rules, which let players in and out of the game after
every play, allowed coaches to call shots from the bench. Innovative
offenses and defenses also inspired one-upmanship as coaches scrambled
to keep up with their colleagues. For players, it was like going from
playing checkers to playing chess. "If you just stuck with one scheme,"
remarked a bemused Ray Overton, "it would eventually come back
around. . . . People will come in with a defense and stop a particular
type of wing-T, and then they'll turn to the one back [offense] and start
to throw the ball . . . and then they'll revert back to some other version
of the wing-T."

As Overton suggested, the game at times suffered from "improvements," and by the end of the 1960s it was clear that football had settled
into a modern age. Coaches generally cited the free substitution rule, face
masks, plastic helmets, and more and better pads as the most wide-sweep-
ing changes. In the 1970s, the coaches added, artificial turf stepped up
the pace of the game as well. Darrell Tully commented: "When you went
just one way, you not only had fresh kids in there, but you had them in
these plastic helmets and shoulder pads—actually, they were weapons.
That's when spearing came into the game—sticking that head gear in
there. They had to make rules to stop it."

In 1960, the year Tully served as president of the Texas High School Coaches Association, he attended the NCAA rules meeting at Miami. Free substitution was a hot topic that year, supported enthusiastically by some coaches and vehemently opposed by others. Among the proposal's detractors was Rice's Jess Neeley, whose opinion carried considerable weight with Texas high school coaches. "He thought you couldn't be a complete player unless you played both ways," said Tully. In Texas the UIL generally adopted NCAA practices, and between 1954 and 1964, both bodies gradually liberalized the substitution rule. Then, starting in 1965, any number of players could enter the game when the ball changed hands, and two fresh players could go into the game at any time.[1]

Nevertheless, many Texas high school coaches were reluctant to give up a proven formula. Permian's Gene Mayfield commented: "We won the state championship in 1965, and I think nine out of the eleven played both ways. I'd be foolish to make that argument today." Mayfield nevertheless asserted: "I believe a well-conditioned high school athlete can play more than just half the time, and you have some athletes who are simply better than the others wherever they're playing." While still at Borger, Mayfield traveled down the highway to pay his respects to Amarillo's new coach, Bum Phillips. The Sandies' mentor confided to Mayfield that he was thinking about two-platooning. Referring to a high school all-American on his Borger team, Mayfield asked: "Well, Bum, what would you do in my case with a guy like John LaGrone? And he said: 'You know, you've got a point there.'"

Yet Phillips and Mayfield began to take advantage of the liberalized substitution rules. Most teams continued to feature an occasional star who played both ways, but eventually coaches came to see greater advantages in two-platooning, because it allowed them to develop specialists at each position. Coaches also saw it as a way to get more of their players in the game. The rule also came along at a time when a much more profound change gave them more boys from which to choose—integration.

Integration

In near unanimity, coaches professed that no single change wielded a greater impact on high school football, and indeed, in all areas of their careers, than integration. It not only changed the way they approached the game, but it also affected their relationships with players and the way they administered discipline both on and off the field. Regarding coaches' values, philosophies, and methods, integration presented many new challenges. Indeed, some of the routine decisions that earlier had seemed so clear began taking on shades of gray.

Coaches felt particularly qualified to reflect upon integration because they were deeply involved from the very beginning and had a tremendous stake in making it work. Their commitment to youth as well as the burdens of having to build winning programs required coaches to foster goodwill among staff members and players, yet the racial climate that prevailed in Texas during that dramatic time did not portend a smooth transition. White coaches, of course, hailed from traditionally poor, southern backgrounds, and many of them were racists at heart. Their black counterparts, cast into uncertain secondary roles in unfamiliar environments, had to answer to white men who headed both coaching staffs and school administrations. The humiliation of losing their own head coaching positions understandably produced bitter resentments among many black coaches. The state, moreover, did not compel school districts to integrate all at once, and there was no plan to prepare the pioneers for what lay ahead. The result was a mixed bag.

In 1956, two years after the Supreme Court struck down public school desegregation, the slow process began. While white-dominated school districts routinely resisted, some more vociferously than others, communities in more diverse regions, especially in South and West Texas, reluctantly pushed forward. Naturally, local race relations were complex. Sentiments often hearkened back to original patterns of settlement, or they might even revolve around some festering incident of long ago. But, by and large, wherever Tejanos and small black populations lived under the shadow of firmly entrenched Anglos, integration seemed less threatening to the social order. Black star Warren McVea of San Antonio Brackenridge commented that in the Alamo City, "the Spanish people kind of leveled off the racial tension between blacks and whites."[2]

Society at large was less tolerating. In 1958 Donald Jay was coaching at Kingsville, which, along with a handful of cities such as San Antonio, Austin, Corpus Christi, San Angelo, El Paso, Harlingen, and Kerrville, had erased the color line. When the team traveled to Abilene for the state championship game that year, they walked out of several places that said their African American athletes would have to eat in the kitchen. Even finding a place to stay was difficult. Finally, a persistent Jay was able to gain the concession of a motel manager who said, "O.K., but would you just not let them walk up and down in front of the hotel in the daytime?"

Such attitudes were pervasive and assured that integration would be a long process. Herb Allen, who in the early 1960s was at Carver, Anahuac's black school, when the district began piecemeal integration—by a policy colloquially termed "freedom of choice"—believed that "it both helped and hurt. It helped where people were ready for it." Yet not everybody was ready, insisted Cotton Miles, who experienced integration troubles at Skyline High School in Dallas. "We didn't ask for the church to do it, we didn't ask the school, we were told by the court." Ed Logan contended, perhaps optimistically, that on the playing fields, at least, integration "forced a positive contact between the races. Athletics opened a door of communication between blacks, whites, and Hispanics. To the extent that the kids were successful in making the transition, the rest of the population also followed."

Such was the case at Longview High School, proclaimed Maurice Cook. "Our school was having trouble trying to get things integrated, but in the heat of that, when things were probably at their worst, the football team started winning. And all of a sudden, people got their mind a little bit more on that football team and Friday night than they did about wanting to fight someone. And then, the black players and the white players were getting along on the football team and having some success. And then, the more we won, the more 'into it' the school got. Finally, when we started getting to the play-offs, approaching an undefeated season, it got us through some really tense times, and I attribute this to a winning football team."

Jap Jones, who, along with fellow Prairie View Interscholastic League veteran Walter Day, is busy compiling PVIL records, cast integration in the unvarnished terms of what it initially meant to coaches of different races. For white coaches integration meant that "they got some 'jewels.'" For black coaches, it meant starting over. "What we accomplished will never be known other than through the [research] that Day and I are doing—and how many people now are even going to believe it?"

Many white coaches frankly admitted that their first reaction to integration was exactly what Jones asserted. They realized that they would be surrounded by a wealth of talent. Morris Southall stated succinctly what many of them expressed: "They're better athletes, period." Maurice Cook elaborated: "It changed the game; I don't think there's any question about that. . . . The athletic ability of the black player made you immediately, as a coach, just try to figure out a way to utilize all that speed." Before integration, Cook remarked, "very few people threw the ball. . . . Oh, I guess they had a split end maybe, but you never threw to him," he laughed. "Everybody had seven- and eight-man fronts on defense. . . . It was just a run-oriented, hard-nosed, three-or-four-yards-at-a-time game. Then, when all the good black athletes came in, you could begin to see where speed came in—reverses, a lot of option, throwing the ball. . . . Therefore, defenses had to adapt. As far as the strategy, I saw a big difference on both sides of the ball."

White coaches, of course, long had appreciated black athleticism, and many of them had enjoyed attending PVIL games. "I watched Burnett High for years here in Terrell, because I opened up the stadium for them," remarked Leon Vinyard. Noting that many black Texas gridders ended up on Big Ten rosters as well as in other traditionally white universities outside of the South was evidence enough that "they played good football," Vinyard proclaimed. "I knew a kid named Englehart—he later played several years of pro ball—who lined up and kicked the ball plumb over the fence and over the bushes and everything. . . . I saw him do it several times."

Black athletes did some other things that tended to perplex white coaches, rather than "wow" them. While African Americans had always observed Anglos from the fringes of society, whites most often viewed

Raymond Hollie. *Photograph courtesy
Texas High School Coaches Association,
Austin.*

blacks only through the negative lenses of stereotypes. Upon integration,
white coaches and fans largely failed to appreciate that African Americans
could impart to the game some unique aspects of their culture, as well as
their speed. Although coaches and fans did not immediately recognize it,
perhaps the black athletes' most significant contribution was simply
putting some fun back into football at a time when it was beginning to
take on some businesslike qualities.

Donald Jay said that during workouts, especially, the black players added
some lightheartedness to the drudgery. "I used to tell my kids: 'Hey,
you're working out in that heat, and there's not a whole lot to enjoy, and
if you see something to laugh at, laugh.'" And usually, he remarked, it was
his black athletes who were quickest to find some fun in the otherwise dismal routine. Bum Phillips echoed Jay. He had long known that on practice
fields at all-black schools, coaches routinely broke the monotony by keeping a loose mood. And, he insisted, "it did not affect the game." In fact,
white players often followed the lead. To expect either race to adapt to the
other's ways would be "arrogant," Phillips concluded.

One black custom that whites only at length came to emulate was celebrating after touchdowns and big plays. "With the black kids it was natural—a cultural thing," said John Hugh Smith, "it's a way that they
express their exuberance and pride." Donald Jay agreed: "Football
should be fun and games, and end zone dancing might just put football
in its proper perspective."

Observing PVIL games, Joe Bob Tyler had assumed that black athletes
were undisciplined, but once he began coaching them, he came to learn
that they "were well prepared and well trained. . . . They just exhibited
their emotions differently." The way they "got ready for a ball game" also
"took me a long time to appreciate," remarked Tyler. White coaches had

always created a meditative environment. By contrast, many of the black players "would put on their earphones and listen to that jive music." After reflecting on the differences, he remarked, "I began wondering if meditating and focusing on the game might just make your tension build up instead of relaxing you."

Coaches who viewed such exhibitions negatively admitted they formed their judgments through their own cultural biases. Before integration, said Bill Shipman, "if a player had done a touchdown dance or any other of the oddball things that players frequently do now, they would have been laughed at, ridiculed, and pitied—as well as benched." He was still not ready to admit that it was not better to "act like you'd been in the end zone before." Gene Mayfield, too, expressed that he was opposed to "hot-dogging." But now, he said, "I feel that maybe I was out of step."

Elmer Redd believed that his white colleagues also misinterpreted the fluid athleticism that African American gridders often exhibited for a lack of effort. "Black players were 'looser' because of grace and speed and natural ability." Sometimes white coaches felt "that the black athlete was loafing, that he wasn't putting out, because he wasn't the guy with his face all wrinkled, his teeth clenched, his fists and muscles all balled up. He had been taught to relax and accelerate, and most of them had great motor skills. This is the thing we had to get [white] coaches to overcome. . . . I had a white coach one time look at a black player and say: 'Well, he's just not trying!' And I said: 'Well, he's averaging five-point-two yards a carry!'"

In a practical sense integration "was a godsend," said Clarence McMichael, who was at all-black E. J. Campbell until Nacogdoches High absorbed it. He pointed out that financing a dual school system was an unnecessary economic burden on communities. More important, it helped foster understanding between the races. Also, he said with a smile, "it made East Texas a powerhouse."

Many coaches seized on McMichael's latter sentiment, and stressed that in retrospect it seemed ridiculous to keep the races on separate football fields. Cotton Miles declared that "the adjustment was needed, and athletics was a good forum to do it." Robert Lowrance observed that at Hawkins: "Integration brought problems, but that's life. . . . We should have integrated much earlier than we did. It was not fair to deprive [African Americans] of an opportunity to achieve greatness, whether it's in the classroom or an athletic endeavor. . . . I don't mean that athletics solved all the problems, but the fact that we discovered other races have abilities and aspirations and can achieve, well, it brought about respect both ways."

On the other hand, for all its noble intentions, integration created some unintended consequences for black communities. Lufkin's Elmer Redd stated: "The three institutions that make up any community are the home, school, and church. When you take any one of them away, the community suffers because that place becomes hollow. . . . As long as you have a school in your community, there's a certain day-to-day life that goes on around it, and it just helps the people to survive as a community." And football, Redd professed, was one of the ties that bound African Americans statewide.

Years after the event, Jap Jones recalled what his high school coach, Raymond Hollie, told him about the ruinous potential of integration. It occurred on "picture day," just before the season began, when the Dallas newspapers produced action poses of the area's potential white stars. Before practice that afternoon some of Jones's teammates were "joking around, saying things like: 'Watch me look like Pete Sultis.'" As Hollie looked on, he commented that "we'd be sorry when we integrated, because the past would be forgotten." Jones heard him, but it did not make much of an impression on him at the time—"I was just a kid," he remarked. The large Dallas newspapers, such as the *Morning News* and the *Times Herald*, did not cover black athletics at all, but neither, lamented Jones, did the black newspapers. Only later did he realize that Hollie's comment "was one of the greatest truths I have known."

Integration, as Hollie had predicted, spelled the end of the Prairie View Interscholastic League, which finally folded in 1970, and all of its memories. Its slow demise, moreover, meant that African American coaches crossed the color line only a handful at a time, which left them politically impotent within their profession. Jap Jones declared: "When we were allowed to become associate members of the Texas High School Coaches Association in the 1950s, we could not vote, we could not coach all-star teams, we could not hold offices. . . . We would pay our money and sit in the coaching clinics and regional meetings as an invisible man, because there was no recognition given to you at all. When they got ready to take a vote . . . they wouldn't count the black hands that were raised."

When school districts decided to integrate, whether by freedom of choice or by judicial fiat, black coaches were left with few career options. Some became vice principals, others assistant coaches, and still others took what they could get. Most of them dreaded integration because they knew it would mean losing the prestige they enjoyed in the black community. Clarence McMichael, reflecting on being demoted, declared: "I had never been an assistant coach in my life, and it was a slap in the face to me, to my family, to my community. For economic reasons, I had to stay. I have a little ranch here . . . and I had five kids in school and college. . . . And I really didn't want to move, because I had deep roots here." The Nacogdoches I.S.D. at least gave McMichael a head coach's pay, which "soothed the pain a little bit. But it was tougher on a lot of coaches I know."

One of them was Herb Allen. When Anahuac integrated, the district asked him to become the team's trainer, whereupon he began to look for another job. Allen had arrived at Anahuac Carver three years earlier to establish a program in a black community that had never enjoyed high school football, and in just three seasons he had produced a district champion. Yet to the white community such accomplishments did not matter. "I don't think that was right, but that's the way it was," Allen recalled.

A handful of black coaches avoided ignominy by moving up to the college level. Elmer Redd, for example, won a position at the University of Houston on the strength of producing an enviable résumé that included four PVIL state champions, a runner-up, and three semifinalists. Between Arp Industrial, where he began his career, and Lufkin Dunbar, his teams had posted a combined 178–38–3 record. In one seven-year span at Lufkin he had placed fifty-seven kids in college, and with black athletes beginning to command scholarships at formerly all-white Texas institutions, his ability to coach and to attract recruits made him a valuable asset.

However unfair, black coaches understood that the dominant white society was not prepared to hand any of them something as visible as a head coaching position. Yet at every level, from junior highs to universities, once men of different races found themselves on the same staff, they soon learned that coaching provided a common ground. Many white coaches, in fact, insisted that despite their backgrounds and the social realities that prevailed from the late 1950s and into the 1970s, they believed integration was long overdue.

When black and white coaches began mixing at clinics in the mid-1950s, individuals began to cultivate new professional ties that transcended issues of race. Bum Phillips declared: "The coaches I liked, I liked because they were good football men. Willie Ray Smith was a good football man. Joe Washington was a good football man. It never occurred to me that they were black and I was white. Hell, they were friends of mine, and they were great football coaches." Maurice Cook added: "Coaches made the transition to integration smoothly because of common bonds and common goals and their understanding of teamwork. Their minds were more on Lufkin or Texarkana or Marshall than each other."

One way that coaches established trust was "just by laying everything on the table," as Allen Boren expressed. During Edna's first team meeting after the South Texas school integrated, head coach Boren opened by saying: "Sooner or later I'm going to slip and say the 'N' word, so I might as well apologize now." He went on to tell his team "that's just how I was raised," but he also promised a policy of colorblindness that would not tolerate racial problems. However awkward, he believed that the straightforward approach, along with putting his words into action, eventually won him a large measure of respect.

At many Texas high schools, building bridges of trust between white staffs and black athletes did not come as easily. Sometimes otherwise conscientious coaches made simple mistakes in judgment. For example, when fifteen black athletes came out for two-a-days at Terrell at the beginning of the 1965 season, Leon Vinyard was determined to stick to his drillmaster ways as if nothing were different. "The next day they were back at the other school," he lamented. In other cases, said Darrell Tully, "black players were quick to rebel because of the times." Most often, however, the long, collective memory of the African American experience left many players dubious about their coaches' commitment to students of color.

Gene Mayfield admitted feeling occasionally frustrated. "There was never anything said; I could just sense it."

Bill Carter was at Amarillo Tascosa when the city's black school, Carver High, closed. Although he did not experience any significant problems after integration, a particular incident made him reconsider his relationships with the team's African American athletes. When a black player missed a Saturday practice, Carter went to the boy's home to check on him. "In those days, you just didn't miss a practice unless something was wrong. The people inside said they didn't know anyone by his [the player's] name, but when I asked some kids playing if they knew him, they said: 'Yeah, he lives right there,' and they pointed to the same house." Experience, Carter reckoned, had taught them that "when white folks came calling it probably wasn't good news."

Among the first to integrate were schools in West and South Texas. When Big Spring made the decision to close its black facilities in 1960, the white coaching staff decided to visit the moribund Lakeview High School and invite its athletes to join the team for the 1961 season. Telling his own players what to expect, Big Spring coach Emmett McKenzie also told them he would brook no hostility—"That's just the way it's going to be." He believed that establishing a climate of trust paid significant dividends. "Individually, there was some resentment on both sides, . . . [but] it was a good move to go over and ask the black kids to come out. Otherwise they might have wondered if they were welcome."

Very often, remarked Bill Patrick, black athletes "came in thinking they'd have to take a back seat to the white kids, . . . but it just took a few weeks for them to realize that whoever was best would play, and everything was OK." At least one, however, had to wonder—Eddie Lewis Smith. "He was as good a football player as we had; quick as a cat," remarked Patrick. But "he wouldn't start working out very hard until about Wednesday of every week." Consequently, Smith found himself on the second team behind Mike Brazier, a boy who was not his peer athletically, but one who "gave a hundred percent." He also happened to be white. "We were running the veer," continued Patrick, "and I told him: 'Eddie, you ought to be our other starting back. Do you have any idea why you're not?' To which he replied: 'No, I sure don't, but by God, I ought to be, I'm better than anybody else out here.'" When Patrick made Smith realize that it was his lack of effort, rather than his race, that was keeping him on the bench "there was nothing stopping him from then on."

The athletic arena was the one place in society where color did not matter, declared Donald Jay; "Football is very democratic; you can't fool kids by playing people who aren't the best ones." Joe Washington echoed: "The cream will rise. You can't muzzle athletic ability. You might contain a guy in an office, but when you put him out there on the field, the fastest and strongest will finish first."

The individual players who developed hard feelings after integration were usually those whose positions were taken away by more talented

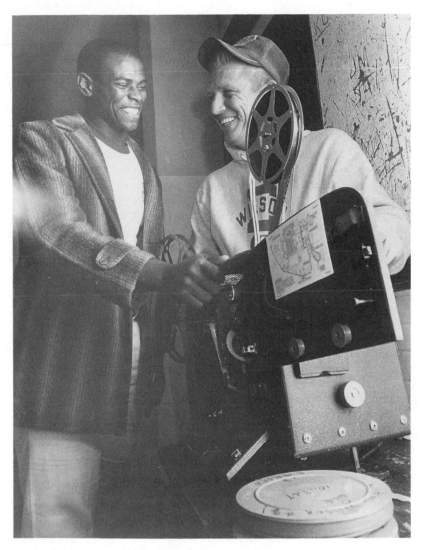

John Paul McCrumbly, "The Big Train," with Coach Cotton Miles, Woodrow Wilson High, 1969. *Photograph courtesy Cotton Miles.*

players, whether white or black. While many African American former quarterbacks found themselves lining up at other positions, many more Anglo former running backs and receivers found themselves on the bench. Cotton Miles said "many coaches believed that the greatest equalizer was a black halfback. To an extent this was the truth." His first, in fact, John Paul McCrumbly, "could run for touchdowns. We called him 'The Big Train.' We gave the ball to John Paul, and we got into the play-offs right quick." The team's only other black player was

McCrumbly's brother, Donald Ray. "Boy, they made the difference," Miles said.

Yet the Big Train's leading role came at the expense of a white player who had started the previous year. "The guy that McCrumbly replaced had a lot of character, and he took it in stride. . . . In the world of competition, if a guy's better than you are, you don't resent him playing," concluded Miles. "Maybe I was just lucky to have coached players with so much character," he said, "but I never had a problem with who started or who played." Others, he intimated, were not always so fortunate.

For a system that showed some surprising signs of promise, integration nevertheless developed severe strains that spread to the football field, said many coaches. One reason, the coaches speculated, was because the court system handled integration so poorly. Joe Hedrick remarked that "if the courts had let it alone it might have accomplished its purpose in twenty years. Now, I don't know." Cotton Miles, who at Woodrow Wilson had seen some encouraging progress under desegregation by "freedom of choice" also witnessed the deleterious effects of forced integration shortly after he moved to Dallas's Skyline High School. When the 1970s began, the predominately Anglo school of about twelve hundred students was nevertheless an integrated institution. Then, in 1971, "a Dallas judge issued this 'great court order' that bused in seventeen hundred black students." The attendant social problems of busing and immediate, forced integration yielded turmoil. The seventy-seven black players whom the court order injected into the football program certainly created some disharmony. Nevertheless, insisted Miles, "it worked smoother in athletics than in any other phase of school."

Yet some admitted that things were never that smooth, even on the football field. Herb Allen contended: "At some schools, there were two standards. . . . The white coaches had a dilemma. They worked the white kids hard, but not the black kids. Then, when it came time to run a black kid off, it would get very ugly."

Issues of race undoubtedly affected traditional methods of administering discipline. In segregated schools, teachers and coaches had routinely meted out harsh, uncompromising punishments, confident that parents and the community would support their actions. Whether paddling players, making them run laps, or relying on peer pressure, coaches, especially, held a tight rein. Integration, however, bred uncertainty, indecision, and compromise in locker rooms as well as classrooms. A deteriorating social climate that was quick to paint traditional measures as abusive, or even racist, when figures of authority crossed the color line, also fostered a tentative will on the part of educators, including many coaches, to exercise discipline.

"Integration," insisted James Brewer, "was needlessly a major factor in school decline." He believed that because teachers were afraid of being charged with discrimination, they invited discipline problems. "This was not the kids' fault, it was society's. Kids would do anything you wanted them to if you'd instill discipline, but society took the easy way out by deciding not to enforce the rules."

Elmer Redd charged that upon integrating: "A lot of schools went out and hired the black male teacher that was extremely passive, extremely 'easy,' one that would agree with everything and would not rock the boat. . . . Anybody that's not gutsy enough to rock the boat when the boat starts to list, you don't have guts enough to keep it afloat either."

Both Redd and Brewer, like many of their colleagues, pointed out that the first students to experience integration had been conditioned by teachers of their own race who did not tolerate disrespect. As the steady progression of matriculation took those memories with it, many said, so too did it take away the chance to make integration work. Allen Boren remembered that when Edna desegregated, the former principal of the black school brought a butt-worn leather strap to his new job as vice principal. Occasionally, when a black student committed a particularly opprobrious offense: "He would slam the door and stretch them across his desk and put whelps on them. He only did this with the black kids. Whenever he disciplined white kids it was always over some minor matter. This situation ended very quickly."

At Brownwood, a few years after the school system integrated, the coaches began detecting discipline problems among some of their black athletes. Morris Southall had a hard time figuring out what had gone wrong after such a promising beginning. During practice one day, he and the team's black manager were talking, and the student gave him some insight. A senior, he was among the last group that had attended an all-black school. "He told me: 'In my elementary school we were all black, and we had black teachers, and when one of those kids got out of line, the teachers would slap the tar out of them—or a lot worse if they could.'" Southall remarked: "Those kids understood how to act, how to do things, and that they were to turn their work in, and there were no discipline problems. And if there was one, that teacher handled it, and they handled it tough." After integration, he said, the white teachers were reluctant to discipline black children. "And, consequently, there's a bunch of them that are not studying, they're not turning in their work, and they're not getting an education."

Elmer Redd laid much of the blame on administrators who failed to support women teachers adequately. "The average lady schoolteacher is afraid to discipline the black boy. As a result, they come up with gimmicks—all types of detention halls, and all types of disciplinary schools. The fact is, they're really scared of him. And if you don't discipline him, the macho white boy says: 'To hell with you, if you don't discipline him, you aren't going to discipline me.' As a result, you've lost discipline in the male segment of the school, and when you've lost that, you've lost discipline entirely."

Defenders of Traditional Values

Discipline problems, however, were much larger in scope than the ills fostered by tentative race relations. The youth counterculture that emerged in the 1960s further separated schoolchildren from those who sought to guide them. Bill Shipman asserted: "During the era of the hippies, things such as long hair, odd clothing, and exhibitionist behavior began to infiltrate even into the best of schools and programs. Hair policies and clothing policies were instituted. Discipline became more difficult, and the coaches' and teachers' authority began to be questioned more often. Automobiles, more money to spend, more liberal parents, television, rock music, relaxed sexual standards, drugs, poor role models, and trashy literature—all these things thrived, and still thrive, to the detriment of our society."

At a coaching school in the early 1970s, Bill Carter and Charles Qualls were discussing their alarm over the way their players were changing. Carter remembered commiserating with his friendly rival over their kids' readiness to voice whatever was on their minds and their tendency to dress sloppily and wear their hair longer. "Charlie said he felt like telling them: 'I can't hear what you're saying, because what you're doing distracts me way too much!'"

Prohibiting players from wearing long hair, in particular, seemed to be a subject over which coaches drew a line in the sand. Looking back, Donald Jay expressed: "We paid more attention to hair than we should have. My gosh, that hair used to give me more trouble! Of course, to us, that was a sign of rebellion." James Brewer remarked: "People say that having to get their hair cut doesn't have anything to do with playing, that it's their right. But if you're out for football, and there is a rule against it, then you ought to conform to it. If you don't have to conform to that, then why should you conform to any other rules?"

As defenders of traditional values, football coaches fervently believed that it was their duty to compel conformity among the young men on their teams. And universally, they depended on their players to serve as a bulwark against the kinds of social changes the coaches perceived as destructive. Where in an earlier day coaches had been trusted to set standards for grooming and behavior, parents and special interest groups increasingly challenged the coaches' role. Referring to the litigious society that began to emerge in the late 1960s, Maurice Cook observed, "it seemed like the words 'our rights' came up more and more." Coaches collectively contended that kids and parents started becoming more concerned about their rights than their responsibilities. At one time, continued Cook, parents commonly looked at the relationship between their sons and coaches as "an investment that would pay dividends in character." Yet increasingly, he lamented, the parents began asking: "What are they doing to my boy?"

At Gregory-Portland, as the seventies were just beginning, the standards that Ray Akins set for his team came under fire by the League of United Latin American Citizens (LULAC). Hair length provoked the incident, but the larger issue was discrimination. "I had always told my kids that I wanted them groomed properly or they wouldn't play," declared Akins. Some of the students in the largely Hispanic community of Gregory included an occasional boy who not only wore his hair long, but also sported an earring. "There's no way a kid is ever, *ever*, going to wear an earring and play for me!" the coach fumed. And, predictably, they did not.

When a complaint reached the LULAC office in Corpus Christi, the organization sent some representatives to the school to investigate. Admittedly, the coach was not very cooperative. "Here they are telling me how to run my business, and they weren't even dry behind the ears!" he railed. Showing Akins a picture of a boy with long hair, they asked if he could play for him. "I can't answer that question because he's not here," the coach responded. "If he was here in our program, he might not want to look that way."

Frustrated when they were unable to elicit the answers they wanted, the LULAC representatives asked Akins to leave the room and called in several students to ask if they had been pressured into conforming. One of them was senior class president Robert Early, whose once-long hair had fallen under the scissors at Akins' command. Nevertheless, he came to his coach's defense. According to Akins, "I heard he told them: 'I feel like I have the right to be on a team where we have discipline and dress properly and do what the coaches and teachers ask them to do.'" Then one of the Hispanic players posed his own question to the LULAC representatives: "Did any of you play football?" When they said no, he followed up: "Maybe you ought to try it sometime."

Akins continued: "So they got mad and sent them out of the room and called me back in. And they said: 'I want to tell you something Akins. You've brainwashed these kids!'" The meeting fell apart shortly after that, but not before the principal and superintendent agreed that the coaching staff would have to suspend its grooming requirements because of the legal pressure. "I didn't say anything, but I'd made up my mind that, OK, if that's what they want, I'll do it," Akins said.

That evening, Akins started getting feedback from the community. "I bet I had twenty-five parents call me and say: 'Coach, I hope you don't give one inch on this stuff. . . . This is what we want for our kids.'" The next day Akins could not bring himself to suspend the team's grooming policy. Gathering his players together, he told them: "I'm being pressured to let you do what you want, but as long as I'm coaching here, I want you to be presentable enough to meet the president." Akins held fast, and "ninety-nine percent" of the parents stood behind him. And fortunately, nobody sued.

Gregory-Portland was composed of the two small, stable towns that gave the school its name. The cultural growing pains that the more mobile, populous parts of the state experienced had not yet made significant inroads there, according to Akins. He also believed that the Hispanic community, especially, stood behind him because he had visited his players' parents in their homes. Although he had never known many Tejanos, he found that he readily identified with them because so many shared his work ethic and impoverished background. He also believed they appreciated his effort to establish trust and loyalty.

Coaches in post-World War II Texas did not generally detect much racial strife between white and Hispanic players. Many pointed out that white players and Hispanic players enjoyed close bonds that would never have formed if not for football. The coaches also expressed that issues of class had as much to do as race in determining the course of their players' relationships off the field. A "Little Mexico," of course, could be found in any community that possessed more than a handful of Hispanic families. And, while many schools in the larger South Texas towns ended up being predominately Hispanic or Anglo based simply on residential patterns, segregating Hispanics on the scale that excluded African Americans was never institutionalized. And again, football, further leveled the social playing field.[3]

In some ways coaches found the culture beyond the state's northern borders more foreign to their ways and values. Hoot Smith and Bill Bookout, for example, recalled an episode at Hurst Bell in 1966 that signaled the changing times, an incident that grew out of their attempt to stop a student demonstration designed to end the school's strict dress code, including the hair length policy.

Hurst and its sister town, Euless, were typical of the rapidly growing suburbs that drew out-of-staters, including many whose attitudes conflicted with the Bible Belt convictions of the former rural inhabitants. Demographically, the area was a product of the postwar defense buildup, which drew factory people, engineers, and scientists from all over the country. The "Mid Cities," which would soon take in the crossroads hamlet of Bedford as well, named their high school after defense contractor Lawrence D. Bell, whose plant was then building helicopters destined for Southeast Asia.

One afternoon an administrator called Smith and told him there was going to be a demonstration. "It was organized by the parents and the kids. . . . They were going to bring some placards and get the TV people out there and try to break the rules of Bell High School. He asked me to take care of it. I told Bill, and he got with the student manager and about seven football players and told them: 'Don't let them have that demonstration.' Well, they went out there and broke it up all right, and they 'whipped' about twenty kids," Smith grimaced.

"They were going to march around our flagpole," Bookout added. "This was a challenge to everything our kids believed. . . . These people were northerners, and they didn't understand the Texas program. . . . What set it off was that one of the protesters took a placard and hit one of our boys." Of course, the player was trying to wrest it from him, Bookout admitted.

"It was a bad scene," Smith stated. "We did not anticipate it going that far, but hey, they didn't have any more demonstrations." The incident did not end there, however. "For the next six months we stayed in court, and they had board meetings over us, and we were on the front page of the newspaper for weeks," he bemoaned. At one meeting, a parent provoked the coaches' defender, principal Frank Johnson, to leap over the table that separated them. "I had to grab him by the belt and pull him back down," Smith laughed. Turning more serious, he reflected: "These were some very trying times. They wanted to change our image, our policies, and our programs and values, and we wanted to maintain a good, pure school."[4]

Many of the boys who agreed with their coaches about what constituted "good and pure" behavior unjustly earned the label "dumb jock." Certainly there had always existed a belief that God rarely endowed individuals with both brawn and brains. Yet beginning in the mid-1960s a growing youth culture demanded a self-awareness that transcended intelligence. A generation gap was clearly distancing young people from their parents, and kids who clung to traditional values were often considered out of touch socially. John Reddell remarked: "I always told my players 'look right, act right, be respectful, and don't embarrass the team.'" In an age of protest, he suggested, those who followed that maxim were often dismissed by their peers as dumb jocks.

John Hugh Smith contended that the stereotype was conceived in an earlier age by Hollywood, and that the role was recast to fit the times. But "it just wasn't true," he insisted. "A dumb kid was not a good player, unless he had uncommon talent, and even then, he couldn't always cut it." Smith drew a parallel between the old World War II movies and stereotypes of athletes. "You always had that Bronx kid with street smarts, and you had a midwestern boy with common sense, but then, there was always that big ol' dumb, ignorant southern kid. And they applied that same formula when it came time to portray kids in school, and it was always the football player who was the dummy."

Coaches, however, conceded that on every team were at least a few boys who seemed to affirm the image. Bob Barfield related: "I was sitting in my office one day and heard a knock on the door. I opened it, and there stood one of my ex-football players. We shook hands and he said: 'Gosh coach it's good to see you. I ain't seen you in two years.' And I said: 'Son, you are a graduate of Pasadena High School and a sophomore at Rice Institute. You shouldn't say I ain't seen you.' And he said: 'Coach, what I meant to say, is that I haven't saw you.'"

Carlos Berry pointed out that "every team has at least one or two kids who flunk out, but many more are straight-A students." Berry felt typical in being able to count among his former players "scores of lawyers, doctors, CPA's, and men of every successful walk in life." He also claimed that studies have shown that "students who participate in extracurricular activities have better grades than those who do nothing after school."

Gordon Brown was proud to note that among the top six graduating seniors at Katy High School in 1960 were five members of his state championship team. "I always found a strong correlation between effort in the classroom and effort on the field. A coach who does not place the importance of academic success first will never have the respect of the players and the support of parents and the community that is necessary to achieve the richest rewards of coaching."

Speaking for the athletes of his own day, Doyle Reynolds commented: "Go to any town and it looks that way because of the 'jocks.' They have gone on to be the community leaders of today. The same type of discipline they developed on that football field, they went on to use after they got out of school."

Ray Overton echoed that sentiment in recalling "one of the greatest thrills I ever had in football. It was my first day on the job at Irving MacArthur." As he walked down to the coaches' office, he noticed that "there was a big guy in the hall, standing there waiting. When I got close enough to see who it was, it turned out to be Mitch Robinson, whom I'd coached at Abilene. He had gone on to establish a successful air freight business at D/FW [Airport]. When I picked up my mail, I got a letter from Bobby White, who played for me there, and he was also president of one of the biggest banks in downtown Dallas. Then I got a phone call. It was Kenny Stevens, who had been our tailback, and he was in one of the big law firms in Dallas. Every one of them wanted to wish me luck and told me that the lessons they had learned in football were the things that helped them get to the position they were in."

Overton was among the few coaches who professed that he never saw much difference in the boys he shepherded. "I don't think kids changed so much as things around them changed." Beginning in the 1960s, and increasingly afterward, "they were certainly confronted with a lot more." At a time when kids began questioning their coaches and teachers, he routinely challenged his players to live up to the high opinion in which the students seemed to regard themselves. "I tried to sell them on the idea that they're part of the best educated generation the world's ever known. But, I said: 'We're holding the count out as to whether you're smart or not. We'll have to wait and see what you leave for your children.'"

Many others perceived distinct differences between boys who played for them in the late 1960s and afterward, and those they had coached just a few years earlier. Cotton Miles declared: "In this time, our society was affected by a lot of things. . . . Cassius Clay comes along and becomes a world hero, and he was 'I,' 'me,' and 'my.'" Miles also singled out Joe Namath as one who "suddenly held up that one finger and said: 'I am the best.'" Such expressions of self-confidence led people "to put 'self' before 'team.' . . . In the early days players would do exactly what the coach said without asking questions." Then, continued Miles, "Students and people in general got to where they wouldn't accept explanations and opinions on face value. They wanted 'to know why.' We had to explain every move. . . . Kids got more sophisticated and you had to have reasons."

About the time that Donald Jay retired from coaching in 1972, he noticed the same things that Cotton Miles related. "You'd say: 'We're going to do this,' and some kid might say: 'Why are we going to do it that way coach?'" When Jay himself was playing, a boy would never have been so bold. "If the coach said: 'You put on this helmet and try to run

Bill Carter, Arlington High. *Photograph courtesy Bill Carter.*

through that wall,' we didn't say: 'Why, coach? Wouldn't it be better to run around it?'"

If there ever was a coach who was loath to tolerate any form of second guessing, it was Joe Bob Tyler. Not until the mid-1970s did he encounter a player at Haltom High School who possessed the temerity to question him regularly. And, he remarked, "when it happened, it changed my whole philosophy about coaching." Some of the staff at a feeder school, North Oaks Junior High, had warned him to watch out for a boy named Greg Hunter. "I had the attitude that Greg was a smart aleck, and when he came on the scene, I just knew that he was going to be a problem— and I wasn't going to have any problems.

"But there was something about that kid that struck me as being 'real,'" Tyler remarked. "You know, we lived by the old adage: 'Ours is not to reason why, ours is but to do or die.' But Greg asked me questions, and some way or another, he reached me enough that I answered him. And I learned something from that young man. He wasn't a smart aleck, he just wanted to 'know.' When I explained things to him, he responded." In fact, Hunter played both ways and made some of the all-state teams "despite the fact that he had some severe asthma and did not possess just a whole lot of athletic ability."

Looking back on his career, Tyler remarked that the game from which he retired had changed considerably since his own playing days. Chatter Allen, reflecting on a career that ended in 1951, added some resonance to Tyler's comment. "I did all the things you don't dare do today. When a boy used profanity I washed his mouth out with soap, used the paddle freely, and made players run laps after practice for goofing off. I put the gloves on boys so they could settle their differences. Even put them on myself with some of my players. I put kids through long sessions without water until I learned better, and they never complained—bragged about it later. The game made men out of boys."

Buzz Allert, whose professional football career was just beginning when Allen retired, contended: "You can still get the same results as you used to." Like Ray Overton, Allert believed: "Kids today are no different than they've ever been, but now a coach has to understand more psychology, he has to ask himself: 'What am I going to do to get kids motivated?'" The answer, according to Quin Eudy, is "you've got to reach them in different ways."

And the easiest way, said Bill Carter, is one that most coaches seldom considered in an earlier day—"You've got to show your feelings." "It doesn't make you a weak coach to tell kids you love them," added Eddie Joseph. "If you coach kids, they need to have good feelings for you, otherwise you're in an empty job." For all of the ills that society has suffered, he expressed, "the greatest change is that a man can be more sensitive now. Kids remember what you tell them. . . . As long as a kid knows you love him, you can do anything to him you want. But a stroke is better than a strike." Coaches "always had feelings," continued Carter, "but they just didn't show it. This 'my way or the highway' type of attitude was just a projection of what they had gone through themselves in just about every aspect of their life. As society has changed, so have the coaches. And the changes have made coaching more fun."

Chapter 10

Circling the Wagons: Coaches' Reflections on Their Lives and the Game

"**Y**ou need to be mad part of the time in football," stated Joe Kerbel in a 1972 interview. "This is a tough game; this isn't one of those sweet games. This is one of these games where people have to go out there and have to be tough." Football players "pay the price" for being part of the game. Take linemen, for example. Playing any position "is drudgery, especially an offensive lineman. He doesn't even get to grab anybody, see. He can't even use his hands. People don't understand this." Still, kids continue to come out for football. "People say they should quit having spring training, but they don't have any knowledge of the game. . . . It's like having a chess master. He couldn't be good playing only part of the time, and football's that kind of game. It's not like basketball, either, and it's a shame it's not. But, it just isn't, because basketball is all fun. You can dribble the ball and shoot, and it's great. It's just great, I love to play it." Baseball, he said, is the same way. "But you take track; it's like football. Working out for it is just old drudgery, and that old football is the same way, except you're carrying equipment with you, plus you've got a headache every day." The routine of football, Kerbel continued, is boring, too. But, "you get something out of this that you don't get out of other places. You don't get it in the classroom or in all these other sports." Through all of this "there is something in the human mind that says: 'I can do some of those other things that I want to do that are . . . [more] . . . fun, but to get to that place in life [where I want to be], am I willing to make these sacrifices?' I think you can get this in some sports, and football is one of them."

Since the early twentieth century, Texas high school coaches such as Joe Kerbel have used the football field as a proving ground on which they initiated young boys into manhood. The rites of passage generally demanded discipline, sacrifice, and unquestioned loyalty. Coaches also held players accountable for their actions, in hopes that the lessons their boys learned on the football field would breed self-reliance and a survival instinct that would help them succeed in the world beyond the school yard. Since retiring, however, many old-time coaches have seen a society emerge that neither understands nor appreciates their values and methods. Many sports sociologists, in fact, have gone so far as to say that coaches have had no positive influence on youth, dismissing their efforts at character building as a "sports myth."[1] Other voices have charged that the old-time coaches taught violence and brutality, fostered unhealthy competition, and emphasized athletic skills at the expense of their players' educations. Whether those accusations hold true in today's society is open to scrutiny, yet critics can do no greater injustice to the old-time coaches than to condemn them by projecting contemporary values backward.

Texans today are a much better educated and more sophisticated people than they were when the old-time coaches grew up and developed their system of beliefs. With no informed point of reference, men and women who criticize the football culture tend to view coaches in stereotypes and blame the game for distorting the state's priorities. That most of the old coaches are only one generation removed from poverty and, in some cases, illiteracy, is easy to overlook. Considering their backgrounds, the extent to which the old-time coaches responded to the radical changes around them is commendable. And the good ones did change with the times in spite of the well-ingrained southern and rural traditions that shaped their values and priorities, ways that contrasted starkly with the values of the emerging cosmopolitan society.

Blasting the Stereotype

Joe Hedrick complained: "Sometimes people think football coaches are some type of Neanderthal who can't spell, and he has to have his wife write letters for him. I always resented the hell out of that." Pointing to the stereotype of the "overweight, sloppily dressed, crude, tobacco-chewing coaches that you see on TV," Maurice Cook lamented that "there's always one around, and he's the one that sticks out because he's the one who's in charge of the thing that parents prize the most—their kid. This slob cancels out all the others because of the potential for being a bad role model."

Buzz Allert commented: "People who knock coaches are uninformed. If they'd go to the source, then they'd see. The kids will defend their coaches against parents, critics, and anybody else." When asked how he dealt with criticism in the community, Homer Johnson remarked: "I didn't have to. There were always some of my former players around who'd fight my fights for me."

If a culture's institutions reflect its values, then certainly some of the abuses and darker manifestations of present-day society have infected this popular sport. In the long view, football in Texas is a uniquely twentieth-century phenomenon. A hundred years from now the sport might well cease to exist, yet even if football thrives, it most certainly will persist as a reflection of the values that future generations of men embrace. In any event, curiosity will compel historians, sociologists, and sports fans to wonder who the game's architects were, what motivated them, what they believed, and why the game was so important to them.

Most of the old-time coaches insisted that football provided a full, rewarding life that otherwise would have eluded them. Giving back to young men the dividends that the coaches enjoyed was their professed mission. "What are you in coaching for?" Buzz Allert asked rhetorically. "Are you in coaching to say when you get through that 'I won 210 games and lost 110?' Or, are you going to say: 'Well, I won a few and lost a few, but I never cheated a kid?'" Ray Overton underscored the feelings of his fellow coaches by proclaiming: "Third and goal is not pressure. I've been trained for that. Every day I have to make a decision that affects young men's lives. That's pressure."

Looking back on his career, Bill Shipman wrote: "When I got up in the morning, I never had the feeling that I was going to work. I always felt that I was going to try to contribute to the quality of the lives of young people and to enjoy the fellowship and friendship of the teachers and coaches with whom I worked. A few weeks ago I received a Christmas card from a quarterback of many years ago. It said simply: 'Coach, thanks again for touching my life.' That type of thing is the real reward of coaching.

"I think—although their jobs are a lot harder and more involved today—that teaching and coaching is still a great way to touch the lives of young people," Shipman continued. Most of the old-time coaches, in fact, expressed the conviction that their successors, on the whole, still comprise a profession of earnest, well-intentioned men whose first priority is the welfare of their players. Most of the old coaches nevertheless conceded that now, more than ever, coaches' priorities have changed along with those of the larger society.

Ray Overton observed that during his career he watched coaching grow into "a science, a true profession that required a different kind of dedication than in earlier times." Referring to the times in which he grew up, he remarked: "A lot of young coaches haven't gone through all this and don't understand what it's all about." Now, he commented: "I look at so many in this day and time that just walk in and want the top coordinator's job, and they beat the kids out of the parking lot when the day's over."

At the bottom line, Overton asserted: "The community and the people are going to perceive coaches for what they are. If we're professional people and we coach kids and treat them right . . . then people will accept us for what we are. If we're going to go out and be crude and be brawlers, then people are going to condemn us for what we are. . . . I know there was an era in there when people thought you had to be tough as nails, and you had to cuss and fight and do all that, but I've always told my coaches: 'I don't want you to be seen using profanity or tobacco or alcohol. I won't tell you how to live your life, I just don't want anybody in our community to see you do it, because I think you live in a glass house.' There are some in every profession that you're not proud of, but I'd like to think our profession is doing pretty well."

Assessing Players of the Present Generation

Nevertheless, at a time when newspapers and television regularly trumpet the transgressions of football players who are involved with drugs or
implicated in rapes and robberies, it is difficult to believe that behind
them was a man who preached the importance of character. In some
instances, the coaches did not live up to the ideal; in other cases, players
simply failed to listen. Confronted with the gulf between the coaches'
exhortations and recalcitrant players' actions, coaches discharged a torrent
of opinions about the environment that has cut short many promising
athletic careers.

Kids in this age are bombarded by the morals of MTV, beer commer-
cials, and Generation X iconoclasts, expressed James Brewer. "A lot of
them are lost. The generation of sixties and seventies kids who questioned
authority are now parents," he added. Ray Akins, in concluding his interview, mourned: "The country is in trouble because young people cannot
relate to a lot of what I have said here."

According to Ray Overton: "The big change was that in the early days
there were not many broken homes. Now, I'd guess that it's about fifty
percent." He also noted, "society is not child-centered anymore because
both parents are working." Of his last years in coaching, he complained,
"I didn't get much help from the homefront."

Clarence McMichael echoed: "Parents don't call as much anymore,
[and] 'Mom' has become the greatest influence in many households
because of broken homes. Families used to have prayer before eating a
meal together, and they would discuss family issues at dinner. Now, they
don't eat together because they don't have the same work schedules and
don't see each other a lot. And when kids leave the field house, they're on
their own. Even coaches have lost a lot of that closeness we used to have
with our boys. Gangs, dope, and all that get in the way, too."

Maurice Cook emphasized: "Used to these [wayward athletes] were big
exceptions to the general rule. A coach could help them, and they'd want
to rise above their situation. Now there are so many that coaches can't
help them all. This forces coaches to do one of two things: turn their back
and just coach, or become quasi-social workers. They have a job—and
that is to coach, not to be a social worker. Used to, it came with the territory, now it can be overwhelming to some, and many of the most sensitive get out of the profession because of it."

In his last years as a coach and teacher, Cook set aside an hour every
day to counsel at-risk students. Once in the field house, he encountered
more kids every year who "stay in athletics just to have a father figure who
cares and fusses about grades and discipline. . . . Being a coach is draining
today. Used to, you just coached, and you always had a few problem kids.
Now, you have to give, give, give, and it's tough to replenish yourself."
Yet he did so for years. "When a young man just pours himself out for
you and your school, and he's totally dedicated, he's very polite, he's a

good student, he's got ambition—it affects you. And in athletics, you get to be around a lot of young men that way."

On the other hand, coaches at times have no choice but to be around young men who are not "that way." H. G. Bissinger, in *Friday Night Lights*, discussed at length an Odessa Permian player who made a mockery of the time-honored lessons of character that the old-time coaches tried to impart. Bissinger's portrait of Boobie Miles tried to evoke pity for a supposed victim of football, a portrayal, however, that was often confused and conflicting. On one hand Bissinger tried to suggest that Permian's coaches discarded the player when his usefulness to the team had run its course, yet his own evidence argued otherwise. In a larger context, Bissinger's observations exposed many of the reasons why some good athletes today fall beyond the reach of coaches who are truly concerned for their players' welfare.[2]

The Boobie Miles that Bissinger portrayed was as immature as he was gifted. The overinflated sense of importance that the town of Odessa thrust upon him kept Miles from realizing that he needed football more than football needed him. To this extent his coaches felt responsible, since their sport had sown the seeds of his self-destruction. In an earlier age, when humility was a common virtue, coaches might have simply kicked such a boy off the team. In this age, however, the staff evidently realized that Miles had the chance to make something of himself with football in his life; without the sport, he most certainly would fail.

Yet Miles went over the edge, and Bissinger seemed to lay the blame for his fall on everyone but the player himself. The author implied that the boy's coaches abandoned him, but did not attempt to explain why the staff continued to indulge Miles after injuries during his senior year gave another player the opportunity to fill in and outshine him.

Watching Permian warm up without him, Miles "seemed devoid of any emotional connection to the team." When he tried to walk out of the locker room, a coach stopped him and tried to reason with the young man. Clearly the player who replaced him demonstrated that despite what Miles thought, he was not indispensable. Bissinger did not speculate why the coaches exhorted Miles to remain on the team at this point, when they no longer needed him. The author seemed not to appreciate the fact that the staff might have been acting selflessly, nor did he express the understanding that it is impossible to help a kid who will not help himself.[3]

In other respects, Boobie Miles manifested all the negative character traits for which sports sociologists have condemned high school athletics. His conceit was evident in a riddle he both asked and answered: "Why are the scores of Permian games so lopsided? Because they only have one Boobie." When he learned that his injured knee would keep him out of action for half the season, he directed a blue streak of disrespect at the doctor who donated his service on Friday nights to the team: "Oh fuck, man! . . . You got to be full of shit, man!" He expressed contempt toward his schoolwork: "Where are your notes from yesterday?" a teacher asked

Miles. "'I left 'em,' he said with a smile. . . . 'I watched you. You didn't take any notes.' . . . He smiled some more." Upon finding that he was no longer a starter, he evinced selfishness. "They jacked me. If I don't play, I'm not going to suit up."[4]

Commerce's Steve Lineweaver, a contemporary of Permian's Randy Mayes, made some observations about such players as Boobie Miles and noted: "The coach is in a quandary. The team has to come first, and then, the individual. But still you have to be tolerant, you have to be humane. You can't just knock a chip off a kid's shoulder and tell him: 'It's my way or the highway.' Is it best, then, under whatever circumstances to kick a kid off the team and take away what is most important to him? Or, can you find some other way to discipline him and at the same time not lose the respect of the rest of the team? . . . A lot of us have taken courses on child psychology and on the dynamics of how people interact. Nowadays at coaching school they'll tell you that you need to take some sociology classes and pay as much attention to your people skills as your 'X's and O's.'"

The tidy models that sports sociologists normally conceive for their studies leave little room for all the variables that affect their subjects. Left out of the equation, of course, are coaches and their efforts to make the "sports myth" a reality. In Boobie Miles's case, his coaches showed dogged patience and restraint. Yet, in the end, the product that stepped from the locker room into society certainly made the words that men such as Ty Bain preached ring hollow: "Courage, self-sacrifice, loyalty, self-discipline, and determination." Certainly, many of Miles's teammates would profess that they acquired some of those traits on the football field at Permian. But, as Herb Allen stated: "Sometimes those lessons take and sometimes they just don't."

Violence, Brutality, and Unhealthy Competition

Critics contend that rather than teaching values and character, coaches emphasize violence and brutality. One of the most outspoken critics of football is Shirl James Hoffman, department head of Exercise and Sports Science at the University of North Carolina at Greensboro. The professor has raised serious questions about the way coaches "manipulate the emotions of students for the purpose of winning football games." Among his examples was that of a Florida high school coach "who regularly concluded his pregame pep talks by ceremoniously biting off the head of a live frog." And once, before playing their arch-rivals, the "Golden Eagles," this coach "painted a chicken gold . . . and stood by as the team chased down the bird and stomped it to death." Hoffman charged that coaches, by appealing to their players' basest emotions, encourage them to disregard their personal safety. Referring to the superior athleticism that football players exhibit, he asserted: "These amazing feats should not cause us to overlook the brutishness that forms the

Courtesy Kevin KAL Kallaugher, Baltimore Sun, *Cartoonists and Writers Syndicate.*

backdrop for their exhibitions." Football, he concluded, "remains in a class by itself, outside the orbit of academic redemption."[5]

Not many good coaches would disagree with Hoffman's assertion that such reprehensible actions as those displayed by the Florida coach have no place in football, and not many coaches have resorted to such object lessons. Even Hoffman conceded that coaches' insistence on sportsmanship taught players to leave violence on the field. Donald Jay, discussing how he handled the natural rivalries that sports cultivates, intoned: "Every school had one. . . . I never promoted revenge, because I felt it was a very poor factor. If you build up on revenge and they get that revenge, what are you going to do next week? There were teams that you had to pump your kids up for, but there were others, that, shoot, you just mention the name and the kids are ready to play."

Regarding football's brutishness, Cotton Miles confessed: "It is not human nature to want to go out there and 'bang' somebody; you had to teach them to do that." At the same time, Hoot Smith cautioned: "If we ever do away with football, kids will still look for the same thrill that they get from the violent aspect of the game." Reconciling those views, Bill Shipman stated: "Despite all the modifications of modern football, it's still a game of blocking and tackling and hard body contact." Nevertheless,

Shipman insisted: "The rules and ethics of high school football promote fair, clean play, and while football is violent, it is not brutal except in the case of a badly outmatched team. And no sport places as much emphasis on safety as football does."

The old coaches also pointed out that football today is the legacy of a much tougher age, when participants went both ways for sixty minutes, and, beginning only in the 1940s, for forty-eight minutes, without face masks and with only cotton wadding in their uniforms for padding—all without the benefit of trainers. Chatter Allen remarked: "To some people football may be a brutal game, but life itself is sometimes brutal. Football teaches young men to cope with life's brutal side."

Gordon Wood was quick to distinguish that there was a big difference between teaching kids how to cope with brutality and teaching them how to employ brutality. At Stamford one of his district opponents had a player "whose sole purpose was to hurt quarterbacks. This kid was an artist. He even took a count! He'd follow quarterbacks after the play and throw elbows and 'cheap shot' them." During Wood's first season on the Gulf Coast, he and Morris Southall attended a Victoria Junior College game, and both of them sat upright in their seats when they spotted the young "assassin" on the visiting team. "We knew it was him right away, because of the way he laid out that quarterback." Wood emphasized that the player's actions did not help his team. "Hell, they lost most games. What he was doing was a bunch of crap. He was trying to hurt people, not trying to win."

Maurice Cook reflected at length on football and brutality. "It's not the intent of the game to be brutal," he began. "If you want to see the teaching of brutality, turn on your TV, don't look at a high school football game if you're looking for brutality." Football players, he continued, "go through a very strenuous off-season program to prepare themselves to be able to give a lick and also to be able to take a lick. We have weight-training that's unbelievable nowadays. Also, equipment is much improved over what we used to have—face masks, the new type air-suspension helmets, and all kinds of new products. It's top-notch, especially the material that shoulder pads and [other protective gear] are made out of. Plus the rules undergo a scrutinizing, year after year after year. Dangerous situations are corrected—like the crack-back block. . . . And, when coaches say 'Let's get out there and kill 'em,' its a figure of speech. I don't want a player to go out and kill somebody," Cook said condescendingly. Then, he said with a chuckle, "you can take your fist and try to beat somebody in a football uniform to death, and you'd find out pretty soon that you're going to hurt your hand."

On the football field itself, the rare occasions when players experienced fatal injuries revealed the coaches' deep revulsion to the literal manifestation of "getting out there and killing 'em." Darrell Tully landed his first head coaching job at Galveston Ball in the early 1950s following the departure of Coach Bill Bush, who never recovered from watching one of his players die after breaking his neck. "He was a good man and a good coach . . . but he got 'gun shy' and wouldn't work them out." And when the team began losing, said Tully: "They ran Bill off. They rocked his house and made phone calls at all hours of the night. And finally, they had to let him go."

Joe Washington identified a player's fatal accident as the low point not only of his career, but also of his life. It happened in an early season contest, during the waning minutes of a tight game. A defensive lineman was closing in on the quarterback, and when the ball handler eluded him, the lineman collided with another player, which shattered a vertebra in his neck. "I don't remember that season, games we won or lost or anything." For Washington, the incident put coaching into perspective. "Winning seemed so minor after that."

Hoot Smith, a former Texas A&M corpsman and ex-Marine, told of a similar experience. When he began his career at Grand Saline in the early 1950s, Smith's approach was typical of his military background. "We coached that old blood and guts. When a kid got hurt, we'd tell him to get up. We thought a kid was supposed to be tough; they were supposed to endure pain. We thought that if they weren't bleeding, they weren't hitting." Then, during two-a-days in 1954, he recalled: "We had a little boy, Kenneth Williams. Something happened in a shell drill, and we sent him to get some water—he said he had a headache and wasn't seeing very well. So, he turned and walked about twenty yards and fell, and went to sleep. . . . We carried him to Dallas, where they operated on him, but he never woke up."

The incident, said Smith, "brought immediate terror on the community. We lost a lot of kids off the team because folks panicked." Afterward Smith was never the same. "It affected me personally. I felt responsible. Those were the most trying years a man could ever want, and for the rest of my career, every time a kid took a good lick, I was very aware of what could happen."

Both Hoot Smith and Joe Washington admitted that they had many second thoughts about the nature of football, yet they never came to view what they were doing as part of something unhealthy. Instead, they tried to find solace in the fact that life itself carries great risks. "Somehow," related Smith, "you've just got to go on."

Homer Johnson emphasized that such tragedies were rare. "Kids were much safer playing football than some other things they could be doing after school. Only one kid in my experience was taken out of football by his mother because she felt he might get hurt," he related. "And one day, while we were working out, he died in a car wreck on the Wylie highway while going over a hundred miles an hour."

Many parents who steer their boys away from football today not only fear for their sons' safety, but they also consider the lessons of competition as something inconsistent with their values. Many educators have come to regard conflict resolution in higher esteem than competition. Influenced by a New Age approach that is less concerned with achievement than equality, the new theory contends that win-lose games are unhealthy and undermine self-esteem. Moreover, editor John Leo, in a *U.S. News & World Report* article, asserted that Rita Kramer, who wrote *Ed School Follies*, believes that in part the attack on competition is gender-motivated as well. "This is one of those hidden agenda items for feminists. . . . Some of them don't want masculine skills to be valued too highly in the schools."[6]

But, to argue that competition is unhealthy, expressed Ed Logan, is an even more radical view than anything coaches can say. "Competition is primordial; it's got thousands of years of experience to back it up. . . . We try so hard to make the school environment a perfect world, but it's just not that way. School is supposed to prepare kids for life," Logan said, and "some competition is critical. The first thing a student is going to do when they get out of high school is compete to see who is going to get into the best colleges. When they get out of college, they're going to be competing to see who'll get the best jobs. Kids who go to work right after they get out of high school are going to be competing for jobs right away." In an age when opportunities in some fields are declining, concluded Logan, "it would damn sure behoove our teachers to instill a sense of competition, because these kiddoes are sure going to get it when they get out. . . . Life is not a no-risk, no-fault proposition."

Alfie Kohn, author of *No Contest: The Case Against Competition*, is a leader in the New Age attack against team athletics. "Competition," Kohn asserted, has a "toxic effect on our relationships." It makes the losers envy the winners and doubt their own self-worth. It also makes the winners look at opponents as obstacles to their success and enables them to dismiss the vanquished as losers. "Winning," Kohn concluded, "doesn't build character. It just lets us gloat temporarily."[7]

Every emotion that Kohn cited, however, finds its source at the lowest level of maturity. He failed to acknowledge that gloating is only one of many emotions that winning evokes. Winning also produces the satisfaction of having worked diligently to achieve a goal. In a sport such as football, skills are developed over years of endless training and, during the season, teams spend many hours each week preparing for a single opponent. After such a considerable investment, winning seldom leaves room for gloating.

Every Friday night provides scores of examples. One of Ray Overton's fondest memories inspired him to wax eloquent: "Man reaches his greatest hour when he lies on the field of battle completely exhausted, but in victory." That moment for him came at the end of a play-off game in 1985 when his MacArthur Cardinals faced a heavily favored Midland Lee team. The lead had changed hands several times, and at one point the Rebels moved the ball inside MacArthur's five-yard line only to be turned away. After Lee went ahead late in the game, a kickoff return the length of the field quickly swung the contest back in MacArthur's favor. And when it was all over, the two teams—in fine Texas tradition—met in the middle of the field and shook hands before kneeling and praying together.

If competition was the name of the game, coaches made sure their boys kept it in perspective by placing a premium on good sportsmanship, and coaches practiced what they preached. Chena Gilstrap asserted: "You become very well acquainted with your competition. And if you beat them, or they beat you, you don't think about having outcoached them. . . . All you want to do, is to do well against them—you want their respect."

And, many added, whether in victory or defeat, you accepted the final score with humility. When an overmatched Pharr-San Juan-Alamo team beat Orange in the 1962 Class 3-A semifinals, the victorious coach was heading for the dressing room when his defeated opponent, Ted Jeffries, spun him around. "Are you Charlie Williams?" he asked. Remembered Williams: "He had such a fire in his eyes, I was almost afraid to say yes! But I did, and he said: 'I just want to congratulate you on a fine job of coaching.'" Williams was quick to respond that if not for an early departure of Orange's quarterback, the outcome might have been different. "Well, my quarterback didn't play defense, and the University of Texas couldn't have scored twenty points on y'all today," Jeffries intoned. "Now this was a guy, an older coach, who had won state championships before," continued Williams, "and it's tough to lose one like that. But, you know, he was truly happy for me, and I'll never forget that."

Abilene's Chuck Moser was a kindred soul of Jeffries. Although loath to accept defeat, he nevertheless expressed some vicarious satisfaction toward Bob Harrell, whose San Angelo Bobcats had finally beaten the Abilene Eagles in the coaches' fourth meeting. During the previous three seasons the game had decided who would represent the district in the play-offs, and both of them had fielded some great teams during that stretch. As Moser extended his congratulations, he told his rival: "Bob, you haven't won your share."

Both Moser and Harrell were successful and highly respected coaches who believed that maintaining strict discipline provided the key to victory. O. W. Follis, who played for and later coached under Bob Harrell, claimed "he was tougher than Bear Bryant." What Follis intended as a compliment, however, might not be interpreted as such today. The old-time coaches, whose methods once went unquestioned, have been increasingly frustrated at having to defend themselves against critics who judge the methods they used twenty-five years ago by present-day standards. Perhaps no area of the coaching profession has drawn as much criticism as the administration of discipline.

Corporal Punishment

Herb Allen declared: "After integration, the biggest change was that teachers could no longer discipline kids in a manner that suited their discretion because of the threat of lawsuits." Allen Boren complained that such actions undermined the coaches' authority "because attorneys and judges can rule against teachers and coaches, even though everyone knows that what they're doing is right."

Coaches, especially, tailored punishment to fit the offense; and, very often, their justice would be swift. Moon Mullins, for example, told about the time he walked by a San Angelo barber shop and saw a player in the chair smoking a cigarette. Entering the room, he pulled the cigarette from the boy's mouth and laid it, still lit, on the boy's chest, and then left without uttering a word. "As far as I know, the kid never again smoked," Mullins said.

Yet now, said Hoot Smith, "a coach has to watch every move, every statement, and he has to be on guard every minute." At one time he never had to hold discussions with his assistant coaches about their side-line behavior. "Now it's a big topic." Carlos Berry remembered that during a game years ago in which a boy was ejected, a school board member "chewed me out for patting the kid on the back." Fans had convinced the man that Berry should have "let him have it" instead of consoling him. "But what you see is not always the whole story," Berry said, for while he was patting the boy on the back, he was also looking sternly through a tight smile into the boy's face, hissing: "If we lose this game, I'm going to kill you."

Today, said Bill Bookout: "If you see a coach on the sideline who pulls a kid out, you'll see him with hands on his side. That coach is saying the same thing that they said twenty years ago, but twenty years ago you'd see him grabbing that kid by the face mask or even boxing him on the headgear."

Because the concept of unity was so crucial to a team's success, coaches did not tolerate dissension among their players. "I had a rule," remarked Herb Allen, "teammates did not fight each other." But when they did, he often let them "slug it out." Once, however, two of his players got into a bitter argument that turned into a fistfight, and he broke it up. When the pair resumed their fight in the locker room, Allen separated them again and marched them into the gym. "OK," he said, "I'm going to let y'all fight, but here's what you're going to do . . . I want only one of you to walk out of here." When the combatants considered the consequences, they decided to talk it out. "I figured it would end that way. People don't often fight when there's no one there to stop it," Allen said. The solution worked so well that he tried it again and again. "I never had one that would fight under those conditions." Still, he conceded, "you couldn't do that today."

John Hugh Smith knew of coaches at some places who had their kids form a ring around the belligerents and let them "bare knuckle it." Bill Hartley admitted, "I put the gloves on them, you bet." During the lunch hour one day, when he spotted two of his players arguing, "I took them between two buildings and let them box until they couldn't lift their fists. When it was over, they shook hands and took it in stride. Today they're still friends and they laugh about it."

"Kids crave discipline as long as it's fair," added Bill Carter. His standard punishment for missing practice was having the offenders run "until their tongues were hanging out." At a recent reunion, he asked a group of former players if they had ever thought about quitting. "To the man, they said: 'No way!' They were going to prove to me they could do it."

In Morris Southall's opinion: "When a kid quits, the coach failed. It was his job to teach him what life was all about." The coach's creed brought to mind Perry Young, whom, in that respect, he had almost failed. "Perry was a great receiver, but he got a little wild after his sophomore year. When his junior year came around, we couldn't get him to toe the line, so we kicked him off the team." That action stirred Young's older brother to appeal to the staff: "If you don't help Perry, then no one else is going to." So, Southall recalled, "we gave him five licks for three days and thirty laps for thirty days and this saved him." Today, he added, "Perry is coaching in San Antonio."

That kind of punishment used to be routine. Not many coaches ever gave a second thought to using "the board." Within the past generation, however, corporal punishment has been condemned as backward and barbaric. Gender equality, progressive thinking, and the fact that the dispensers of discipline must at times cross racial lines have precluded its use in all but a handful of communities today. Even so, many old-time coaches continue to defend their use of corporal punishment.

Ed Logan fervently believed: "It's a mistake not to have corporal punishment. Not being able to use the board puts you in the position of haggling over discipline. . . . Paddling is immediate, and it's swift justice. It doesn't leave anything hanging. If you're a good kid, it's embarrassing, but it reminds you that someone is in charge, and if you mess up, there will be consequences."

"The paddle never hurt anything but your butt," asserted Moon Mullins. "When the paddle was taken away, you lost discipline. You paddle them, you put your arm around them, and the kids love you for it. Now, I have grown men that I used to beat their butt with a board come up and say: 'Coach, do you remember me?' They always reinforce the belief that paddling helped them and that they deserved it." James Brewer added: "Busting them showed them that the coach cared. I always told them: 'It's when I quit busting your butt that you'd better worry.'"

At Stamford, early in his career, Gordon Wood developed misgivings about paddling his players after a teacher berated him for it. "I had twenty-five kids that year, and I told them that I was going to take a poll and see if they wanted me to quit doing it. I gave them all a pencil and some paper, and we took a secret ballot, and all twenty-five of them said they wanted to continue it."

At an East Texas State Teachers College training school in Commerce, where Darrell Tully coached the sons of professors and graduate students, he added their names to the "Board of Education" whenever they misbehaved. "It got to where they'd mess up on purpose just to get their name on it," he laughed. Mayfield Workman also used the paddle to get his players' attention. "One time I had a boy refuse to take licks, so I ran him extra laps," he recalled. Then, years later, Workman said, he was in the coaches' office when a man "about six-foot-four and two-hundred-and-twenty pounds showed up at my door and told me he was that kid. Said he'd come back to take his licks." Workman, of course, just laughed, and "we sat down for a long time and visited."

James Brewer echoed: "Busting them was not judging them, it was to help them. These are the ones who still come back and see me." Just recently, a former North Side player whose son was enrolled at Aledo learned that the retired Brewer was volunteering in the afternoons to help the coach there. Approaching the principal, the man told him: "I want you to let Coach Brewer discipline my son just like he did me." The principal agreed, but he required the father to sign a release, which provoked the old coach to growl: "People can't discipline now, because the courts will get you."

While Allen Boren acknowledged that paddling "was easy, immediate, and effective," he also commented that "taking away the board did not completely undermine authority; it only took away one tool. We've got to be smart enough to figure out other ways to discipline kids." Buzz Allert agreed. "You can communicate with players in any number of ways, and the board is only one of them." He was never one to rely on paddling, although he did occasionally resort to the practice. "I had a good kid, an all-stater at [Houston] Spring Wood. When he was disrespectful in class, I gave him five or six licks, and he said that he wouldn't act up anymore. But he did anyway. That next time I told him I wasn't going to hit him again. I just said that if you ever come back in here for any kind of disciplinary reason whatsoever, or, if you ever miss a practice, then you're through. This got his attention."

Other coaches, such as John Hugh Smith and Jewell Wallace, never used the paddle. And, while admitting they were in a definite minority, the coaches also asserted they were by no means alone. Others said that they resorted to corporal punishment "only in extreme cases." At some point in their careers, commented Bob Harrell and Ray Overton, they realized that making their players run laps allowed them to exercise discipline while conditioning their recalcitrant players.

"I stopped paddling as soon as I got to Amarillo in 1955," remarked John Reddell. "We had a junior high coach there carry around a paddle in his back pocket. I told him: 'We don't do that.' You can run them or you can give them physical exercises. But the paddle is demeaning in my opinion, particularly when it's connected with 'Did you block that man?' or 'Did you miss your assignment?'"

Quin Eudy was another who did not lament the passing of corporal punishment. "You can still have tough discipline. You've just got to reach them in different ways," he said. Eudy's way was "the hundred-mile rule," reserved for players he caught breaking training. At Needville, during track season one year, he walked into a convenience store and spotted one of his players buying a beer. Falling in behind him, Eudy asked: "'Don't you think you need to put that back?' He said: 'No, I'm thirsty.'" The next day Eudy called the boy into the coaches' office and told him: "You owe me a hundred miles." Another catch was that the player could not compete again until he fulfilled the obligation. "This kid was a great track man, and he loved getting his medals," Eudy said. Although Eudy gave the player two weeks, he ran the hundred miles in six days. When he had thirty miles to go, Eudy told him that if he wanted to get it out of the way, he would run with him. "Word got around that we were doing this run, and when we went through Boling, the banker there drove by us, rolled down his window and hollered: 'You're crazy as hell!' Another lady told us that when we passed by on the way back that she'd have some iced tea ready for us."

"Kids do crave discipline," commented Carlos Berry. "When they come back to visit, they talk about the hard times the coaches put them through and laugh about it." And many of them, he noted, are college-educated men who capitalized on their athletic abilities to earn scholarships. Many coaches expressed deep resentment about the perception that they cultivated gridiron talent at the expense, or even disregard, of education. They emphasized that football kept legions of boys in school who otherwise would have seen little point in completing their secondary education, and many former players went on to enjoy success in business and professional fields, the coaches claimed.

Placing a Value on Education

Charlie Williams, who arrived at Pharr-San Juan-Alamo in 1959, became part of a program that had not enjoyed much success. "And that extended into life, too. Only about five percent of the boys on the team went on to college." Yet he noted that over seventy percent of his 1962 and 1963 Class 3-A state finalists eventually earned college degrees. "I attribute this to learning the prerequisites to success in life," Williams declared. In recounting those prerequisites, he beat a familiar drum: "Self-discipline, pride, accountability."

"Football was a means to an end," insisted Bob Barfield. "Grades came first." Surveying his career, Barfield stated that he measured his success by the number of doctors, lawyers, businessmen, and coaches who had played for him. "Football is just a way to get there. If you've played three or four years of ball, in my opinion, you've got about all you're going to get out of football except a scholarship."

O. W. Follis said: "I tried to make my kids see that athletics was just a part of school. School came first. They were not always going to be playing, and they needed to be prepared for life." Bum Phillips added: "I always told them you play for eight or ten years, and then you go maybe forty or fifty more without it. Education is going to get you the easy forty years instead of the easy four years that you spend playing in college."

Many coaches, in fact, expressed pride in their own classroom performance. Some of them, even after they became head coaches, continued to teach full loads by choice. At Crane, for example, Dan Anderegg taught three science classes in addition to being athletic director and head football and track coach. Walt Parker earned the respect of his classroom peers by teaching bookkeeping, shorthand, and business law while holding down the same coaching duties as Anderegg.

"I believed that [my] students deserved the same effort out of me as the athletes," declared Gordon Brown. During football season teaching often required late-night preparation, which was difficult, he said. But, "I wanted other teachers to respect me as a good teacher." It was a respect that came more grudgingly in his own household. Once, Brown related: "My second-grade son came home and asked me the relationship of the sun and moon. I went into detail to explain it, after which he said: 'That is not right. Mrs. Legget says it is so-and-so and she is a teacher and you are just a coach.'"

"One of the biggest misperceptions is that coaches and teachers are at odds," commented Bill Patrick. On the contrary, he said, teachers considered coaches a stabilizing influence. Maurice Cook agreed. Wherever he coached, he always remained in the math department at his own insistence. That way, "I can be elbow-to-elbow with the other teachers, and that was the way I liked it." Coaches, he said, made themselves available as disciplinarians. Coaches also believed that in most schools their presence in the classroom provided a measure of comfort, especially to female teachers, who knew that in a pinch, there was a coach down the hall who could handle any matter.

One morning before the school day began at Aldine Carver, for example, Herb Allen was in his classroom when "Mrs. Slater, the science teacher" rushed in to tell him that a madman had entered the building and was standing at the crossing hall "ranting and raving." So, Allen snapped the handle off of a mop and "went to take care of it." One pop set the man to flight, with the coach right on his heels. "I beat him all the way through the hall and across the baseball field, over a barbed wire fence, and right off the school property." Allen said.

Where athletes were concerned, teachers in most schools simply expected the coaches to demand good conduct. Just like mothers keep their children in line by threatening to "tell daddy," a teacher's threat to "tell coach" had the same effect on football players. Gordon Wood recalled "a mean English teacher—'stronger than onions'"—who, he thought, did not care for football. One day, however, he had to ask her how some of his athletes were doing in her class. "And she said: 'I never have problems with athletes, they're the best disciplined students I have.'"

At Lufkin Dunbar, related Elmer Redd, each gridder who earned a letter was required to get three-fourths of his teachers to sign a form stating "that he was the type of person with enough character to represent the school and wear the 'D.' See, the 'D' was an honor, an award that was not just for playing football, but for being a citizen and the type of person that we wanted to represent our school." During the year, Redd said, "there comes a time when that kid knows, I'm going to need that English teacher, or math teacher, or history teacher to sign that paper."

Despite their emphasis on good behavior and academic performance, there is nevertheless a great degree of validity to the fact that coaches often made poorer teachers than they cared to admit. According to Chatter Allen: "Many did not have, or did not take, the time for classroom preparation. Most of them knew that they could be outstanding teachers, but if they had a poor football team, they lost their job."

Until after World War II, many coaches also believed that developing a work ethic built upon physical sacrifice was equally as important as book knowledge. When many coaches began their careers, Texans were overwhelmingly a rural people, and since more jobs were outdoors in the sunshine, college was neither universally accessible nor considered to be of paramount importance.

In 1976 Joe Golding stated very frankly: "Being in the field of education all my life, and being connected with competitive sports for as long as I can remember . . . I do have this profound feeling that our [coaches'] objective in education is perhaps the responsibility of developing young manhood and young womanhood, even more important than developing academic excellence. Both are important, but I don't think you can have academic excellence without having developed [character]."

That did not mean that coaches failed to place a high premium on schooling. Many of them pointed to where they started out and asserted that no group of men could better appreciate an education. Before Congress passed the GI Bill just after World War II, athletics provided one of the few paths to college for young Texans of modest means. And even then, they had to realize they were capable of clearing such a hurdle. Football, coaches asserted, had opened the door to higher education for them, and they felt that it was an incumbent responsibility to pass along that lesson to players whose families possessed no college tradition.

Yet, said Andrew Miracle and Roger Rees in *Lessons of the Locker Room*, "The idea that the high school athlete—usually a male from a blue collar family—can use an athletic scholarship to complete a college education that he otherwise would have not been able to afford is one of our great cultural myths." The authors, of course, drew the debatable conclusion by looking at evidence compiled only during the past generation. The models they cited did not examine how athletes fared in an earlier time. Nor did they acknowledge that a great many coaches got their educations in that very manner.[8]

With due credit to sports sociology, the conditions that prevailed during the old coaches' adolescence have changed considerably. Rather than

opening doors, the current demands of having to perform for those athletic scholarships today can present obstacles rather than opportunities.
Poor kids, especially, might be better off forgetting about athletics and
taking advantage of the numerous grants, scholarships, and low-interest
loans available to them.

Confronted with the critical view of sports sociology, Emory Bellard
roared: "I think that's a bunch of hogwash as a starting point!" While
conceding that times have changed, he countered: "If you look at football
for no other reason than the number of people who went to school who
otherwise wouldn't have gone, then it's good." As far as those fortunate
enough to make a lucrative living from athletics, he challenged: "What
would they be doing if they didn't have that opportunity?" Citing the
scandals in which particular athletes have become involved, Bellard
lamented that "the total sport has to absorb the punishment for it, or, in
some cases, the lack of respect." But, he continued, "for every one of
those you see, there are a hundred others who are fine and outstanding."

Such arguments routinely fall on deaf ears among football's critics. Few
would expect a coach to do anything less than defend his players and his
system. And again, as the present-day society has grown more critical of
its institutions, coaches have lost the unquestioned trust they once
enjoyed. Nothing brought that fact into focus more clearly than the
storm of controversy that surrounded "no-pass/no-play." The proposal,
enacted as part of House Bill 72, became a political football in the larger
debate about general education reform in Texas during 1984.[9]

No-pass/no-play, which generated a backlash of resentment, was
supported by men and women who believed that high school football
symbolized the state's misplaced priorities. To coaches the proposal
came to symbolize their loss of prestige. In fighting the measure, they
found few sympathetic ears. Coaches' protests, in fact, seemed to verify
in the public mind that they were concerned only with winning.

"The new rules make coaches look like they never cared about education," Morris Southall claimed. "But, a good coach was very concerned
with grades and preparing kids for a living." His own coaches, Wilson
Gilmore and Pat Jarrell, he said, always looked at their athletes as students
first, and "I coached like I was taught." Ray Overton added that in principle, "every coach I know agrees with no-pass/no-play. But, there are
some factors about it that were just wrong." The coaches' chief complaint
was that the rule removed athletes from the influence of their coaches and
teammates for as long as they were ineligible to play.

Eddie Joseph, as executive director of the Texas High School Coaches
Association, was involved in the House Bill 72 affair from the beginning.
Before no-pass/no-play became state law, he contended, Texas already
had in place some of the most stringent eligibility rules in the country.
The University Interscholastic League, in fact, had imposed its first academic standards in 1913 and continued to be a model for the rest of the
country. Over the decades the league's requirements changed, and at the

time that House Bill 72 was proposed, the UIL held athletes accountable for passing four out of five "core" courses seven days before competing.

Joseph admitted that "some schools became lax, but most did enforce it." Ignoring or sidestepping the rule also meant running the risk of having to forfeit games, he added. Like Joseph, James Brewer believed that "stewardship and scholarship in football was good for the most part, but the importance attached to football did lead to some misplaced priorities." Coaches, he conceded, brought no-pass/no-play woes on themselves in part by a spotty record of enforcing the week-to-week rules. John Reddell added that because grades came out only every six weeks, paperwork became a problem and left room for creative math.[10]

Summing up the attitude of many coaches, Leon Vinyard remarked that he always had "three or four good players who were 'borderliners.' I always found a way to get them to make up the slack in another course." But when they did not, he confessed, the superintendent and principal would usually relax the rules until the season was over. Then, he added, failing grades equaled "a good butt-busting."

On the other hand, just as many coaches insisted that they toed the line. Dan Anderegg, at Crane, remarked that he and "Dr. Miller, our superintendent, sent a form around to all the teachers each Monday morning. They had to sign it 'passing or failing.' . . . Kids with failing grades went to the teacher at 3:30 instead of practice, and if they had two failing grades they couldn't play." Gene Mayfield commented: "I always had no-pass/no-play. Our coaches were always talking to teachers and asking what we could do. Even in the fifties and sixties we had study halls for our players who weren't making the grades." Bob Cashion made sure that players who failed grade checks stood on the sidelines on Friday nights wearing a jersey over their street clothes. The ignominy, he believed, was an appropriate motivator.

Then, in 1984, all of that changed when Governor Mark White, who was running for re-election, enlisted Texas billionaire Ross Perot to reappraise the state's educational system. Donald Jay, who had retired from the head post at the THSCA, remembered getting a call from Perot. "Donald, I've got a list of allegations against these coaches that's a mile long, and I'd like to meet with some of you," Jay recalled Perot saying. So Jay and his successor, Eddie Joseph, selected five coaches who met Perot at the Hyatt in Dallas. "I thought being a computer person, he was really going to pull out a computer list a mile long," Jay said.

What happened instead, asserted Jay, was that Perot simply passed along to them some anecdotes he had heard while visiting Texas high schools. For example, an English teacher had told him that one of their coaches spent too much time at the golf course. At another school someone had complained that a Vocational Agriculture student had missed forty days of school to show a chicken. "Well, Ross," said the coaches, "a lot of our football coaches are golf coaches. Did you ever stop to think he might be the golf coach? . . . Did you ever stop to think that when those people [showing animals] win first prize that they get enough money to make a scholarship?"

Perot did not listen. Jay at least gave him credit for being forthright. Before the meeting broke up, Jay said: "He told us: 'I'm not going to attack all sports, I'm going to attack football, because that is king in Texas. . . . The only way I'm going to get any ink in Texas is to attack what's most important, and that's football.'" And the legislature, Jay lamented, "bought it hook, line, and sinker." House Bill 72, he continued, was presented as "the most progressive educational bill ever passed." Speaking ten years after the fact, he said, "the only thing left in that dadgummed bill right now is no-pass/no-play."

The negative consequences that followed the measure were just as the coaches had predicted. Like so many laws, the coaches expressed, legislators did not take into consideration the best interests of the schoolchildren the bill was designed to benefit. What the bill provided was simply a document its sponsors could point to and say: "Look what we accomplished." But a close inspection, coaches said, would reveal that it most severely affected the marginal students who needed help the most. Another unintended consequence was that the bill adversely affected programs such as accelerated classes.

Several of the old-time coaches who were still active when no-pass/no-play was enacted noticed that some of their brightest players dropped honors courses because the new rules left no room for error. To remain eligible, students not only had to pass all their courses, but the floor for a failing grade was raised from 59 to 69. "Nothing is based on 100 percent! But this is!" Buzz Allert protested. And Ross Perot, Allert suggested, was a fool if he thought that declaring students ineligible would inspire them to use the extra time to study. "What they did instead was get a job or go out and just kill time."

In the Garland schools, remarked athletic director Homer Johnson, "we had kids who were good at chemistry or calculus, kids who liked a challenge. Now, instead of risking making an 'F,' they just don't take the hard courses." Among their athletes, he continued, was "a girl gymnast who was an all-honors student on her way to the state finals. She made a 68 and could not compete. At the same time we had a running back who could barely read and write, and he played because of the courses he took."

Bill Bookout called no-pass/no-play "the cruelest thing that's ever happened to Texas's extracurricular activities. . . . People thought that it was only going to affect varsity football players." What happened instead, he pointed out, was that "it gutted the bands, the drill teams, and everything else." Not many realized, moreover, that "it applied to schoolchildren from the seventh grade on up."

Joe Hedrick stated: "The tragic thing is that in the big schools and cities, the people most affected by it for a lifetime are those junior high kids. They haven't got enough judgment to know why they're in school in the first place. Some kind of extracurricular activity is often the thing that keeps them there, and once they are ineligible, they just quit school, and the next thing you know, you don't see those kids anymore." Indeed, at one of the Irving junior highs, Ray Overton addressed a boy's P.E. class not long after they had received their report cards. "Their coach told me, watch and see who those students that failed walk off with. Sure enough, they left with the druggies."

"Most of the kids who flunk out do so because they have no discipline, not because they are stupid," remarked Clarence McMichael. Coaches, he said, lose very few players who go on to be productive, responsible, citizens and leaders. "It's the marginal ones that need the break, that need to be under the supervision of the coach." On almost every team are players who remain in school simply because of football. Although H. G. Bissinger did not admit it, he certainly provided an example in Boobie Miles. In the epilogue, when the player lost his eligibility, he simply dropped out of school.[11]

Perhaps Quin Eudy encapsulated the opinions of his fellow coaches best: "House Bill 72, Education 0." It was Ray Overton, however, who produced what he considered the most tragic example about the bill's consequences. On Overton's freshman team at Irving MacArthur was a young Hispanic player, Jessy Sanmiguel, who started both ways. Overton recalled: "He failed one class with a 68. I can understand that he can't play, but that House bill says that he can't work out with the kids after school. . . . Now, what you've done is force him to find a new set of friends, because all of his friends are playing football. And nine times out of ten, he doesn't find the quality friends he had before."

Overton continued: "From the day he became ineligible, he began to get in trouble at school; had fights, got in a scrape at the park and shot a guy. Finally, he dropped out of school." Then, one night, Sanmiguel and his new friends walked into a Taco Bell and herded the five employees inside the freezer, where the former athlete shot and killed them all. "So there's five lives that are gone," Overton said, "and you always wonder if we could have kept him in the program, could we have averted all of that?"[12]

For a dozen years after the enactment of no-pass/no-play, Eddie Joseph spearheaded a lobbying effort to change the law. Finally, in 1996, he convinced legislators to adopt the plan he had advocated from the time the measure was first proposed. Joseph asked that ineligible players be allowed to continue participating in extracurricular activities, although they would continue to be barred from actually competing. That way their coaches could still have an influence on them, and the peer pressure would make the students want to bring up their grades. Coaches, he contended, "are—and always have been—a player's best hedge against mediocrity, whether on the football field or in class. When we disenfranchise a kid and label him a dummy, he will find a new group to join."

The priorities of Texans are changing, as shown by the treatment that coaches received over no-pass/no-play. Judging by their actions, however, neither the state legislature nor Texans in general are truly committed to financing a top-flight education system. Today Texas continues to rank below the average in most national benchmarks.[13] Coaches expressed that instead of assailing athletics, critics of sports would do better to bring the rest of the system up to the level of excellence that they so long ago achieved. Making scapegoats of coaches and athletes was certainly a weak substitute for the lofty goals that House Bill 72 claimed to embody.

Yesterday, Today, and Tomorrow

Texans of long ago who enjoyed high school football made it a superior institution when it was the only game in town. In places such as Odessa or Plano or Converse, or in dozens of small towns, it still enjoys a prominent place in the local culture, yet the sport has clearly lost some of its luster. Beginning in the 1960s, said James Brewer, "your pros were coming in, and the colleges were starting to play on television. . . . And that started watering down interest in high school football." Today, moreover: "You don't have the community spirit like you used to. . . . At one time, when a big game was coming up, it was common for businessmen in one town to get together and put up some money and bet the businessmen in the other town. It was just a community thing; it was about pride. The money wasn't important; hell, they'd usually give it away. . . . Used to, the radio and the newspapers would be saturated with [news of the game]. Everywhere you went there would be signs up and banners and shoe polish on people's windshields. You couldn't get away from it if you tried. This year [1993], there were six state championship games played in two weeks, and on the sports at ten o'clock they were showing some damn hockey team."

John Reddell echoed: "There was a time if you went 8–0, you'd fill the stadium, I don't care where you were. Now, you see some of them do that, and there might be twenty-five hundred, maybe. There are several reasons. One of them is the economy. There is only a certain amount of entertainment dollar per family. Here, where we are [between Fort Worth and Dallas], you might want to go see the Rangers play, or you might want to go see the Mavericks or the Cowboys. Or, you might just want to go to a good show or something. And that's your entertainment money. Well, to go to the high school game, if you don't have a kid playing, or if you're not part of the booster club, you don't have much walk-in traffic. There was a time when you'd look around and there would be a big game and everybody would want to come watch it. But I don't think that's true any more."

Nevertheless, Reddell hedged, sometimes it still is. The material support of wealthy school districts continues to yield some high-profile programs, and occasionally, when a consistently mediocre team suddenly

Pine Tree Pirates coach Maurice Cook celebrates his team's first-ever victory against the rival Longview Lobos. *Photograph by Ricky Russell, courtesy Longview* News-Journal.

enjoys a winning streak, it can bring communities together just like it always has. Tim Edwards, recently retired from Hurst Bell, and the only coach to have served at the helm of a school in every classification—Class B through 5-A—expressed that although "high school football is no longer *the* thing, it has never been as big in some ways as it is right now." The team that he took to the 5-A state finals in 1982 played that contest in the Astrodome. Earlier in the season his Blue Raiders twice played Reddell's Trinity Trojans, the first time in a district-deciding contest in which the two undefeated teams drew twenty-nine thousand people; the second time, in the play-offs, thirty-three thousand fans watched them play. Both games had to be moved to Texas Stadium because the "old" Pennington Field that the two Hurst-Euless-Bedford schools shared could not accommodate crowds that large.

By the mid-1980s popularity among diehard sports fans attracted television exposure for some of the state championship games. Now, as many as four in various classifications are broadcast annually, hyped by one cable sports channel as the "Texas Bowl." And these days, at the schools where Edwards and Reddell ended their careers, their legacy plays at "new" Pennington Field, a multi-million dollar facility that features artificial turf and an elevator-accessed, soundproofed, two-story press box tall enough to command a clear view of both the Fort Worth and Dallas skylines.

Ironically, the very fact that high school football has gotten so "big" has also left it in a tenuous position, Edwards intoned. "This isn't the eighties anymore; we don't have barrels full of money to throw around, and when we've reached a point where 'Johnny can't read,' but he can play football in some of the stadiums that you see in these 5-A school districts, then you've invited a backlash." He pointed out that when the Arlington I.S.D. recently faced a fiscal crisis, administrators fleetingly entertained the thought of cutting athletics to save money. "It wasn't more than a passing thought, but I think that some time in the future you will see some school districts seriously consider those kinds of measures."

A veteran of the no-pass/no-play battle against Ross Perot, Edwards appeared on *Donahue* and ABC's *Nightline* and was quoted in state newspapers and national news magazines defending his institution. Behind closed doors he helped beat back some of Perot's demands, such as that school districts drop physical education classes that encompassed sports in the curriculum. From the sidelines, Miracle and Rees sneered that Edwards's chief motivation was to preserve the high salary that he enjoyed as head coach and athletic coordinator.[14]

Edwards, however, countered that if the sociologists had listened to what he was saying, they would have heard some well-reasoned arguments that centered on the concern that the internecine measures football's critics pushed would rob future generations of schoolboys of an important part of their youth. "Whose interests would it serve to do away with athletics? How would it make society better?" he implored. "The discipline that athletes get today is not as rigid and tough as it used to be, it's fairer and more diplomatic; but, if you compare the discipline that athletes get now to what society's discipline is in general, then it's probably stronger than it was when you had all that 'kick 'em in the tail and shake that face mask' kind of discipline, because at home they were getting a strap across their butt." Coaches, Edwards insisted, "are as much a positive influence on these boys right now as they have ever been, if not more so, because for some of them the coach is the only one in their life that is placing any demands on them. You take that away, and you're going to lose a lot of young men."

In a recent historiography, "Why Sports Matter," novelist Wilfrid Sheed wrote: "It's hard to say exactly when the new era began, but at some point lost in the smog of the 19th century, sports went from being officially a bad thing to being a very good thing." Judging by the conclusions of sports sociologists and the way the public pilloried coaches over no-pass/no-play, then society has come full circle. Yet lost somewhere in the "smog of the 1960s" perhaps was the fact that sports really did provide a good influence on youth. According to the old-time coaches, it still does.[15]

"I think any adult who played football in a reasonably good situation will say that no other area of education contributed more to what he has become," contended Bill Shipman. And for the coaches, too, he added, their relationship with young men provided "a life that counted." At eighty-two, Gordon Wood remarked: "If I could come back, I'd come back as a coach."[16] Just a few weeks before Ed Varley passed away in 1996, he reflected upon his career and expressed succinctly the sentiments that most of his peers in one way or another imparted: "Coaching is a wonderful profession—if you like kids. I loved it and enjoyed it. We—the kids and I—worked hard during hard times, but we had a lot of fun, too. . . . I have wonderful memories of those days. These were good kids who turned out well. . . . I treasure the times we had together and am proud of the contact I still have with most of them—and love to hear them say: 'Coach, you made a difference in my life.'"

Appendix

Interviews

All interviews were conducted by the author, except for a series conducted by researchers at Texas Tech's Southwest Collection. Each of these is noted. All entries also list the date of the interview (or postmark for correspondence). The coaches' birth dates and the years spanning their careers are followed by each high school where they coached. Data for those who coached at the college or professional level as well as those who coached at private schools or out-of-state schools is listed in parentheses.

Akins, Ray. January 12, 1994, August 12, 1996. Born 1925. Career 1950–1988: Rosebud, Lometa, Goldthwaite, Tomball, Tidehaven, Freer, Gregory-Portland.

Allen, Herbert Hoover (Herb). December 20, 1993, January 24, 1994. Born 1928. Career 1952–1985: Sulphur Springs Douglas, Hearne Blackshear, Diboll Temple, Anahuac Carver, Aldine Carver, Houston Klein.

Allen, Chester Lee (Chatter). December 10, 1993, June 23, 1996 (by correspondence); May 30, 1995. Born 1908. Career 1932–1951: La Grange, Overton, McAllen, Corpus Christi High, Beaumont High (also University of Corpus Christi).

Allert, H. L (Buzz). December 6, 1993. Born 1932. Career 1958–1982: Navasota, Houston Smiley, Port Arthur Jefferson, Edinburg, Houston Lamar Consolidated, Houston Spring Woods, Houston Spring Branch Northbrook.

Anderegg, Dan. November 22, 1993 (by correspondence); January 3, 1994. Born 1922. Career 1950–1982: Sherman, Crane.

Barfield, Robert (Bob). December 3, 1993 (by correspondence); May 22, 1995. Born 1919. Career 1940–1977: Cedar Bayou, Corrigan, Rosenberg, Robstown, Pasadena (also Baylor University).

Bellard, Emory. February 28, 1995. Born 1927. Career 1949–1993: Alice, Ingleside, Breckenridge, San Angelo, Spring Westfield (also University of Texas, Texas A&M University, Mississippi State University).

Berry, Carlos. September 24, 1993. Born 1935. Career 1957–1991: Haskell, Henrietta, Fort Worth Richland (also Hardin-Simmons College).

Blount, R. E. (Peppy). November 30, 1995. Author, *Mamas, Don't Let Your Babies Grow Up to Play Football.*

Bookout, William (Bill). October 2, 1993. Born 1932. Career 1954–1977: El Paso Austin, El Paso Burgess, Hurst Bell, Euless Trinity (also Midwestern University).

Boren, Allen. December 15, 1993. Born 1934. Career 1956–1991: Wharton, Sweeny, Bellville, Edna, Humble, Houston Klein (also Sam Houston State University).

Brewer, James. December 22, 1993. Born 1929. Career 1955–present: Fort Worth North Side, Fort Worth Polytechnic, Fort Worth Paschal, Aledo, Fort Worth Castleberry (also Arlington State University, North Texas State University).

Brown, Gordon. December 6, 1993 (by correspondence). Born 1930. Career 1951–1987: Groesbeck, Fort Hood, Tyler, Houston Katy, Nacogdoches (also Stephen F. Austin State University).

Carter, William (Bill). January 24, 1994. Born 1922. Career 1948–1981: Wichita Falls, Holliday, Iowa Park, Amarillo Tascosa, Fort Worth Western Hills, Arlington, Euless Trinity.

Cashion, Robert (Bob). September 7, 1993. Born 1933. Career 1955–1991: Kilgore, Longview, Hurst Bell, Fort Worth Haltom, Lancaster, Fort Worth Richland.

Christian, Jack, interview by David Murrah, September 17, 1971 (Southwest Collection). Born, c. 1910. Career c. 1935–1965: Abilene, Colorado City, Spur.

Cook, Maurice. January 12, 1994. Born 1939. Career 1962-present: Longview, Hurst Bell, Longview Pine Tree, Longview Spring Hill.

Conover, Brooks. February 27, 1994 (by correspondence); May 23, 1995. Born 1907. Career 1930–1960: Mart, Ennis, Odessa, Borger, Brownsville, Orange, Temple, Cleburne.

Curtis, Charles (Chuck). January 20, 1994. Born 1937. Career 1959–1989: Holliday, Jacksboro, Garland, Cleburne, Aledo (also Southern Methodist University and Arlington State University).

Edwards, Tim. March 21, 1997. Born 1944. Career 1968–1995: New Waverly, Hallettsville, Copperas Cove, Hurst Bell.

Ellington, William (Bill). January 17, 1994. Born 1921. Career 1946–1979: Winters, Pleasant Grove, Garland, Amarillo Tascosa (also University of Texas).

Eudy, Quin. January 27, 1994. Born 1937. Career 1961–present: Crockett, Honey Grove, Needville, Big Spring, Midland, (also Rayville, Louisiana, Dallas Lake Hill Preparatory).

Follis, O. W. January 4, 1994. Born 1920. Career 1946–1960: Lamesa.

Gaines, Gary, February 5, 1996. Born 1952. Career 1975–present: Fort Stockton, Monahans, Odessa Permian, Abilene, San Angelo (also Texas Tech University).

Gilstrap, Claude (Chena). July 5, 1995. Born 1914. Career 1937–1965: Leverett's Chapel, Crockett, Wharton, Cleburne (also Paris Junior College, Schreiner Institute, Arlington State College).

Golding, Joe, interview by Neil Sapper, August 21, 1975, interview by Steven Gamble, August 26, 1976 (both Southwest Collection). Born c. 1918. Career 1940–1961: Denison, Wichita Falls.

Goolsby, Perry. January 26, 1996 (by correspondence). Career 1948–1962: Wichita Falls.

Hamm, Hugh. September 9, 1993. Born 1930. Career 1956–1989: Big Spring, Carrolton-Turner, Hurst Bell, Fort Worth Richland.

Harrell, Robert (Bob). January 9, 1994. Born 1915. Career 1938–1963: DeLeon, Odessa, Denison, Greenville, Lamesa, Corpus Christi Miller, San Angelo, Irving (also Tulsa University).

Hartley, Billy James. Born 1924. Career 1949–1965: Columbus.

Hedrick, Joseph L. May 5, 1994. Born 1922. Career 1946–1985: Franklin.

Henderson, Zac Sr. July 11, 1995. Born 1923. Career 1950–1970: Slaton, Cisco, Breckenridge, Burkburnett, Wichita Falls (also Hanesville and Jena, Louisiana).

Jay, Donald. May 26, 1994. Born 1928. Career 1951–1972: Kingsville, Lamesa, West Orange.

Johnson, Homer. September 21, 1993. Born 1927. Career 1948–1962: Garland.

Jones, Marion T. (Jap). December 6, 1994. Born 1923. Career 1948–1971: Hallsville Galilee, Dallas Booker T. Washington, Fort Worth I. M. Terrell, Fort Worth Dunbar.

Jones, Thurman (Tugboat), interview by Steven Gamble, August 4, 1976 (Southwest Collection). Born c. 1920. Career 1943–1965: Electra, Wichita Falls, Midland, Highland Park (also Midwestern State College, Texas A&M College, University of Washington).

Joseph, Eddie. October 25, 1993, November 20, 1995. Born 1933. Career 1957–1981: Victoria, Corpus Christi Carroll, Wharton (also Oklahoma City McGinnis).

Kerbel, Joe, interview by Neil Sapper, July 27, 1972 (Southwest Collection). Born c. 1921. Career 1947–1960: Breckenridge, Amarillo (also Bartlesville and Cleveland, Oklahoma, West Texas State University, Texas Tech University).

Kirkpatrick, Hunter. January 26, 1996 (by correspondence). Born 1916. Career c. 1935–1975: Cooper, Denison, Wichita Falls.

Lerma, E. C. November 8, 1993. Born 1915. Career 1938–1966: Benavides, Rio Grande City.

Logan, Edward (Ed). September 27, 1993. Born 1930. Career 1956–1966: College Station A&M Consolidated, Fort Worth Haltom.

Lowrance, Robert. April 27, 1994. Born 1913. Career 1936–1975: Longview, Sabine, Ennis, Iraan, Hawkins.

McKenzie, Emmett, interview by Steven Gamble, August 4, 1976 (Southwest Collection). Born c. 1933. Career 1955–1962: Nederland, Big Spring.

McMichael, Clarence. October 23, 1993. Born 1920. Career 1947–1980: Crockett Ralph Bunch, Nacogdoches E. J. Campbell, Nacogdoches (also Texas College).

Marshall, Bailey. January 31, 1994. Born 1934. Career 1956–1964: Gladewater, White Oak.

Martin, Ralph. October 22, 1993, July 18, 1995. Born 1911. Career 1930–1931: Rio Grande City (also San Antonio YMCA).

Mayes, Randy. June 17, 1996. Born 1955. Career 1979–present: Odessa Permian, Ennis.

Mayfield, Gene. February 2, 1994. Born 1928. Career 1956–1977, 1982–1987: Littlefield, Borger, Odessa Permian, Levelland (also West Texas State University).

Miles, Theo C. (Cotton). January 26, 1994. Born 1924. Career 1948–1975: White Oak, Dallas Wilson, Skyline.

Morris, Eddie. November 20, 1995. Born 1940. Career 1962–1980: Gainesville, Archer City.

Moser, Charles (Chuck). September 14, 1993. Born 1918. Career 1940–1959: McAllen, Abilene (also Lexington, Missouri).

Mullins, Fagan (Moon). May 18, 1994. Born 1918. Career 1943–1982: Crane, Anson, San Angelo Lakeview (also Hardin-Simmons College, Cisco Junior College).

Overton, Ray. November 29, 1993, January 17, 1994. Born 1924. Career 1948–1994: Paint Creek, Haskell, Abilene Cooper, Irving MacArthur.

Parker, Walter E. (Walt). June 22, 1994. Born 1917. Career 1940–1954: Farmersville, Palestine, Arlington Heights, Fort Worth Carter-Riverside, Denton.

Patrick, William D. (Bill). Born 1931. Career 1957–1990: Garrison, Hooks, Port Arthur, Bridge City, Houston Galena Park, Houston C. E. King.

Phillips, Oail Andrew Jr. (Bum). March 2, 1994. Born 1923. Career 1950–1985: Nederland, Port Neches, Jacksonville, Amarillo (also Texas A&M College, University of Houston, Oklahoma State University, University of Texas at El Paso, San Diego Chargers, Houston Oilers, New Orleans Saints).

Phillips, Weldon (Stoney). May 22, 1995. Born 1915. Career 1938–1957: Cedar Bayou, Beeville, Harlingen, Pasadena (also Peacock Military Academy, San Antonio).

Prescott, Harold (Ace), interview by Richie Cravens, November 21, 1976 (Southwest Collection). Born c. 1925. Career 1950–1974: Falfurrias, Raymondville, Ranger, Burkburnett (also Cisco Junior College).

Pulattie, Frank. July 6, 1995. Born 1922. Career 1949–1984: Itasca, Hamilton, Childress, Livingston, Riesel, Lubbock Monterrey, Kermit, Big Spring, Caldwell, El Paso Ysleta (also Sacramento Lincoln, California).

Qualls, Charles (Charlie). January 19, 1994. Born 1930. Career 1953–1978: Kingsville, McKinney, Mesquite, North Mesquite (also University of Texas at Arlington).

Redd, Elmer. November 29, 1994. Born 1928. Career 1950–1987: Arp Industrial, Lufkin Dunbar (also University of Houston).

Reddell, John. October 13, 1993. Born 1930. Career 1953–1991: DeKalb, Amarillo Palo Duro, Arlington, Midland, Euless Trinity (also Oklahoma City Classen).

Reynolds, Doyle. October 2, 1993. Born 1929. Career 1956–1977: Pharr-San Juan-Alamo, Breckenridge, Abilene Cooper, Euless Trinity (also McMurry College).

Robbins, Cooper, interview by Steven Gamble, August 3, 1976 (Southwest Collection). Born c. 1907. Career 1929–1956: Fort Worth North Side, Fort Worth Diamond Hill, Breckenridge, Odessa (also Texas A&M College).

Shipman, William (Bill). January 12, 1994 (by correspondence); January 24, 1994. Born 1926. Career 1949–1983: Irving, Denton, Lewisville, Abilene, Andrews (also Bowlegs, Oklahoma).

Shotwell, P. E. (Pete), interview by Richie Cravens, November 5, 1975 (Southwest Collection). Born 1893. Career 1916–1952: Cisco, Abilene, Breckenridge, Longview (also Sul Ross State College, Hardin-Simmons College).

Smith, Hulen (Hoot). October 2, 1993. Born 1927. Career 1950–1968: Grand Saline, Hurst Bell.

Smith, John Hugh. September 24, 1993. Born 1916. Career 1940–1966: La Vega, Belton, Cypress-Fairbanks, Fort Worth Haltom.

Southall, Morris. September 29, 1993. Born 1921. Career 1947–1986: Seminole, Winters, Victoria, Brownwood.

Taylor, M. B. (Joe), June 22, November 7, 1996. Born 1907. Career 1938–1969: Gladewater, Galveston Ball, Houston Spring Branch (also East Texas State Teachers College).

Tully, Darrell. January 10, 17, 1994. Born 1917. Career 1940–1964: Dallas Crozier Tech, Galveston Ball, Houston Spring Branch (also East Texas State Teachers College).

Tyler, Joseph Robert (Joe Bob). November 3, 1993. Born 1923. Career 1949–1990: Burkburnett, Wichita Falls, Wichita Falls Rider, Fort Worth Haltom.

Varley, Edward L. February 15, 1994 (by correspondence); February 14, 19, 1994. Born 1914. Career 1938–1964: Fort Worth Birdville, Fort Worth Diamond Hill.

Vinyard, Leon. February 21, 1994. Born 1917. Career 1940–1968: Alpine, Canton, Terrell.

Wallace, Jewell. September 30, November 16, 1993. Born 1907. Career 1935–1953: El Paso Bowie, El Paso, Greenville, San Angelo, San Antonio Jefferson (also University of Houston, Texas Christian University).

Washington, Joe. January 11, 1995. Born 1929. Career 1951–1993: Bay City Hilliard, Port Arthur Lincoln.

Whitley, Jack. February 22, 1994. Born 1920. Career 1948–1966: Fort Worth Masonic Home, Fort Worth Polytechnic.

Williams, A. C., November 2, 1997. Born 1919. Career 1940–1942: Greenville Booker T. Washington.

Williams, Charlie. November 3, 1997. Born 1930. Career 1958–1989: Pharr-San Juan-Alamo, Alice, McAllen, Harlingen.

Wood, Gordon. October 4, 1993. Born 1914. Career 1938–1985: Spur, Rule, Roscoe, Seminole, Winters, Stamford, Victoria, Brownwood.

Wood, Toby. November 20, 1995. Born 1939. Career 1961–1982: Quanah, Gainesville, Archer City, Jacksboro, Uvalde, Fort Worth Richland.

Workman, Mayfield (Bull). January 10, 1994. Born 1917. Career 1947–1962: Arlington.

Notes

Chapter 1

1. Nick Patoski, "The World According to Coach," *Texas Monthly*, 15 (Oct., 1987), 128 (Lamberson quote).

2. Ibid., 130.

3. Mark Busby, *Larry McMurtry and the West: An Ambivalent Relationship* (Denton: University of North Texas Press, 1995), 98, 102.

4. Ibid., 8

5. For a review of the series, see John J. O'Connor, "'Against the Grain': Football and Family Values," *New York Times*, Oct. 15, 1993, sec. D, p. 17.

6. Harold Ratliff, *Autumn's Mightiest Legions: History of Texas Schoolboy Football* (Waco: Texian Press, 1963); Ratliff, *Texas Schoolboy Football: Champions in Action* (Austin: University Interscholastic League, 1972). Bill McMurray, *Texas High School Football* (South Bend, Indiana: Icarus Press, 1985), 505–509, includes a fine biographical vignette on Ratliff.

7. R. E. "Peppy" Blount, *Mamas, Don't Let Your Babies Grow Up To Play Football* (Austin: Eakin Press, 1985), 10.

8. Ibid., 16–18, 23 (quotations).

9. Ibid., 2 (quotations), 12–14.

10. R. E. Blount to Ty Cashion, interview, Nov. 30, 1995.

11. Until 1980, when a Class 5-A was created, the state's largest classification was 4-A. Until 1948 all schools competed for the state title regardless of size. From 1948 through 1950, teams competed for a championship in three divisions: 1-A, 2-A, and City. In 1951 the City division was dropped and 3-A and 4-A divisions were added. A Class-B division began playing for a title in 1972. Also beginning that year, six-man and eight-man teams competed for a championship. Eight-man football was dropped after the 1975 season. See George Breazeale (comp. and ed.), *Tops in Texas: Records and Notes on UIL State Football Champions, 1920–1992* (Austin: Martin Communications, 1993).

12. Carlton Stowers, *Friday Night Heroes: A Look at Texas High School Football* (Austin: Eakin Press, 1983).

13. Jan Reid, *Vain Glory* (Fredericksburg, Texas: Shearer Publishing, 1986), xi, xv.

14. Ibid., 208–229.

15. Bum Phillips to Ty Cashion, interview, Mar. 2, 1994.

16. Reid, *Vain Glory*, 3, 27.

17. Ibid., 21, 31.

18. Ibid., 40–42.

19. Ibid., 21.

20. Ibid., 31, 59, 97–98.

21. H. G. Bissinger, *Friday Night Lights: A Town, A Team, and a Dream* (New York: HarperCollins Publishers, 1990), xi.

22. Ibid., 1st quotation, 31–32; 2nd and 3rd quotations, 90; 4th quotation, 34–35; 5th quotation, 130; 6th quotation, 215.

23. Ibid., 149.

24. Ibid., 12 (quotation), 68.

25. Ibid., 125.

26. Ibid., 1st quotation, 125; 238–239; 2nd quotation, 239; 3rd quotation, 320; 355.

27. Ibid., 231.

28. Associated Press release from Dallas *Morning News*, Sept. 16, 1981, sec. B, p. 5; letter, George Merlis, Executive Producer, ABC Entertainment, to Eddie Joseph, Assistant Executive Vice President, Texas High School Coaches Association, Oct. 7, 1981, THSCA files, Austin. Gordon Wood did not comment on this incident in accordance with a settlement he reached with ABC Entertainment.

29. "Quote of the Week," Austin *American-Statesman*, Sept. 27, 1995, sec. D, p. 10.

30. Reid, *Vain Glory*, 97–98.

31. Andrew W. Miracle Jr. and C. Roger Rees, *Lessons of the Locker Room* (New York: Prometheus Books, 1994), 8.

32. Ibid., 17–18; 1st quotation, 18; 2nd quotation, 179; 3rd quotation, 82; 4th quotation, 90–91; 5th quotation, 94; 6th quotation, 133; 7th quotation, 121; 8th quotation, 96.

33. Ibid., 7; Paul Redekop, *Sociology of Sport: An Annotated Bibliography* (New York: Garland Publishing, Inc., 1988), 22–42; Andrew W. Miracle, "Crime, Sport, and American Mythology," Fort Worth *Star-Telegram*, July 24, 1994, sec. C, p. 8.

34. University of Washington professor Charles Berquist adeptly encapsulated the shortcomings of sociologists and historians whose writings tresspass into the others' disciplines. See "In the Name of History," *Latin American Research Review*, 25, no. 3 (1990), 156–176.

35. Patoski, "The World According to Coach," 125.

Chapter 2

1. Guy M. Lewis, "Teddy Roosevelt's Role in the 1905 Football Controversy," *The Research Quarterly*, 40 (Dec., 1969), 717–724.

2. Kern Tips, *Football, Texas Style: An Illustrated History of the Southwest Conference* (Garden City, N.Y.: Doubleday & Co., 1964), 1, 2.

3. McMurray, *Texas High School Football*, 3.

4. Roy Bedichek, *Educational Competition: The Story of the University Interscholastic League* (Austin: University of Texas Press, 1956), 344–345.

5. Ibid., 341–343, 348; 1st and 2nd quotations, 341; 3rd quotation, 343.

6. "Caesar "Dutch" Hohn Describes Football at Texas A&M, 1909," in J'Nell Pate (ed.), *Document Sets for Texas and the Southwest in U.S. History* (Lexington, Mass.: D. C. Heath and Co., 1991), 127.

7. Tips, *Football, Texas Style*, 2–3.

8. McMurray, *Texas High School Football*, 3; Bedichek, *Educational Competition*, 346.

9. Bedichek, *Educational Competition*, 345–346, 351–352. Quotation on 346.

10. Ratliff, *Texas Schoolboy Football*, 3; Hohn, "Hohn Describes Football," 126.

11. Hohn, "Hohn Describes Football," 124 (1st and 2nd quotations), 126; McMurray, *Texas High School Football*, 478; Tips, *Football, Texas Style*, 8 (3rd quotation).

12. James Smallwood, "The Greatest Challenge: Education in Texas," in Donald W. Whisenhunt (ed.), *Texas: A Sesquicentennial Celebration* (Austin: Eakin Press, 1984), 393–394.

13. Bedichek, *Educational Competition*, 349; McMurray, *Texas High School Football*, 483.

14. Bedichek, *Educational Competition*, 37, 349–350, 352; McMurray, *Texas High School Football*, 483–485.

15. Bedichek, *Educational Competition*, 352; McMurray, *Texas High School Football*, 141.

16. Ratliff, *Autumn's Mightiest Legions*, 4.

17. Fred Russell, "Football in the South," in Allison Danzig and Peter Brandwein (eds.), *Sport's Golden Age: A Close-Up of the Fabulous Twenties* (New York: Harper & Row Brothers Publishers, 1948), 154–155.

18. McMurray, *Texas High School Football*, 4, 478.

19. Ibid., 365.

20. Bedichek, *Educational Competition*, 396; Ratliff, *Autumn's Mightiest Legions*, 4, 29.

21. Ratliff, *Autumn's Mightiest Legions*, 16.

22. McMurray, *Texas High School Football*, 2–3.

23. Ibid., 484. As a result of consolidations, the number is now about 1,200 high schools and 1,500 middle schools.

24. Bobby D. Weaver, "Black Gold: Oil Development in Texas," in Whisenhunt (ed.), *Texas: A Sesquicentennial Celebration*, 272.

25. Ratliff, *Autumn's Mightiest Legions*, 50–52.

26. Ibid., 47–49.

27. Smallwood, "The Greatest Challenge," 393; Ratliff, *Autumn's Mightiest Legions*, 66–67.

28. Ratliff, *Autumn's Mightiest Legions*, 16.

29. Harold Ratliff, "Mr. Schoolboy Football Names His All-Time Greats," in Dave Campbell (ed.), *Dave Campbell's Texas Football* (1968), 101–106.

30. Bill McClanahan, "The Hydrophobia Play and Other Crowd Pleasers," in Campbell (ed.), *Dave Campbell's Texas Football* (1969), 122–127.

31. Ibid., 123.

32. Ratliff, *Autumn's Mightiest Legions*, 59.

33. For a more detailed account of the Fields murder, see the *Williamson County Sun* (Georgetown), Oct. 24, 1924, p. 2.

34. McMurray, *Texas High School Football*, 8, 11, 73; Ratliff, *Autumn's Mightiest Legions*, 39, 41–45.

35. Ratliff, *Autumn's Mightiest Legions*, 44.

36. McMurray, *Texas High School Football*, 8, 11, 73; Ratliff, *Autumn's Mightiest Legions*, 41–45.

37. Eddie Joseph to Ty Cashion, interview, Oct. 25, 1993; Ratliff, *Autumn's Mightiest Legions*, 24, 27, 31, 41–45; McMurray, *Texas High School Football*, 8–11, 73.

38. Ratliff, "Mr. Schoolboy Football," 101–106.

39. McMurray, *Texas High School Football*, 522.

40. Ratliff, *Autumn's Mightiest Legions*, 24–27; 44.

Chapter 3

1. David Burner, *Herbert Hoover: A Public Life* (New York: Alfred A. Knopf, 1978), 201.

Chapter 4

1. Hart, "Football in the Southwest," in Danzig and Brandwein (eds.), *Sport's Golden Age*, 144, 149.

2. Tips, *Football, Texas Style*, 59–89.

3. Ibid., 38.

4. Ratliff, *Texas Schoolboy Football*, 76–77.

5. Bedicheck, *Educational Competition*, 54–5, 57–63.

6. Ibid., 59–63.

7. Ratliff, *Autumn's Mightiest Legions*, 91; Troy Phillips, "Uncrowned Champion," Fort Worth *Star-Telegram*, Oct. 23, 1994, sec. B, p. 16.

8. Bedicheck, *Educational Competition*, 369–370; McMurray, *Texas High School Football*, 478–479.

9. McMurray, *Texas High School Football*, 485–487 (quotation 485).

10. Ibid., 485–487 (quotation 485).

11. Ibid., 370.

12. Ratliff, *Autumn's Mightiest Legions*, 70–71 (quotation 71).

13. Ibid., 60–61.

14. McMurray, *Texas High School Football*, 364.

15. Frank X. Tolbert, "Mighty Mites," *Collier's*, 108 (Nov. 22, 1941), 45, 75–76.

16. Ratliff, *Autumn's Mightiest Legions*, 72–74 (quotation 72); Ratliff, *Texas Schoolboy Football*, 72–74.

17. McMurray, *Texas High School Football*, 375–379 (1st quotation, 375); Ratliff, *Autumn's Mightiest Legions*, 72–74 (2nd quotation, 73); Ratliff, *Texas Schoolboy Football*, 72–74.

18. Ratliff, *Autumn's Mightiest Legions*, 69–70.

19. Phillips, "Uncrowned Champion."

20. McMurray, *Texas High School Football*, 380, last quotation.

21. Ratliff, *Texas Schoolboy Football*, 81.

Chapter 5

1. Ratliff, *Autumn's Mightiest Legions*, 101–102.

2. McMurray, *Texas High School Football*, 389.

3. Will Wright, "Unheralded Achievement," Fort Worth *Star-Telegram*, Oct. 30, 1994, sec. B, p. 13.

4. Ratliff, *Autumn's Mightiest Legions*, 110.

5. Ratliff, *Autumn's Mightiest Legions*, 96–100; McMurray, *Texas High School Football*, 523–524.

Chapter 6

1. A popular work of the time, Lewis Cotlow, *Amazon Head Hunters* (New York: Henry Holt and Co., 1953), spread the Jivaros' reputation.

2. McMurray, *Texas High School Football*, 519.

3. Ibid., 388–390.

4. Actually, the 1950 census figures from the *Texas Almanac and State Industrial Guide, 1952–1953* (Dallas: A. H. Belo Corporation, 1951), listed the populations of Wichita Falls and Breckenridge at 67,709 and 6,605, respectively.

5. Emory Bellard to Ty Cashion, interview, Feb. 28, 1995; Whit Canning, "Best of the Best," Fort Worth *Star-Telegram*, Dec. 18, 1994, sec. B, p. 24.

6. Canning, "Best of the Best."

7. Ibid.

8. For a more thorough account of the series, see Ty Cashion,

"Remembering the 'Big 33,'" *Sound Historian: Journal of the Texas Oral History Association*, 2 (Fall, 1994), 48–57.

9. Robert H. Boyle, "Beef, Bones and Hershey Bars," *Sports Illustrated*, 21 (Aug. 10, 1964), 18.

10. John Underwood, "Texas Teeners Strike Back," *Sports Illustrated*, 23 (Aug. 23, 1965), 20–21.

11. Since 1994, California and Texas have played a high school all-star game. California has won each time. Just as in the first Big 33 game, the date has fallen before the Texas all-star contest, thus rendering the interstate participants ineligible to play in the North-South game. In this case, Texas officials have not moved to change the dates to their advantage.

Chapter 7

1. Patoski, "The World According to Coach," 128.

Chapter 9

1. McMurray, *Texas High School Football*, 478.

2. Richard Pennington, *Breaking the Ice: The Integration of Southwest Conference Football* (Jefferson, N.C.: MacFarland and Co., Inc., 1987), 26. Also see the author's chapter "Before the Thaw," which presents an objective and well-conceived overview of the racial climate that existed in Texas during these years.

3. For a good primer on the complexities of racial patterns in South Texas, see D. W. Meinig's *Imperial Texas: An Interpretive Essay in Cultural Geography* (Austin: University of Texas Press, 1969).

4. See "HEB School Officials Get Verbal Threshing," *Mid-Cities News Texan*, Mar. 15, 1966, p. 1. Follow-ups appeared in a series, "Text of Statement to H-E-B School Board," *Mid-Cities News Texan*, Mar. 16, 1966, p. 4, Mar. 17, 1966, p. 9, Mar. 18, 1966, p. 10. A final article also appeared, "Bell High School Athletes Cleared in Assault Case," *Mid-Cities News Texan*, Mar. 25, 1966, p. 1.

Chapter 10

1. In Miracle and Rees, *Lessons of the Locker Room*, the authors introduce this idea in the preface and concentrate on this "myth" as a central theme.

2. Gary Gaines to Ty Cashion, interview, Feb. 5, 1996, and Randy Mayes to Ty Cashion, interview, June 17, 1996. For Bissinger's observations on Boobie Miles, see *Friday Night Lights*, 53–69, 150–151, 195–202, 363.

3. Ibid., 195–197. Quotation on 197.

4. Ibid., 1st quotation, 52; 2nd quotation, 56; 3rd quotation, 151; 4th quotation, 196.

5. Shirl James Hoffman, "Football's Brutishness Does Not Belong in

Higher Education" *Chronicle of Higher Education*, Nov. 11, 1992, sec. A, p. 44.

6. Alfie Kohn, "Sports Create Unhealthy Competition," in *Sports in America: Opposing Viewpoints* (San Diego: Greenhaven Press, 1994), 20, reprinted from *Women's Sports and Fitness* (July/Aug., 1990); John Leo, "Phys Ed, or Self-Esteem?" *U.S. News & World Report*, 114 (May 31, 1993), 21.

7. See Alfie Kohn, *No Contest: The Case Against Competition* (Boston: Houghton Mifflin, 1986).

8. Miracle and Rees, *Lessons of the Locker Room*, 134 (quotation); 149, n. 14.

9. Miracle and Rees, in *Lessons of the Locker Room*, produced an interpretation of no-pass/no-play based on the assumption that coaches opposed the measure simply because it meant that they would lose athletes, which would decrease their chances of winning. They neither considered seriously the opposition to no-pass/no-play, nor did they explore the consequences of the act. See pp. 21, 177–200. See also State of Texas, *House Bill 72 and Subsequent Educational Legislation: Comprehensive References and Explanations*, Texas Educational Code, 69th Legislature (Austin, 1985), 21, 920.

10. Bedichek, *Educational Competition*, 365–381, 396–408.

11. Bissinger, *Friday Night Lights*, 363.

12. Nita Thurman, "4 Killed at Irving Taco Bell," Dallas *Morning News*, Jan. 26, 1991, sec. A, pp. 1, 10.

13. See various categories ranking each state in *CQ's State Fact Finder: Ranking Across America, 1998* (Washington, D.C.: Congressional Quarterly, Inc., 1998), 190–216. Note particularly that Texas ranks forty-second in the percentage of population over twenty-five with a high school diploma (195) and forty-ninth in high school completion rates (197). See also Paul Burka, "Save Our Schools," *Texas Monthly*, 108 (Apr., 1990), 124–128.

14. Miracle and Rees, *Lessons of the Locker Room*, 191–192.

15. Wilfrid Sheed, "Why Sports Matter," *Wilsonian Quarterly*, 19 (Winter, 1995), 11.

16. Frank Luksa, "High School Football is Heart-Hitting," Dallas *Morning News*, Sept. 6, 1996. sec. B1, p. 15.

Index

(Illustrations are indicated by boldfaced page numbers)

295

Colophon

The typeface used for the text is Galliard, designed by Matthew Carter. Helvetica Compressed was used for the subheadings and page headings. The display face is Impact.

Two thousand copies printed at Edwards Bros., Inc., Lillington, North Carolina, on 55 lb. Glatfelter.